Microsoft® Word 2000 Illustrated Introductory

Jennifer A. Duffy
Marie L. Swanson

COURSE TECHNOLOGY
Thomson Learning™

MICROSOFT OFFICE USER SPECIALIST
APPROVED COURSEWARE

ONE MAIN STREET, CAMBRIDGE, MA 02142

Australia • Canada • Denmark • Japan • Mexico • New Zealand • Philippines
Puerto Rico • Singapore • South Africa • Spain • United Kingdom • United States

Microsoft Word 2000—Illustrated Introductory is published by Course Technology

Senior Product Manager:	Kathryn Schooling
Product Managers:	Jennifer A. Duffy, Rebecca VanEsselstine
Associate Product Manager:	Emily Heberlein
Senior Production Editor:	Catherine G. DiMassa
Developmental Editor:	Pam Conrad
Marketing Manager:	Karen Bartlett
Acquisitions Editor:	Christine Guivernau
Editorial Assistant:	Stacie Parillo
Composition House:	GEX, Inc.
QA Manuscript Reviewers:	John Freitas, Jeff Schwartz, Jon Greacen, Matt Carroll
Text Designer:	Joseph Lee, Joseph Lee Designs
Cover Designer:	Doug Goodman, Doug Goodman Designs

For more information contact:

Course Technology
One Main Street
Cambridge, MA 02142
or find us on the World Wide Web at: www.course.com

Trademarks

Disclaimer

ISBN 0-7600-6066-5

Printed in the United States of America

3 4 5 6 7 8 9 BM 04 03 02 01 00

The Illustrated Series Offers the Entire Package for your Microsoft Office 2000 Needs

Office 2000 MOUS Certification Coverage

The Illustrated Series offers a growing number of Microsoft-approved titles that cover the objectives required to pass the Office 2000 MOUS (Microsoft Office User Specialist) exams. After studying with any of the approved Illustrated titles (see list on inside cover), you will have mastered the Core and Expert skills necessary to pass any Office 2000 MOUS exam. In addition, the **Word 2000 MOUS Certification Objectives** at the end of the book map to where specific MOUS skills can be found in each lesson and where students can find additional practice.

Helpful New Features

The Illustrated Series responded to Customer Feedback by adding a **Project Files List** at the back of the book for easy reference, changing the red font in the steps to green for easier reading, and adding new conceptual lessons to units to give students the extra information they need when learning Office 2000.

New Exciting Case and Innovative On-Line Companion

There is an exciting new case study used throughout our books, a fictitious company called MediaLoft, designed to be "real-world" in nature by introducing the kinds of activities that students will encounter when working with Microsoft Office 2000. The **MediaLoft Web site**, available at **www.course.com/illustrated/medialoft**, is an innovative Student Online Companion which enhances and augments the printed page by bringing students onto the Web for a dynamic and continually updated learning experience. The MediaLoft site mirrors the case study used throughout the book, creating a real-world intranet site for this chain of bookstore cafés. This Companion is used to complete the WebWorks exercise in each unit of this book, and to allow students to become familiar with the business application of an intranet site.

Enhance Any Illustrated Text with these Exciting Products!

Course CBT

Enhance your students' Office 2000 classroom learning experience with self-paced computer-based training on CD-ROM. Course CBT engages students with interactive multimedia and hands-on simulations that reinforce and complement the concepts and skills covered in the textbook. All the content is aligned with the MOUS program, making it a great preparation tool for the certification exams. Course CBT also includes extensive pre- and post-assessments that test students' mastery of skills.

Course Assessment

How well do your students really know Microsoft Office? Course Assessment is a performance-based testing program that measures students' proficiency in Microsoft Office 2000. Previously known as SAM, Course Assessment is available for Office 2000 in either a live or simulated environment. You can use Course Assessment to place students into or out of courses, monitor their performance throughout a course, and help prepare them for the MOUS certification exams.

Create Your Ideal Course Package with CourseKits™

If one book doesn't offer all the coverage you need, create a course package that does. With Course Technology's CourseKits—our mix-and-match approach to selecting texts—you have the freedom to combine products from more than one series. When you choose any two or more Course Technology products for one course, we'll discount the price and package them together so your students can pick up one convenient bundle at the bookstore.

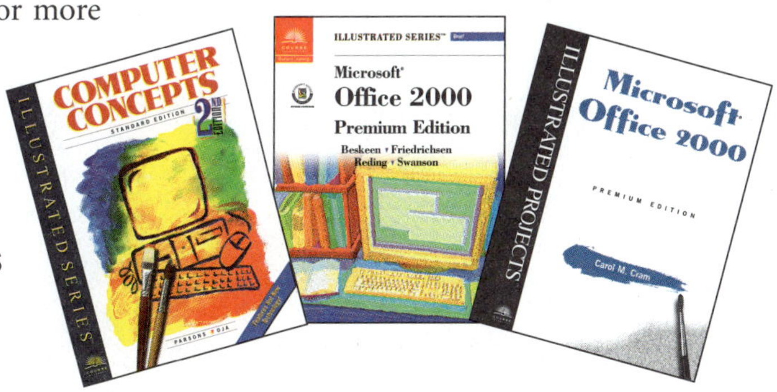

For more information about any of these offerings or other Course Technology products, contact your sales representative or visit our Web site at:

www.course.com

Preface

Welcome to *Microsoft Word 2000—Illustrated Introductory*. This highly visual book offers users a hands-on introduction to aspects of Microsoft Word 2000 and also serves as an excellent reference for future use. If you would like additional coverage of Microsoft Word 2000, we also offer *Microsoft Word 2000—Illustrated Second Course*, a logical continuation of the Introductory Edition.

▶ Organization and Coverage

This text contains eight units that cover basic through intermediate Word skills. In these units, students learn how to create, edit, and format documents and tables, create a Web page, and merge Word documents.

▶ About this Approach

What makes the Illustrated approach so effective at teaching software skills? It's quite simple. Each skill is presented on two facing pages, with the step-by-step instructions on the left page, and large screen illustrations on the right. Students can focus on a single skill without having to turn the page. This unique design makes information extremely accessible and easy to absorb, and provides a great reference for after the course is over. This hands-on approach also makes it ideal for both self-paced or instructor-led classes.

Each lesson, or "information display," contains the following elements:

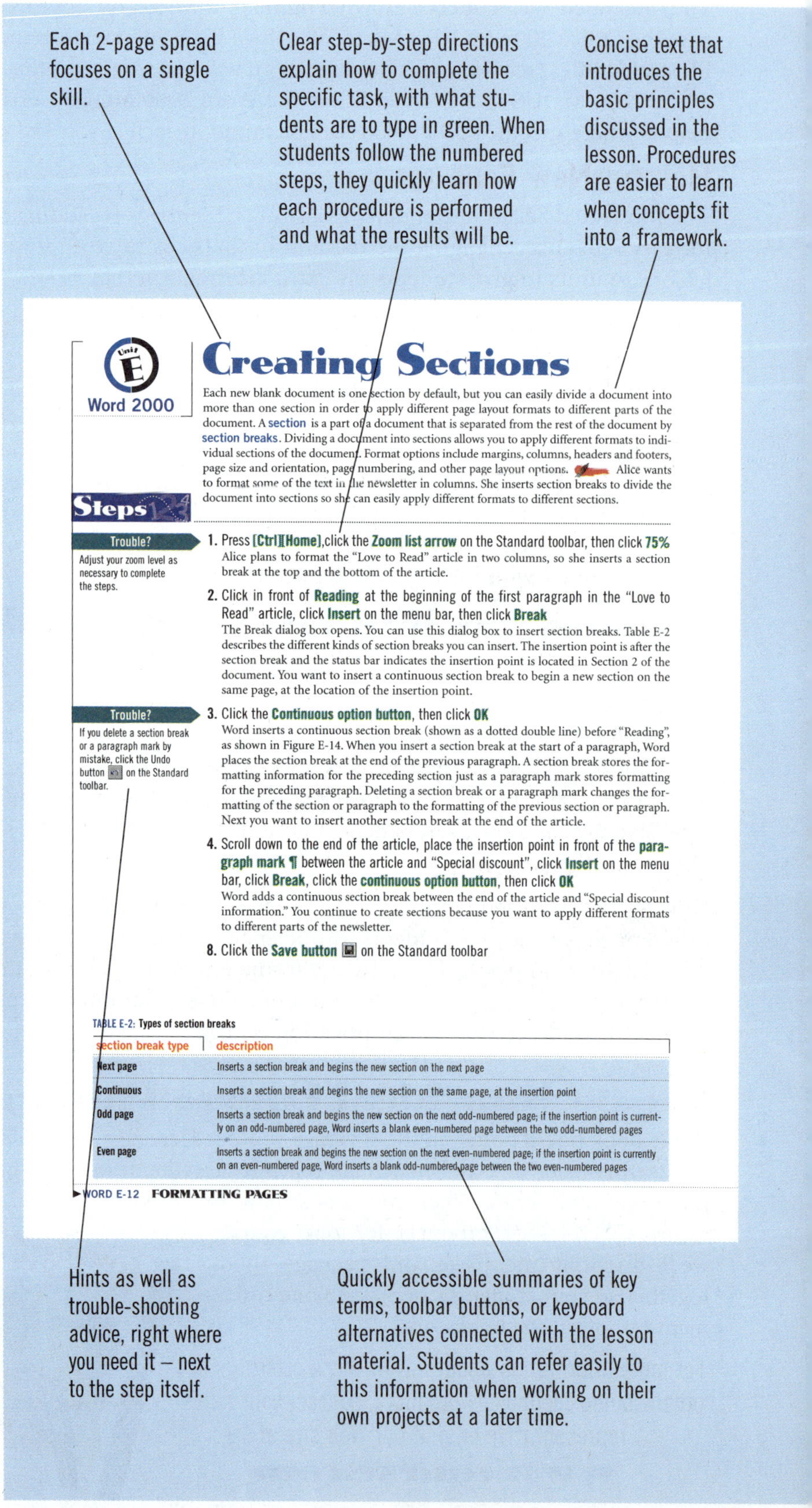

Unit E Word 2000

Creating Sections

Each new blank document is one section by default, but you can easily divide a document into more than one section in order to apply different page layout formats to different parts of the document. A **section** is a part of a document that is separated from the rest of the document by **section breaks**. Dividing a document into sections allows you to apply different formats to individual sections of the document. Format options include margins, columns, headers and footers, page size and orientation, page numbering, and other page layout options. Alice wants to format some of the text in the newsletter in columns. She inserts section breaks to divide the document into sections so she can easily apply different formats to different sections.

Steps

1. Press **[Ctrl][Home]**, click the **Zoom list arrow** on the Standard toolbar, then click **75%**
   Alice plans to format the "Love to Read" article in two columns, so she inserts a section break at the top and the bottom of the article.

Trouble? Adjust your zoom level as necessary to complete the steps.

2. Click in front of **Reading** at the beginning of the first paragraph in the "Love to Read" article, click **Insert** on the menu bar, then click **Break**
   The Break dialog box opens. You can use this dialog box to insert section breaks. Table E-2 describes the different kinds of section breaks you can insert. The insertion point is after the section break and the status bar indicates the insertion point is located in Section 2 of the document. You want to insert a continuous section break to begin a new section on the same page, at the location of the insertion point.

Trouble? If you delete a section break or a paragraph mark by mistake, click the Undo button on the Standard toolbar.

3. Click the **Continuous option button**, then click **OK**
   Word inserts a continuous section break (shown as a dotted double line) before "Reading", as shown in Figure E-14. When you insert a section break at the start of a paragraph, Word places the section break at the end of the previous paragraph. A section break stores the formatting information for the preceding section just as a paragraph mark stores formatting for the preceding paragraph. Deleting a section break or a paragraph mark changes the formatting of the section or paragraph to the formatting of the previous section or paragraph. Next you want to insert another section break at the end of the article.
4. Scroll down to the end of the article, place the insertion point in front of the **paragraph mark ¶** between the article and "Special discount", click **Insert** on the menu bar, click **Break**, click the **continuous option button**, then click **OK**
   Word adds a continuous section break between the end of the article and "Special discount information." You continue to create sections because you want to apply different formats to different parts of the newsletter.
8. Click the **Save button** on the Standard toolbar

TABLE E-2: Types of section breaks

section break type	description
Next page	Inserts a section break and begins the new section on the next page
Continuous	Inserts a section break and begins the new section on the same page, at the insertion point
Odd page	Inserts a section break and begins the new section on the next odd-numbered page; if the insertion point is currently on an odd-numbered page, Word inserts a blank even-numbered page between the two odd-numbered pages
Even page	Inserts a section break and begins the new section on the next even-numbered page; if the insertion point is currently on an even-numbered page, Word inserts a blank odd-numbered page between the two even-numbered pages

▶WORD E-12 FORMATTING PAGES

Other Features

The two-page lesson format featured in this book provides the user with a powerful learning experience. Additionally, this book contains the following features:

Every lesson features full-color representations of what the students' screen should look like after completing the numbered steps.

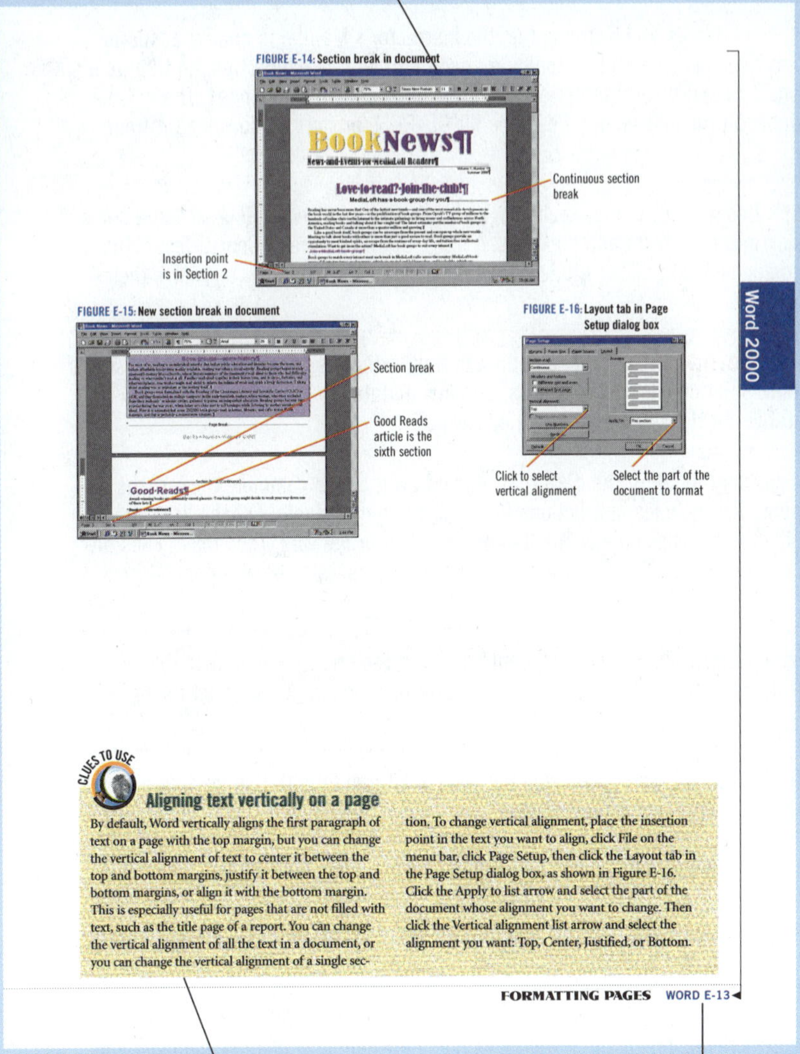
FIGURE E-14: Section break in document

FIGURE E-15: New section break in document

FIGURE E-16: Layout tab in Page Setup dialog box

CLUES TO USE

Aligning text vertically on a page

By default, Word vertically aligns the first paragraph of text on a page with the top margin, but you can change the vertical alignment of text to center it between the top and bottom margins, justify it between the top and bottom margins, or align it with the bottom margin. This is especially useful for pages that are not filled with text, such as the title page of a report. You can change the vertical alignment of all the text in a document, or you can change the vertical alignment of a single section. To change vertical alignment, place the insertion point in the text you want to align, click File on the menu bar, click Page Setup, then click the Layout tab in the Page Setup dialog box, as shown in Figure E-16. Click the Apply to list arrow and select the part of the document whose alignment you want to change. Then click the Vertical alignment list arrow and select the alignment you want: Top, Center, Justified, or Bottom.

FORMATTING PAGES WORD E-13

Clues to Use boxes provide concise information that either expands on one component of the major lesson skill or describes an independent task that is in some way related to the major lesson skill.

The page numbers are designed like a road map. WORD indicates the Word section, E indicates the fifth unit, and 13 indicates the page within the unit.

► MOUS Certification Coverage

Each unit opener has a MOUS next to it to indicate where Microsoft Office User Specialist (MOUS) skills are covered. In addition, there is a MOUS appendix which contains a grid that maps to where specific Core Word MOUS skills can be found in each lesson and where students can find additional practice. This textbook thoroughly prepares students to learn the Core skills needed to pass the Word 2000 MOUS exam. *Microsoft Word—Illustrated Complete, 0-7600-6068-1,* teaches students the Expert skills needed for the Word 2000 Expert MOUS exam.

► Real-World Case

The case study used throughout the textbook, a fictitious company called MediaLoft, is designed to be "'real-world" in nature and introduces the kinds of activities that students will encounter when working with Microsoft Word 2000. With a real-world case, the process of solving problems will be more meaningful to students.

Students can also enhance their skills by completing the Web Works exercises in each unit by going to the innovative Student Online Companion, available at **www.course.com/illustrated/medialoft.** The MediaLoft site mirrors the case study by acting as the company's intranet site, further allowing students to become familiar with applicable business scenarios.

► End-of-Unit Material

Each unit concludes with a Concepts Review that tests students' understanding of what they learned in the unit. The Concepts Review is followed by a Skills Review, which provides students with additional hands-on practice of the skills. The Skills Review is followed by Independent Challenges, which pose case problems for students to solve. At least one Independent Challenge in each unit asks students to use the World Wide Web to solve the problem as indicated by a Web Work icon. The Visual Workshops that follow the Independent Challenges help students develop critical thinking skills. Students are shown completed Web pages or screens and are asked to recreate them.

Instructor's Resource Kit

The Instructor's Resource Kit is Course Technology's way of putting the resources and information needed to teach and learn effectively into your hands. With an integrated array of teaching and learning tools that offers you and your students a broad range of technology-based instructional options, we believe this kit represents the highest quality and most cutting edge resources available to instructors today. Many of these resources are available at www.course.com. The resources available with this book are:

MediaLoft Web site Available at **www.course.com/illustrated/medialoft**, this innovative Student Online Companion enhances and augments the printed page by bringing students onto the Web for a dynamic and continually updated learning experience. The MediaLoft site mirrors the case study used throughout the book, creating a real-world intranet site for this ficticious company, a national chain of bookstore cafés. This Companion is used to complete the WebWorks exercise in each unit of this book, and to allow students to become familiar with the business application of an intranet site.

Instructor's Manual Available as an electronic file, the Instructor's Manual is quality-assurance tested and includes unit overviews, detailed lecture topics for each unit with teaching tips, an Upgrader's Guide, solutions to all lessons and end-of-unit material, and extra Independent Challenges. The Instructor's Manual is available on the Instructor's Resource Kit CD-ROM, or you can download it from **www.course.com**.

Course Test Manager Designed by Course Technology, this Windows-based testing software helps instructors design, administer, and print tests and pre-tests. A full-featured ptogram, Course Test Manager also has an online testing component that allows students to take tests at the computer and have their exams automatically graded.

Course Faculty Online Companion You can browse this textbook's password-protected site to obtain the Instructor's Manual, Solution Files, Project Files, and any updates to the text. Contact your Customer Service Representative for the site address and password.

Project Files Project Files contain all of the data that students will use to complete the lessons and end-of-unit material. A Readme file includes instructions for using the files. Adopters of this text are granted the right to install the Project Files on any standalone computer or network. The Project Files are available on the Instructor's Resource Kit CD-ROM, the Review Pack, and can also be downloaded from www.course.com.

Solution Files Solution Files contain every file students are asked to create or modify in the lessons and end-of-unit material. A Help file on the Instructor's Resource Kit includes information for using the Solution Files.

Figure Files Figure files contain all the figures from the book in bitmap format. Use the figure files to create transparency masters or in a PowerPoint presentation.

WebCT WebCT is a tool used to create Web-based educational environments and also uses WWW browsers as the interface for the course-building environment. The site is hosted on your school campus, allowing complete control over the information. WebCT has its own internal communication system, offering internal e-mail, a Bulletin Board, and a Chat room.

Course Technology offers pre-existing supplemental information to help in your WebCT class creation, such as a suggested Syllabus, Lecture Notes, Figures in the Book / Course Presenter, Student Downloads, and Test Banks in which you can schedule an exam, create reports, and more.

Brief Contents

Contents

Word 2000

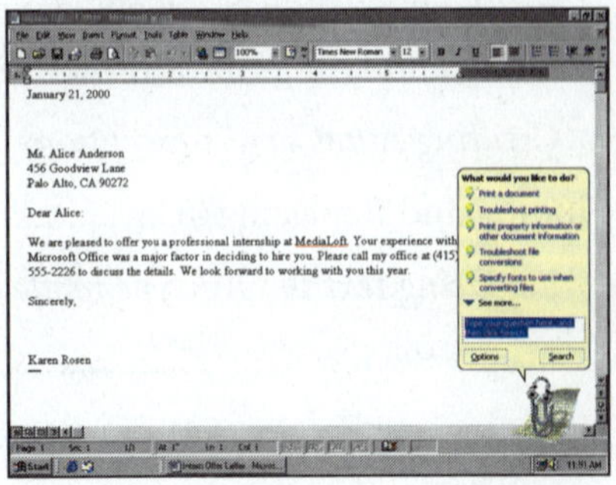

Contents

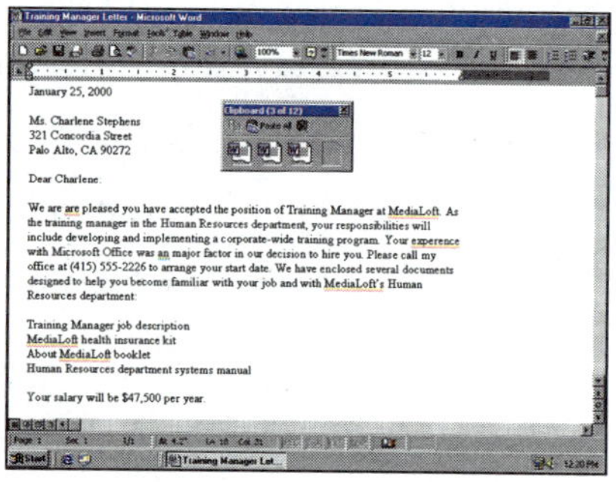

January 25, 2000
Ms. Charlene Stephens
321 Concordia Street
Palo Alto, CA 90272
Dear Charlene:

Formatting a Document — WORD C-1

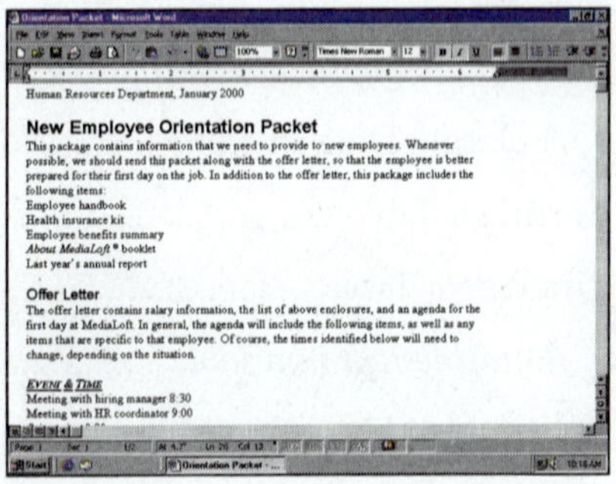

Contents

Working with Tables

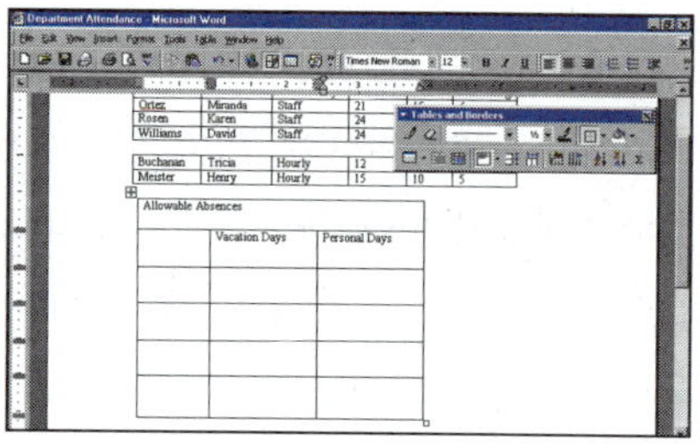

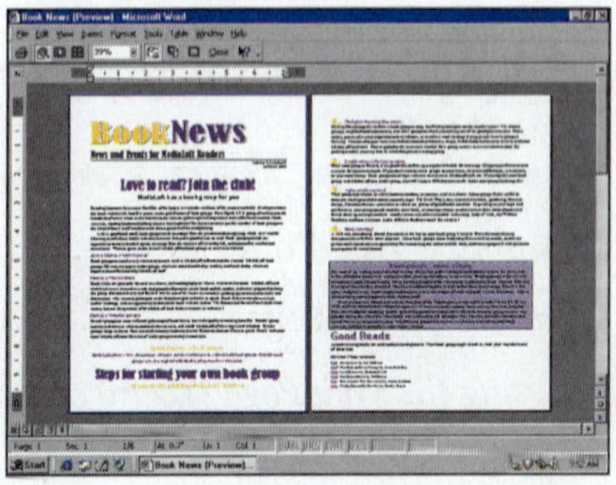

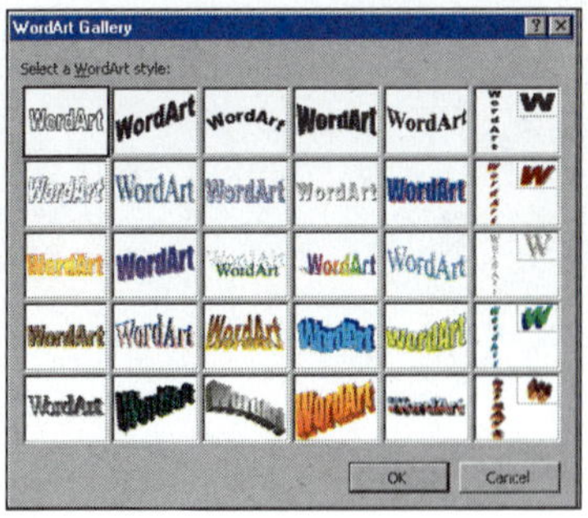
WordArt Gallery
Select a WordArt style:
OK
Cancel

Contents

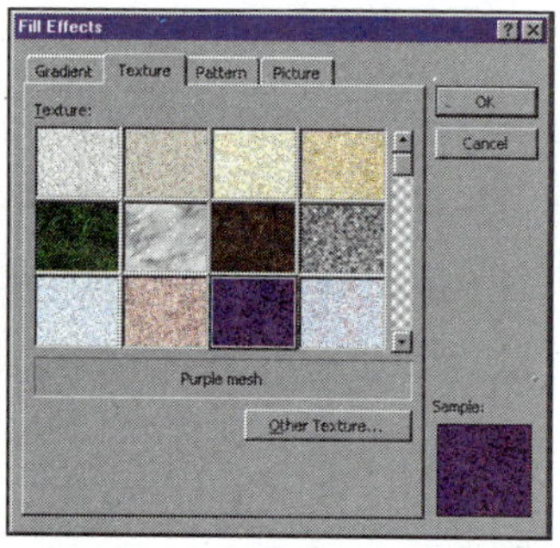

Fill Effects
Gradient
Texture
Pattern
Picture
Texture:
OK
Cancel
Purple mesh
Other Texture...
Sample:

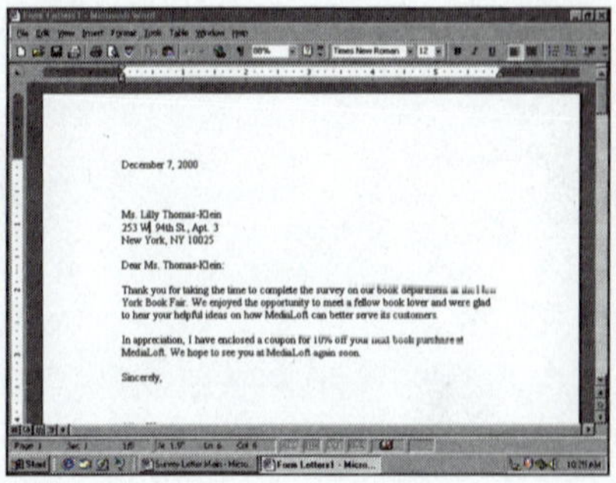
December 7, 2000
Dear Ms. Thomas-Klein:
Sincerely,

Getting Started with Word 2000

Objectives

- Define word processing software
- Start Word 2000
- View the Word program window
- Create a document
- MOUS Save a document
- MOUS Preview and print a document
- MOUS Get Help
- Close a document and exit Word

Welcome to Microsoft Word 2000. Microsoft Word is a powerful computer program that helps you create documents that communicate your ideas clearly and effectively. It includes sophisticated tools for editing text, creating tables and graphics, formatting pages, and proofing a document, to name just a few of its features. The lessons in this unit introduce you to the basic features of Word and familiarize you with the Word environment as you create a new document. Karen Rosen is the director of human resources at MediaLoft, a nationwide chain of bookstore cafés selling books, videos, and CDs. Karen's responsibilities include communicating with employees about company policies and benefits. She uses Word to create attractive and professional-looking documents.

Unit A

Word 2000

Defining Word Processing Software

Microsoft Word is a full-featured word processing program. A **word processing program** is a software program that allows you to create attractive and professional-looking documents quickly and easily. Word processing offers many advantages over typing. The information you type in a word processing document is stored electronically on your computer, so it is easy to revise text and reuse it in other documents. Editing tools allow you to insert and delete text, move information from one part of a document to another, and check spelling and grammar. In addition, you can enhance your documents by changing the appearance of text, adding lines or graphics, and creating tables. Figure A-1 illustrates some of the word processing features you can use to create and enhance your documents using Word.

Details

Word allows you to:

Enter and revise text

Using Word's editing tools, you can easily enter and delete text, insert new text in the middle of a sentence, undo a change, and find and replace text throughout a document.

Copy and move text without retyping

You can copy or move text from one part of a document to another part of the same document, or from one document to a different document.

Locate and correct spelling mistakes and errors in grammar

Word's proofreading tools identify misspelled words and grammatical errors in your documents. You can correct the mistakes yourself or allow Word to suggest a correction.

Format text and design pages

By formatting the text and pages in your document to highlight important ideas, you can create documents that convey your message more effectively to your readers. In Word you can change the size and appearance of text, create bulleted or numbered lists, apply formatting styles, and add borders and shading to words and paragraphs. You can also organize text in columns, change margins, line spacing, and paragraph alignment, and adjust tabs and indents.

Align text in rows and columns using tables

You can create tables in Word to present information in an easy-to-read grid of rows and columns. You can format the tables to emphasize important points, and use the information contained in Word tables to create charts and graphs.

Enhance the appearance of a document using images, lines, and shapes

Word's graphic tools make it easy to illustrate your documents with graphic elements. You can draw lines and shapes, add color, and insert photographs and professionally-designed images into your documents.

Use Mail Merge to personalize form letters and create mailing labels

Mail merge allows you to customize form letters when you need to send the same letter to many different people. When you perform a mail merge, you merge a standard letter with a separate list of names and addresses. Mail merges are useful for creating labels and for sending frequent correspondence to the same group of people.

FIGURE A-1: Features of a word processing document

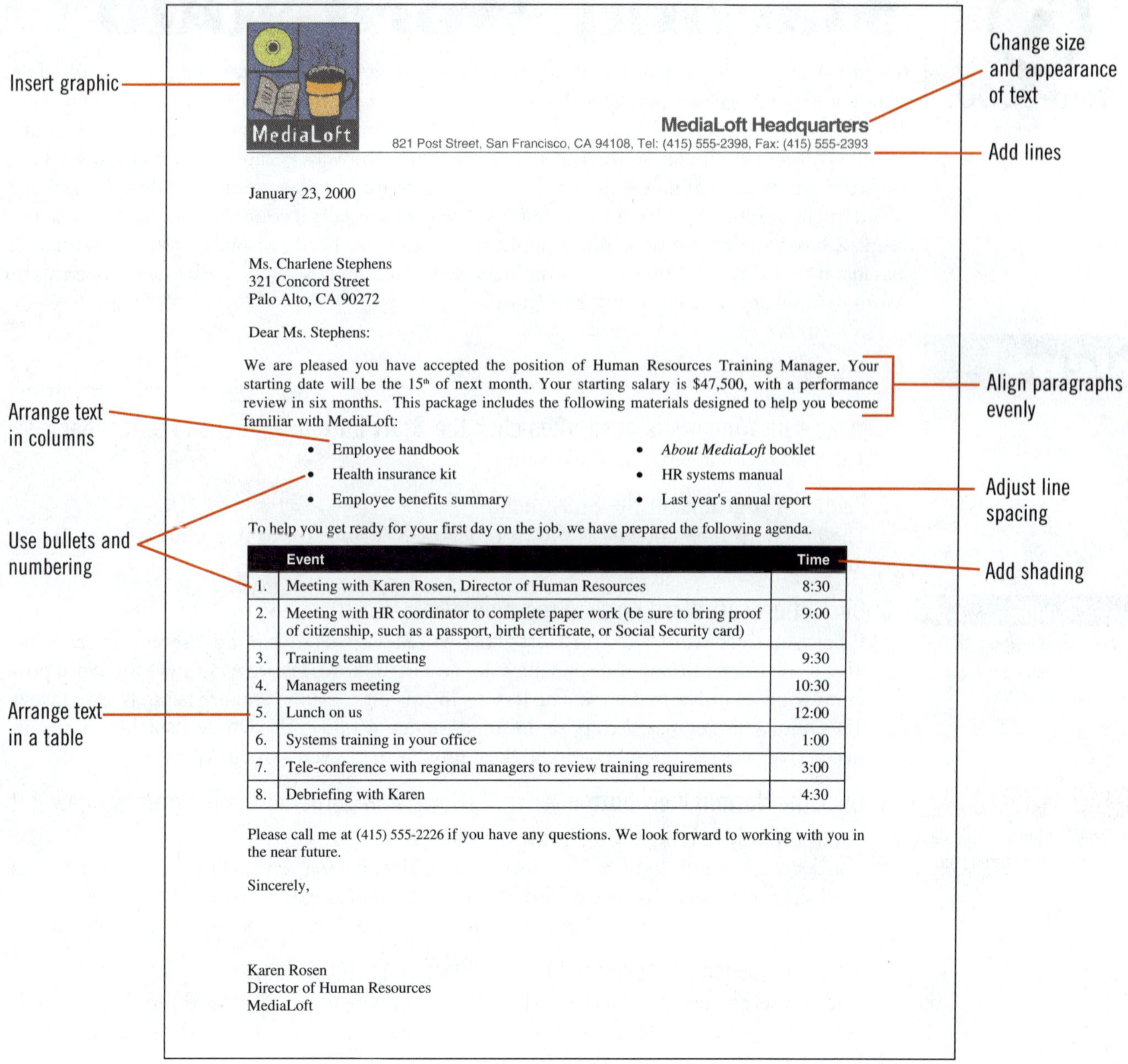

MediaLoft Headquarters
821 Post Street, San Francisco, CA 94108, Tel: (415) 555-2398, Fax: (415) 555-2393

January 23, 2000

Ms. Charlene Stephens
321 Concord Street
Palo Alto, CA 90272

Dear Ms. Stephens:

We are pleased you have accepted the position of Human Resources Training Manager. Your starting date will be the 15th of next month. Your starting salary is $47,500, with a performance review in six months. This package includes the following materials designed to help you become familiar with MediaLoft:

- Employee handbook
- Health insurance kit
- Employee benefits summary
- *About MediaLoft* booklet
- HR systems manual
- Last year's annual report

To help you get ready for your first day on the job, we have prepared the following agenda.

	Event	Time
1.	Meeting with Karen Rosen, Director of Human Resources	8:30
2.	Meeting with HR coordinator to complete paper work (be sure to bring proof of citizenship, such as a passport, birth certificate, or Social Security card)	9:00
3.	Training team meeting	9:30
4.	Managers meeting	10:30
5.	Lunch on us	12:00
6.	Systems training in your office	1:00
7.	Tele-conference with regional managers to review training requirements	3:00
8.	Debriefing with Karen	4:30

Please call me at (415) 555-2226 if you have any questions. We look forward to working with you in the near future.

Sincerely,

Karen Rosen
Director of Human Resources
MediaLoft

Unit A

Word 2000

Starting Word 2000

To start Word, you must first start Windows by turning on your computer. You can start Word on your computer by clicking the Start button on the taskbar, pointing to Programs, and then clicking Microsoft Word on the Programs menu. The Programs menu displays the list of programs installed on your computer, so you can start any program this way. Because computer systems have different setups depending on the hardware and software installed, your procedure for starting Word might be different from the one described below, especially if your computer is part of a network. See your instructor or technical support person if you need assistance. MediaLoft has just installed Word 2000 on the computers in the Human Resources department. Karen starts Word to familiarize herself with the program.

Steps

1. Make sure Windows is open, then click the **Start button** Start on the taskbar
   The Start menu appears on the desktop.

2. Point to **Programs** on the Start menu
   The Programs menu opens, as shown in Figure A-2. Your list of programs will depend on the programs installed on your computer.

3. Click **Microsoft Word** on the Programs menu
   When you start Word, the **Word program window** opens in the most recently used view. **Views** are different ways of displaying a document in Word. Figure A-3 shows the Word program window in Normal view. The lessons in this unit assume you are using Normal view. The Office Assistant may also appear in your program window. The **Office Assistant** is an animated character that appears periodically to provide tips as you work in Word.

4. Click the **Normal View button** in the lower-left corner of the program window if it is not already indented, as shown in Figure A-3
   The document window changes to Normal view. The blinking vertical line | at the left edge of the document window is called the **insertion point.** It indicates where text will appear when you begin typing. When you start Word, you can enter text and create a new document right away.

5. Move the mouse pointer around in the Word program window
   The mouse pointer changes shape depending on where it is in the Word program window. When the mouse pointer is in the document window in Normal view, the pointer changes to an **I-beam** I. Table A-1 describes other Word mouse pointers.

6. If the Office Assistant appears in your program window, move the pointer over the Office Assistant, then click the **right mouse button**
   Right-clicking displays a pop-up menu of commands related to the item you click. You can choose to hide the Office Assistant until you want to get help with Word.

7. Click **Hide** on the pop-up menu
   The Office Assistant disappears from the window.

8. Click **Tools** on the menu bar, click **Customize**, click the **Options tab** in the Customize dialog box, click **Reset my usage data** to restore the default settings, click **Yes** in the alert box, then click **Close**
   You'll learn about restoring default settings for toolbars and menus in the next lesson.

Trouble?

If an Office Assistant dialog balloon appears, click Start using Microsoft Word.

QuickTip

An indented button indicates that a feature is turned on.

Trouble?

If the Office Assistant does not appear, continue with Step 8.

Trouble?

See your instructor or technical support person for assistance.

FIGURE A-2: Starting Word from the desktop

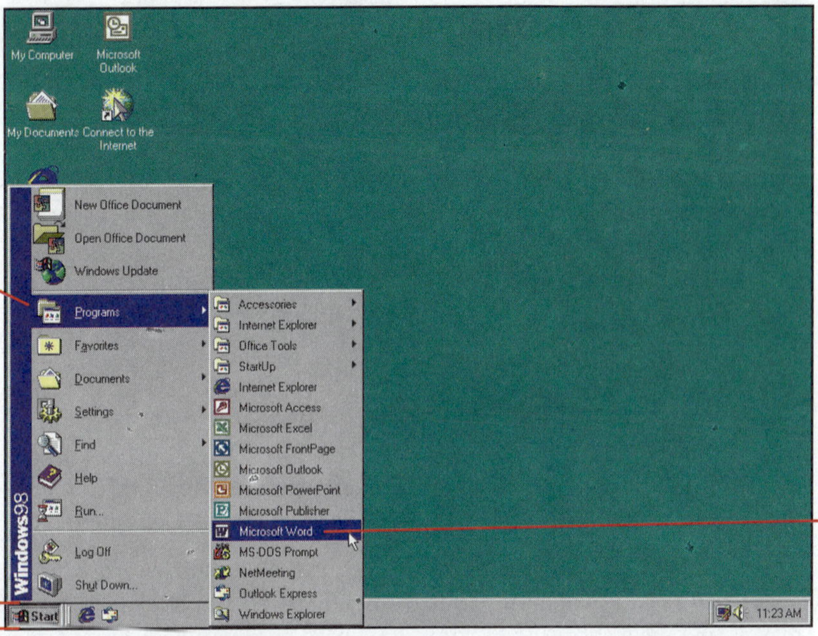

FIGURE A-3: Word program window in Normal view

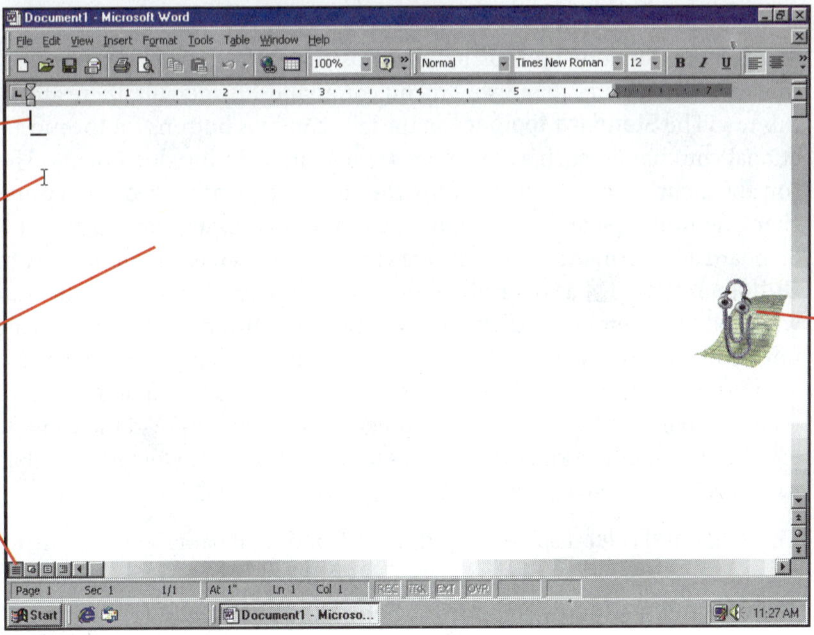

TABLE A-1: Pointers in Word

pointer	description
	Appears in the document window when working in Normal, Web Layout, and Outline views; use to move the insertion point in the document, or to select text to edit
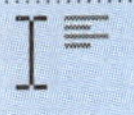	Appears in the document window when working in Print Layout view; use to move the insertion point in the document or to select text to edit
	Appears when you point to a menu, toolbar, ruler, status bar, or other areas that are not part of the document window; use to click a button, menu command, or other element of the Word program window
	Appears when you point to the left edge of a line of text; use to select a line or lines of text
	Appears when you click the What's This command on the Help menu; click this pointer over text to view the format settings applied to the text, or click an element of the Word program window or a dialog box to view information about that tool, option, or feature

Unit A

Word 2000

Viewing the Word Program Window

When you start Word, the Word program window opens with a new, blank document in the document window. Refer to your screen and Figure A-4 as you locate the elements of the Word program window described below.

Details

Trouble?

If your Word program window does not fill your screen, click the Maximize button on the title bar.

- The **title bar** displays the name of the document and the name of the program. Until you save the document and give it a name, its temporary name is Document1.
- The **menu bar** lists the names of the menus that contain Word commands. Clicking a menu name displays a list of commands from which you can choose. When you open a menu, you may at first see a short list of commonly used commands. After the menu remains open for a few seconds, additional commands appear on the menu. Menus stay open until you point to another menu, click outside the menu, or press [Esc].
- The **toolbar** contains buttons for the most frequently used commands. Clicking buttons on a toolbar is often faster than using menu commands. By default, there are actually two toolbars in this row. The **Standard toolbar** (on the left) contains buttons for the most commonly used operational commands, such as opening, saving, and printing documents. The **Formatting toolbar** (on the right) contains buttons for the most frequently used formatting commands, such as changing font type and size, applying bold to text, or aligning text. Not all the buttons on the Standard and Formatting toolbars are visible on the screen. To view other buttons, click the **More Buttons button** at the right end of each toolbar. Throughout the lessons in this book, you will need to remember to click the More Buttons button if a button you are instructed to click is not visible on your screen. When you use a button from the More Buttons list, Word adds it to your visible toolbar. That's why each user's toolbars look unique. You can return your toolbars to their original state by resetting your usage data. Be sure to read the Clues to Use in this lesson to learn more about working with Word's toolbars. Word also includes toolbars related to other features, such as a toolbar that contains drawing tools.
- The **horizontal ruler** displays tab settings, left and right paragraph indents, and document margins.
- The **document window** is the area where you type text and format and organize the content of your documents. The blinking insertion point is the location where text appears when you type.
- The **vertical and horizontal scroll bars** display the relative position of the text displayed in the document window. You use the scroll bars and **scroll boxes** to view different parts of your document.
- The **view buttons**, which appear in the horizontal scroll bar, allow you to display the document in one of four views: Normal, Web Layout, Print Layout, and Outline. Each view offers features that are useful for working on different types of documents.
- The **status bar** displays the current page number, section number, total number of pages in the document, and the position of the insertion point (in inches, in lines, and in columns, from the upper-left corner of the document).
- **ScreenTips** appear when you place the pointer over a toolbar button or some other element of the Word program window. A ScreenTip is a label that identifies the name of the button or feature.

FIGURE A-4: Elements of the Word program window

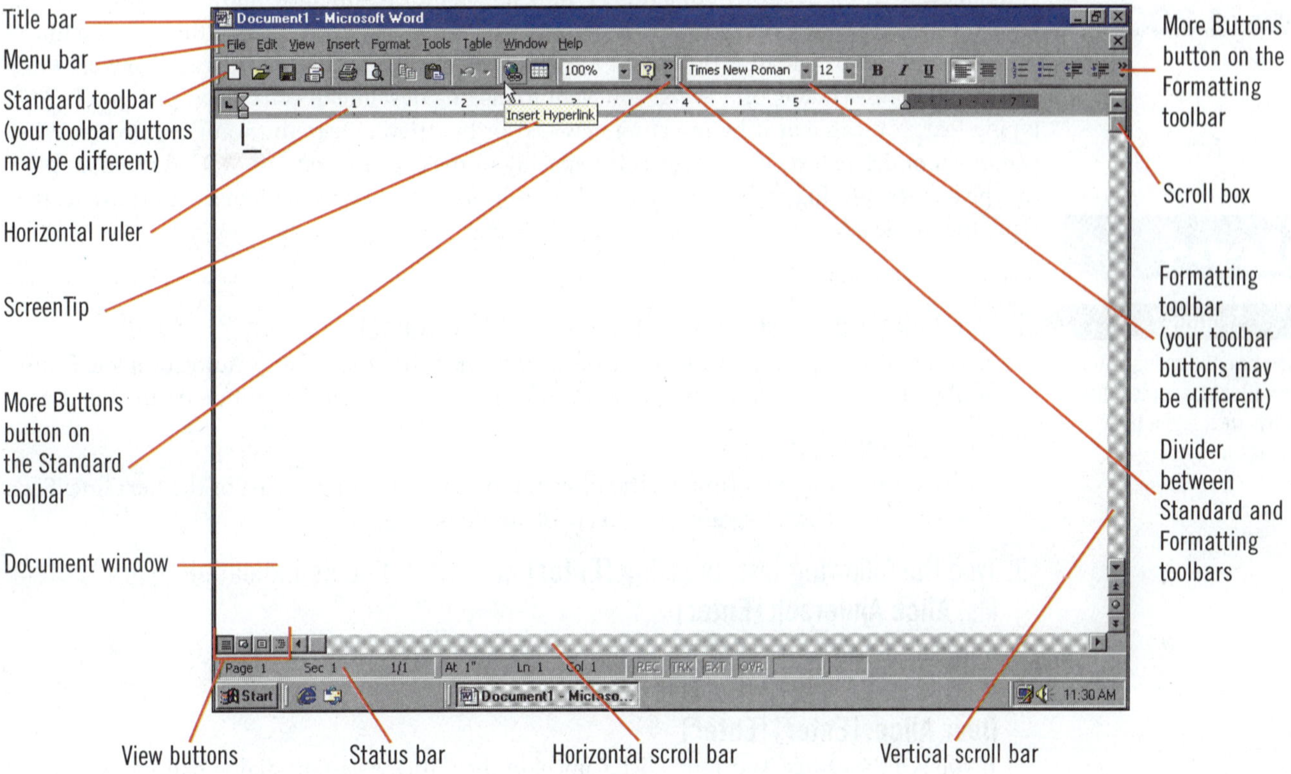

Word 2000

CLUES TO USE

Personalized toolbars and menus in Word 2000

Word toolbars and menus modify themselves to your working style. The Standard and Formatting toolbars you see when you first start Word include the most frequently used buttons. To locate a button not visible on a toolbar, click the More Buttons button on the Standard or Formatting toolbar to see the list of additional toolbar buttons. As you work, Word adds the buttons you use to the visible toolbars, and moves the buttons you haven't used in a while to the More Buttons list. Similarly, Word menus adjust to your work habits, so that the commands you use most often automatically appear on shortened menus. Click the double arrow at the bottom of a menu to view additional menu commands. You can return toolbars and menus to their default settings by clicking Tools on the menu bar, then clicking Customize. On the Options tab in the Customize dialog box, click Reset my usage data. An alert box or the Office Assistant appears asking if you are sure you want to do this. Click Yes, then click Close in the Customize dialog box. Resetting your usage data erases changes made automatically to your menus and toolbars. It does not affect the options you set yourself. The lessons in this book assume you are using personalized menus and toolbars, but you can also turn off this feature if you'd like, so that your Standard and Formatting toolbars appear on separate rows, and your menus display the full list of commands. To turn off these features, remove the checks from the Standard and Formatting toolbars share one row and the Menus show recently used commands first checkboxes in the Customize dialog box, then click Close.

Unit A

Word 2000

Creating a Document

You can begin a new document by simply typing text in the document window. Entering text with a word processor is different from typing with a typewriter. When you reach the end of a line as you type with Word, the insertion point moves to the next line. This feature is called **wordwrap**. You need to press [Enter] only when you want to insert a new line or start a new paragraph. After typing text, you can edit it by inserting new text or by deleting text you want to remove. When you insert or delete text, Word adjusts the spacing of the existing text. Karen uses Word to type a letter offering an internship to Alice Anderson. She begins her letter with the date, then types the inside address, salutation, body, and closing.

Steps

Trouble?

If you type the wrong letter, press [Backspace] to erase the incorrect letter, then type again.

1. Type **today's date**, starting with the month (for example, January 21, 2000)
   As you type the space after the name of the month, notice that Word's AutoComplete feature displays today's date. You can ignore AutoComplete for now and continue typing the date.
2. Press **[Enter]** four times
   The first time you press [Enter], the insertion point moves to the start of the next line. Each time you press [Enter] again, you create blank lines.
3. Type the following text, pressing **[Enter]** after each line as indicated:
   Ms. Alice Anderson [Enter]
   456 Goodview Lane [Enter]
   Palo Alto, CA 90272 [Enter] [Enter]
   Dear Alice: [Enter] [Enter]
   If you see the Office Assistant, click Cancel in the Office Assistant dialog balloon. If you see a wavy, red line under words it means that these words are not in Word's dictionary and might be misspelled. You can ignore the wavy lines for now. Don't worry if you make typing errors. You can fix them after you finish typing the letter.

QuickTip

Word processing programs have made it unnecessary to type two spaces after a period. Typing one space provides enough space after a period to separate sentences because the space is automatically adjusted by the word processing software.

4. Type the following, pressing **[Enter]** twice at the end of the paragraph as indicated:
   We are pleased to offer you an internship at MediaLoft. Your experience with Microsoft Office was a major factor in deciding to hire you. Please call my office at (415) 555-2221 to discuss the details. We look forward to working with you this year. [Enter] [Enter]
5. Type **Sincerely**, press **[Enter]** four times, then type your name
   Your letter should resemble Figure A-5. Don't be concerned if your text wraps differently than the text shown in the figure. Text wrapping can depend on your monitor or printer. Now that you have finished typing the letter, you can edit it by inserting and deleting text as necessary.
6. Position the pointer I after the word **an** (but before the space) in the first sentence, then click to place the insertion point
   The insertion point is now located between the words "an" and "internship" in the first sentence. Anything you type will be added to the document here.

Trouble?

If your typing overwrites existing text, double-click OVR in the status bar to switch back to Insert mode. See your instructor or technical support person for assistance.

7. Press **[Backspace]**, press **[Spacebar]**, then type **professional**
   Pressing [Backspace] removes the character before the insertion point.
8. Place the insertion point between **2** and **1** in the third sentence, press **[Delete]** to remove the character **1**, then type **6**
   Pressing [Delete] removes the character after the insertion point. Fix your other typing mistakes using [Backspace] or [Delete], then compare your document to Figure A-6. You'll learn how to save your new document in the next lesson.

FIGURE A-5: Text in a Word document

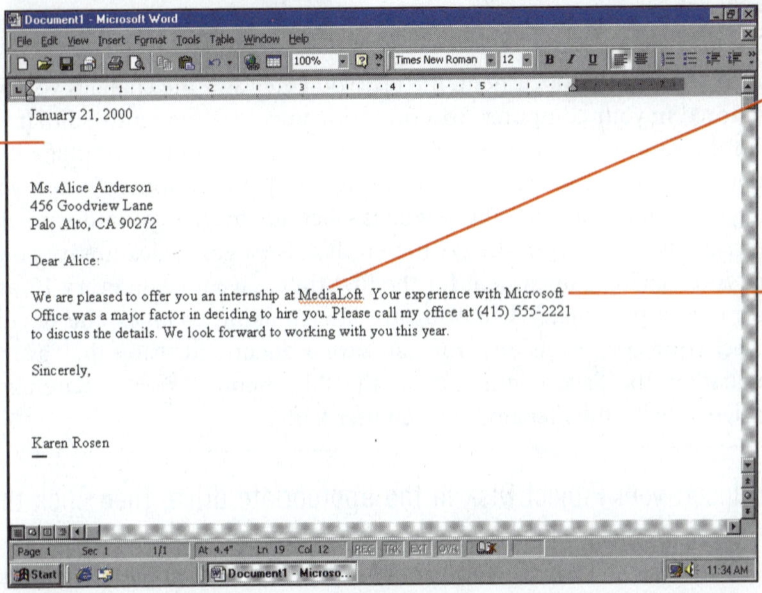

FIGURE A-6: Edited document

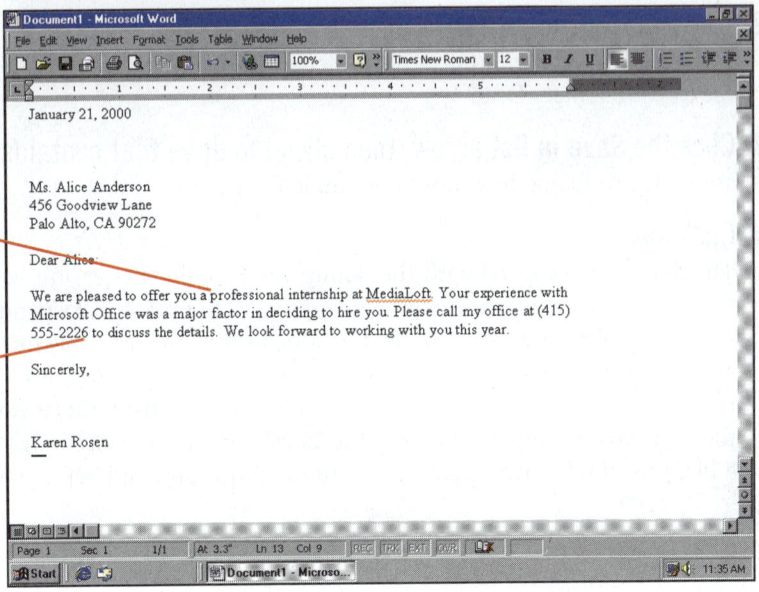

CLUES TO USE

Working with AutoCorrect

Certain kinds of spelling or typographical errors are automatically corrected as you type. This feature is called **AutoCorrect**. For example, Word corrects some common spelling mistakes (such as typing "adn" instead of "and") as soon as you type the first space or punctuation mark after the word. Similarly, if you type two uppercase letters in a row, the second character is automatically changed to lowercase as you continue typing (except in a state's abbreviation, such as "WA"). If Word makes a correction that you do not want to use, click the Undo button on the Standard toolbar. If you type a word that is not in Word's dictionary, the word is underlined with a red, wavy line to indicate it may be misspelled. If you make a possible grammatical error, the error is underlined with a green, wavy line. Right-click red- or green-underlined text to display a pop-up menu of correction options, then click a correction to accept it and remove the underlining.

Saving a Document

When you create a document, the text you enter and the changes you make are only temporarily stored in your computer. To store a document permanently so that you can retrieve and edit it in the future, you must **save** your document to your computer's internal hard disk or to a floppy disk. Documents are saved as **files** on your computer. When you save a document you give it a name, called a **filename**. It's helpful to give your documents brief filenames that describe the contents of the document. It's also a good idea to save your work soon after starting. After saving a document for the first time, save it again every 10 or 15 minutes and always save before printing. When you save after making changes, the document file is updated to reflect your latest revisions. You can save a document using the Save button on the Standard toolbar or the Save command on the File menu. Karen saves her letter to Alice Anderson with the filename Intern Offer Letter.

Steps

1. **Insert your Project Disk in the appropriate drive, then click the Save button on the Standard toolbar**
   The first time you save a document the Save As dialog box opens, as shown in Figure A-7. In this dialog box, you assign a name to the document (replacing the default filename) and indicate the location where you want the file to be stored. The default filename is based on the first few words of the document, in this case today's date.

2. **Type Intern Offer Letter in the File name text box**
   The name of the current drive or folder appears in the Save in list box. You want to save the file to your Project Disk.

3. **Click the Save in list arrow, then click the drive that contains your Project Disk**
   Your Save As dialog box should resemble Figure A-8.

4. **Click Save**
   The document is saved with the name "Intern Offer Letter" on your Project Disk. Notice that the new name of the document appears in the title bar. Depending on your computer's settings in Windows Explorer, the filename in your title bar may include the DOC extension after the period. All Word documents automatically include this extension to help you distinguish Word documents from other files on your disks. Once you save a document as a file, you can continue to work on it in Word, or you can close it. If you continue to work on a file, you should save it again every 10 or 15 minutes and before you close it.

QuickTip

This book assumes your Project Disk is in drive A. Substitute the correct drive if this is not the case. See your instructor or technical support person for assistance.

Clues to Use

Using the AutoRecover feature

The AutoRecover feature in Word automatically saves your document every few minutes in a temporary file, so that all your work is not lost in case of an interruption to power or some other problem that abruptly stops Word. If Word shuts down unexpectedly, a temporary version of the document you were working on opens automatically the next time you start Word. You can then save the temporary document with a filename and continue to work on it. AutoRecover is not a substitute for using the Save command frequently, so be sure to save a new document right away and to save often. To change how often AutoRecover saves a document, click Tools on the menu bar, click Options, change the number of minutes on the Save tab, then click OK.

FIGURE A-7: Save As dialog box

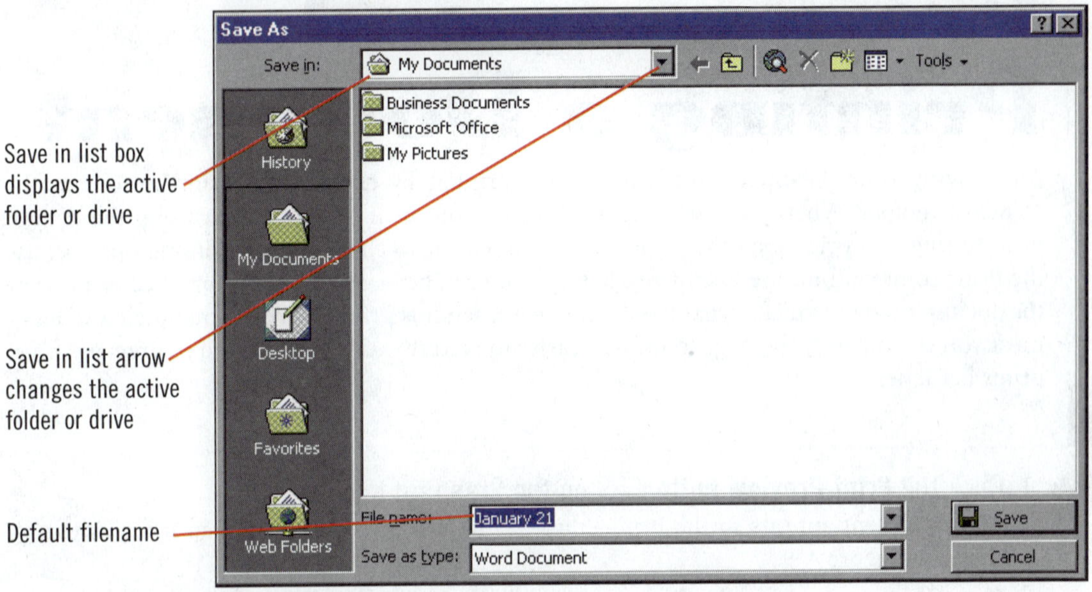

FIGURE A-8: File to be saved to the A drive

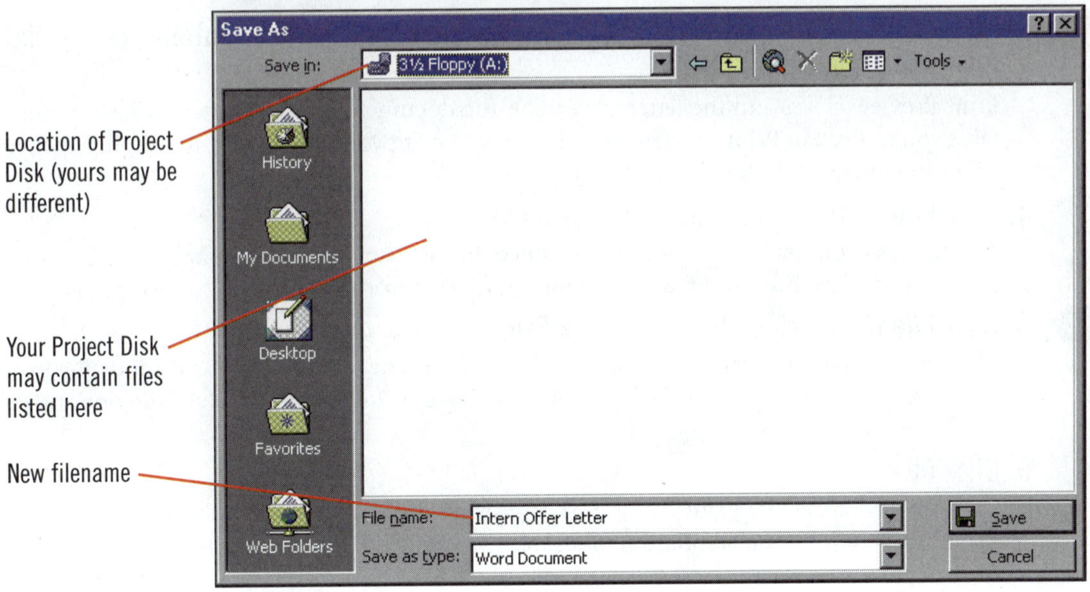

Word 2000

Unit A
Word 2000

Previewing and Printing a Document

After saving your document, you can quickly print it by clicking the Print button on the Standard toolbar. When you use the Print button, you print the document using the default print settings. To print a specific page of a document or to choose other printing options, use the Print command on the File menu. Before printing, however, it is good practice to preview the document to see exactly what it will look like when it is printed. When you preview a document you can magnify the page to make it easier to read the text. Karen previews, then prints her letter.

Steps

Trouble?

If does not appear on your Standard toolbar, click the More Buttons button to view additional toolbar buttons.

QuickTip

Click the Print button on the Print Preview toolbar to print the document directly from Print Preview.

Trouble?

If you are not connected to a printer, ask your instructor or technical support person for assistance.

1. Click the **Print Preview button** on the Standard toolbar
   The document appears in the Print Preview window as it will look when it is printed, as shown in Figure A-9.
2. Move the pointer over the page until it changes to , then click the letter
   Clicking with magnifies the document in the Print Preview window, allowing you to read the text. When the document is magnified the pointer changes to . Clicking with reduces the size of the document in the Print Preview window.
3. Examine your letter for mistakes, then click the **Close Preview button** on the Print Preview toolbar
   Print Preview closes and the letter appears in the document window. After fixing any mistakes you noticed in Print Preview, you are ready to print your document. You should always save a document right before printing it.
4. Click **File** on the menu bar, then click **Save**
   Any changes you made to the document since the last time you saved it are saved. You can also click the Save button on the Standard toolbar or press [Ctrl][S] to save changes.
5. Click **File** on the menu bar, then click **Print**
   The Print dialog box opens, as shown in Figure A-10. The settings in your Print dialog box might be different, depending on your printer. Table A-2 describes some of the options in the Print dialog box.
6. Click **OK**
   Clicking OK closes the Print dialog box and prints your document. You can also use the Print button on the Standard toolbar to print the document using the default settings.

TABLE A-2: Options in the Print dialog box

print option	use to
Printer Name	Change the current printer
Properties	Display the printer's Properties dialog box; use it to change settings for the size or type of paper in your printer, the orientation of the paper, the resolution you want your printer to use, and other printer properties
Page range	Indicate what pages of a document to print
Copies	Specify the number of copies to print, and whether or not you want the copies to be collated
Zoom	Specify the number of pages you want to print on each sheet of paper
Print what	Select which aspect of a document to print, such as the document itself (the default) or other associated text
Print	Specify the portion of the document you want to print

FIGURE A-9: Print Preview window

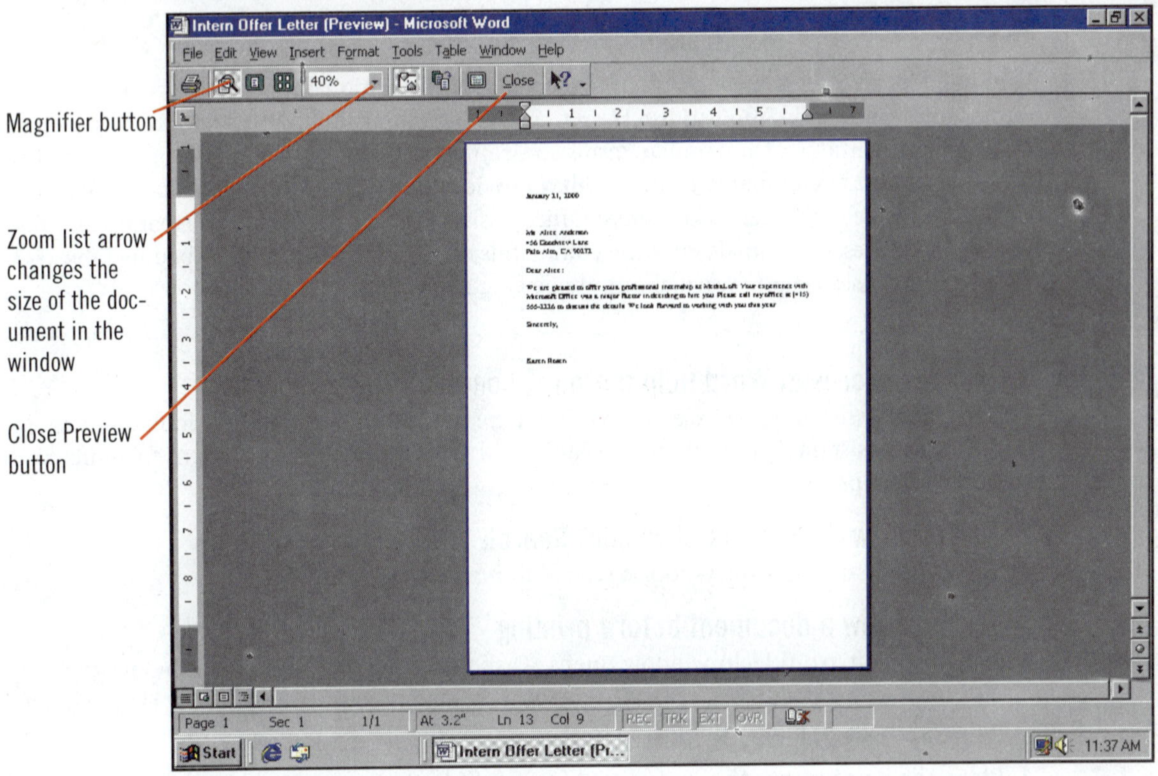

FIGURE A-10: Print dialog box

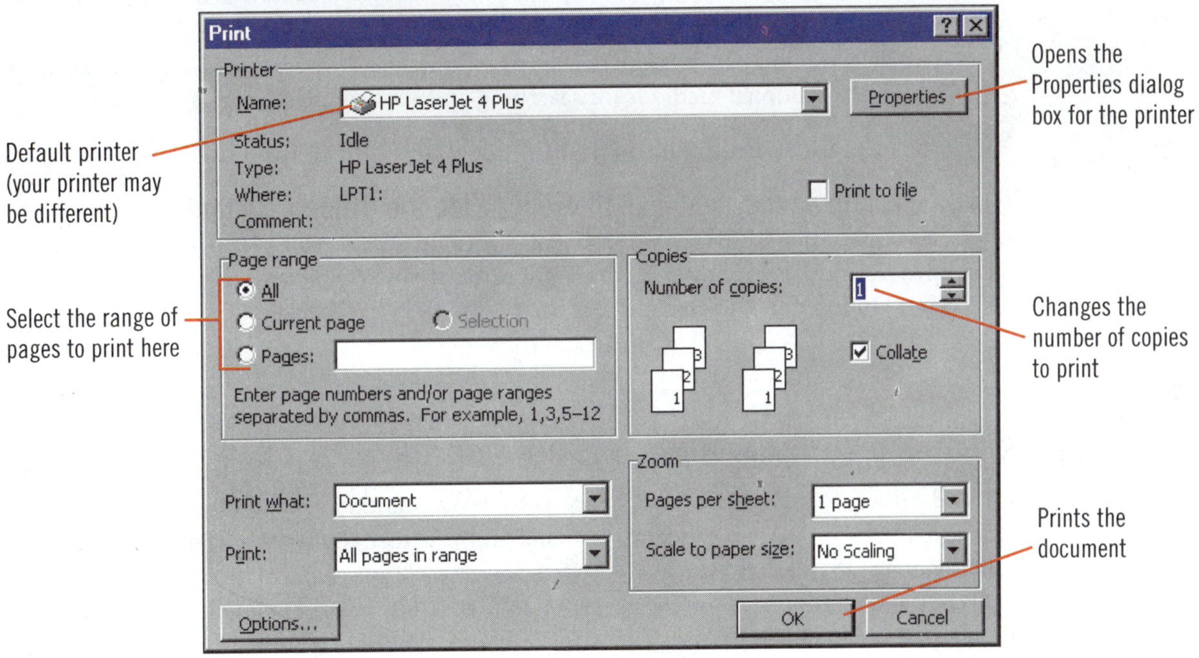

Unit A

Word 2000

Getting Help

Word includes an extensive Help system that provides information and instructions about Word features and commands. You can use Help to get as little or as much information as you need, from quick definitions of unfamiliar terms to detailed steps for completing a procedure. The **Office Assistant**, an animated character that provides tips while you are working in Word, is one way to get help. You can also use the Office Assistant to display Help information and discover new features. You can also use the commands on the Help menu, described in Table A-3.
Karen uses Help to learn about previewing a document.

Steps

Trouble?

If the Help window opens instead of the Office Assistant, someone turned the Office Assistant off on your computer. Click the Close button in the Help window, click Help on the menu bar, click Show the Office Assistant, then repeat Step 1.

1. Click the **Microsoft Word Help button** on the Standard toolbar
   The Office Assistant appears, as shown in Figure A-11. Your assistant may look different. In the Office Assistant dialog ballon, you can enter key words or whole questions for which you would like more information.
2. Type **preview documents**, then click **Search**
   The Office Assistant displays topics related to previewing documents.
3. Click **Preview a document before printing**
   The Microsoft Word Help window opens, as shown in Figure A-12. Read the information on previewing a document before you continue. The underlined text in the Help window indicates a link to a related topic.
4. Place the pointer over the underlined topic **edit text in print preview** until the pointer changes to, then click
   A new Help window opens displaying the steps for editing text in print preview.
5. Click the **Magnifier button** in the Help window
   A pop-up description of this button opens. Read the description before you continue.
6. Click the description to close it, then click the **Show button** on the Help window toolbar
   The Help window expands and displays the Contents, Answer Wizard, and Index tabs. These tabs offer additional methods for searching and accessing Help topics.
7. Click the **Close button** in the Help window to return to Word
8. Click **Help** on the menu bar, then click **Hide the Office Assistant**
   Selecting Hide the Office Assistant hides it temporarily; it will reappear later to give you tips. To turn off the Office Assistant completely, right-click the Assistant, click Options, and deselect the Use the Office Assistant checkbox.

CLUES TO USE

Using the Contents, Index, and Answer Wizard tabs to get Help

The Contents, Index, and Answer Wizard tabs offer different methods for searching Word's Help system. Use the Contents tab as you would use a table of contents in a book. Scroll through the list of general topics to find the topic that best relates to the topic that interests you, then click the plus sign next to each closed book icon to display a list of subtopics in that topic. Click a subtopic to display information about it in the Help window. The Answer Wizard tab works like the Office Assistant: type a question (or even just the name of the feature you want to learn about), then click Search to display information about your question in the Help window. Use the Index tab to search for topics that relate to a keyword. Type your keyword in the first box, click Search, then double-click the keyword in the second box that best describes your topic. In the third box, click the topic you want to view in the Help window.

FIGURE A-11: Word's Office Assistant

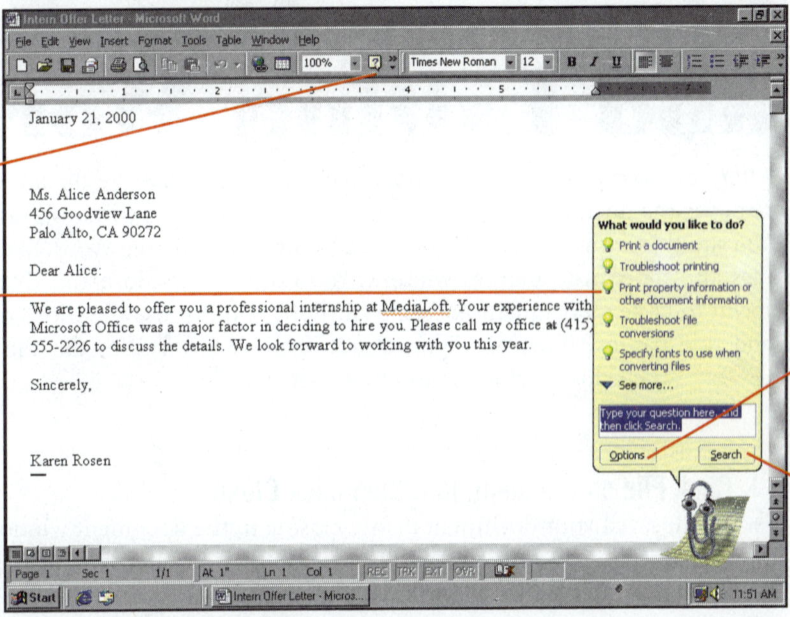

FIGURE A-12: Microsoft Word Help window

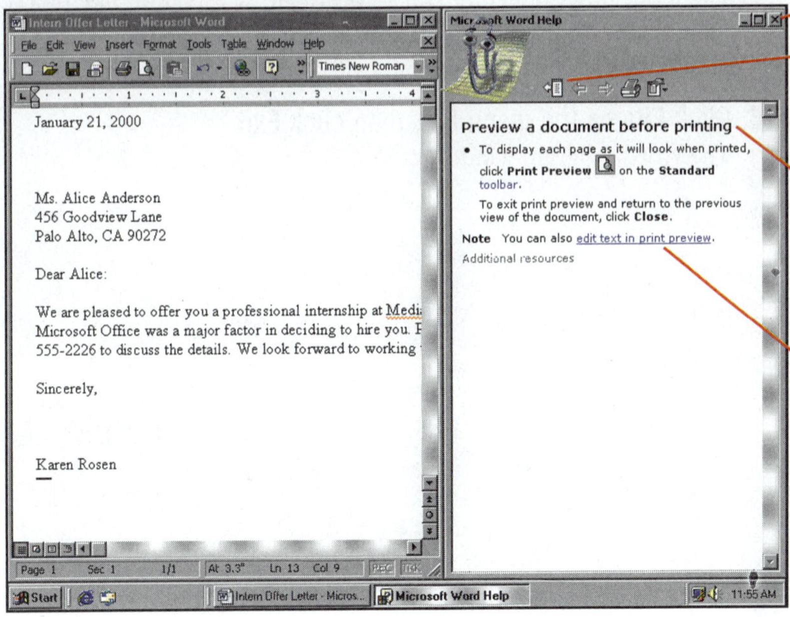

TABLE A-3: Help menu options

help menu option	function
Microsoft Word Help	Opens the Office Assistant if the Office Assistant is turned on; opens the Microsoft Word Help window if the Office Assistant is turned off
Show/Hide the Office Assistant	Opens/closes the Office Assistant
What's This?	Changes the mouse pointer to ; click a button or menu option to view a brief explanation
Office on the Web	Connects to Microsoft's Web site, where you can find additional information and articles; you must be connected to the Internet to use this option
About Microsoft Word	Provides the version and Product ID of Word

Unit A
Word 2000

Closing a Document and Exiting Word

After you save your work on a document, you can close the document. Closing a document removes the document window from the Word program window, but it does not close Word. You should save and close all open documents before exiting Word. Exiting Word closes all open files and the Word program window. You can use the Close and Exit commands on the File menu to close a document and exit Word, or you can use the Close buttons on the menu bar and title bar, as shown in Figure A-13. Table A-4 describes the Close and Exit commands. Karen closes her letter and then exits Word.

Steps

QuickTip

You can also close a document by clicking the Close Window button on the menu bar.

1. Click **File** on the menu bar, then click **Close**

   If you saved your document before closing it, the document window closes immediately. If you did not save your changes before closing it, an alert box or the Office Assistant opens, asking if you want to save your changes.

2. Click **Yes**, if necessary

   The Word program window remains open, as shown in Figure A-14. After you close a document you can use the menus and toolbars to create a new document or to open an existing Word document, or you can exit Word.

QuickTip

You can also exit Word by clicking the Close button on the title bar.

3. Click **File** on the menu bar, then click **Exit**

   The Word program window closes.

TABLE A-4: The Close and Exit commands

command	function
Close	Closes the current document; leaves Word open so that you can open another document or use Help
Exit	Closes all open Word files; closes the Word program window and returns you to the Windows desktop

FIGURE A-13: Closing the document and program windows

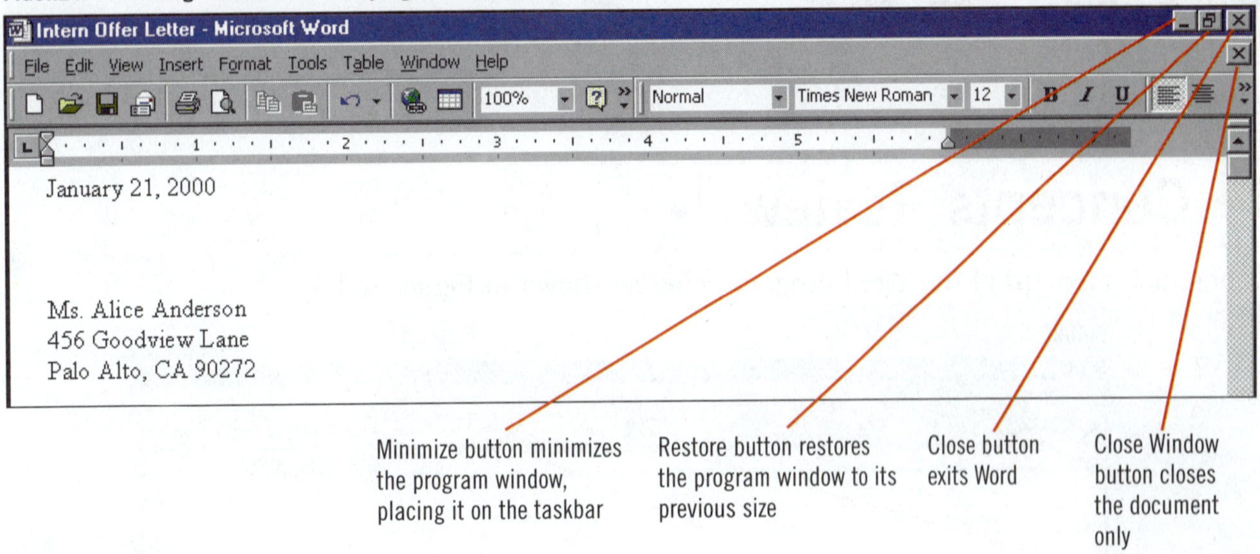

FIGURE A-14: Word program window with no documents open

Practice

Concepts Review

Label each element of the Word program window shown in Figure A-15.

FIGURE A-15

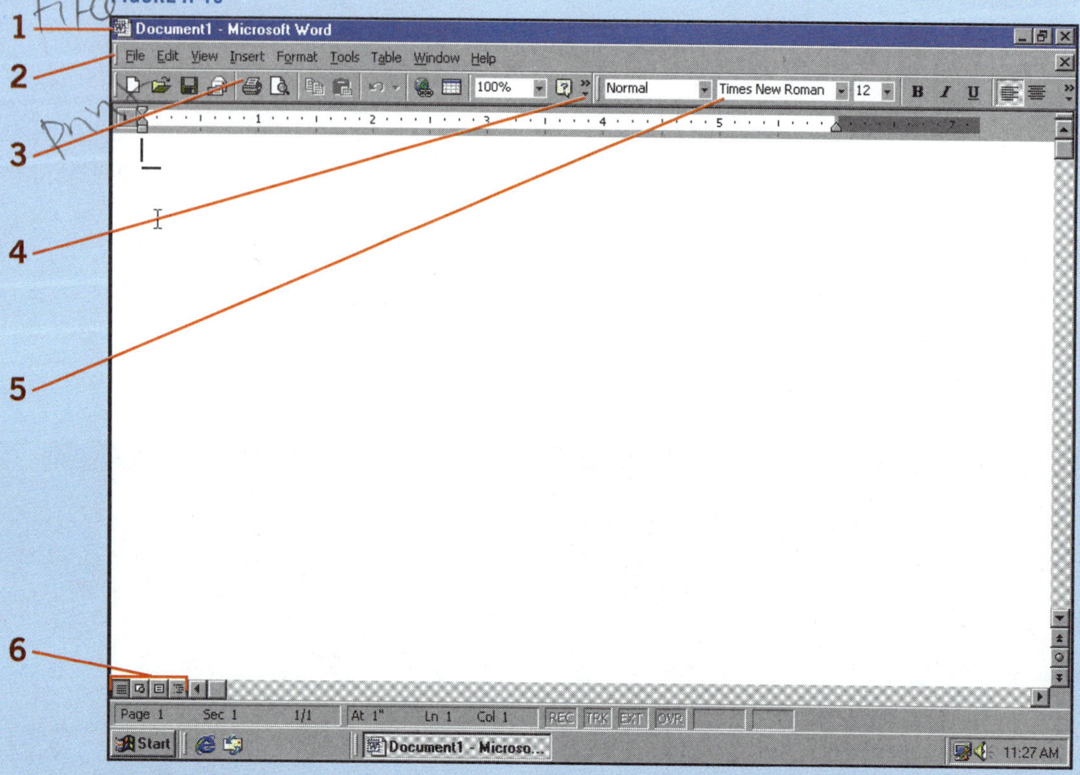

Match each term with the statement that describes it.

7. **Standard toolbar**
8. **Formatting toolbar**
9. **Document window**
10. **Ruler**
11. **Status bar**
12. **AutoCorrect**
13. **More Buttons button**
14. **Office Assistant**

- **a.** The part of the Word program window in which you enter text
- **b.** Identifies the location of the insertion point
- **c.** Contains buttons for commands such as Save and Print
- **d.** Changes the spelling of misspelled words as you type
- **e.** Displays tab settings and paragraph and document margins
- **f.** Provides tips and information about using Word
- **g.** Contains buttons for commands that change the appearance of text
- **h.** Displays buttons not currently visible on the toolbar

Select the best answer from the list of choices.

15. How is word processing different from typing with a typewriter?
- **a.** Word processors allow you to enter new text in the middle of a sentence
- **b.** Word processors use word wrap
- **c.** Word processors automatically adjust the spacing between characters
- **d.** All of the above

16. To view a document as it will look when printed, you
- **a.** Click File on the menu bar, then click Print.
- **b.** Click the Normal View button on the horizontal scroll bar.
- **c.** Click the Print Preview button on the Standard toolbar.
- **d.** Click View on the menu bar, then click Document Map.

17. You can get Help in any of the following ways, except
- **a.** Viewing topics on the Contents tab.
- **b.** Double-clicking anywhere in the document window.
- **c.** Clicking the Microsoft Word Help button on the Standard toolbar.
- **d.** Clicking Help on the menu bar.

18. The Close command on the File menu
- **a.** Closes Word without saving any changes.
- **b.** If you have made changes to the document, asks if you want to save them, then closes the document.
- **c.** Closes all open Word documents.
- **d.** Closes the document without saving changes.

19. To close the Word program window, you must
- **a.** Click File on the menu bar, then click Close.
- **b.** Click the Exit button on the Standard toolbar.
- **c.** Click File on the menu bar, then click Exit.
- **d.** Click the Close Window button on the menu bar.

20. The Standard toolbar does not include
- **a.** The Save button.
- **b.** The More Buttons button.
- **c.** The Bold button.
- **d.** The Print button.

Skills Review

1. Start Word 2000.

- **a.** Click the Start button on the Windows taskbar.
- **b.** Click Microsoft Word on the Programs menu.
- **c.** Click the Normal View button if necessary.
- **d.** Hide the Office Assistant if it appears.
- **e.** Reset your usage data to return your toolbars and menus to the default settings. (*Hint*: Click Tools on the menu bar, click Customize, click the Options tab in the Customize dialog box, click Reset my usage data, click Yes, then click Close.

2. View the Word program window.

- **a.** Identify as many elements of the Word program window as you can.
- **b.** Click each menu and drag the pointer through all the commands on each menu.
- **c.** Point to each button on the toolbars and read the ScreenTips.
- **d.** Click the More Buttons buttons on the Standard and Formatting toolbars and read the ScreenTips for the buttons on the More Buttons lists.

3. Create a document.

- **a.** Begin a short letter to your local newspaper. Type today's date.
- **b.** In the inside address, type "Editor," the name of the paper, a street address, and the city, state, and zip code. Make up the information if you don't know it.
- **c.** For a salutation, type "To Whom It May Concern:" (If the Office Assistant appears, click Cancel.)
- **d.** In the body of the letter, state that you are interested in a career in journalism, and mention that you have strong Word 2000 skills. Request an informational interview with the editors to learn more about working for newpapers.
- **e.** For a closing, type "Sincerly," press [Enter] four times, then type your name. (Notice that Word corrects your typing for you.)
- **f.** Insert the sentence "I can be reached at 555-3030." after the last sentence in your letter.
- **g.** Correct any spelling and grammatical mistakes you made as you typed the letter. (*Hint*: Use the [Backspace] or [Delete] key to correct your typing.)
- **h.** Using the [Backspace] key, change the inside address to:
  Ms. Alexandra Thomas
  Hamilton Transcript
  35 Conval Street
  Hamilton, NH 02468
- **i.** Using the [Delete] key, change the salutation to "Dear Ms. Thomas:"

4. Save a document.

- **a.** Click File on the menu bar, then click Save.
- **b.** Save the document on your Project Disk with the filename "Information Letter."
- **c.** Change the date on the letter to tomorrow's date.
- **d.** Save your changes to the letter.

5. Preview and print a document.

- **a.** Click the Print Preview button on the Standard toolbar.
- **b.** Click to zoom in on the document in Print Preview, then proofread the letter.
- **c.** Click to zoom out on the document and then close Print Preview.
- **d.** Print a copy of the letter using the default print settings. (*Hint:* Don't forget to save the document before you print it.)

6. Get Help.

- **a.** Click the Microsoft Word Help button on the Standard toolbar.
- **b.** Type "Print" in the Office Assistant dialog balloon, then click Search.
- **c.** Click Print a document, and read about printing more than one copy at a time. (*Hint:* Click "See More" in the dialog balloon if necessary.)
- **d.** Click the Show button, then type "How do I print a help topic?" on the Answer Wizard tab.
- **e.** Read about printing a help topic, then close the Help window.
- **f.** Hide the Office Assistant.

7. Close a document and exit Word.

- **a.** Close the Information Letter document, saving your changes if necessary.
- **b.** Exit Word.

▶ Independent Challenges

1. Your company's employee newsletter includes a technology question-and-answer page. This month you have been asked to write a short article about using Word's toolbars for the page. You consult the Help system to learn more about toolbars before writing your essay.

To complete this independent challenge:

- **a.** Start Word.
- **b.** Use the Office Assistant to search Help for information about using toolbars.
- **c.** Write a brief essay that provides a definition of a toolbar, identifies the two default toolbars, and explains how to display a button that is not visible on a toolbar.
- **d.** Type your name at the top of the document.
- **e.** Proofread your document and correct any errors.
- **f.** Save the document on your Project Disk with the filename "Toolbar Article," then preview and print the document.

2. As a co-chair for the Lake City High School class reunion planning committee, you are responsible for recruiting classmates to help with reunion activities. Four reunion subcommittees need volunteers:

- The entertainment committee, which arranges for music, hall rental, and prizes, and organizes different reunion weekend events.
- The hospitality committee, which arranges for lodging discounts and deals with spouses and children of alumni.
- The meals committee, which works with the entertainment committee to coordinate meals at each event.
- The transportation committee, which addresses the logistical issues of transporting alumni to and from airports and to and from reunion events.

Using Word, draft a letter to your fellow alumni asking for volunteers for the four subcommittees.
To complete this independent challenge:

a. Start Word and create a document called "Reunion 2000 Letter" on your Project Disk.
b. Type today's date. For the inside address, type any name and address you wish, then add a salutation, such as "Dear Fellow Alum:".
c. In the first paragraph, describe the responsibilities of the reunion committee and your need for volunteers.
d. In the next paragraph, describe the responsibilities of each of the subcommittees.
e. In the final body paragraph, include one more plea to encourage people to sign up, and give instructions for contacting you.
f. Include your name and phone number in the closing.
g. Correct all spelling and grammatical errors.
h. Save your changes, then preview and print the letter.

3. Your initiative and enthusiasm for learning to use Word has resulted in you becoming a Word resource for your colleagues. To assist your co-workers in helping themselves (rather than interrupting your own work), you decide to provide them with a summary of Word's built-in Help features.
To complete this independent challenge:

a. Start Word.
b. Write a brief essay that describes each of the following help features, including how to access the feature and an example of when you would use it: Microsoft Word Help, Office Assistant, What's This?, and Office on the Web.
c. Be sure to create a new paragraph for each topic (separated by a blank line).
d. Insert your name at the top of the page, proofread the document, then correct your spelling and grammatical errors.
e. Save the document with the filename "Help Overview" on your Project Disk.
f. Preview and print a copy of your essay.

WEB WORK

4. You are an intern in the Human Resources department at MediaLoft. You recently interviewed for a position in the Systems department, and you want to follow up with a thank-you letter to the office manager who interviewed you. You want to make sure you spell his name correctly, so you consult the MediaLoft intranet site. An intranet is a group of connected networks owned by a company or organization that is used for internal purposes. Intranets use Internet software to handle the data communications, such as e-mail and Web pages, within an organization. These pages often provide company-wide information. As with all intranets, the MediaLoft intranet limits access to MediaLoft employees.

To complete this independent challenge:

a. Start Word.
b. Connect to the Internet, go to the MediaLoft intranet site at http://www.course.com/illustrated/MediaLoft, then click the link for the About page.
c. Write down the address of the San Francisco headquarters.
d. Click the link for the Human Resources page, and locate the Personnel database on that page.
e. Note the correct spelling of the office manager's name, then disconnect from the Internet.
f. Start a thank-you letter to the office manager. Be sure to type today's date, an inside address, and a salutation at the top of the page.
g. In the first paragraph, express your thanks for the interview and reiterate how much you learned about the Systems department during your interview.
h. In a separate paragraph, mention your experience with Word 2000 and describe a recent project where you used Word.
i. Include your name in the closing.
j. Proofread your document, correct any mistakes, then save it with the filename "Office Manager Letter" on your Project Disk.
k. Preview and print the letter.

▶ Visual Workshop

Using the skills you learned in this unit, create the document shown in Figure A-16. Save it on your Project Disk with the filename "Acceptance Letter," then print a copy of the letter.

FIGURE A-16

April 2, 2000

Mr. David Matthews
Management Systems Enterprises
Human Resources Department
128 Technology Drive
Needham, MA 02128

Dear Mr. Matthews:

Thank you for offering me the systems coordinator position in your department. I am writing to accept this position under the terms you described in your letter. I am eager to put my Microsoft Office experience to practical use at Management Systems Enterprises.

Again, thank you for your offer. I look forward to working with you and your team.

Sincerely,

Your Name

Word 2000

Unit B

Editing and Proofing Documents

Objectives

- Plan a document
- MOUS Open and save a new document
- MOUS Select and replace text
- MOUS Understand the Office Clipboard
- MOUS Move text
- MOUS Copy text
- MOUS Check spelling and grammar
- MOUS Create AutoCorrect entries
- MOUS Find and replace text

Word's editing and proofing tools make it easy to edit and fine-tune your documents. In this unit, you will learn a variety of techniques for copying and moving text and for replacing specific occurrences of text throughout a document. You will also use Word's proofing tools to find and correct misspelled words and grammatical errors. To begin, you'll create a new document by saving an existing document with a new name, leaving the original unchanged. Karen Rosen wants to write a letter to the woman she just hired to be the new training manager at MediaLoft, confirming the terms of her employment. She bases this letter on a similar letter she wrote to another recently hired employee.

Unit B

Word 2000

Planning a Document

Details

It is important to plan a document before you create it. Planning a document involves determining the purpose of the document, identifying its audience, developing the content, organizing the content logically, and then deciding the tone the document should take to achieve its purpose. The **tone** of a document is the way it "sounds." It affects how someone feels while reading it. A document's tone should match its audience and purpose. For example, the tone of an invitation to a company picnic is different from the tone of a letter requesting payment for an overdue invoice. Planning a document also involves thinking about its visual appearance. You want the layout and design of a document to complement its purpose, audience, content, organization, and tone. For example, you would never design a business letter to look like a newspaper article. Karen plans her letter to MediaLoft's new training manager. She jots down her ideas as shown in Figure B-1.

In planning her letter Karen is careful to:

Identify the audience and purpose of the document

The audience for this letter is the new training manager. Its purpose is to welcome her to MediaLoft and to confirm the terms of her employment.

Choose the information and important points to cover in the document

If you later want to add or remove information from a document, you can easily insert and delete text. Karen wants to confirm the new training manager's title, responsibilities, and salary in the letter. She also wants to mention why MediaLoft decided to offer her the position, and to include several enclosures.

Decide how the information will be organized

If you decide to rearrange the structure of your document later, you can use Word's editing features to move, copy, and cut text. Because the information about the position is most important, Karen decides to present it first, followed by a list of enclosures.

Choose the tone of the document

You can edit your documents until you achieve exactly the tone you want. The document is being sent to a new employee, so Karen plans to use a businesslike tone that is welcoming and enthusiastic. She wants the new training manager to be excited about her new job and to feel comfortable with her decision to work at MediaLoft.

Plan the layout and design of the document

Planning the layout of a document involves thinking about its overall appearance: selecting the fonts to use, organizing text under headings, sketching ideas for tables and lists, and planning to include lines and shading to highlight important points and help to organize content, among many other formatting options. If you change your mind about the format of a document, you can make adjustments later. Karen wants to use a simple business letter format for her document.

FIGURE B-1: Document plan

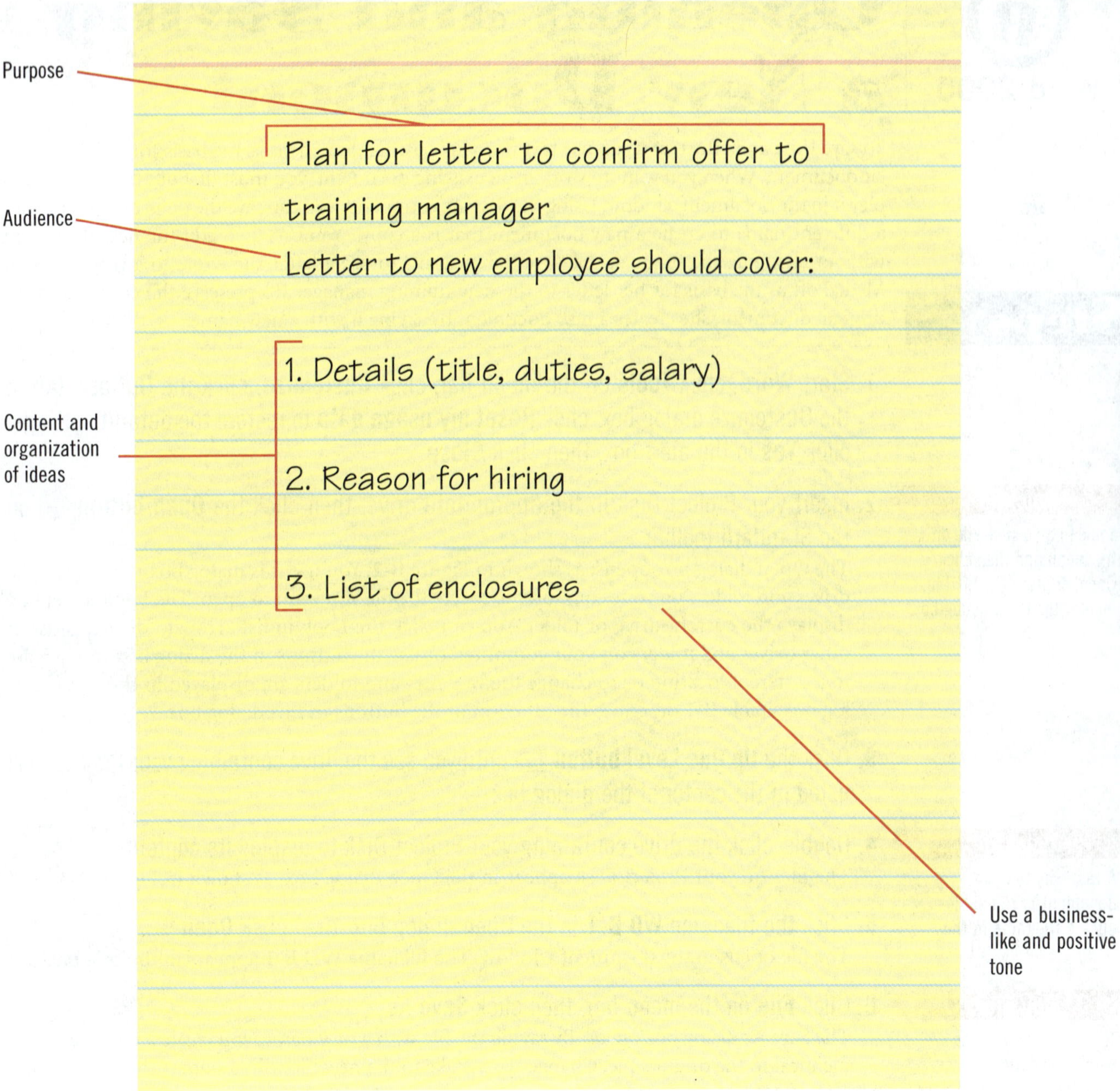

Word 2000

CLUES TO USE

Creating new documents using wizards and templates

Word includes wizards and templates that help you create a variety of professionally designed documents, including resumes, memos, faxes, letters, and other publications. **Document wizards** are interactive coaches that guide you through the process of creating a document, prompting you to enter information and to choose the design and appearance of a document. **Templates** are pre-formatted documents that contain placeholder text that you replace with your own words. Either method gives you a great head start in developing attractive and effective documents, because wizards and templates offer formatting options that fit many common purposes and tones, such as a professional memo. All you do is provide the text. To create such a document, click File on the menu bar, then click New. In the New dialog box, click the tab containing the type of document you want to create, then double-click the icon for the wizard or template you want to use.

Unit B

Word 2000

Opening and Saving a New Document

To save time and effort, you can use text from an existing document as the basis for another similar document. When you want to work in an existing document, you must first **open** it, that is, display it in the document window. Using the Save As command, you can save the open document with a different name to create a new document that is a copy. You can then edit the new document without changing the original. Karen wants to use a letter she wrote to a new intern at MediaLoft as the basis for her letter to the new training manager. To preserve the contents of the original document, she creates a new document by saving it with a new name.

Steps 1 2 3 4

1. Start **Word**, click **Tools** on the menu bar, click **Customize**, click the **Options tab** in the Customize dialog box, click **Reset my usage data** to restore the default settings, click **Yes** in the alert box, then click **Close**

QuickTip

You can also click File on the menu bar, then click Open, or press [Ctrl][O] to display the Open dialog box.

2. Insert your Project Disk in the appropriate drive, then click the **Open button** on the Standard toolbar

   The Open dialog box opens, as shown in Figure B-2. You use this dialog box to navigate the drives and folders on your computer to locate the file you want to open. The Look in list box displays the current drive or folder. You can click the Look in list arrow to display a list of other drives and folders on your computer, or use the buttons in the dialog box to navigate to a different location or to change the way files and folders are displayed in the Open dialog box. Table B-1 describes the function of the buttons in this dialog box.

3. Click the **Up One Level button** until you see the drive containing your Project Disk listed in the center of the dialog box

QuickTip

A fast way to open a document is to double-click a filename in the Open dialog box.

4. Double-click the drive containing your Project Disk to display its contents

   The files on your Project Disk appear in the Open dialog box, as shown in Figure B-3.

5. Click the filename **WD B-1** in the Open dialog box, then click **Open**

   The file opens in the document window. The filename WD B-1 appears in the title bar.

QuickTip

To create a new folder within the current folder, click the Create New Folder button, type a name for the folder, then click OK.

6. Click **File** on the menu bar, then click **Save As**

   The Save As dialog box opens. By saving the file with a new name, you create a new file that is identical to the original file. Changes you make to the new file will not affect the original file.

7. Navigate to the drive or folder where you store your project files (if necessary), type **Training Manager Letter** in the File name text box, then click **Save**

   The original document closes and the Training Manager Letter file is displayed in the document window, ready for you to edit. Note the name of the new document appears in the title bar.

CLUES TO USE

Save command vs. Save As command

The Save and the Save As commands are different in important ways. Use the Save command the first time you want to name a new document and store it permanently on a disk. When you save a document for the first time, the Save command displays the Save As dialog box, in which you name your document. Using the Save command after naming a file writes your latest changes to the document file on the disk. The Save As command has a different purpose. Use the Save As command to create a new document that is a copy of an existing document. Using Save As allows you to make changes in a copy of a document while leaving the original intact.

FIGURE B-2: Open dialog box

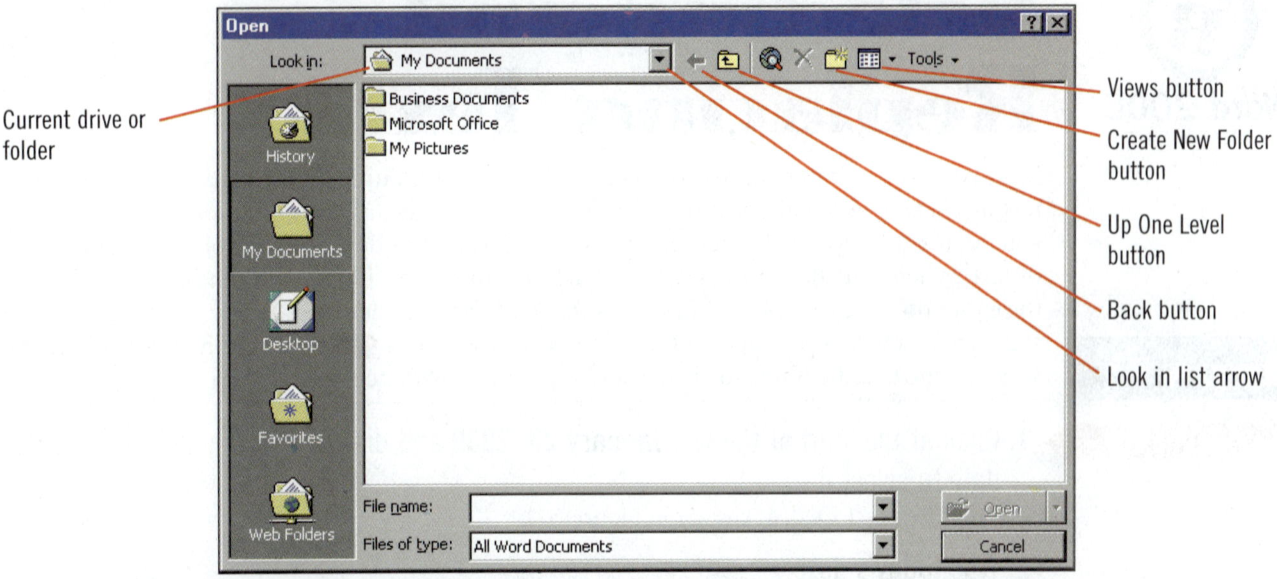

FIGURE B-3: Document file to open

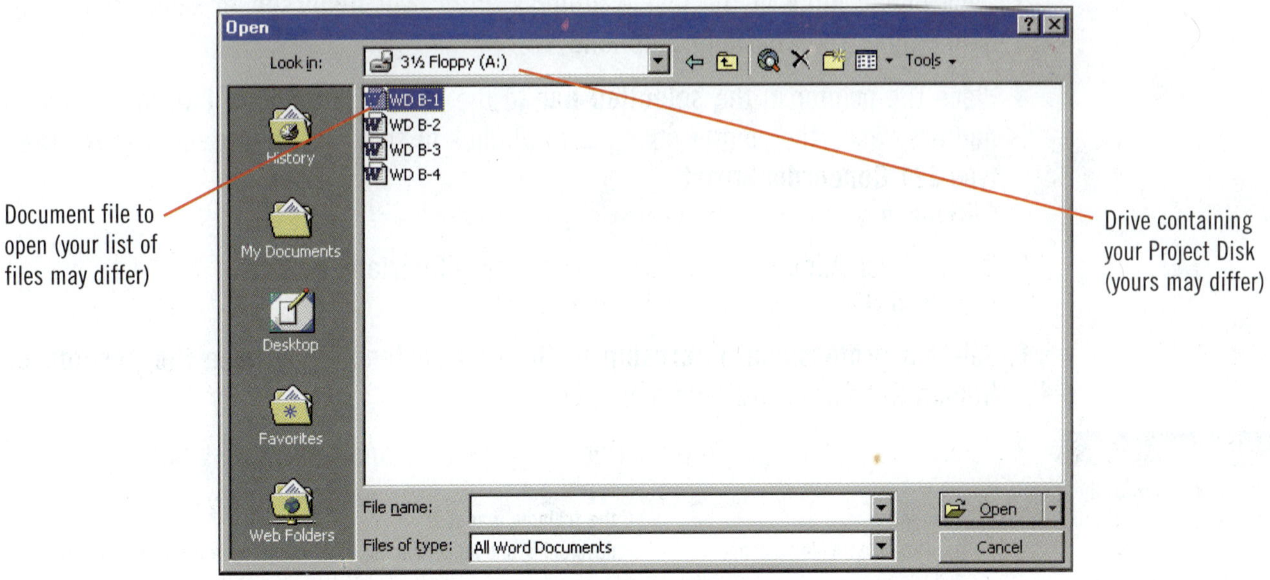

TABLE B-1: Open dialog box buttons

button	function
Back	Navigates to the previously active folder or drive; the ScreenTip for this button displays the name of the previously active folder or drive
Up One Level	Navigates to the next highest folder in the folder hierarchy (to the folder or drive that contains the current folder)
Search the Web	Connects to the World Wide Web to locate a file
Delete	Deletes the currently selected file
Create New Folder	Creates a new folder in the current drive or folder
Views	Changes the way file information is displayed in the Open dialog box; click to scroll through each view—List, Details, Properties, and Preview—or click the list arrow to choose a view

Unit B

Word 2000

Selecting and Replacing Text

Most Word operations require that you **select** text before editing or formatting it. You can select text by clicking before the text you want to select and dragging the mouse pointer across it, or you can use the selection bar to select lines of text. The **selection bar** is the blank area to the left of text. When you click in the selection bar you can select a line, several lines, a paragraph, or the entire document. Table B-2 describes different ways to select text. When you select text and start typing, the text you type replaces the text you selected. Karen revises her letter by selecting the text she wants to change and replacing it with new text.

Steps

QuickTip

You can click anywhere in the document window to deselect text.

1. Click at the start of the text **January 23, 2000** and drag the mouse pointer over the date to select it
   The date is selected, as shown in Figure B-4.
2. Type **today's date**
   The text you type replaces the selected text.
3. Click before **Alice** in the inside address, drag over **Anderson** to select the entire name, then type **Charlene Stephens**
4. Place the pointer in the **selection bar** to the left of the **second line** in the inside address, when the pointer changes to ↗ click to select the entire line of text, then type **321 Concordia Street**
   Clicking once in the selection bar selects a line of text.
5. Double-click **Alice** in the salutation, then type **Charlene**
   Double-clicking a word selects the word.
6. Select **a professional internship** in the first sentence, then type **the position of Human Resources Training Manager**
7. Select and replace text in the letter using the following table as a guide:

select:	type:
an intern	**the training manager**
assisting the training manager and myself on a variety of projects	**developing and implementing a corporate-wide training program**
9.25 per hour	**47,500 per year**

Trouble?

Click the down arrow at the bottom of the vertical scroll bar to display text that is not currently visible in the document window.

8. Click the **Save button** on the Standard toolbar
   The changes you made to the letter are saved. Compare your document with Figure B-5.

CLUES TO USE

Reversing and repeating changes

Word keeps track of the operations you perform in a document so that you can reverse and repeat any action (with the exception of saving, opening, closing, and printing documents). You can repeat the last action by clicking Edit on the menu bar, and then clicking the Repeat command. The name of the Repeat command changes to reflect your most recent action. You can also press [F4] to repeat the last action. In addition, clicking the Undo button reverses the most recent change you've made. To reverse a series of changes, click the Undo list arrow and scroll through the list of actions to find the last action you want to undo. Click the action and Word reverses all the changes you've made to that point. If you decide to keep a change you just reversed, click the Redo button. To reverse a series of changes, click the Redo list arrow and click the last change you want to reverse.

FIGURE B-4: Selected text

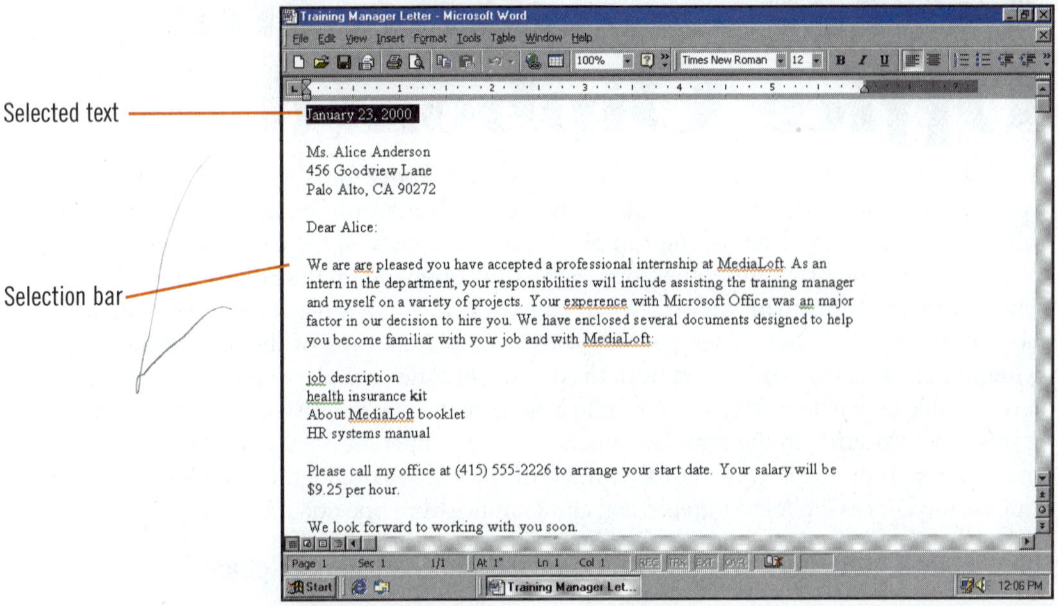

FIGURE B-5: Edited letter

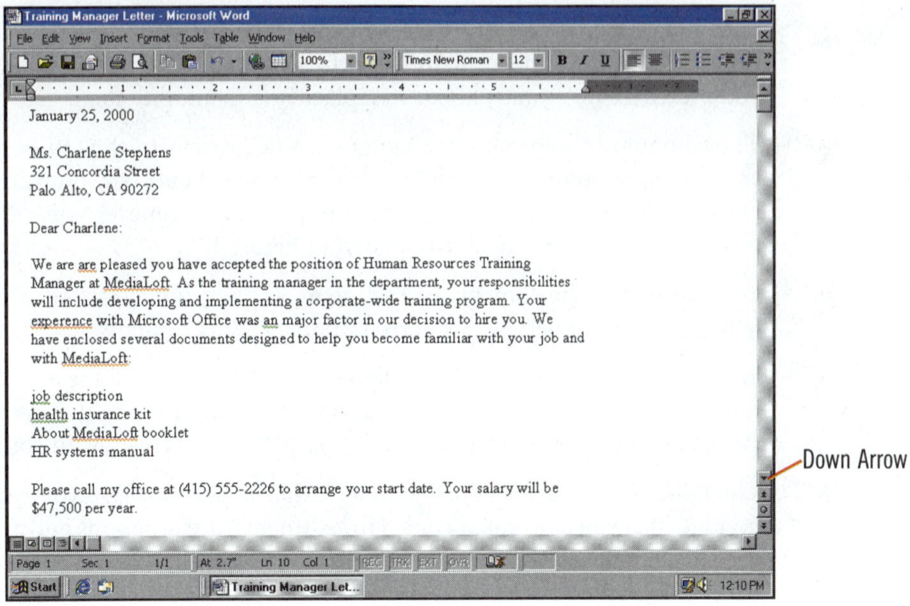

TABLE B-2: Mouse selection techniques

to select	do this
A word	Double-click the word
A sentence	Press and hold [Ctrl], then click the sentence
A paragraph	Triple-click the paragraph, or double-click the selection bar next to the paragraph
A line of text	Click the selection bar next to the line
An entire document	Press and hold [Ctrl], then click anywhere in the selection bar, or triple-click the selection bar
A vertical block of text	Press and hold [Alt], then drag through the text
A large amount of text	Place the insertion point at the beginning of the text, press and hold [Shift], then click the end of the text

Understanding the Office Clipboard

The **Clipboard** is a temporary area in the computer's memory for storing text and graphics that you want to reuse. When you use an Office program such as Word, you use the **Office Clipboard**, which can hold up to 12 items. You can place text or graphics on the Clipboard by selecting the text or graphic and using either the Copy or the Cut command on the Edit menu or the Copy or Cut button on the Standard toolbar. When you **cut** text, you remove it from the document and place it on the Clipboard. When you **copy** text, you place a copy of the text on the Clipboard without removing the original text from the document. After you place an item on the Clipboard it is available for you to **paste**, or insert, into a document using the Paste command. You can paste it into a new location in the same document, or into a different document. Table B-3 describes the commands on the Edit menu that work with the Clipboard. Figure B-6 illustrates how you can use the Office Clipboard to reuse text and graphics from one document in other documents.

Details

It is important to understand the following about the Office Clipboard:

- Like a physical paper clipboard, the Office Clipboard allows you to place multiple items on it. In Word (and in other Office programs), you can place up to 12 items on the Clipboard.
- Each item you place on the Clipboard can be pasted into a document an unlimited number of times. When you paste an item from the Clipboard, the item remains on the Clipboard until you exceed 12 items and choose to replace it with another item.
- The Clipboard toolbar holds the items copied or cut to the Office Clipboard. You can view the Clipboard toolbar by clicking View on the menu bar, pointing to Toolbars, and then clicking Clipboard. It also appears automatically whenever you cut or copy multiple selections. The Clipboard toolbar is shown in Figure B-7.
- You can review the contents of each item on the Clipboard toolbar by pointing to the item. When you point to an item, a ScreenTip displays its contents.
- To paste an item from the Office Clipboard toolbar, you click the item on the Clipboard to paste it to the location of the insertion point in a document. You can also use the Paste command or the Paste button on the Standard toolbar to paste the most recent item you collected.
- The Office Clipboard is available in all Office applications, so you can use it to paste text and graphics that you have cut or copied from other Office programs into a Word document, and vice versa. For example, you can use the Office Clipboard to insert a spreadsheet or chart created in Excel or a graphic from a PowerPoint presentation into your Word documents.
- Items remain on the Office Clipboard until you close all open Office applications.

TABLE B-3: The Edit menu Clipboard commands

command	description
Cut	Removes the selected text or graphic from the document and places it on the Clipboard
Copy	Copies the selected text or graphic to the Clipboard; the selection remains in the document
Paste	Inserts the last item you cut or copied at the insertion point in the document
Paste Special	Inserts an item created in another Office program (such as a spreadsheet or a picture) in a document; you can create a link so that changes to the source file are reflected in the document or embed objects so that you can edit the object in its original program

FIGURE B-6: Using the Office Clipboard

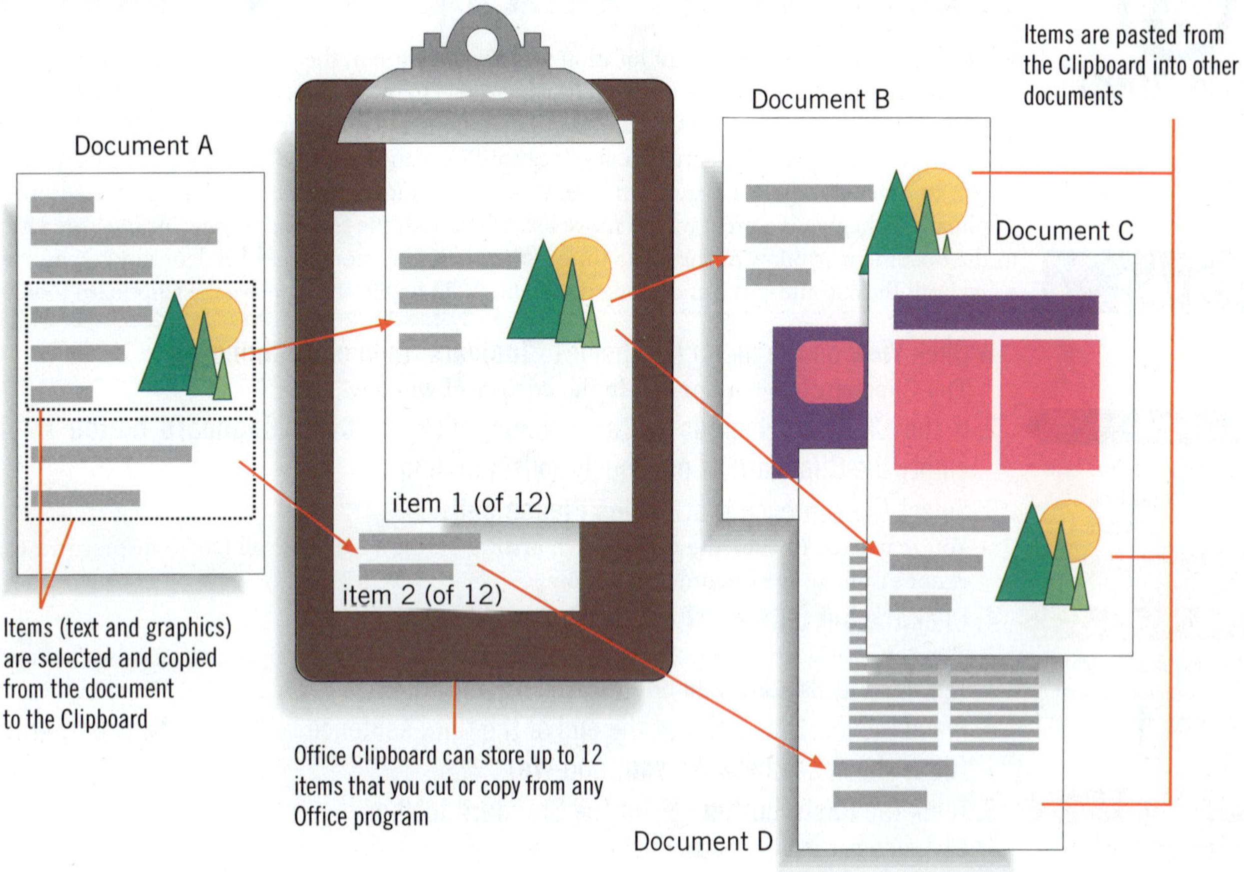

FIGURE B-7: Clipboard toolbar

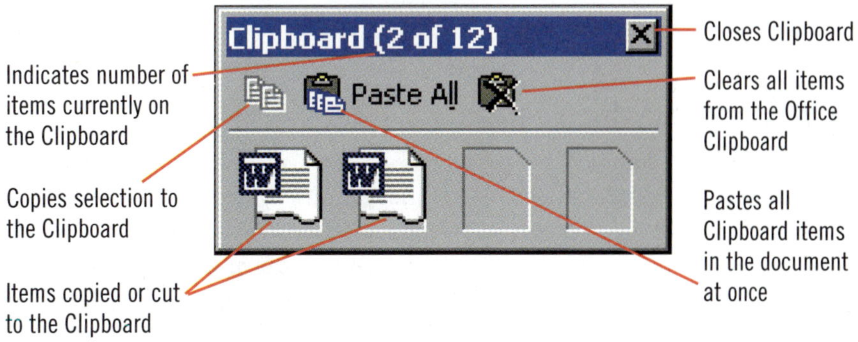

Unit B

Word 2000

Moving Text

You can move text from its current location to a new location in the same document or to a different document. Before you move text, you must select it. To **move** text, use the Cut command or the Cut button to place the text on the Clipboard, then use the Paste command or the Paste button to insert the text from the Clipboard in a new location. You can also move text by selecting it and dragging it to a new location using the mouse. When you drag text, however, it is not placed on the Clipboard. Dragging is a great way to move text when both the text and its new location are visible in the document window at the same time. Karen reorganizes her letter by moving text using both the cut-and-paste and dragging methods. To begin, she displays the Clipboard toolbar.

Steps 1 2 3 4

Trouble?

If the Clipboard toolbar is in your way, click the toolbar title bar, then drag it to a different location.

QuickTip

Click the More Buttons button on the Standard toolbar to locate buttons that are not visible on your screen.

QuickTip

You can also click Edit on the menu bar, then click Paste, or press [Ctrl][V] to paste text.

Trouble?

If you make a mistake, click the Undo button on the Standard toolbar, then repeat Steps 8 and 9.

1. Click **View** on the menu bar, point to **Toolbars**, then click **Clipboard**
   The Clipboard toolbar appears in the document window.
2. If the Clipboard toolbar contains items, click the **Clear Clipboard button** to empty the Clipboard of previously collected items
3. Select the sentence that begins **Please call...**
   You may need to click the up or down arrows on the vertical scroll bar to display text that is not visible in the document window.
4. Click the **Cut button** on the Standard toolbar
   The sentence is removed from the document and placed on the Clipboard, as shown in Figure B-8. You can also click Edit on the menu bar, then click Cut, or press [Ctrl][X] to cut text.
5. Place the insertion point at the end of the third sentence in the first body paragraph (after the space between **you.** and **We**)
6. Click the **Paste button** on the Standard toolbar
   The sentence is inserted in the first paragraph.
7. Select **Human Resources** in the first sentence, then press and hold the mouse button over the selected text until the pointer changes to (do not release the mouse button)
8. Drag the pointer's vertical line in front of the word **department** in the next sentence, as shown in Figure B-9
9. Release the mouse button
   The text is moved from its original location in the first sentence to its new location in the second sentence.
10. Click anywhere in the document window to deselect the text, then click the **Save button** on the Standard toolbar
    Compare your letter to Figure B-10.

CLUES TO USE

Working with multiple documents

If you want to copy or cut text from one document and paste it into another, it is easiest to work with both documents open in the program window at the same time. To open multiple documents, you can open one document and then open subsequent documents one by one, or you can open several documents at once by holding [Ctrl] as you click the filename of each document you want to open in the Open dialog box, and then clicking Open. To move between open documents in the document window, click Window on the menu bar, then click the filename of the document you want to display. You can also view multiple documents at once in the program window, by clicking Window on the menu bar, and then clicking Arrange All. All the open documents will appear on the screen, each in its own program window. To activate a document, click its program window. With multiple documents open, you can easily copy and move text between documents by selecting the text you want to copy or move in one document, and then pasting it in another document. To quickly save or close all open documents at the same time, press and hold [Shift] as you click File on the menu bar, then click Save All or Close All.

FIGURE B-8: Cut item on the Clipboard toolbar

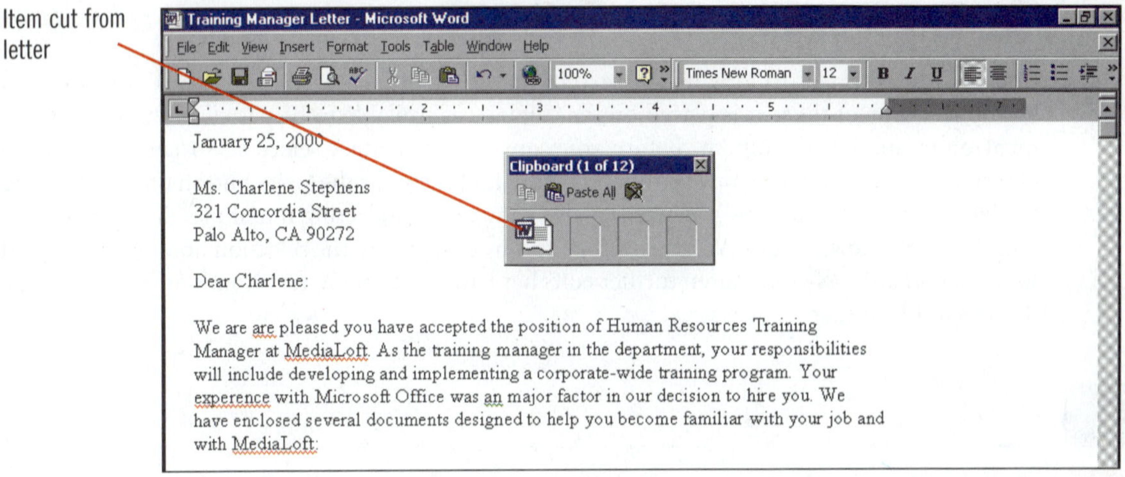

FIGURE B-9: Dragging to move text

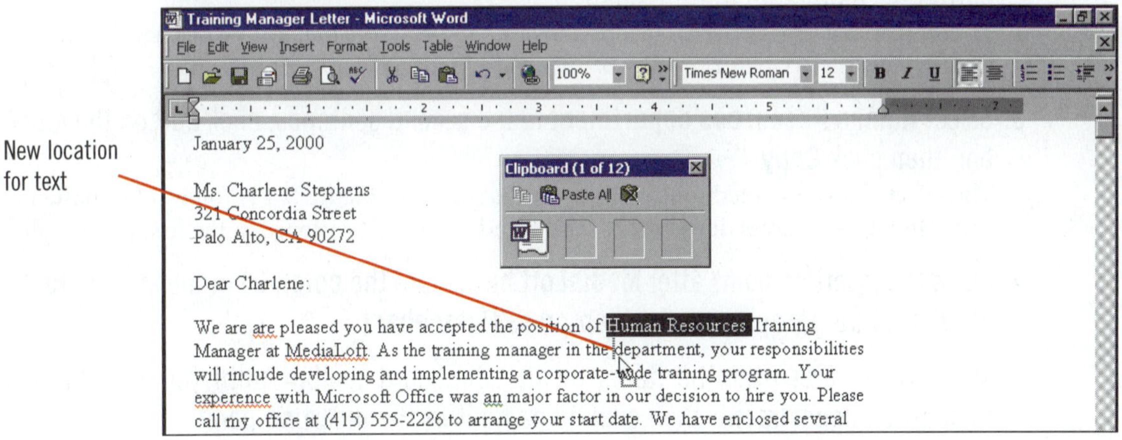

FIGURE B-10: Moved text in document

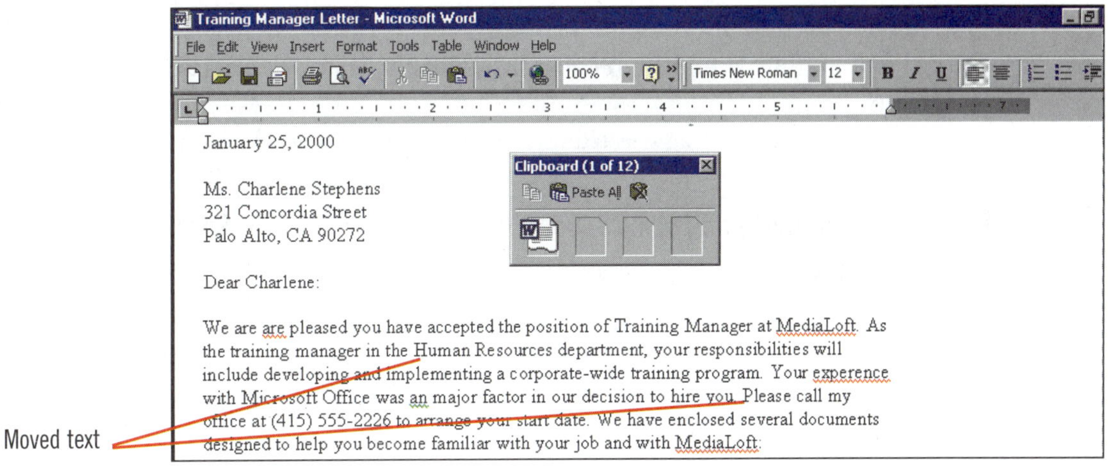

Unit B
Word 2000

Copying Text

Copying text is similar to moving text, except that when you copy text it remains in its original location. A copy of the text is placed on the Clipboard, available to be pasted in the same document or in another document. Before you copy text you must select it. To copy text to the Clipboard you can use the Copy command on the Edit menu or the Copy button on the Standard toolbar or the Clipboard toolbar. You can also copy text by selecting it and pressing [Ctrl] while you drag it to a new location. When you copy text by dragging it, the selection does not get copied to the Clipboard. Karen further edits her letter by copying text from one location in the document to another.

Steps

QuickTip

You can also click the Copy button on the Clipboard toolbar to copy text to the Clipboard.

1. Select **Training Manager** in the first sentence, then click the **Copy button** on the Standard toolbar
   The selected text is copied to the Clipboard. You want to place a copy of this text in front of "job description" in the list.
2. Place the insertion point in front of **job description** in the list, then click the **Paste button** on the Standard toolbar
   "Training Manager" is inserted before "job description." Note that Word automatically inserts a space between "Manager" and "job." "Training Manager" also remains on the Clipboard.
3. Select **Human Resources department** in the second sentence, click **Edit** on the menu bar, then click **Copy**
   The selected text is copied to the Clipboard, as shown in Figure B-11. You want to paste the text "Human Resources department" at the end of the last sentence in the first paragraph.
4. Place the insertion point after **MediaLoft** but before the **colon (:)** in the last sentence of the first paragraph, type **'s**, then press **[Spacebar]**
5. Move the pointer over the items on the Clipboard toolbar until you find **Human Resources department**, then click to paste it at the insertion point
   The text is pasted at the end of the sentence.
6. Select **HR** in the list, then click **Human Resources department** on the Clipboard toolbar
   The pasted text replaces the selected text in the document.
7. Select **MediaLoft** in the first sentence, press and hold **[Ctrl]**, then press and hold the mouse button over the selected text until the pointer changes to
8. Drag the pointer in front of **health insurance kit** in the list to position the pointer's vertical line in front of **health**, release the mouse button, release **[Ctrl]**, then deselect the text
   Pressing [Ctrl] while you drag selected text copies the text to a new location. Compare your document with Figure B-12.
9. Click the **Close button** on the Clipboard toolbar, then click the **Save button** on the Standard toolbar

QuickTip

Click the Undo button on the Standard toolbar if you make a mistake, then try again.

FIGURE B-11: Copying to and from the Clipboard toolbar

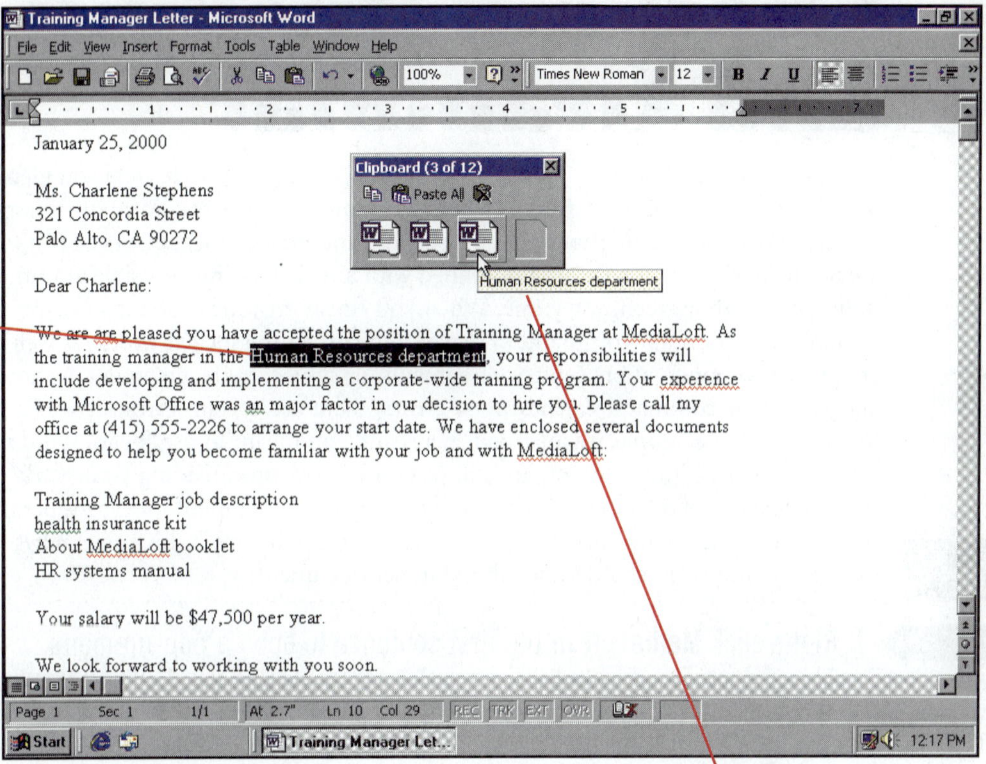

FIGURE B-12: Copied text

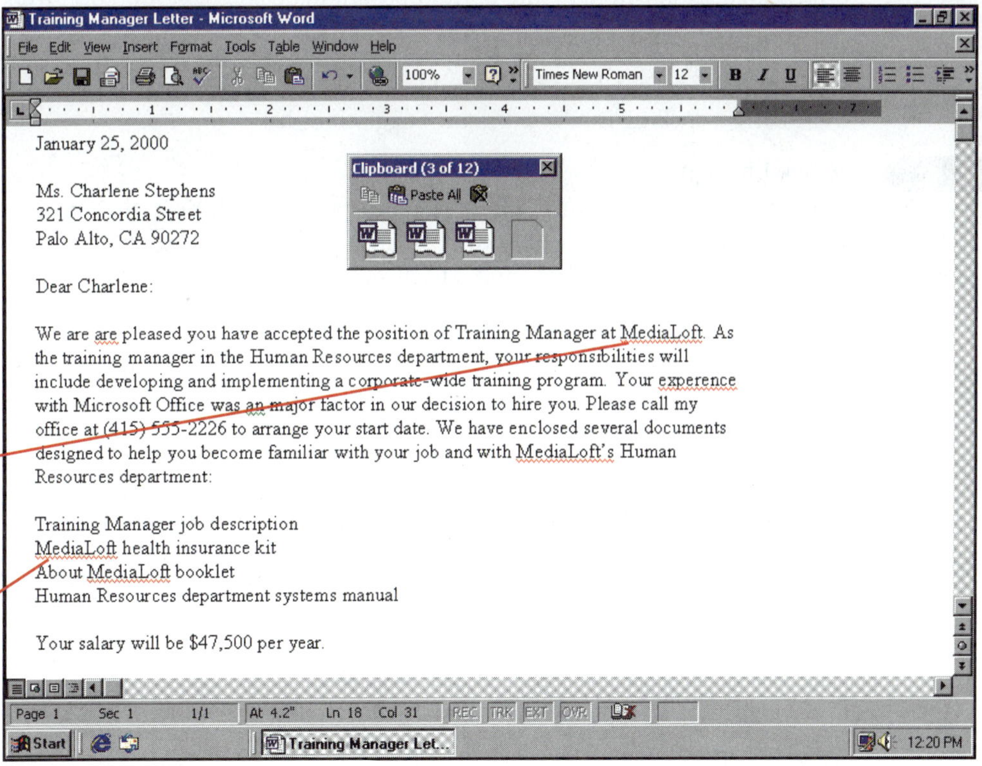

Unit B

Word 2000

Checking Spelling and Grammar

You can use Word's Spelling, Grammar, and AutoCorrect features to help you identify and correct mistakes in your document. **AutoCorrect** automatically corrects commonly misspelled words as you type. Word also underlines possible spelling and grammatical errors as you type. Words that are not in Word's dictionary are underlined with a red, wavy line. Possible grammatical errors are underlined with a green, wavy line. When you finish creating a document, you can use Word's Spelling and Grammar command to review and correct misspelled words, as well as grammatical errors such as punctuation, sentence fragments, or subject-verb agreement. Although the Spelling and Grammar command catches most errors, there are certain errors it will not find, such as homonyms. For example, if you typed "here" and you meant to use "hear," Word will not identify this as an error. Ultimately, you are still responsible for proofreading your work. Karen uses the Spelling and Grammar command to search her document for errors. Before searching the document, she sets AutoCorrect to ignore the word "MediaLoft," which she knows is not in Word's dictionary because it is underlined in red in her document.

Steps 1 2 3 4

Trouble?

If "MediaLoft" is not underlined, click Tools on the menu bar, click Options, click the Spelling & Grammar tab, click Recheck Document, click Yes, click OK, then continue with Step 1.

1. Right-click **MediaLoft** in the first sentence to open a pop-up menu

   This pop-up menu includes a suggestion for correcting the spelling ("Media Loft") as well as commands for ignoring Word's suggestion and for adding the word to Word's dictionary. Note that Word's suggested correction is wrong in this case.

2. Click **Ignore All** on the pop-up menu, right-click **MediaLoft's**, then click **Ignore All**

   Clicking Ignore All tells Word to ignore all instances of "MediaLoft" and "MediaLoft's" in the current document, and removes the red, wavy lines under these words.

Trouble?

If a word is identified as misspelled, click Ignore to ignore it, or click the correct spelling in the Suggestions list, then click Change.

3. Press **[Ctrl][Home]** to move the insertion point to the top of the document, then click the **Spelling and Grammar button** on the Standard toolbar

   The Spelling and Grammar dialog box opens. The dialog box indicates that the word "are" is repeated, as shown in Figure B-13. You want to delete the second occurrence of the word.

4. Click **Delete**

   The second "are" is deleted from the document. Next, "experence" is identified as misspelled. The correct spelling is selected in the Suggestions list.

Trouble?

Click the Office Assistant button in the Spelling and Grammar dialog box if the Office Assistant does not open.

5. Click **Change**

   The correctly spelled word replaces the misspelled word. Next, the Spelling and Grammar dialog box suggests using the word "a" in place of "an." The Office Assistant displays an explanation of the rule that applies to this error, as shown in Figure B-14.

6. Read the explanation, then click **Change**

   The word "a" is substituted for the incorrect word "an." If you made other errors in your document, you may need to correct them. When Spelling and Grammar check is complete, the dialog box closes.

7. When a message box opens saying the Spelling and Grammar check is complete, click **OK** to close it, then proofread the letter for other errors

8. Press **[Ctrl][Home]**, then click the **Save button** on the Standard toolbar

FIGURE B-13: Spelling and Grammar dialog box

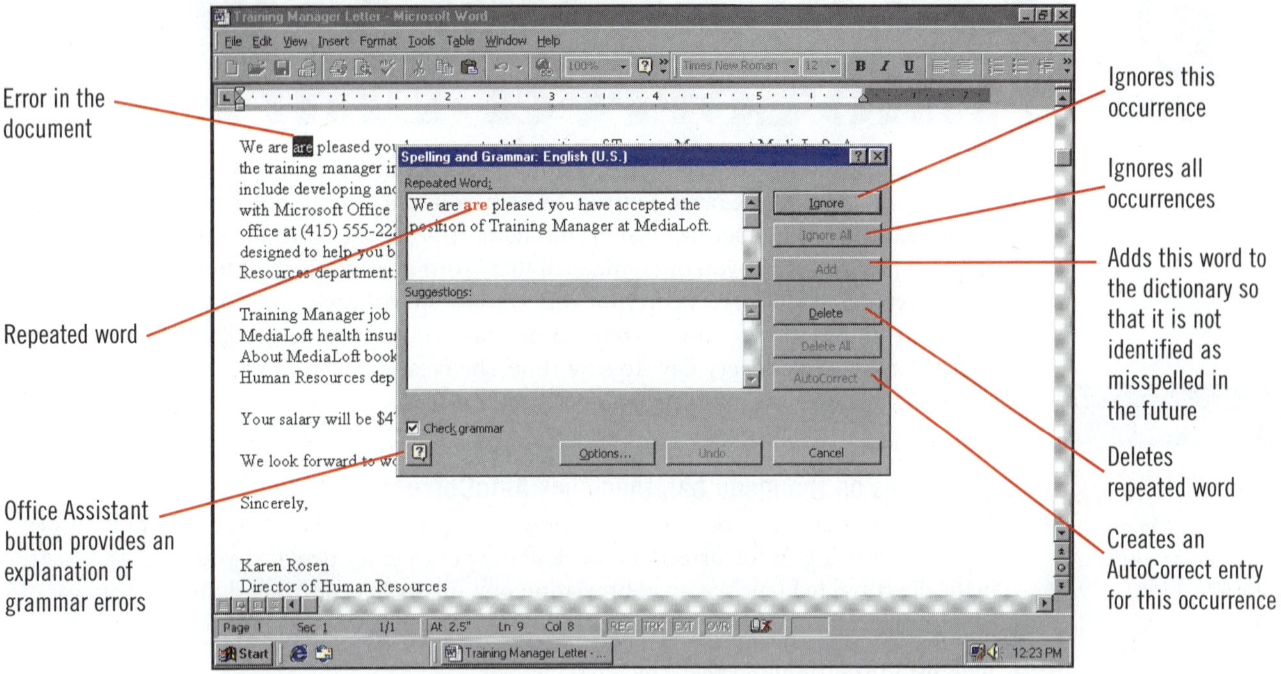

FIGURE B-14: Grammar explanation

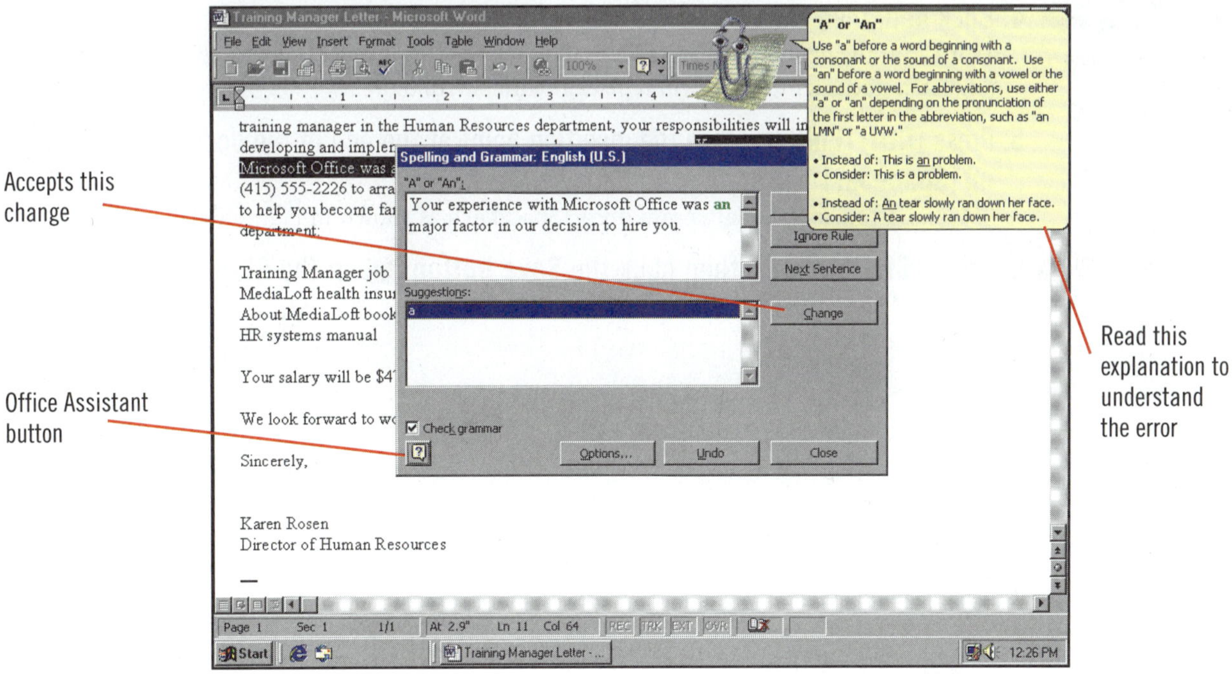

CLUES TO USE

Using the Thesaurus

You can use Word's Thesaurus to look up synonyms for overused or awkward words in your document. For some words, you can also look up antonyms. To use the Thesaurus, select the word for which you want to find a synonym, click Tools on the menu bar, point to Language, then click Thesaurus. In the Thesaurus dialog box, select the synonym you want to use in your document, then click Replace.

Unit B
Word 2000

Creating and Using AutoCorrect Entries

While AutoCorrect automatically corrects hundreds of commonly misspelled words, you can also create your own AutoCorrect entries to help you work more efficiently. You can create entries for text you use frequently, such as your name, title, or the name of your company, or you can create entries for words you often misspell that Word does not correct for you. For example, you could create an AutoCorrect entry for your initials, so that each time you typed your initials Word would automatically insert your name into your document. Karen types "MediaLoft" many times every day. To save time, she creates an AutoCorrect entry that inserts "MediaLoft" whenever she types the abbreviation "ml".

Steps 1 2 3 4

QuickTip

To delete an AutoCorrect entry, select it on the AutoCorrect tab, then click Delete.

1. Click **Tools** on the menu bar, then click **AutoCorrect**
   The AutoCorrect dialog box opens, as shown in Figure B-15. The AutoCorrect tab displays the list of existing AutoCorrect entries. Use the tab to enter new text you want to be automatically corrected (such as an abbreviation or a misspelled word) and the text you want to be automatically inserted in its place.
2. Type **ml** in the Replace text box
3. Press **[Tab]** to move the insertion point to the With text box, then type **MediaLoft**
4. Click **Add**, then click **OK**
   Word adds the new AutoCorrect entry to the list of AutoCorrect entries. Every time you type "ml" in a document, Word will replace it with "MediaLoft".
5. Press **[Ctrl] [End]** to place the insertion point at the end of the document, then type **ml [Spacebar]**
   "MediaLoft" is inserted after you press [Spacebar], as shown in Figure B-16.
6. Press **[Ctrl] [Home]**, then click the **Save button** on the Standard toolbar

Trouble?

If you can't click Add in your AutoCorrect dialog box, someone already created an AutoCorrect entry for "ml". Click Replace, click Yes in the alert box or dialog balloon, then click OK. See your instructor or technical support person for assistance.

CLUES TO USE

Creating AutoCorrect exceptions

There are some situations when you do not want Word to automatically correct what it assumes to be a mistake. For example, AutoCorrect automatically capitalizes the first character you type after typing a period. However, when you type the abbreviation "Cal." (for California) in the middle of a sentence, you do not want AutoCorrect to capitalize the next character. To avoid this, you can create an AutoCorrect exception. Create an AutoCorrect exception by clicking Tools on the menu bar, clicking AutoCorrect, then clicking Exceptions. In the AutoCorrect Exceptions dialog box, click the tab that includes the type of AutoCorrect exception you want to create: First Letter, INitial CAps, or Other Corrections. Type the text you do not want automatically corrected in the text box on the tab, click Add, then click Close. You can later remove an exception by deleting it from the list of exceptions in the AutoCorrect dialog box.

FIGURE B-15: AutoCorrect dialog box

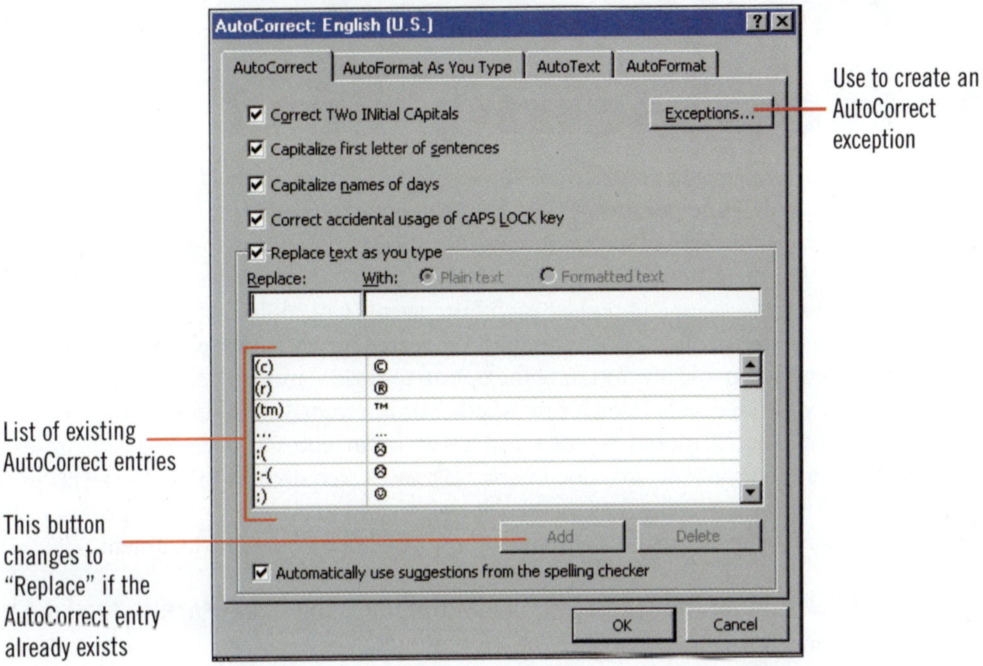

FIGURE B-16: Inserted AutoCorrect entry

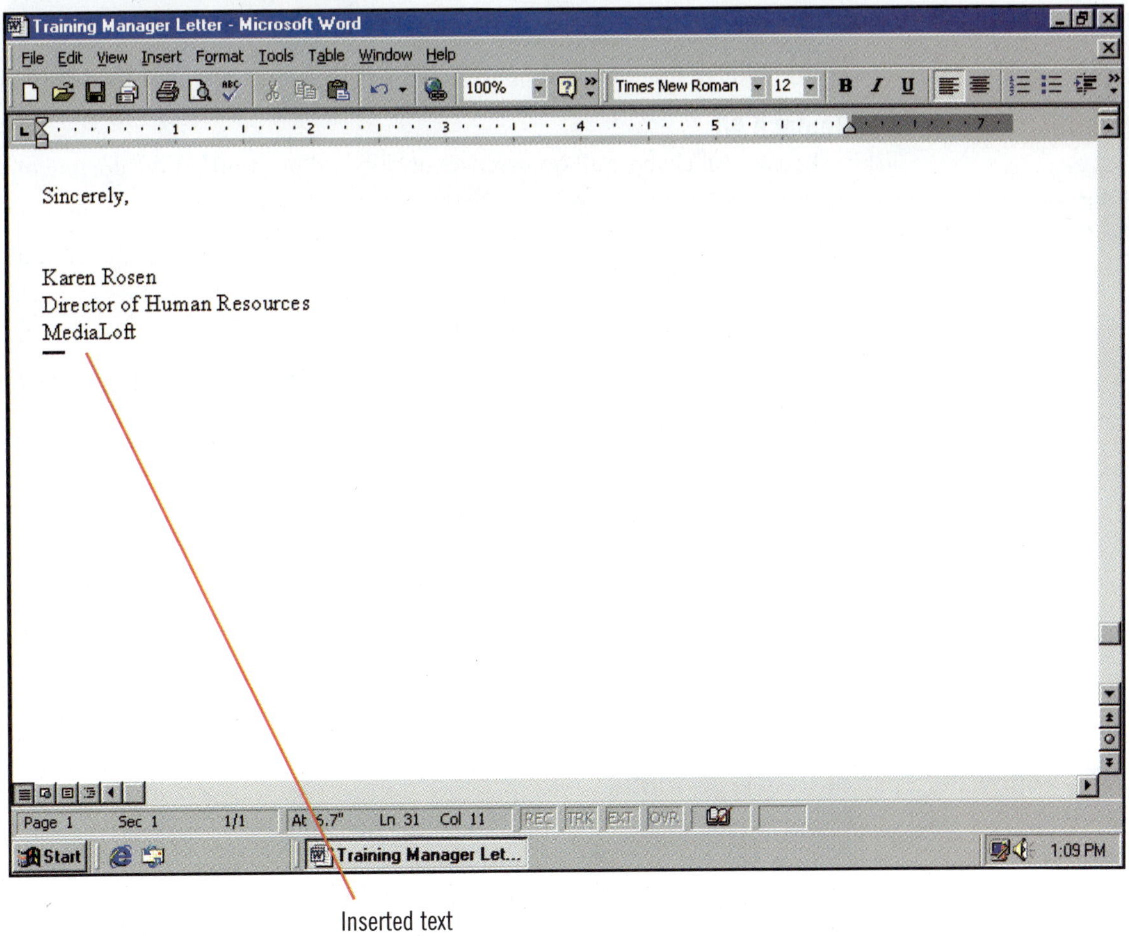

Finding and Replacing Text

Sometimes you need to replace text throughout a document. In a long document, doing this manually would be time-consuming and prone to error. For example, suppose you just finished writing an announcement of a new beverage for the MediaLoft café, when the marketing department decides that the product name should change from "ChocoShakes" to "CocoShakes". Rather than having to find, select, and replace each instance of "ChocoShakes" in your document, it would be much easier to use the Replace command to search for and replace "ChocoShakes" throughout the document automatically. You have the option to review and replace each occurrence one at a time (so that you can decide in each case whether or not to make the substitution), or you can perform a global replace. A **global replace** changes all occurrences at once. You can also use Word's Find command to locate text in a document. Karen decides to use the term "position" instead of "job" in her letter. She uses the Replace command to change "job" to "position" throughout the document. When she is finished, she saves, prints, and closes the document.

Steps 1 2 3 4

1. Click **Edit** on the menu bar, click **Replace**, then click **More** in the Find and Replace dialog box if necessary
   The Find and Replace dialog box opens, as shown in Figure B-17. Clicking More in the Find and Replace dialog box reveals additional options for narrowing a search and replace. Table B-4 describes the search options available in the Find and Replace dialog box.
2. Type **job** in the Find what text box
   This text will be replaced.
3. Press **[Tab]** to move the insertion point to the Replace with text box, then type **position**
4. Click **Replace All**
   Clicking Replace All changes all occurrences of "job" to "position" in the document. A message box or balloon reports that two replacements were made.
5. Click **OK** to close the message box or click to close the message balloon, then click **Close**
   The dialog box closes. Compare your document to Figure B-18.
6. Click **Edit** on the menu bar, click **Find**, type **Karen Rosen** in the Find what text box, click **Find Next**, then click **Cancel**
   "Karen Rosen" is selected in the document.
7. Type your name, click the **Save button** on the Standard toolbar, then click the **Print button** on the Standard toolbar
   A copy of the document prints.
8. Click **File** on the menu bar, click **Close**, click **File** on the menu bar, then click **Exit**
   The documents and Word close.

QuickTip

If you want to review each occurrence before replacing it, click Find Next.

Clues to Use

Replacing text in Overtype mode

Word's Overtype feature allows you to type over existing text without selecting it first. When you work in Overtype mode, Word replaces the existing text with any new text you type. You can turn on Overtype mode by double-clicking the OVR box on the status bar (it appears in light gray when Overtype is off, and in black when Overtype is on). On some keyboards you can also turn on Overtype by pressing [Insert]. To turn off Overtype mode, double-click the OVR box in the status bar again, or press [Insert].

FIGURE B-17: Find and Replace dialog box

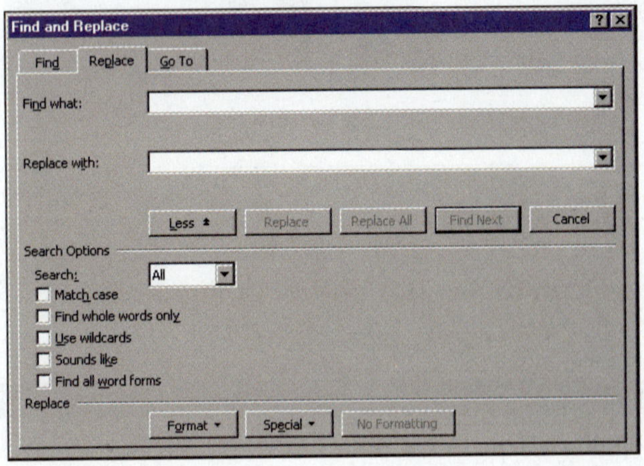

FIGURE B-18: Completed document

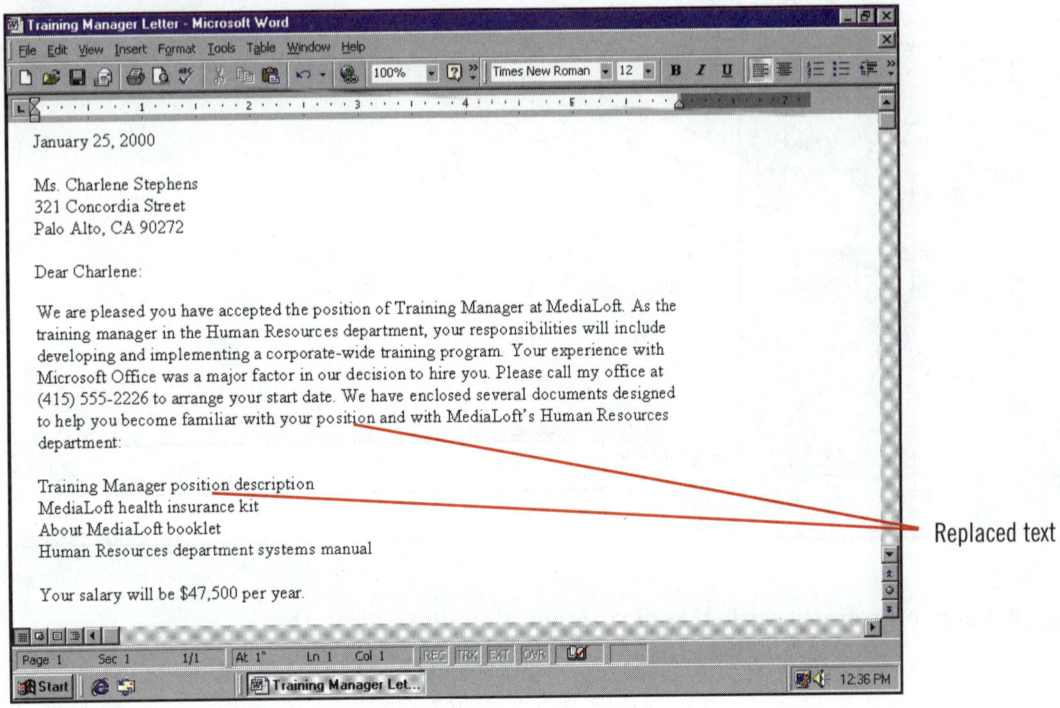

TABLE B-4: Search options in the Find and Replace dialog box

search option	use to
Search	Specify the direction of the search from the current location of the insertion point: Down, Up, or All
Match case	Locate only exact matches for the uppercase and lowercase letters entered in the Find what text box; select to find "President" but not "president"
Find whole words only	Locate only words that are complete and not part of a larger word; select to locate "Asia" but not "Asian"
Use wildcards	Search for a string of characters by using wildcards; select to enter "c*t" to find "cat" and "coat"
Sounds like	Locate words that sound like the text in the Find what text box, but have different spellings; select to find "their" and "there" and "they're"
Find all word forms	Find and replace all forms of a word; for example, specify "find" in the Find what text box to locate "find," "finds," "found," and "finding" and replace each with the comparable form of the replacement word

Practice

► Concepts Review

Label each element of the Open dialog box shown in Figure B-19.

FIGURE B-19

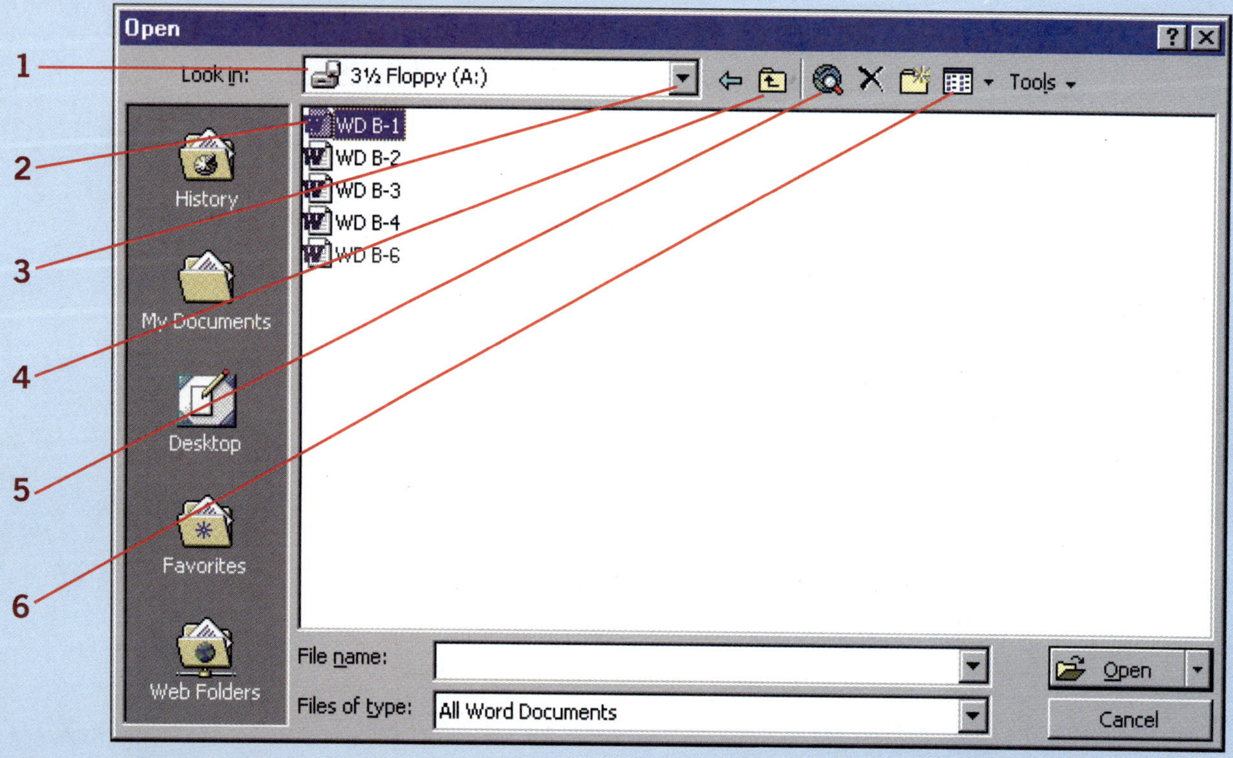

Match each command with the statement that describes it.

7. Copy
8. Paste
9. Spelling and Grammar
10. Thesaurus
11. Cut
12. Replace
13. Save As
14. Paste Special

a. Creates a new document while saving the original document
b. Reviews a document for spelling, punctuation, and usage errors
c. Suggests synonyms and antonyms
d. Removes text from a document and places it on the Clipboard
e. Places text on the Clipboard without removing it from the document
f. Embeds or links an item created in another Office program in a document
g. Locates and replaces occurrences of text in a document
h. Inserts text from the Clipboard in a document

Select the best answer from the list of choices.

15. To place text on the Clipboard, you must first

a. Click the Copy button.
b. Click the Cut button.
c. Click the Paste button.
d. Select the text.

16. **How many times can you paste an item from the Clipboard into a document?**
    a. Once
    b. Twice
    c. 12 times
    d. An unlimited number of times
17. **Which of the following statements best describes the selection bar?**
    a. The selection bar is the empty area to the left of text in the document window.
    b. To display the selection bar, you must click View on the menu bar, then click Selection Bar.
    c. The selection bar contains up to 12 items that you have copied or pasted to the Clipboard.
    d. The selection bar is the empty area to the right of text in the document window.
18. **Which option is NOT available in the Spelling and Grammar dialog box when a spelling error is identified?**
    a. Add the word to the dictionary
    b. Add an AutoCorrect entry
    c. Select a synonym for the word
    d. Choose a suggested spelling
19. **The Spelling and Grammar feature does not**
    a. Check for words that are repeated.
    b. Suggest revisions to make a sentence correct.
    c. Automatically correct all misspelled words.
    d. Explain grammatical errors.
20. **Which of the following is not true about the AutoCorrect feature?**
    a. AutoCorrect corrects common grammatical errors as you type them.
    b. Words underlined with a wavy line indicate possible spelling or grammatical errors.
    c. You can create AutoCorrect entries.
    d. AutoCorrect corrects commonly misspelled words as you type them.
21. **Using the Find and Replace commands, you can do all of the following *except***
    a. Search for all uses of the passive voice in your document.
    b. Search the document for specified text in a certain direction only.
    c. Substitute all occurrences of a word with another word.
    d. Locate all the different forms of a word in a document.

Skills Review

1. **Open and save a new document.**
   a. Start Word.
   b. Open the file WD B-2 from your Project Disk and save it as "Road Map."
2. **Select and replace text.**
   a. Select the date and replace it with today's date.
   b. Select "Wing" in the inside address and replace it with "Carroll."
   c. Select "Wing" in the salutation, then use the Repeat Typing command to replace the name with "Carroll."
   d. Select the street address and replace it with "280 Technology Drive."
   e. Select the line after the street address and delete it.
   f. Undo the deletion, then select "8B" and replace it with "555."
3. **Move text.**
   a. Display the Clipboard toolbar.
   b. Use the cut-and-paste method to move the last two sentences of the first body paragraph to the end of the second body paragraph.
   c. Use the drag method to move the last sentence of the last body paragraph in front of the second sentence in the first body paragraph.
4. **Copy text.**
   a. Copy "Open Roads, Inc." from the first sentence to under "Your Name" in the signature block.
   b. Copy "Open Roads" in the first sentence to in front of "package" in the third sentence.
   c. Close the Clipboard toolbar.

5. **Check spelling and grammar.**
   a. Press [Ctrl][Home], then click the Spelling and Grammar button.
   b. Correct the spelling and grammatical errors in the letter.
   c. Use the Thesaurus to find a substitution for "contact" in the last paragraph, then replace "contact." If the Thesaurus is not installed on your computer, substitute a word of your own.
6. **Create and use AutoCorrect entries.**
   a. Create an AutoCorrect entry for "Account Representative." Use the abbreviation "ar."
   b. Insert a blank line after "Your Name," type "ar," then press [Spacebar].
7. **Find and replace text.**
   a. Press [Ctrl][Home], then use the Replace command to replace all occurrences of "Inc." with "Intl."
   b. Double-click "OVR" in the status bar, place the insertion point in front of "Your Name," then type your name.
   c. Double-click "OVR" in the status bar again to turn Overtype mode off, save your changes, then print the document.
   d. Close the document and exit Word.

Independent Challenges

1. As the co-chair for the Middleburg reunion planning committee, you are responsible for recruiting classmates to help with reunion activities. One of the other people on your committee drafted a letter to your classmates for you to review and edit. You use the editing and proofing tools in Word to revise the letter.

To complete this independent challenge:

a. Start Word, open the file WD B-3 from your Project Disk, and save it as "Reunion Volunteer."
b. Copy the text "Middleburg" and paste it in front of "memories" in the second body paragraph and in front of "Reunion" in the signature block.
c. Move the second body paragraph so that it appears immediately before the last body paragraph.
d. Correct the spelling and grammatical errors in the document.
e. Replace "Your Name" with your name, save your changes, then print and close the document.

2. As an account representative for EasyTemps, a temporary placement service, you often use Word templates to create professional-looking documents. You recently used a template to create a memo to a customer describing your corporate discount program. You use the editing and proofing tools in Word to revise your memo before sending it to the customer.

To complete this independent challenge:

a. Start Word, open the file WD B-4 from your Project Disk, and save it as "Discount Proposal."
b. Copy the company name from the subject line of the memo and paste it in front of "DISCOUNT PROPOSAL" at the top of the document.
c. Use the Replace command to replace all but the second occurrence of "our" with "EasyTemps."
d. Move the second-to-last sentence of the memo so that it is the last sentence in the first paragraph.
e. Use the Thesaurus to look up an alternative word for "sequential," and replace it with a word of your choice.
f. Correct the spelling and grammatical errors in the document.
g. Click HERE in the From line, type your name, save your changes, then print and close the document.

3. Your boss has recognized you as a Word resource for your colleagues. To help everyone in your department learn to use Word more efficiently, she asks you to create a quick reference list of shortcut keys for the commands you use frequently. The shortcut keys are listed next to the commands on the File and Edit menus.

To complete this independent challenge:

a. Start Word and create a new document named "Quick Reference" on your Project Disk.
b. Open the Edit menu and note the keyboard shortcuts for the Paste, Copy, and Cut commands.
c. Create an AutoCorrect entry that inserts "[Ctrl]" whenever you type "ct."

d. Type a list that includes the name of each command and its keyboard shortcut. Use the new AutoCorrect entry to insert [Ctrl] in your document. (For example, enter "Paste: [Ctrl][V]" for the Paste command.)
e. Add keyboard shortcuts for the Undo, Repeat, Find, Replace, New, Open, Save, and Print commands to your list.
f. Cut and paste to rearrange your list so the commands appear in alphabetical order.
g. Delete the [Ctrl] AutoCorrect entry.
h. Type your name at the top of the document, save your changes, then print and close the document.

WEB WORK

4. You work in the Community Relations Department at MediaLoft. A nonprofit organization called Companies for Kids has approached MediaLoft for information about its corporate sponsorship program. Using the plan shown in Figure B-20, draft a short letter to Companies for Kids, describing MediaLoft's community relations programs.

To complete this independent challenge:

a. Start Word, then create a new document using the Letter Wizard. (*Hint:* To start the Letter Wizard, click File on the menu bar, click New, click the Letters & Faxes tab in the New dialog box, click the Letter Wizard, then click OK.)
b. Complete the wizard dialog boxes. Use today's date and choose any page design and letter style you wish. Address the letter to Judy Wexler, Director of Companies for Kids, and use any address. Add any other information you want to the letter, making sure to enter your name as the sender. (*Hint:* When you finish entering information in a dialog box, click Next to proceed to the next dialog box.)
c. Save the document as "Companies for Kids" on your Project Disk.
d. Using Figure B-20 as a guide, type a paragraph in the letter for each topic in the plan. For the second paragraph, collect information from the MediaLoft intranet site.
e. Connect to the Internet, go to the MediaLoft intranet site at http://www.course.com/illustrated/MediaLoft, then click the link for the Community page.
f. Copy MediaLoft's core assumptions from the Community Relations page on the intranet site to your letter. Disconnect from the Internet when you are done.
g. Use editing techniques to rework the text into a readable paragraph. (*Hint:* Delete the bullets.)
h. When you finish typing the letter, use the Replace command to locate each occurrence of "valuable" and replace it with "important."
i. Correct your spelling and grammatical errors.
j. Save your changes, then print and close the document.

FIGURE B-20

Plan for letter describing MediaLoft's community relations policies

Letter to Director of Companies for Kids should cover:

1. Thank you for interest in MediaLoft
2. Describe MediaLoft's core assumptions
3. Suggest a meeting to go over questions/concerns

► Visual Workshop

Create the letter shown in Figure B-21, using the Contemporary Letter template. Save it as "Lakeside Letter" on your Project Disk, then print a copy of the letter.

FIGURE B-21

128 Lakeview Avenue
Brooklyn Valley, MN 55217

International Voices

January 26, 2000

Ms. Leslie Ryden
Banquet Caterer
Lakeside Center
North Bay, MN 55509

Dear Ms. Ryden:

I would like to take this opportunity to reaffirm how delighted we are to be conducting International Voices' Vision Conference at the Lakeside Center. We at International Voices believe it is the perfect setting for our conference's objectives.

As you requested, here are my ideas for the informal dinner that will wrap up the day's events. I would be interested in having a low-fat, healthful menu for this meal. Regarding table centerpieces, I liked your idea of arranging international flags drawn by children of International Voices employees.

I hope these general suggestions will be helpful to you as you plan your menu and price proposal. I look forward to confirming our plans by the end of next month.

Sincerely,

Your Name
Conference Coordinator
International Voices

Children Are The Key To Our Success!

Word 2000

Unit C

Formatting a Document

Objectives

- MOUS ► Change fonts and font sizes
- MOUS ► Apply font effects
- MOUS ► Change paragraph alignment
- MOUS ► Indent paragraphs
- MOUS ► Change line spacing
- MOUS ► Change paragraph spacing
- MOUS ► Align text with tabs
- MOUS ► Create bulleted and numbered lists
- MOUS ► Apply borders and shading

Without some formatting, even a simple document could be almost impossible to read. You can highlight important words or improve the look of a document by changing its typeface or the size of its words. You can organize ideas and add structure to a document by changing the spacing, indentation, and alignment of text in paragraphs. Formatting a document makes it easier to read and easier to understand. Karen Rosen has drafted a description of the orientation packet for new MediaLoft employees. Before distributing the document to her colleagues, she formats the text and paragraphs to improve the document's organization and to emphasize important topics.

Unit C
Word 2000

Changing Fonts and Font Sizes

One of the easiest ways to change the appearance of a document is to change its font. A **font** is a family of characters, which includes letters, numbers, and punctuation, with the same typeface or design. A font can be basic, with clean, simple lines, or more stylized, with a lot of curlicues or a definite "theme." The font you choose affects the tone of your document: stylized fonts can add a note of flamboyance, formality, or sleekness to a document, while a more traditional font can "feel" businesslike or scholarly. You can also change the size of text in your documents by increasing or decreasing the **font size**. Fonts are measured in points (pts). A **point** is 1/72 of an inch. The bigger the number of points, the larger the size of the font. To quickly change fonts and font size, select the text you want to format, then use the buttons on the Formatting toolbar. Karen changes the font and font size of the title and headings in her document, so that readers can quickly find the information they need.

Steps 1 2 3 4

1. Start **Word**, click **Tools** on the menu bar, click **Customize**, click the **Options tab** in the Customize dialog box, click **Reset my usage data** to restore the default settings, click **Yes** in the alert box, then click **Close**
2. Open the file **WD C-1** from your Project Disk, then save it as **Orientation Packet**
   The document opens in Normal view. The name of the font used in the document appears in the Font list box on the Formatting toolbar, and the font size appears next to it in the Font Size list box. The document is formatted in 12 point Times New Roman.
3. Select the title **New Employee Orientation Packet**, then click the **Font list arrow** on the Formatting toolbar
   The Font list opens with Times New Roman selected, as shown in Figure C-1. The name of each font is formatted in the font so you can see what it looks like. Use the scroll box in the list to view the fonts available on your computer. Fonts you have used recently appear at the top of the list.
4. Click **Arial**
   The font of the selected text changes to Arial. Arial is a font that is commonly used in headings. Titles and headings often appear in a font different from that document's body text.
5. Click the **Font Size list arrow** on the Formatting toolbar, then click **18**
   The size of the title increases to 18 points. The headings should also be formatted in the Arial font.
6. Select the heading **Offer Letter**, click the **Font list arrow**, click **Arial**, click the **Font Size list arrow**, then click **14**
   The heading is formatted in 14 point Arial. Headings in a document are usually larger than body text, but smaller than the title. You'll format each heading in the document in the same way.
7. Click the **down scroll arrow** at the bottom of the vertical scroll bar until the heading **Employee Handbook** appears at the top of your screen
   The Orientation Packet document contains more text than will fit in the document window. **Scrolling** allows you to navigate a document to display the text you want to read or edit in the document window.
8. Select the heading **Employee Handbook**, change the font to **Arial**, change the font size to **14**, then change the font and font size to 14 point Arial (scrolling as needed) for each of the following headings: **Health Insurance Kit**, **Employee Benefits Summary**, and **About MediaLoft © booklet**
9. Deselect the text, then click the **Save button** on the Standard toolbar
   Compare your document to Figure C-2.

Trouble?

Click the More Buttons button on the Formatting toolbar to locate the buttons and list arrows that are not visible on your Formatting toolbar.

QuickTip

Take care to limit the number of fonts you use to two or three per document, and be sure to choose fonts that are appropriate for your audience.

FIGURE C-1: Font list

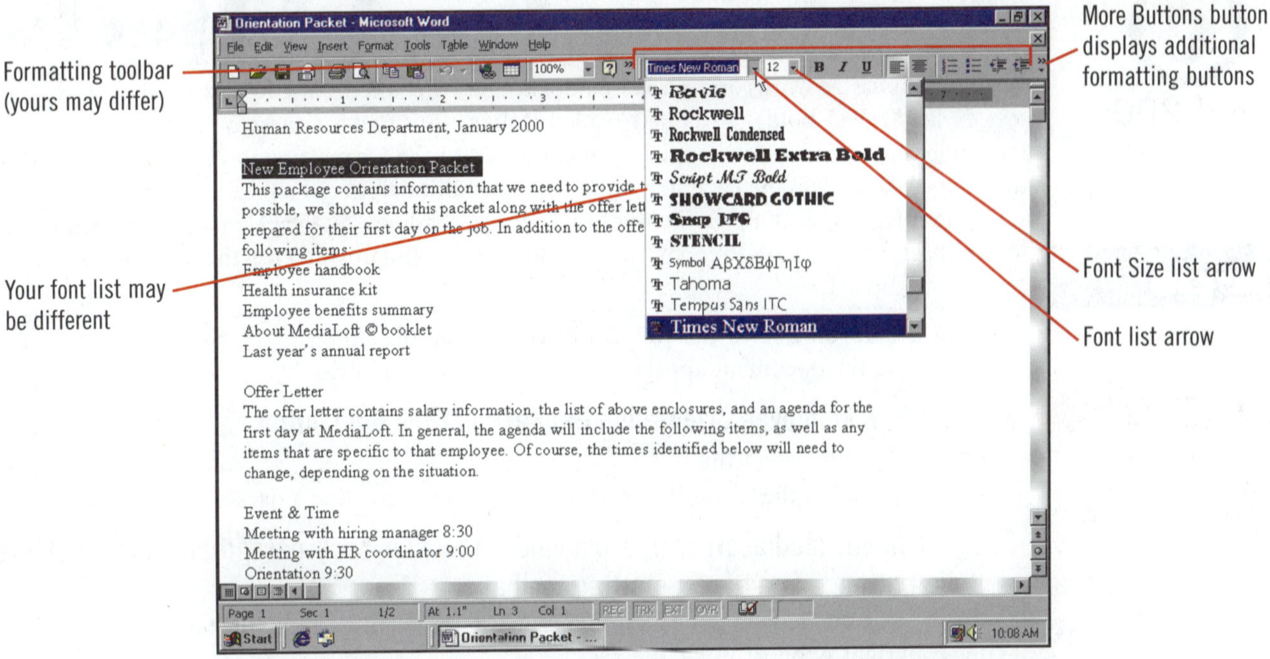

FIGURE C-2: Formatted document

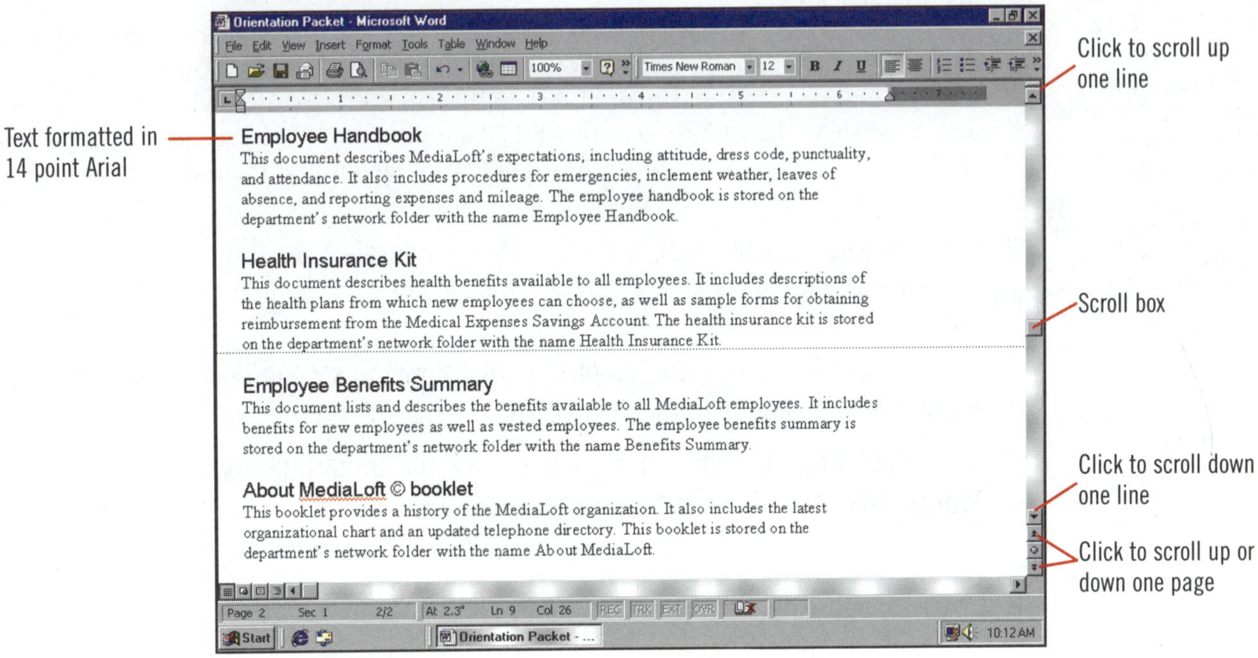

CLUES TO USE

Scrolling a document

If your document contains more text than will fit in the document window, you need to scroll the document to display the text you want to read or edit. Scrolling changes the position of the document window relative to the document text. You can scroll up or down in a document. Scroll one line at a time by clicking the arrows at the top and bottom of the vertical scroll bar, or scroll one document window at a time by clicking the scroll bar above or below the scroll box. If you want to scroll the document one page at a time, click the up or down double-arrows at the bottom of the scroll bar. You can also drag the scroll box to a new location in the scroll bar to move to a specific page in the document.

Unit C
Word 2000

Applying Font Effects

You can emphasize words and ideas in a document by changing the font style, such as making text darker (called **bold**) or slanted (called **italics**). Buttons for these and other font effects, including underlining and changing font color, are on the Formatting toolbar. You can also use the Font command on the Format menu to apply additional special effects to text, such as superscripting it (raising text above the line) or adding a shadow. Karen applies font effects to emphasize important elements in her document, and to italicize the title of the About MediaLoft booklet.

Steps

QuickTip

You can also underline text by clicking the Underline button on the Formatting toolbar.

QuickTip

Use the Character Spacing tab in the Font dialog box to expand or condense the amount of space between characters, adjust the width or scale of characters, raise or lower characters, and adjust kerning (the spacing between standard character combinations). Formatting character spacing can dramatically affect the appearance of text.

1. Drag the **scroll box** to the top of the vertical scroll bar
   The top of the document appears in the document window.
2. Select **New Employee Orientation Packet**, click the **Bold button** on the Formatting toolbar, then deselect the text
   Applying bold to the text makes each character fatter, creating a darker appearance.
3. Select **About MediaLoft** in the list under the first body paragraph, then click the **Italic button** on the Formatting toolbar
   The title of the booklet appears in italics. Next you want to apply the superscript effect to the copyright symbol.
4. Select © (the copyright symbol) after About MediaLoft, click **Format** on the menu bar, then click **Font**
   The Font dialog box opens as shown in Figure C-3. You can use the Font tab to apply many different effects to text, including shadow, superscript, and subscript. You can also change the font, font size, style, and color of text on this tab, and select the style of underline you want to apply to the selected text. Using the Font dialog box, you can apply multiple font effects to text at once. The Preview box on the Font tab displays the combined effects you have chosen for the selected text.
5. Click the **Superscript** check box, click **OK**, then deselect the text
   The copyright symbol is superscripted—formatted in a smaller font size and raised above the line of text.
6. Select **Event & Time** at the top of the list below the second body paragraph, click **Format** on the menu bar, then click **Font**
7. Click **Bold Italic** in the Font style list, click the **Underline style list arrow**, click **Words only**, then click the **Small caps** check box
   The text appears in the Preview box formatted in bold, italic, small caps, with the words (not the spaces between them) underlined. When you change text to small caps, the characters change to uppercase, with the capital letters two points larger than lowercase letters.
8. Click **OK**, deselect the text, then click the **Save button** on the Standard toolbar
   Compare your document to Figure C-4.

CLUES TO USE

Adding color to text

When you want to use color to add visual interest in a document, you can highlight, or apply a transparent layer of color to text, or you can change the color of the text itself. To highlight text, click the Highlight button on the Formatting toolbar and then drag the Highlighter pointer over the text you want to highlight. You can change the highlight color by clicking the Highlight list arrow and then clicking a new color. To turn off the Highlighter pointer, simply click the Highlight button again. If you want to change the color of the characters themselves, select the text you want to color, click the Font Color list arrow on the Formatting toolbar, and then click a new color.

FIGURE C-3: Font dialog box

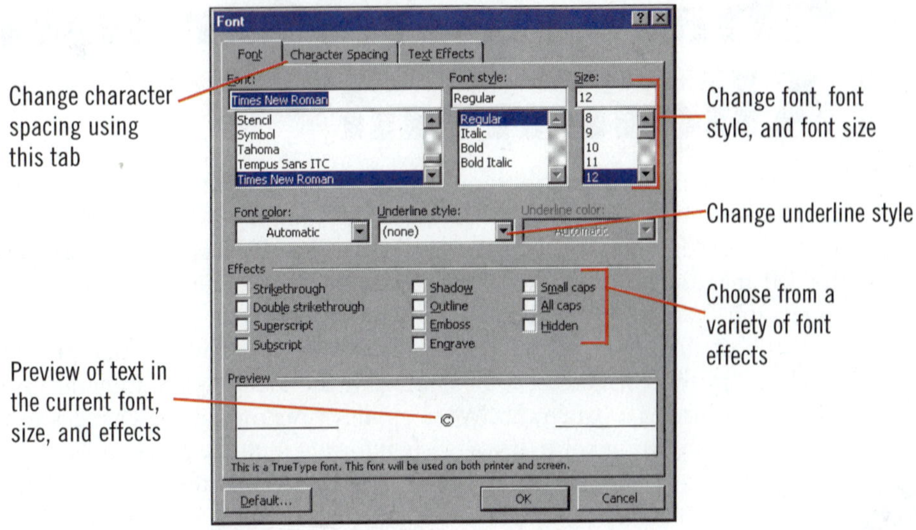

FIGURE C-4: Completed font formatting

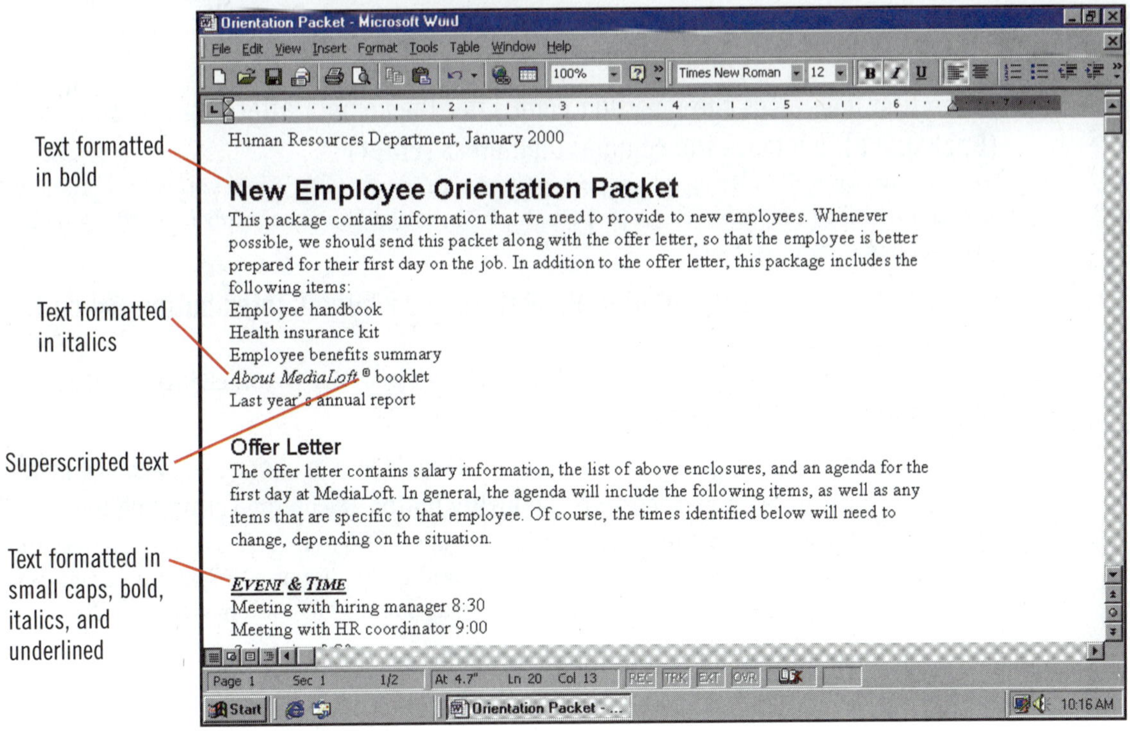

CLUES TO USE

Serif vs. sans serif fonts

Fonts can be divided into two types: serif and sans serif. A **serif font**, such as Times New Roman, has a small stroke, or a **serif**, at the ends of its characters, as shown in Figure C-5. Serif fonts are typically used in business documents, such as letters and resumes, and as the body text in books and other publications. Fonts without serifs, such as Arial, are known as **sans serif fonts.** Sans serif fonts are often used for headings in a document, or as the main font in other types of publications, such as flyers, brochures, and business cards. In a longer document, serif fonts can be easier to read than sans serif fonts.

FIGURE C-5: Serif vs. sans serif fonts

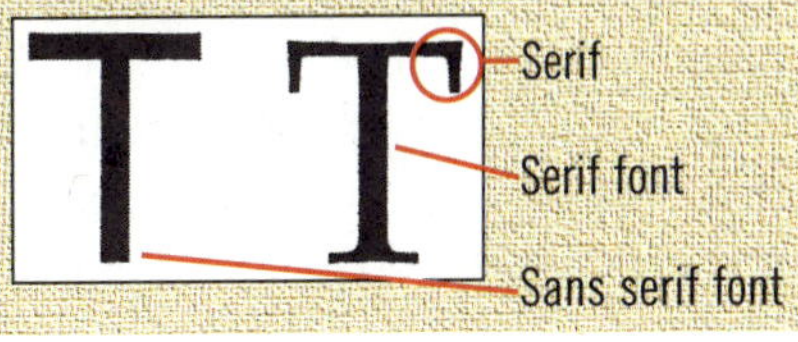

Word 2000

Unit C
Word 2000

Changing Paragraph Alignment

Another way to change the appearance of text in a document is to change the alignment of paragraphs. Paragraphs are aligned relative to the margins in a document. **Margins** are the blank areas between the edge of the text and the edge of the page. By default, text is **left-aligned**, or flush with the left margin. However, you can also **center** a paragraph between margins or **right-align** a paragraph so that its right edge is even with the right margin. You can also **justify** a paragraph so that both the left and right edges are evenly aligned. These paragraph alignment options are available on the Formatting toolbar or with the Paragraph command on the Format menu. When you format a paragraph, Word applies your formatting changes to the paragraph that contains the insertion point. If you wish to format multiple paragraphs, you must first select the paragraphs you want to format. Karen varies the alignment of paragraphs in her document to make it easier to read.

Steps

Trouble?

Click the More Buttons button on the Formatting toolbar to locate buttons that are not visible on your Formatting toolbar.

1. Select the first line of the document, **Human Resources Department, January 2000**, then click the **Align Right button** on the Formatting toolbar
   The text is aligned with the right margin.
2. In the first line, place the insertion point after the comma after **Department**, press **[Backspace]** to remove the comma, then press **[Enter]**
   The new paragraph is also right-aligned, as shown in Figure C-6. When you press [Enter] in the middle of a paragraph, the new paragraph "inherits" the paragraph formatting of the original paragraph.
3. Select **New Employee Orientation Packet**, then click the **Center button** on the Formatting toolbar
   The title is centered evenly between the left and right margins. If you change the margins, this text will always remain centered relative to the margins.
4. Scroll down to locate the paragraph that begins **I would like to share . . .**, place the insertion point in the paragraph, then click the **Justify button** on the Formatting toolbar
   Word adjusts the spacing between words of the paragraph so that each line in the paragraph is the same length, and flush with both the left and right margins. Justifying paragraphs eliminates the ragged right edge, and can make your documents look neater.
5. Click the **Save button** on the Standard toolbar
   Compare your document to Figure C-7.

CLUES TO USE

Using the FormatPainter to copy formatting

You can use Word's FormatPainter to copy text or paragraph formatting to other text that you want to format the same way. This feature is especially useful when you want to copy multiple effects at once. To use the Format Painter, select the text whose formatting you want to copy, then click the FormatPainter button on the Standard toolbar. When the pointer changes to , simply select the text you want to format. The new formatting is automatically applied. If you want to copy the formatting to multiple locations, double-click the FormatPainter button so that the FormatPainter pointer remains active. To turn off the FormatPainter, click the FormatPainter button again.

FIGURE C-6: Right-aligned text

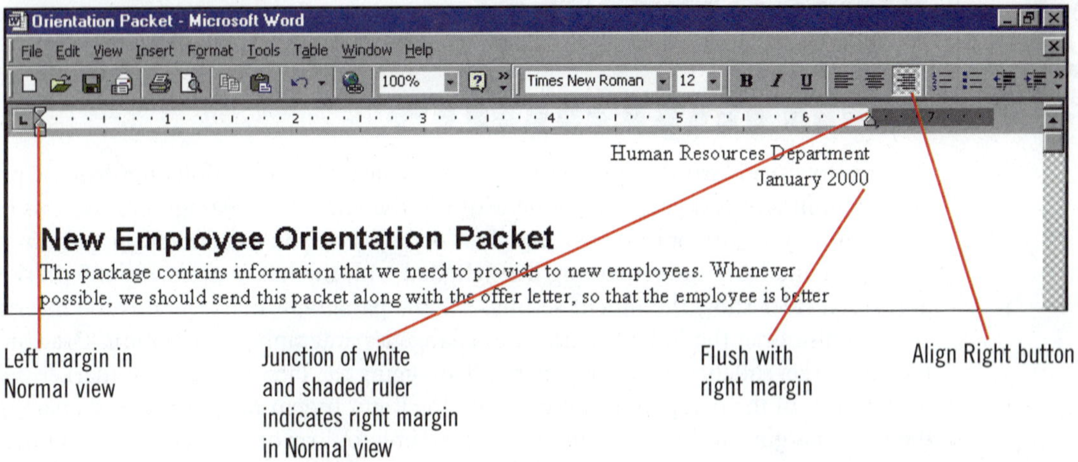

FIGURE C-7: Justified text

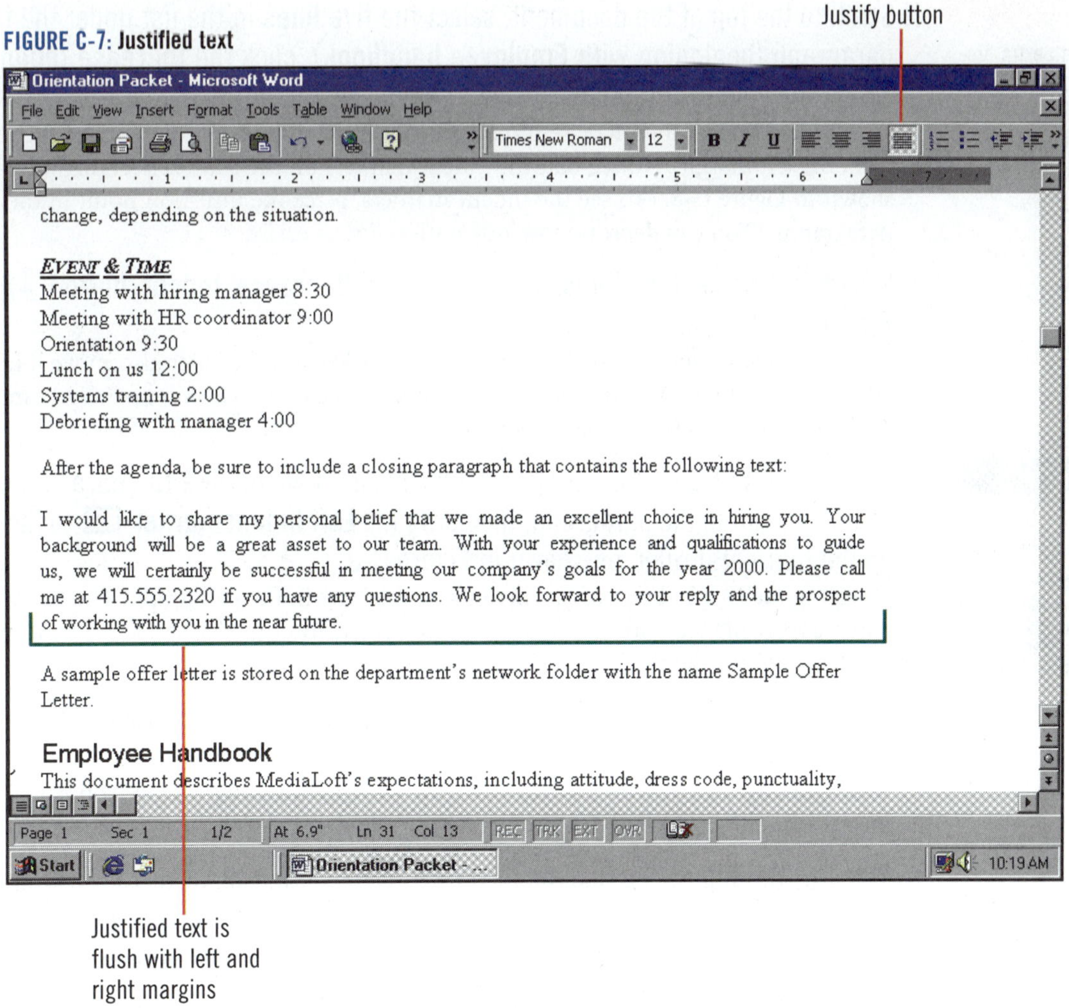

Unit C
Word 2000

Indenting Paragraphs

One way to visually structure a document is to change the indentation of individual paragraphs. When you **indent** text you change the width of the lines in the paragraph. You can modify the indentation from the right or left margins (or both) or you can indent just the first line of a paragraph and leave the remaining lines aligned with the left margin. **Indent markers** on the horizontal ruler show the indent settings for the paragraph that contains the insertion point. You can also drag the indent markers to change a paragraph's indentation. Dragging the Left Indent marker indents an entire paragraph, dragging the First Line Indent marker indents only the first line of the paragraph, and dragging the Right Indent marker indents a paragraph from the right margin. You can also use the Formatting toolbar or the Paragraph command on the Format menu to change a paragraph's indentation. Karen indents several paragraphs to help clarify the structure of her document. She uses the buttons on the Formatting toolbar and the indent markers on the horizontal ruler.

Steps 1 2 3 4

QuickTip

To indent text with extra precision, click Format on the menu bar, click Paragraph, then enter the amount you want to indent in the Paragraph dialog box.

Trouble?

Be sure to drag the Left Indent marker, not the First Line Indent marker or the Hanging Indent marker. Click the Undo button if you make a mistake, then redo the step.

1. Scroll to the top of the document, select the **five lines** in the list under the first body paragraph (beginning with **Employee handbook**), click the **Increase Indent button** on the Formatting toolbar twice, then deselect the text

   Each time you click the Increase Indent button, Word indents the left edge of the text ½ inch from the left margin. Notice that the indent markers on the ruler reflect the indentation, as shown in Figure C-8. (To see the indent markers, place the insertion point in the indented paragraphs.) You can decrease the indentation just as easily.

2. Select the same **five lines**, then click the **Decrease Indent button** on the Formatting toolbar once

   The text moves ½ inch to the left. The indent markers on the ruler also move ½ inch to the left. The indent markers indicate how much the selected text is indented. You can also drag the indent markers to change indentation.

3. Scroll down to locate the paragraph that begins **I would like to share ...**, place the insertion point in the paragraph, then drag the **Left Indent marker** to the **¾" mark** on the horizontal ruler, as shown in Figure C-9

   Dragging the Left Indent marker indents all the lines in the paragraph. The left edge of the paragraph is aligned with the ¾" mark on the ruler. You can also use the indent markers to indent text from the right.

4. With the insertion point in the same paragraph drag the **Right Indent marker** to the **5¾" mark** on the horizontal ruler

   The right edge of the paragraph is indented ¾" from the right margin. You can also indent only the first line of a paragraph by dragging the First Line Indent marker.

5. Scroll to the top of the document, place the insertion point in the first body paragraph that begins **This package contains ...**, then drag the **First Line Indent marker** to the **½" mark** on the horizontal ruler, as shown in Figure C-10

   Dragging the First Line Indent marker indents only the first line of text in a paragraph.

6. Place the insertion point in the **paragraph** directly below each heading in the document (except "Event & Time"), then drag the **First Line Indent marker** to the **½" mark** on the horizontal ruler so that the first line in each paragraph is indented ½"

7. Click the **Save button** on the Standard toolbar

FIGURE C-8: Indented list

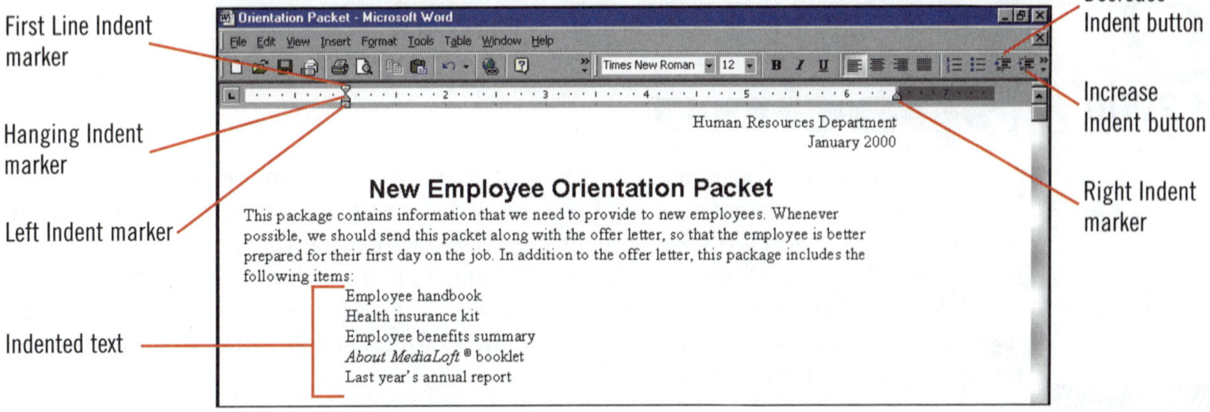

FIGURE C-9: Dragging Left Indent marker

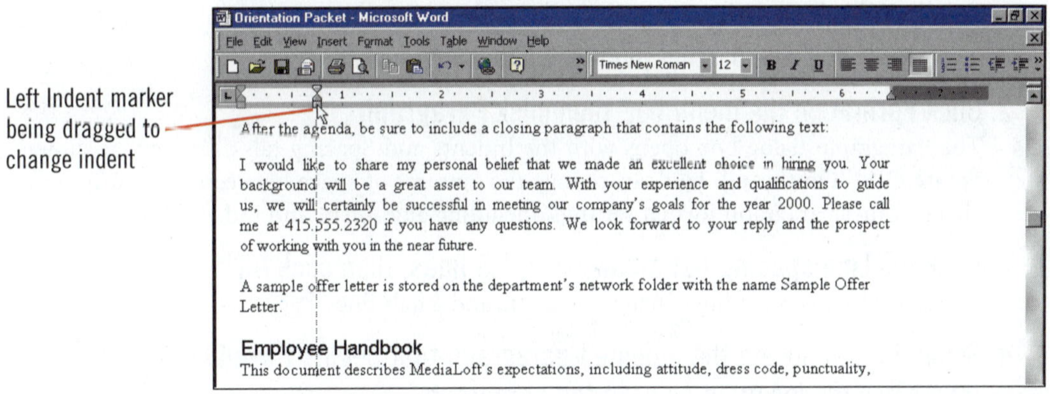

FIGURE C-10: Dragging First Line Indent marker

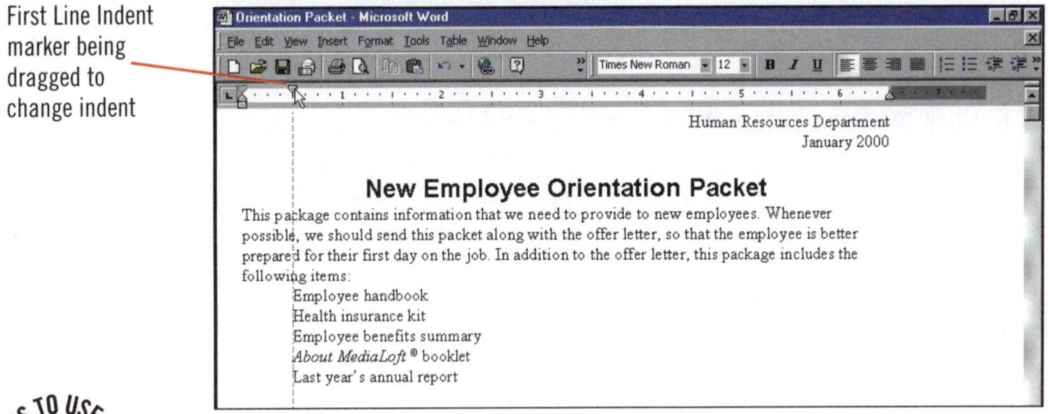

CLUES TO USE

Using hanging indent paragraph formatting

Sometimes you want a paragraph formatted so that the first line of the paragraph is not indented as much as the text in the remaining lines. This formatting is known as a **hanging indent**, shown in Figure C-11. Notice the arrangement of the indent markers on the horizontal ruler and the indentation of the first and remaining lines of the paragraph. You can create a hanging indent by dragging the Hanging Indent marker on the horizontal ruler or by pressing [Ctrl] [T].

FIGURE C-11: Hanging indent

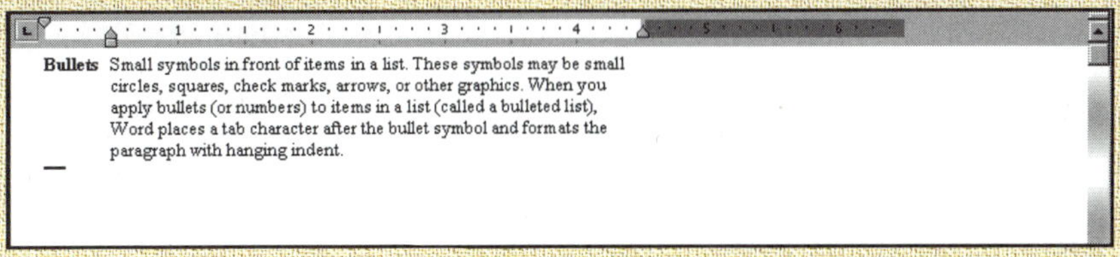

Word 2000

Unit C

Word 2000

Changing Line Spacing

Another way to make a document easier to read is to increase the amount of spacing between lines. For example, thesis papers or draft versions of documents are often double-spaced to allow space for readers to add written comments. Increase line spacing whenever you want to give a more "open" feel to a document. You use the Paragraph command on the Format menu to change line spacing. Table C-1 describes several keyboard shortcuts for formatting paragraphs. Karen wants to provide space for comments from her colleagues, so she increases the line spacing in the document.

Steps

1. Scroll to the top of the document, then place the insertion point in the first body paragraph that begins **This package contains ...**
2. Click **Format** on the menu bar, then click **Paragraph**
   The Paragraph dialog box opens with the Indents and Spacing tab displayed, as shown in Figure C-12. On this tab you can change the amount of space between lines. You can also change other paragraph format settings, including alignment and indentation.
3. Click the **Line spacing list arrow**, click **1.5 lines**, then click **OK**
   The space between the lines increases to one and a half lines.
4. Scroll down to locate the indented paragraph that begins **I would like to share ...**, then place the insertion point in the paragraph
5. Click **Format** on the menu bar, click **Paragraph**, click the **Line spacing list arrow**, click **Double**, then click **OK**
   The space between the lines of the paragraph doubles, as shown in Figure C-13.
6. Click the **Save button** on the Standard toolbar

QuickTip

You can also display the Paragraph dialog box by right-clicking, then clicking paragraph on the Pop-Up Menu.

TABLE C-1: Keyboard shortcuts for aligning text and changing line spacing

to	press	to	press
Left-align text	[Ctrl] [L]	Format text with 1.5 line spacing	[Ctrl] [5]
Center text	[Ctrl] [E]	Single-space text	[Ctrl] [1]
Right-align text	[Ctrl] [R]	Double-space text	[Ctrl] [2]
Justify text	[Ctrl] [J]		

FIGURE C-12: Paragraph dialog box

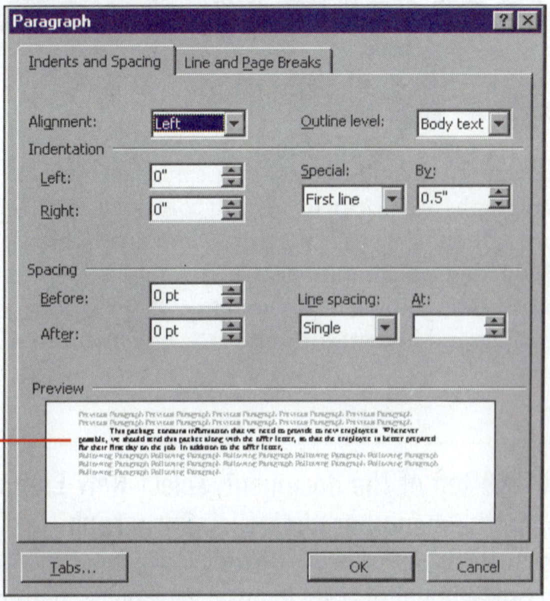

Preview area displays example of formatting

FIGURE C-13: New line spacing in a document

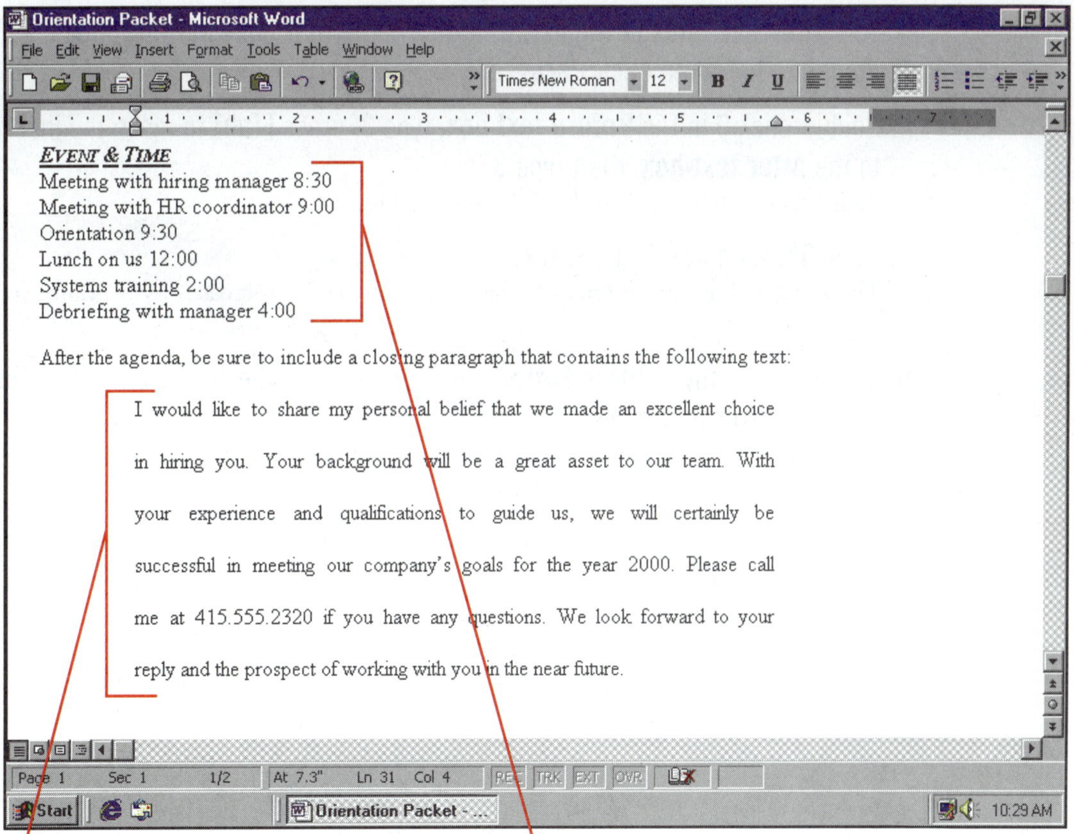

Double-spaced text

Single-spaced text

Unit C

Word 2000

Changing Paragraph Spacing

In the same way increasing line spacing can make a document easier to read, adding space between paragraphs can help to visually organize the content of your document. Spacing between lines and paragraphs is measured in points. Because you can set the number of points you want, adjusting paragraph spacing is a much more precise way to format than simply inserting blank lines between paragraphs. Karen increases the paragraph spacing between headings and body text to make the document more readable.

Steps

1. Scroll to the top of the document, select **New Employee Orientation Packet**, click **Format** on the menu bar, then click **Paragraph**
   The Paragraph dialog box opens with the Indents and Spacing tab displayed. You can use this tab to change the amount of space between paragraphs. You want to increase the amount of space after the title.
2. Click the **After up arrow** twice, then click **OK**
   The space after the paragraph is increased to 12 points. Clicking the Before or After arrows increases or decreases the amount of space above or below a paragraph. Each time you click an up or down arrow, the spacing changes by 6 points. You can also type the specific number of points you want in the Before and After text boxes.
3. Select the **five lines** in the list that follows the first body paragraph, click **Format** on the menu bar, then click **Paragraph**
4. Double-click **0** in the **Before text box**, type **3**, press **[Tab]** to move the insertion point to the **After text box**, then type **3**
   Your Paragraph dialog box should resemble Figure C-14.
5. Click **OK**, then deselect the text
   The space before and after each paragraph in the list increases by 3 points, as shown in Figure C-15.
6. Select the heading **Offer Letter**, click **Format** on the menu bar, click **Paragraph**, click the **After up arrow** once, then click **OK**
   The space between the heading and the paragraph below it increases by 6 points. The other headings should also be formatted with 6 points of space after.
7. Place the insertion point in each remaining **heading** in the document (except "Event & Time"), then format each heading with 6 points of space after it
8. Click the **Save button** on the Standard toolbar

QuickTip

You can press [F4] to repeat the last command.

FIGURE C-14: Paragraph spacing in Paragraph dialog box

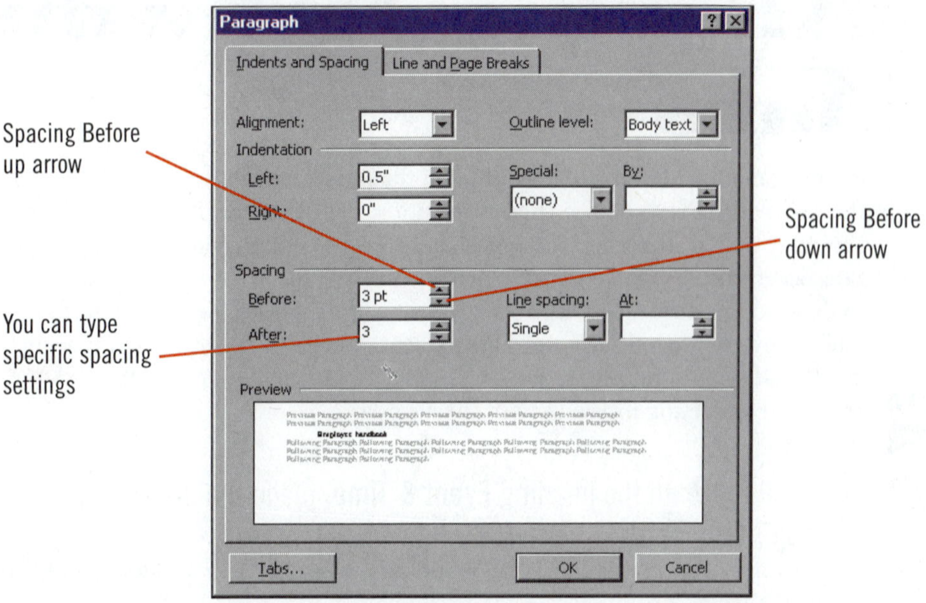

FIGURE C-15: Increased paragraph spacing

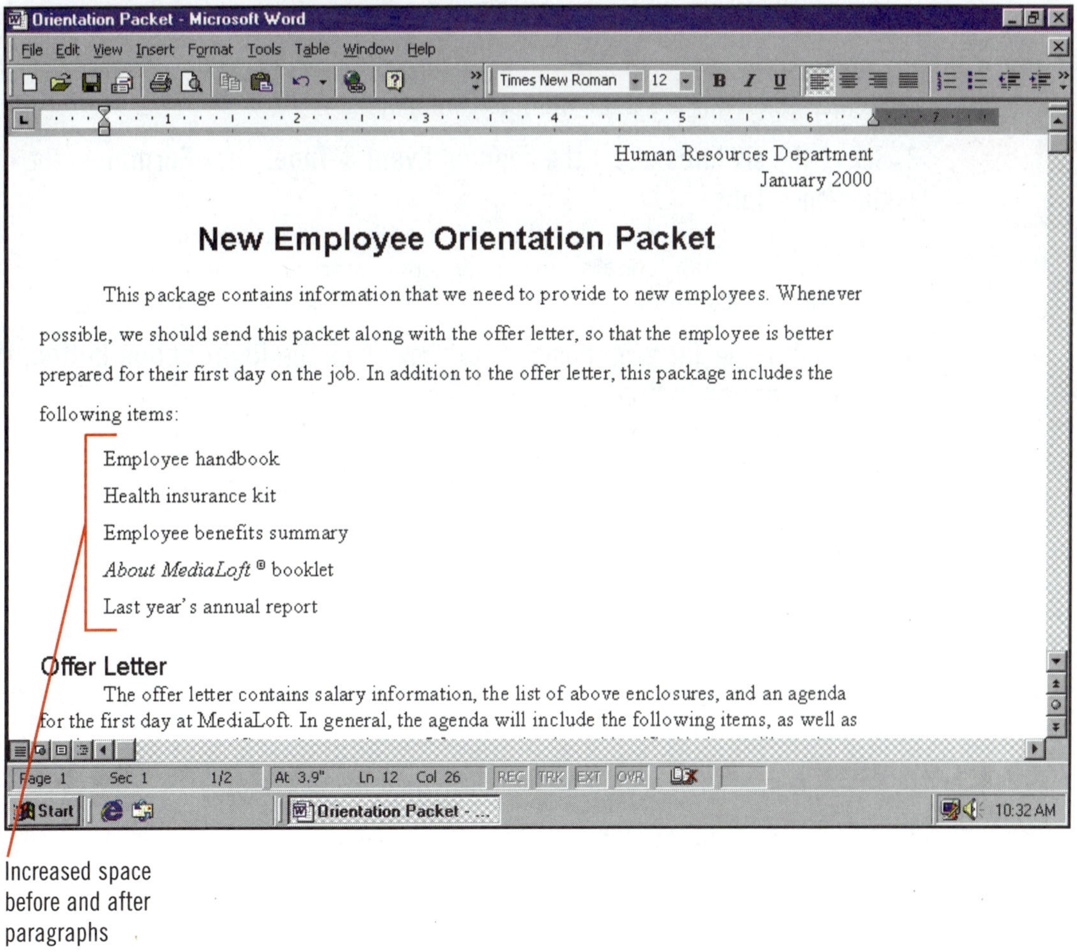

Word 2000

Unit C

Word 2000

Aligning Text with Tabs

Numerical information (such as tables of financial results) is often easier to read when you align the text with tabs. A **tab** is used to position text at a specific location in the document. You should use tabs rather than the Spacebar to vertically align your text because tabs are more accurate, faster, and easier to change. When you press [Tab] in a document, the insertion point moves to the next tab stop. A **tab stop** is a predefined position in the document to which you can align tabbed text. By default, tab stops are located at every ½" from the left margin, but you can also create and modify tab stops. Table C-2 describes the five types of tabs. Karen uses tabs to align the meeting times listed in the agenda.

Steps

QuickTip

Click the Show/Hide button ¶ on the Standard toolbar to reveal tab symbols (→), paragraph marks (¶), and spaces between characters (•) in your document. Click it again to hide the symbols.

1. Scroll to locate the heading **Event & Time**, place the insertion point in front of **Time**, then press **[Tab]**

   Pressing [Tab] moves the word "Time" to the next default tab stop at the 1" mark on the horizontal ruler. You can also set your own tab stops.

2. At the left end of the horizontal ruler be sure the **Left Tab icon** is active, as shown in Figure C-16, then click the **5" mark** on the ruler

   If the Left Tab icon is not visible in the tab indicator at the left end of the ruler, click the tab indicator until the Left Tab icon appears. Clicking the ruler moves the tab stop to the 5" mark, and the tabbed text "Time" moves to the new location as shown in Figure C-16. To align the meeting times under this heading, you need to create a tab stop for each line in the agenda. To do this you'll use the Tabs command.

QuickTip

You can also adjust the location of a tab stop by dragging the tab marker to a new location on the ruler.

3. Select the **six lines** under the heading **Event & Time**, click **Format** on the menu bar, then click **Tabs**

   The Tabs dialog box opens. You can use this dialog box to set tab stop position and alignment and to set **tab leaders** (lines or dots that appear in front of the tabbed text). You can also use the Tabs command to clear tabs. You'll set right-aligned tabs with leaders.

4. Type **5.3** in the Tab stop position text box, click the **Right option button**, then click the **2.... option button**

   Your Tabs dialog box should resemble Figure C-17.

5. Click **Set** to create the tab setting, then click **OK**

   A new right tab marker appears on the ruler just after the 5¼" mark. You'll insert tabs in front of each of the meeting times.

6. Place the insertion point in front of **8:30** in the first line of the agenda, then press **[Tab]**

   The time "8:30" is right-aligned with the 5.3" tab stop with a dotted tab leader in front of it.

QuickTip

You can remove a tab stop by dragging it off the ruler.

7. Place the insertion point in front of each remaining **time** in the agenda, then press **[Tab]**

   The times right-align at 5.3".

8. Select **&** in the Event & Time heading, then press **[Delete]**

9. Click the **Save button** on the Standard toolbar

   Compare your document to Figure C-18. To see the right-aligned tab marker, place the insertion point in the agenda.

FIGURE C-16: Setting a tab stop on the ruler

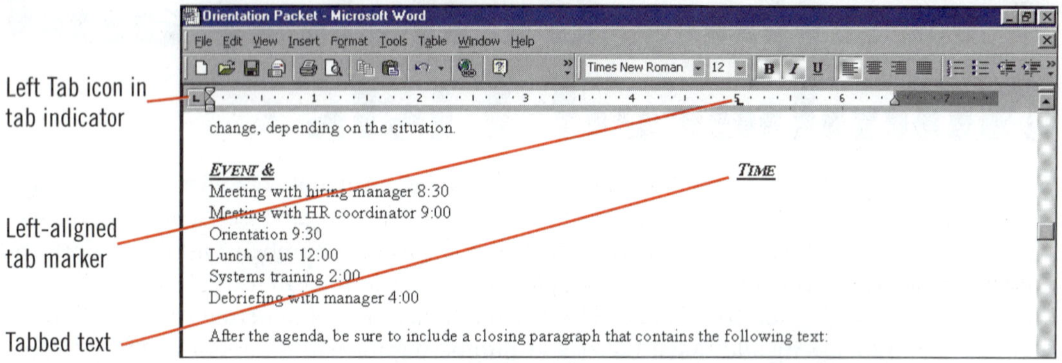

FIGURE C-17: Tabs dialog box

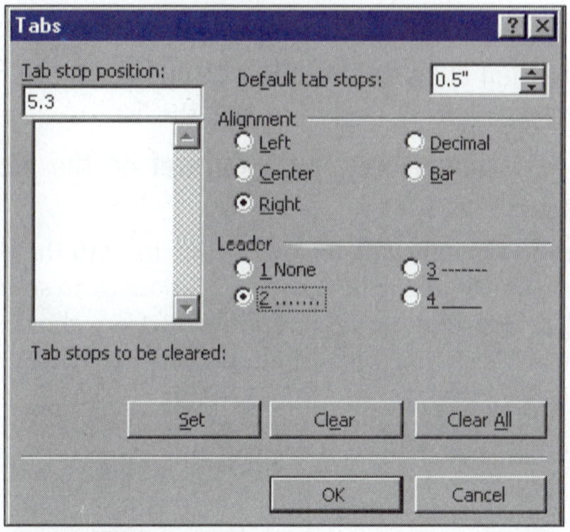

FIGURE C-18: Right-aligned tabs with tab leaders

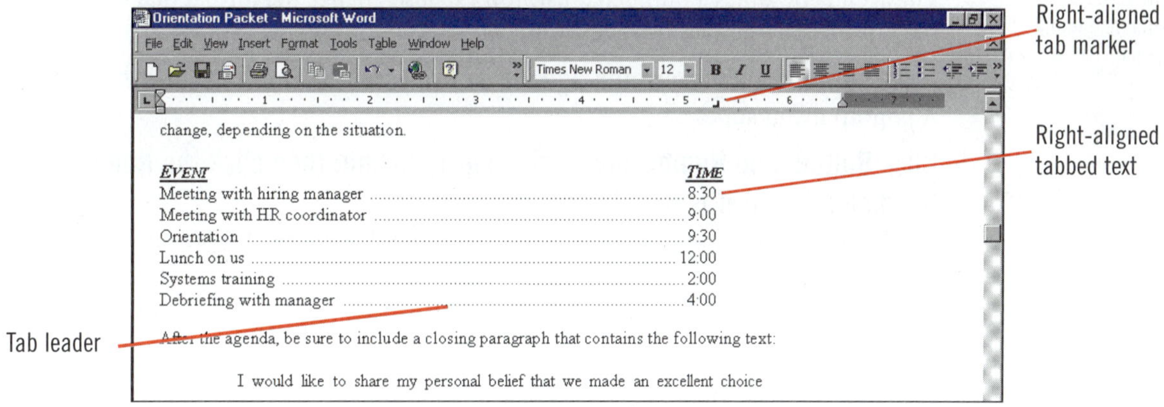

TABLE C-2: Types of tabs

alignment	description	tab indicator
Left	Text left-aligns at the tab stop and extends to the right	
Center	Text aligns at the middle of the tab stop, extending an equal distance to the left and right	
Right	Text right-aligns at the tab stop and extends to the left	
Decimal	Text aligns at the decimal point: text before the decimal point extends to the left, and the text after the decimal point extends to the right (used to align numbers)	
Bar	Inserts a vertical bar at the tab position	

Unit C

Word 2000

Creating Bulleted and Numbered Lists

In a bulleted list, a **bullet**—a small symbol such as a circle or square—precedes each paragraph in the list. Using the Bullets button on the Formatting toolbar, you can insert a bullet in front of each item in a list. When you want to show items in a sequence, a numbered list best reflects the order or priority of the items. To create a simple numbered list, you can use the Numbering button on the Formatting toolbar. You can also use the Bullets and Numbering command on the Format menu to specify additional bullet and numbering formatting options. Karen draws attention to the lists in her document by formatting them with bullets and numbers.

Steps 1234

1. Scroll to the top of the document, select the **five lines** in the list under the first body paragraph, then click the **Bullets button** on the Formatting toolbar
   A bullet appears in front of each item in the list.
2. With the list still selected, click **Format** on the menu bar, then click **Bullets and Numbering**
   The Bullets and Numbering dialog box opens with the Bulleted tab displayed, as shown in Figure C-19. In this dialog box, you can choose from seven different bullet styles. Do not be concerned if your bullet styles are different from those shown in the figure. You can customize your styles to use whatever bullet characters you prefer.
3. Click the **check mark box**, then click **OK**
   The bullet character changes to a small check mark.
4. Scroll to the agenda under the "Event Time" heading, select the **six lines** in the agenda, then click the **Numbering button** on the Formatting toolbar
   The agenda becomes a numbered list. You can also change the format of a numbered list in the Bullets and Numbering dialog box.
5. Make sure the six lines of the agenda are selected, then right-click the **agenda**
   A pop-up menu appears.
6. Click **Bullets and Numbering** on the pop-up menu, then click the **Numbered tab** in the dialog box, if it is not already displayed
   The Numbered tab in the Bullets and Numbering dialog box displays additional numbering options.
7. In the first row, click the **uppercase Roman numeral box**, then click **OK**
   The numbers in the list change to Roman numerals.
8. Deselect the text, then click the **Save button** on the Standard toolbar
   Compare your document to Figure C-20.

QuickTip

To access more bullet or number styles, click Customize in the Bullets and Numbering dialog box, then choose from the options in the Customize dialog box.

QuickTip

When you add or remove any numbered item, Word renumbers the remaining items in the list.

CLUES TO USE

Creating outline style numbered lists

You can create a simple outline style numbered list by applying an outline numbering scheme from the Outline Numbered tab in the Bullets and Numbering dialog box to a list. To create a new outline, choose a numbering scheme (one that does not include headings), then type your outline, pressing [Enter] after each item in the list. After you have applied an outline numbering scheme to a list, you can increase or decrease the indentation of individual paragraphs to change their level of importance in the outline. For example, to demote an item to a lower level in the outline, click in the paragraph, then click the Increase Indent button on the Formatting toolbar. To promote an item to a higher level, click the Decrease Indent button. You can choose to format outline style numbered lists with a combination of letters and numbers, numbers alone, or bullets, or you can create a custom outline style.

FIGURE C-19: Bullets and Numbering dialog box

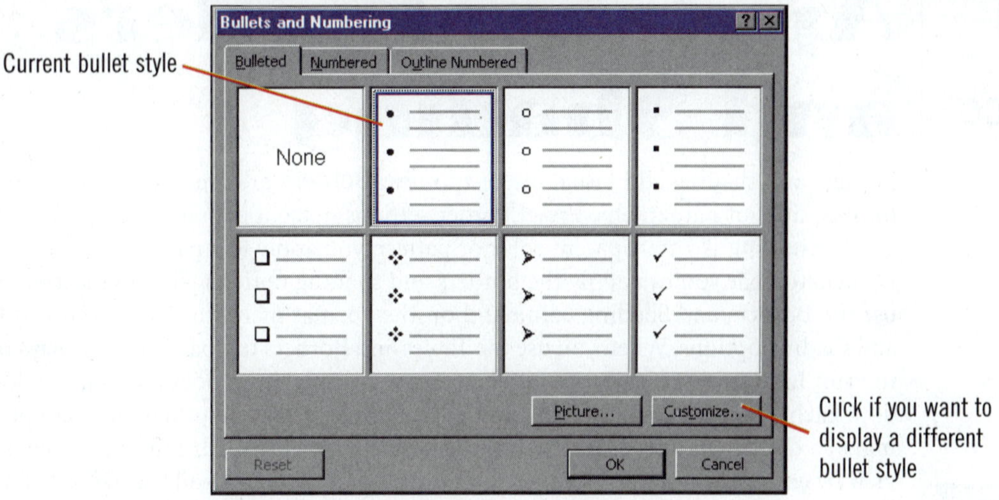

FIGURE C-20: Bulleted and numbered lists

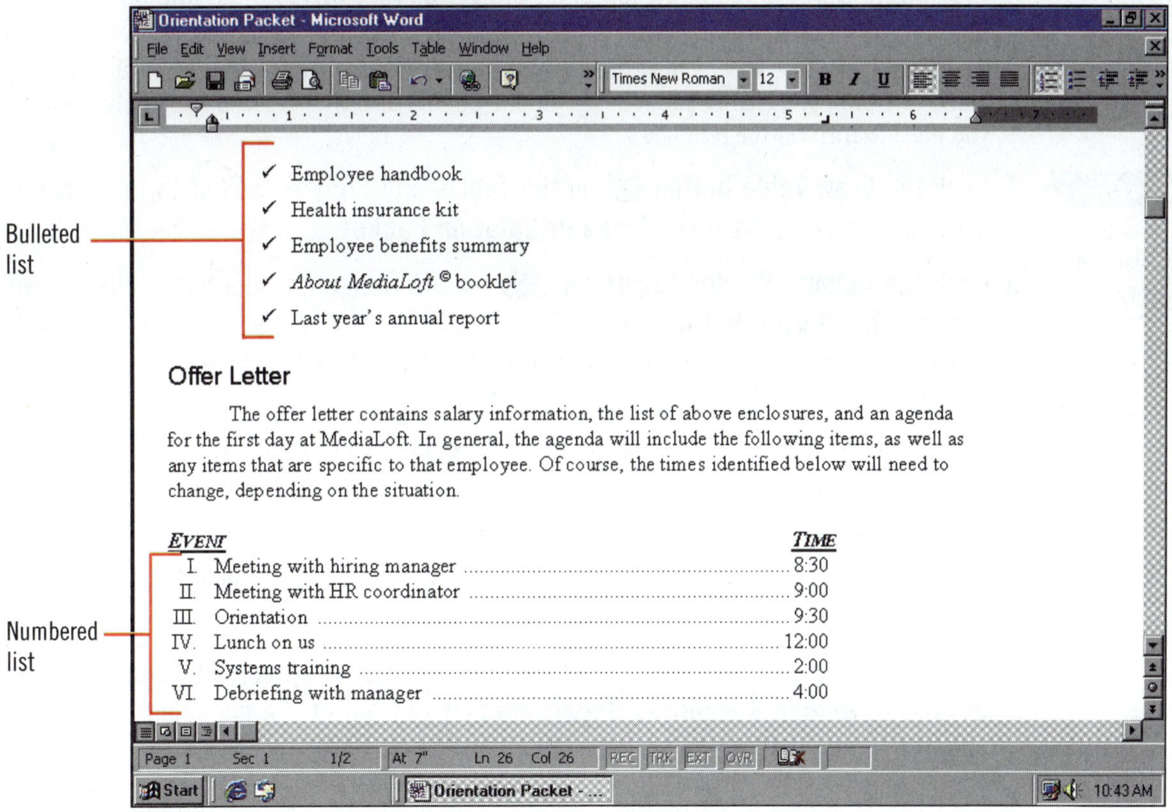

Word 2000

Unit C
Word 2000

Applying Borders and Shading

Borders and shading add visual interest to text. **Borders** are lines you can add to the top, bottom, or sides of paragraphs. Preset border settings make it easy to create a box around a paragraph. **Shading** is a transparent color or pattern you apply to a paragraph. With the Tables and Borders toolbar you can apply the borders and shading options you use most often, or you can use the Borders and Shading command on the Format menu to select from additional border and shading options. When you use the Tables and Borders toolbar, Word displays the document in Print Layout view. **Views** are different ways of displaying a document in the document window. Each view provides different features that are especially helpful in different phases of working on a document. Table C-3 describes different views in Word. You can change the document view by clicking the view buttons to the left of the horizontal scroll bar. Karen uses borders to emphasize the headings and adds shading to draw attention to the closing paragraph.

Steps

Trouble?

Click the More Buttons button on the Standard toolbar to locate buttons that are not displayed on your Standard toolbar. Click Cancel if the Office Assistant appears.

Trouble?

If a box appears, click the Undo button, click the text, then click again.

1. Place the insertion point in the paragraph that begins **I would like to share...**, then click the **Tables and Borders button** on the Standard toolbar
   The Tables and Borders toolbar appears, and the document switches to Print Layout view.
2. Click the **Shading Color list arrow** on the Tables and Borders toolbar, then click the **Gray 20% box**, as shown in Figure C-21
   A transparent gray rectangle covers the paragraph.
3. Scroll to the top of the document, click the **Line Style list arrow** on the Tables and Borders toolbar, then click the **Thick/Thin style** (thick line on top, thin line below) on the Line Style list
   The Thick/Thin line style is now the active line style. It remains in effect for all the borders you create until you change the style again. The pointer also changes to . To apply a border you need to turn off the pointer.
4. Click the **Draw Table button** on the Tables and Borders toolbar to turn off the pointer, then select **New Employee Orientation Packet**
5. Click the **Outside Border list arrow** on the Tables and Borders toolbar, then click the **Top Border button**
   A border of a Thick/Thin line appears above the selected text. You'll change to a new line style before adding a border under the selected text.
6. With the text still selected, click the **Line Style list arrow,** click the **Thin/Thick style** (thin line on top, thick line below), then click to turn off the pointer
7. Click the **Top Border list arrow** on the Tables and Borders toolbar, click the **Bottom Border button** on the menu that appears, then deselect the text
   A border appears below the title, as shown in Figure C-22.
8. Click the **Close button** on the Tables and Borders toolbar, place the insertion point in front of **Human Resources Department** at the top of the document, type your name, then press **[Enter]**
9. Click the **Save button** on the Standard toolbar, then click the **Print button** on the Standard toolbar
10. Close the document, then exit Word

FIGURE C-21: Tables and Borders toolbar

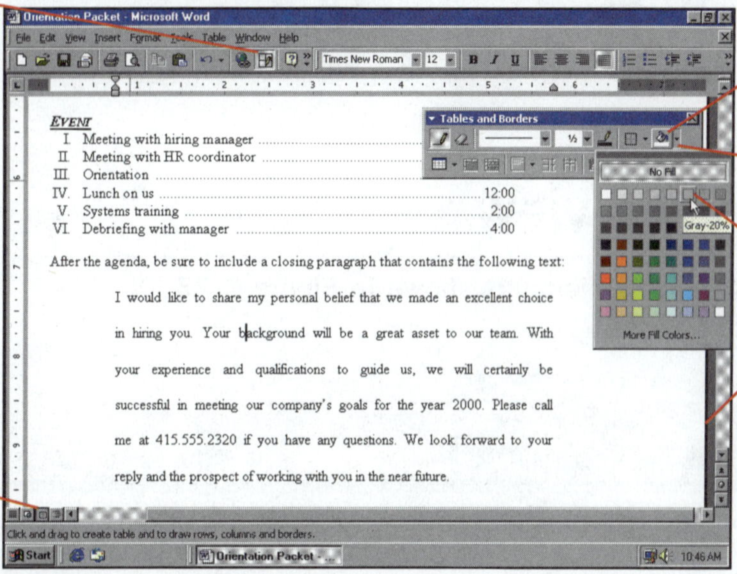

FIGURE C-22: Borders in a document

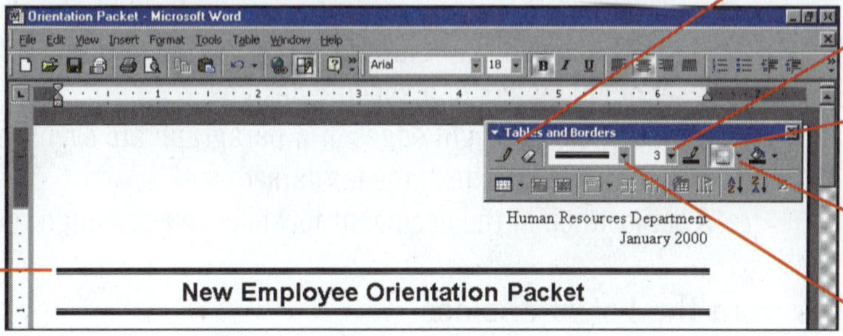

TABLE C-3: Word document views

view	displays	use to
Normal	A simple layout view of the document	Type, edit and format text quickly
Print Layout	The document as it will appear when printed on paper, along with the horizontal and vertical rulers	Edit and view the exact placement of text and graphics on the page, adjust margins, and work with columns and tables
Outline	Selected levels of headings and body text	View major headings and organize ideas in outline format
Web Layout	The document as a Web page	Create a Web page

CLUES TO USE

Adding borders and shading with the Borders and Shading command

The Tables and Borders toolbar includes the most frequently used border and shading options. However, for even more border and shading options use the Borders and Shading command on the Format menu to display the Borders and Shading dialog box. In this dialog box, you can use the Borders tab to select preset box, shadow, and 3-D borders, or design a border of your own using the many line, color, and spacing options available on this tab. Borders can be as simple or as complex as you like. On the Shading tab, you can select a shade pattern, including stripes, checkerboards and grids, and choose the color of the pattern and its background. You can also create a custom shade color and adjust the intensity of the shading you apply to text. Use the Apply to list arrow on both tabs to choose to apply borders or shading to the selected text or to paragraphs.

Practice

▶ Concepts Review

Label each of the formatting elements shown in Figure C-23.

FIGURE C-23

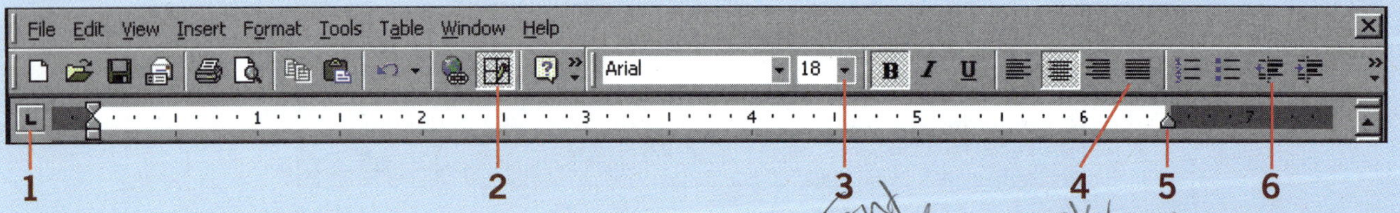

Match each term with the statement that describes it.

7. **Font**
8. **Bold**
9. **Hanging indent**
10. **Tab stop**
11. **Justified**

a. The first line of a paragraph is closer to the left margin than the remaining lines
b. A set of characters of a specific design
c. Both the left and right edges of a paragraph are evenly aligned
d. A style that makes text appear darker
e. A set location in the document to which you can align text

Select the best answer from the list of choices.

12. Which paragraph formatting feature is not available on the Formatting toolbar?
- a. Paragraph alignment
- b. Line spacing
- c. Decrease indentation
- d. Borders

13. Which view would you use to best see the margins on a page?
- a. Normal
- b. Outline
- c. Print Layout
- d. Web Layout

14. Which of the following statements about tabs is not true?
- a. You can use the horizontal ruler to set tab stops.
- b. You can use the Tab command on the Format menu to set tab stops.
- c. You can use the horizontal ruler to create a tab leader.
- d. Tabs are a more accurate way to align text than spaces.

15. Which button on the Tables and Borders toolbar do you click when you want to apply shading to text?
- a. Borders
- b. Shading
- c. Borders and Shading
- d. You can not apply shading with a button

Skills Review

1. **Change fonts and font sizes.**
   a. Start Word, open the file WD C-2 from your Project Disk, and save it as "Press Release."
   b. Format "Press Release" in 26 point Arial Black.
   c. Format the second line of text in 20 point Arial.
   d. In the second sentence, format "RoadMap" in Arial.
   e. Format all occurrences of "Open Roads, Inc." in Arial.

2. **Apply font effects.**
   a. Format the heading, "Package Delivery Company …" in bold.
   b. In the first body paragraph, format "RoadMap" in bold italics with an underline.
   c. Use the Format Painter to apply the same formatting to "RoadMap" in the second body paragraph.
   d. Apply superscript formatting to the copyright symbol after the first occurrence of "RoadMap."
   e. Format the first occurrence of "Open Roads, Inc." in bold, and apply the All caps effect.
   f. Apply the same formatting to all occurrences of "Open Roads, Inc."

3. **Change paragraph alignment.**
   a. Center "Press Release" and "Package Delivery Company …".
   b. Justify the remaining paragraphs in the document.
   c. Type your name and today's date at the bottom of the document, then right-align your name and the date.

4. **Indent paragraphs.**
   a. Drag the First Line Indent marker to indent the first line in the first and second body paragraphs ½".
   b. Indent the three lines after the first body paragraph one inch.
   c. With the insertion point in the last body paragraph, drag the Left Indent marker to the ½" mark on the horizontal ruler.
   d. Right-indent the last body paragraph ½" from the right margin.

5. **Change line spacing.**
   a. Change the line spacing of the body text (not the headings) to 1.5.
   b. Change the line spacing of the last body paragraph to single-spacing.

6. **Change paragraph spacing.**
   a. Format "Press Release" with 12 points of space before and 3 points of space after.
   b. Format "Package Delivery Company …" with 18 points of space before and 6 points of space after.
   c. Format the first body paragraph with 6 points of space after.

7. **Align text with tabs.**
   a. Near the bottom, insert a blank line after "Typical shipping prices:".
   b. Press [Tab], type "Weight," press [Tab], type "Cost," then press [Enter].
   c. Press [Tab], type "Under 1 lb," press [Tab], type "5.25," then press [Enter].
   d. Press [Tab], type "1 - 10 lbs," press [Tab], then type "10.75." Do not press [Enter].
   e. Select all three lines of the list and place a left-aligned tab stop at the 2" mark.
   f. With the same three lines selected, click the tab alignment indicator at the left end of the ruler until you see the decimal tab marker, then place a decimal-aligned tab stop at the 4.5" mark.
   g. Press [Enter] at the end of the last item in the list, press [Tab], type "More than 10 lbs," press [Tab], then type "14.50."
   h. Remove the decimal tab stop from the first line in the table, then set a new left-aligned tab stop at the 4⅜" mark.
   i. Select the next three lines of the table, and format the 4.5" tab stop to have a dotted leader.
   j. Underline each word in the first line of the table.

8. **Create bulleted and numbered lists.**
   a. Number the three-line list under the first body paragraph.
   b. Apply bullets to the list, then change the bullets to another bullet style.

9. **Apply borders and shading.**
   a. Apply a thin double line above and below "Press Release."
   b. Apply 15% gray shading to the last paragraph.
   c. Save your changes to the document, print the document, and exit Word.

Independent Challenges

1. As an account representative for Lease For Less, a company that rents office equipment such as fax machines and large copiers, you need to improve the formatting of a customer proposal.
To complete this independent challenge:

a. Start Word, open the document WD C-3 from your Project Disk, then save it as "Discount Letter."
b. At the top of the document, format the company name in 18 point Arial Black, with the outline effect.
c. Format the company address in 11 point Arial. Right-align the company name and address.
d. Change the font size of the rest of the letter to 12 points.
e. Indent the list of discount rates 1" and format the list as a bulleted list.
f. Justify the body paragraphs in the letter.
g. Type your name in the signature block, and then preview, save, and print the document.

2. Your golf league has asked you to design the announcement for the annual tournament. You already entered information about the tournament in a document; now you need to enhance its appearance.
To complete this independent challenge:

a. Start Word, open the document WD C-4 from your Project Disk, and save it as "Golf Classic."
b. Center the first two lines, change the font to 18 point Arial, bold, italic, and then add 25% gray shading.
c. Indent the first body paragraph one-half inch from the right and left margins.
d. Select the 4 lines under the first body paragraph. Use the Tabs dialog box to format the lines with right tab stops at 1¾" and a left tab stop at 2¼", then press [Tab] before and after "Where", "When", "Who" and "How Much".
e. Center the heading "Schedule." Format this heading in 14 point Arial bold, then add red highlighting.
f. Add numbers to the list of scheduled events.
g. Add a 1½ point border above the line "Send the attached ...", and center the remaining four lines.
h. Double-space the entire document.
i. Replace "Your Name" with your name, preview, save, and print the document.

3. As co-chair for your college reunion planning committee, you need to write a memo about upcoming meetings. You use Word's Memo Wizard to create the memo. This wizard prompts you to enter information in a series of dialog boxes, and then formats the memo for you. After the memo is created, you adjust the formatting to suit your own preferences.
To complete this independent challenge:

a. Start Word and create a new document using the Memo Wizard. (*Hint*: Click File on the menu bar, click New, then double-click Memo wizard on the Memos tab in the New dialog box.)
b. Click Next to begin, click the Professional option button, then click Next to proceed through the wizard.
c. Enter the title "Reunion Memo," the date, your name, and the subject "Meeting dates," clicking Next at the end of each dialog box.

d. Enter "Reunion Planning Committee" in the To text box, deselect the CC check box and all other check boxes in the next two dialog boxes, then click Finish.
e. Format "Reunion Memo" in 36 point Arial bold, then center the title.
f. Type the following memo text:
Thank you for participating in the reunion planning. Here's the schedule for the next three meetings.

Date	Topic
October 18	Deciding a theme
November 15	Contacting alums
March 20	Catering options

g. Select the 4 lines of the schedule. Use the Tabs dialog box to set a right tab stop at 3" and a left tab stop at 3½", then use tabs to align the schedule.
h. Format the schedule with a double-line 1½ point box around it, 20% gray shading, and 6 points of space below each line, then indent the schedule one inch from both margins.
i. Change the font size of the body text to 12 points, then format the schedule headings in 14 point bold.
j. Save the memo on your Project Disk as "Reunion Memo," then preview and print the memo.

WEB WORK

4. As volunteer coordinator at MediaLoft, you are responsible for creating a certificate to award to the volunteer of the month. The name of the winner is posted each month on MediaLoft's intranet site.
To complete this independent challenge:

a. Start Word and create a new document called "Volunteer Award" on your Project Disk.
b. Connect to the Internet, go to the MediaLoft intranet site at http://www.course.com/illustrated/MediaLoft, click the link for the Community page, then click the link for Volunteer of the Month.
c. Copy the name of this month's winner to the Clipboard, then disconnect from the Internet.
d. Using Figure C-24 as a guide, enter and format the text on the award certificate. Add the name of the recipient and your name.
e. Use Garamond for the font. Format "Volunteer of the Month" in 36 point bold italic and apply the shadow effect. Format "MediaMentors" in 36 point bold and apply the small caps effect. Format all other text in 24 points.
f. Center the text and use 1.5 line spacing. Use 12 point spacing before and after "Presented to," "for participating in," "This day," and the date.
g. Add a ½ point border under the recipient's name.
h. Right-align your name and title, and change the font size to 18 points. Add 60 points of space above your name, then place a ½ point border above your name and indent this line to the 2" mark.
i. Add 25% gray shading as shown in the figure.
j. Preview, save, and print the certificate.

FIGURE C-24

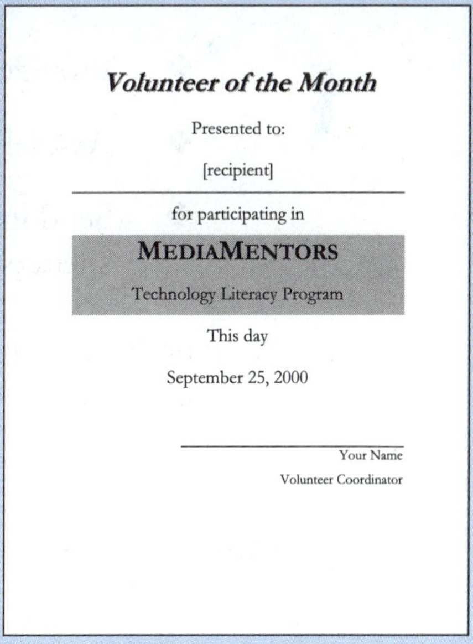

► Visual Workshop

Create the flyer shown in Figure C-25 and save it as "Kids Flyer" on your Project Disk. Use 16 point Garamond for the font and change the font size of the heading to 24 points. Adjust the character spacing of the heading text to expand it and change the scale to 150%. (*Hint*: Use the Character Spacing tab in the Font dialog box.) For the contact information, use a 3 point box border. (*Hint*: Use the Borders and Shading command.) Print a copy of the completed flyer.

FIGURE C-25

COMPANIES FOR KIDS
NEEDS YOUR HELP!

COMPANIES FOR KIDS is a non-profit community program that collects toys, clothing, and books for children in local shelters. We depend largely on local businesses to help fund our efforts.

Each weekend **COMPANIES FOR KIDS** sends out corporate teams to collect clothing, books, and toys from the community. Your company may also choose to help our children in any of the following ways:

- Provide a monetary donation.
- Assemble teams to sort or collect clothing and toys.
- Send individuals to spend time with children in local shelters.

We look forward to your company's participation and support in this valuable community program.

Contact: Your Name
Fundraising Coordinator
COMPANIES FOR KIDS
(415) 555-2020

Word 2000

Unit D

Working with Tables

Objectives

- MOUS ► Create a table
- MOUS ► Adjust table rows and columns
- MOUS ► Add and delete rows and columns
- MOUS ► Format a table
- MOUS ► Calculate data in a table
- MOUS ► Sort a table
- MOUS ► Draw a table
- MOUS ► Split and merge cells

A **table** is text that is arranged in a grid of rows and columns. With Word, you can create a table from scratch or you can convert existing text into a table. Once you have created a table, you can easily modify it, sort and calculate the data in it, and quickly make it attractive using a preset table format. You can also build tables by drawing rows and columns exactly where you want them. Tables are an excellent tool for displaying data that is typically found in lists or columns. Karen Rosen needs to create an agenda for a new employee, a record of earned vacation days, and a record of employee absences. She decides to format this information in tables to make the documents attractive and easy to use.

Unit D

Word 2000

Creating a Table

In a **table**, text is arranged in a grid of rows and columns that is divided by borders. A **column** in a table is text arranged vertically. A **row** is text arranged horizontally. The intersection of a column and a row is called a **cell**. **Borders** surround each cell to help you see the structure of the table. You can create an empty table and then add text to it, or you can convert existing text into a table. When you create a new, blank table, you specify the number of rows and columns you want your table to include. Once the table is created, you can enter information in it. To create a blank table, you can use the Insert Table button on the Standard toolbar, or the Insert Table command on the Table menu. You can later change the structure of the table by adding and deleting rows and columns. Karen creates a table for tracking employee attendance in a new document. As she works, she adds rows to the table.

Steps 1 2 3 4

1. Start **Word**, click **Tools** on the menu bar, click **Customize**, click the **Options tab** in the Customize dialog box, click **Reset my usage data** to restore default settings, click **Yes** in the alert box, then click **Close**
2. Click the **Print Layout View button** on the horizontal scroll bar
   The document displays in Print Layout view and the I-beam pointer changes to
3. Type **Agenda for New Employees**, then press **[Enter]** twice
4. Click the **Insert Table button** on the Standard toolbar
   A grid opens. You use this grid to indicate the number of rows and columns you want the new table to contain.
5. Click the **second box** in the last row of the grid to select four rows and two columns, as shown in Figure D-1
   A blank table containing four rows and two columns appears in the document.
6. Type **EVENT** in the first cell, then press **[Tab]**
   Pressing [Tab] moves the insertion point to the next cell in the row.
7. Type **TIME**, press **[Tab]**, type **Meeting with Karen Rosen, Director of Human Resources**, press **[Tab]**, type **8:30**, then press **[Tab]**
   Pressing [Tab] at the end of a row moves the insertion point to the next cell in the next row.
8. Type the following text in the table, pressing **[Tab]** to move from cell to cell
   Meeting with HR coordinator **9:00**
   Orientation **9:30**
9. Press **[Tab]**
   Pressing [Tab] with the insertion point in the last cell of a table creates a new blank row at the end of the table, as shown in Figure D-2.
10. Type the following text in the table, pressing **[Tab]** to move from cell to cell, and to add new rows
    Lunch on us **12:00**
    Systems training **2:00**
    Tele-conference with regional managers **3:00**
    Debriefing with training manager **4:00**
11. Click the **Save button** on the Standard toolbar, then save the document with the filename **Agenda** to your Project Disk
    Compare your table to Figure D-3.

Trouble?

Click the More Buttons button on the Standard toolbar to locate buttons that are not visible on your toolbar.

QuickTip

Pressing [Shift][Tab] selects the previous cell.

Trouble?

If you pressed [Tab] after the last row, click the Undo button on the Standard toolbar to remove the new blank row.

FIGURE D-1: Creating a table

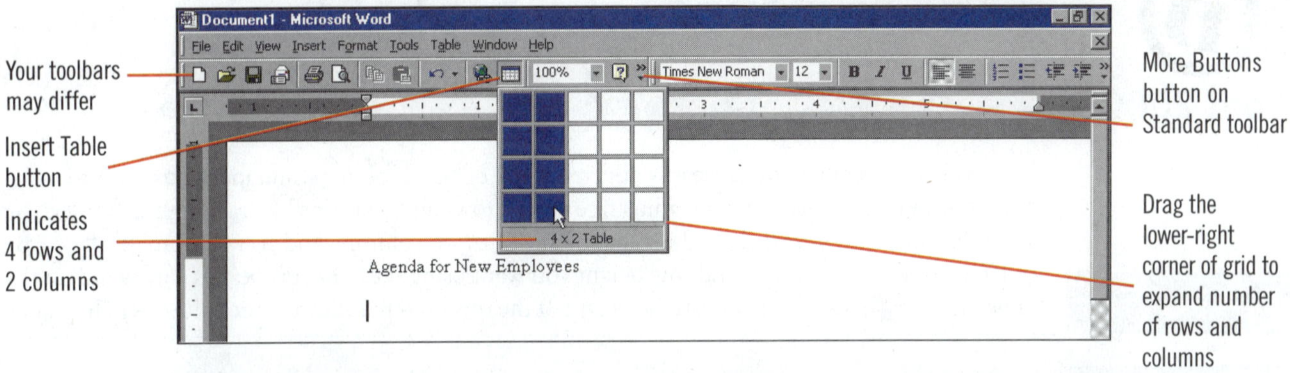

FIGURE D-2: New row

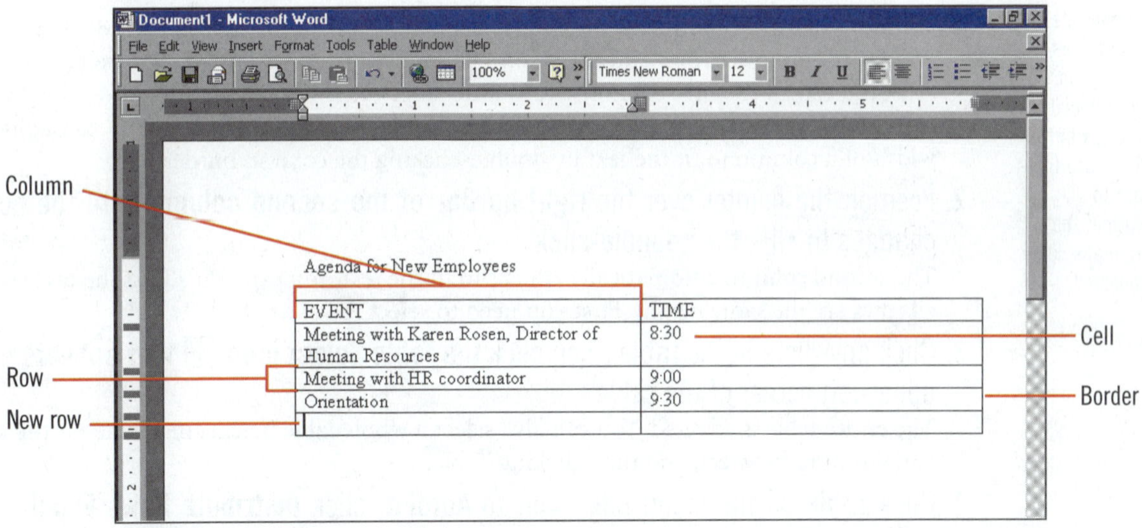

FIGURE D-3: Text in a table

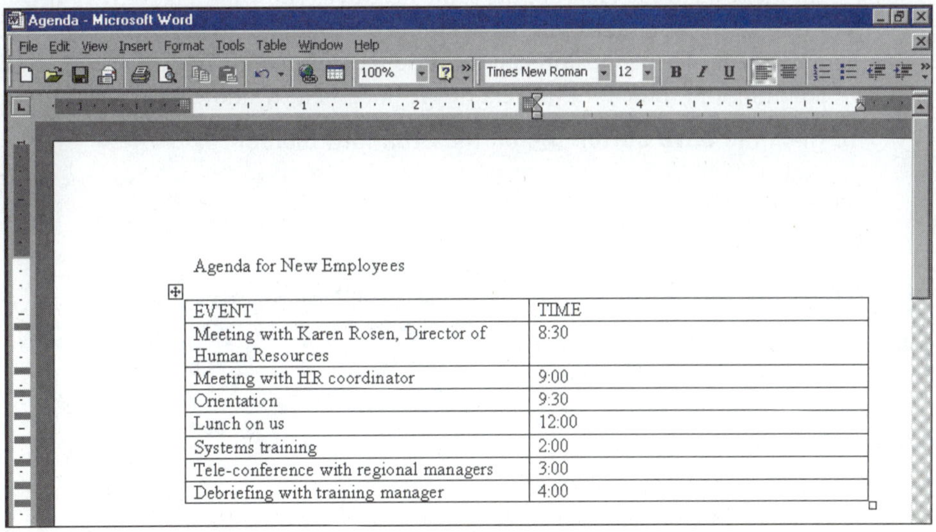

CLUES TO USE

Converting text to a table

Sometimes it is easier to enter text in your document and convert it into a table than to create a blank table and enter the text in the cells. The text you intend to convert to a table must be formatted with tabs, commas, or paragraph marks so that Word can interpret the formatting and create the table. You can create a table based on existing text by selecting the text and then using the Insert Table button on the Standard toolbar or the Convert Text to Table command on the Table menu. In the Convert Text to Table dialog box, you can specify the number of rows and columns you want in your table, along with other table formatting options.

Unit D

Word 2000

Adjusting Table Rows and Columns

Once you create a table, you can easily adjust the size of rows, columns, and individual cells to make your tables easier to read. You can adjust the size of rows and columns by dragging the borders, by using the AutoFit command on the Table menu to resize columns and rows automatically, or by specifying the column width and row height you want using the Table Properties command on the Table menu. Karen adjusts the height of the rows and the width of the columns in her table.

Steps 1 2 3 4

Trouble?

If the width of only one cell in the column changes when you adjust the column width, deselect the cell, then click the Undo button on the Standard toolbar. If you want to adjust the width of the entire column, make sure no cells are selected.

1. Position the pointer over the **right border of the first column** until the pointer changes to +||+, then drag the border to the **2¼" mark** on the horizontal ruler
   The first column narrows and the second column widens as shown in Figure D-5. In some cells, the text in the first column wraps onto a second line. Moving the border for the first column resulted in the second column becoming too wide for the text. You can adjust the width of a column to fit the text by double-clicking the column border.
2. Position the pointer over the **right border of the second column** until the pointer changes to +||+, then double-click
   The second column automatically adjusts to fit the text. You can also adjust the table so that all rows are the same height. First you need to select the entire table.
3. Click anywhere in the table, then click the **Table Select icon** that appears at the upper-left corner of the table
   The entire table is selected. You can also select a whole table by clicking Table on the menu bar, pointing to Select, and then clicking Table.
4. Click **Table** on the menu bar, point to **AutoFit**, click **Distribute Rows Evenly**, then deselect the table
   All the rows in the table are the same height, as shown in Figure D-6. If you had wanted to make all the columns the same width, you would have clicked Distribute Columns Evenly on the AutoFit menu. You can also use the commands on this menu to adjust the size of columns and rows to fit the text or the document window.
5. Click the **Save button** on the Standard toolbar

CLUES TO USE

Setting table properties

You can use the Table Properties command to change the structure and format of the tables you create. This command is especially useful when you want to set a specific row height or column width, or when you want to change the alignment of a table on the page. To open the Table Properties dialog box, click Table on the menu bar, then click Table Properties. On the Row, Column, and Cell tabs you can specify an exact height and width for the columns, rows, and cells selected in your table. You can also change the vertical alignment of text in cells on the Cells tab. To change a table's alignment on the page, choose the alignment you want on the Table tab, shown in Figure D-4. You can also specify the width of the table on this tab and set text wrapping options, if any.

FIGURE D-4: Table Properties dialog box

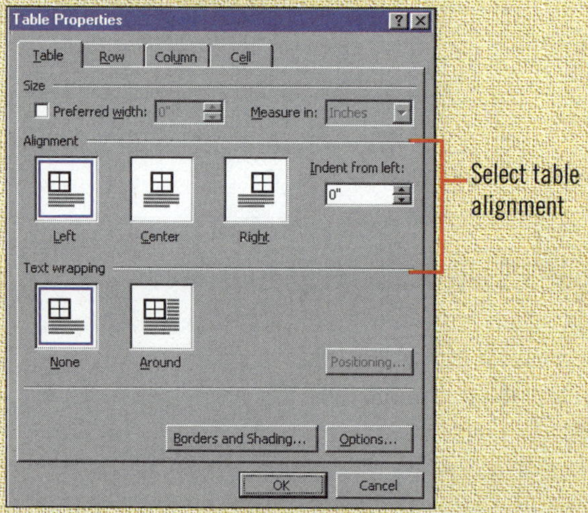

FIGURE D-5: Resized columns

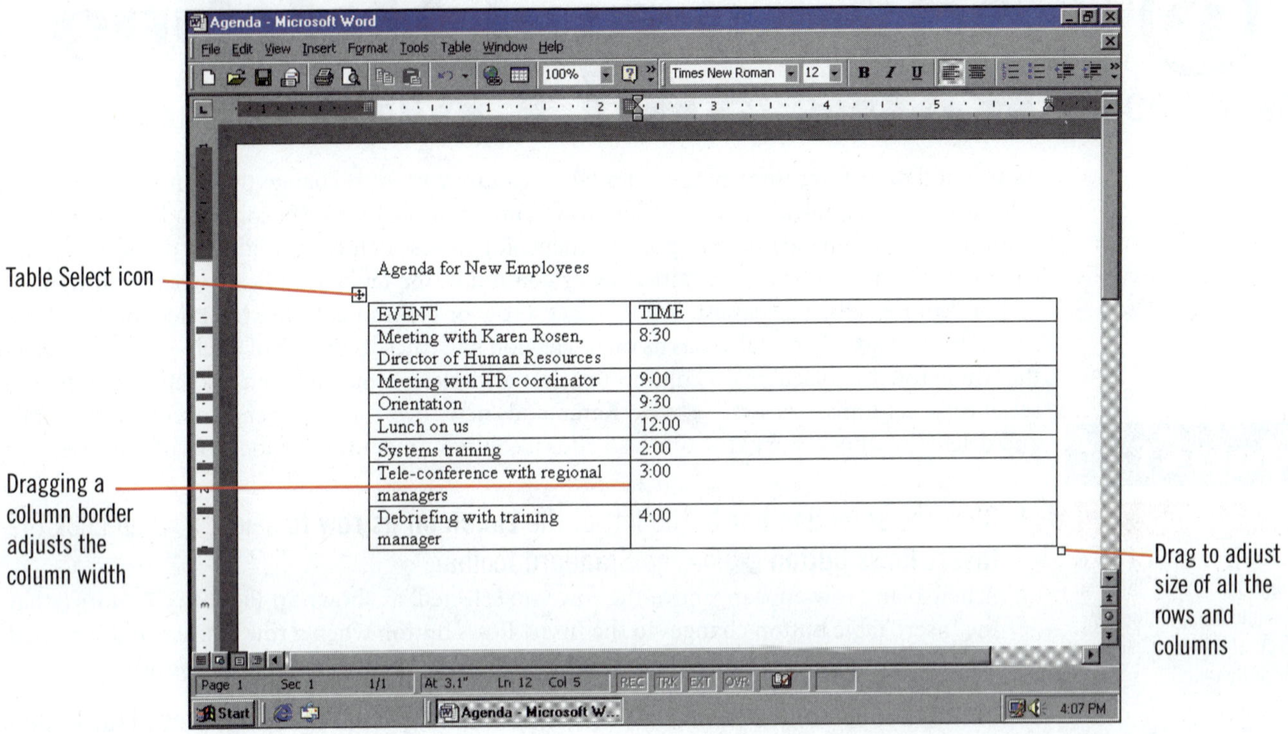

FIGURE D-6: Resized rows and columns

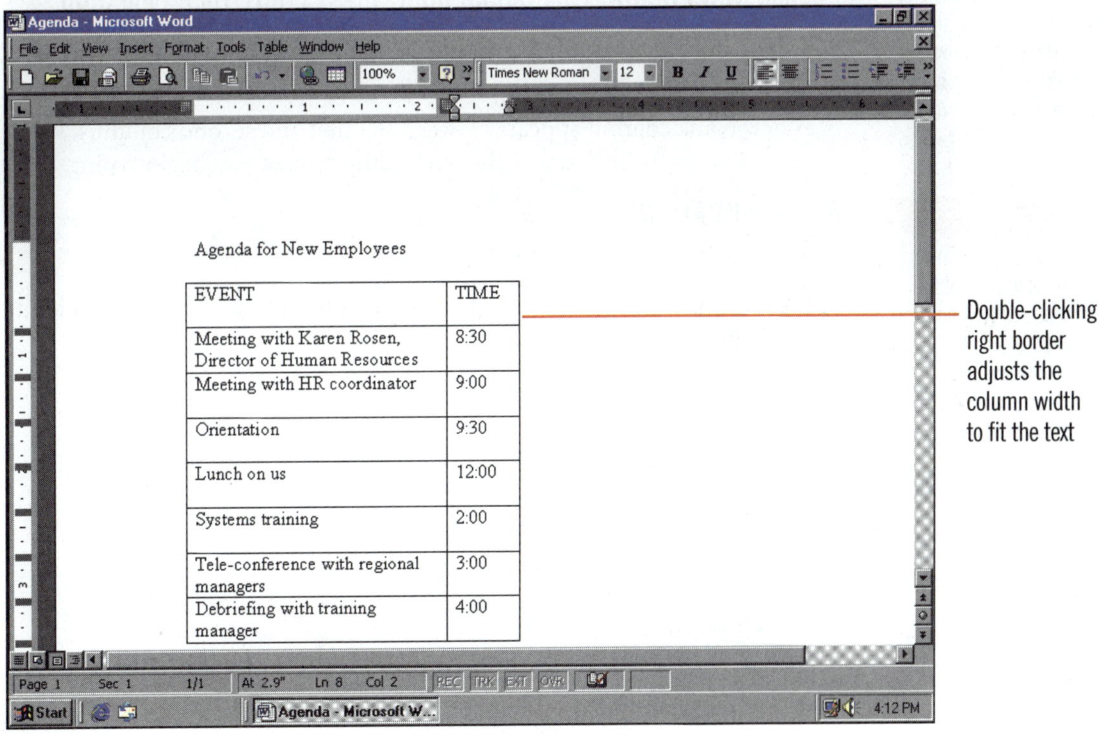

Unit D

Word 2000

Adding and Deleting Rows and Columns

As you add or remove information in a table, you may need to change the number of rows or columns. You can quickly add or delete rows and columns using the commands on the Table menu or the commands on the pop-up menu for tables. Before you add or delete rows and columns, you must select an existing row or column in the table to indicate where you want to add or remove cells. The easiest way to select a row or column is to use the selection bar. Each row, column, and cell in a table has its own selection bar. Click to the left of a cell or a row to select the whole row, or click above a column to select a whole column. You can also click and drag to select cells, columns, or rows. Karen adds new rows for new agenda events to the table, and deletes an unnecessary row. She also adds a column to identify the location of each event.

Steps 1 2 3 4

QuickTip

You can also select a row or column by clicking Table on the menu bar, pointing to Select, and then clicking Row or Column.

QuickTip

To quickly delete a row or column, select it, then press [Shift][Delete] or [Ctrl][X]. You can also click Table on the menu bar, point to Delete, then click Rows or Columns. To remove only the text from a selected row or column, press [Delete].

QuickTip

To insert a new column at the right end of a table, place the insertion point in the last column, click Table on the menu bar, click Insert, then click Columns to the Right. You can also use the Insert command to insert rows above or below the selected cell.

1. Click the **selection bar** to the left of the **Lunch on us row** to select it, then click the **Insert Rows button** on the Standard toolbar
   A new blank row appears above the row you selected, as shown in Figure D-7. Notice that the Insert Table button changes to the Insert Rows button when a row is selected. If you had selected a column, the button would have changed to the Insert Columns button.
2. In the first cell of the new blank row, type **Training team meeting,** press **[Tab]**, then type **10:30**
3. Select the **Tele-conference row**, right-click, then click **Delete Rows** on the pop-up menu
   The selected row is deleted.
4. Place the insertion point in **the last row**, click **Table** on the menu bar, point to **Insert**, click **Rows Below**, type **Social hour**, press **[Tab]**, then type **5:00**
5. Select the entire **second column** in the table, then click the **Insert Columns button** on the Standard toolbar
   A new blank column appears between the first and second columns. Word places the insertion point in the first cell of the new column when you begin typing.
6. Type **LOCATION**
   The column width adjusts to fit the text.
7. Press **[↓]**, then type the following in the remaining cells in the column:
   HR 220 [↓]
   HR 225 [↓]
   Training Center [↓]
   Conference Room 1 [↓]
   Reception Area [↓]
   Your office [↓]
   HR 250 [↓]
   Reception Area
   Compare your document to Figure D-8.
8. Click the **Save button** on the Standard toolbar

FIGURE D-7: Inserted row

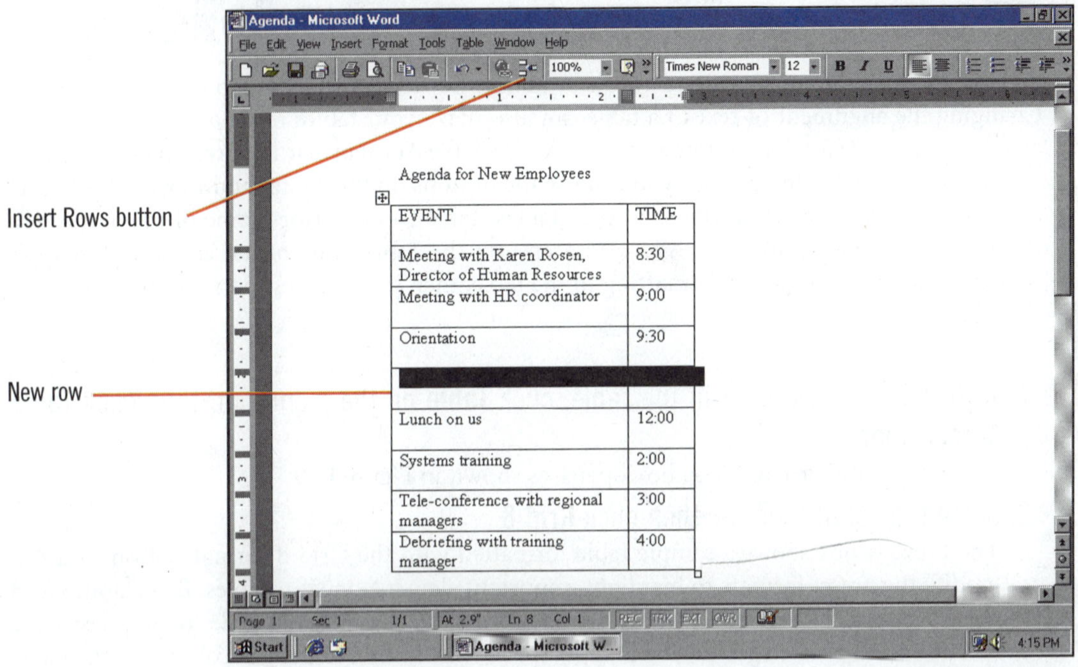

FIGURE D-8: Edited table

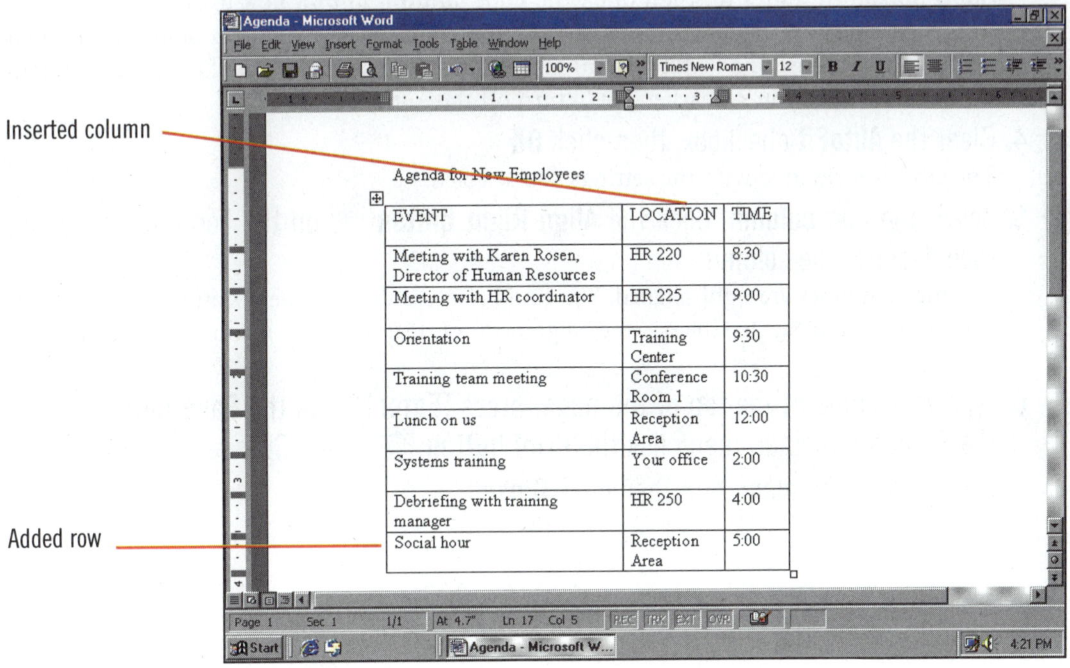

Word 2000

CLUES TO USE

Copying and moving columns and rows

You can use the same techniques to copy and move columns and rows that you use to copy and move text in a document. Be sure to select the entire row or column you want to copy or move, then click the Cut or Copy buttons to place the selection on the Clipboard. Place the insertion point in the location you want to insert the row or column in the table, then click the Paste button. You can also copy or move rows or columns by clicking and dragging them. Again, select the rows or columns you want to copy or move, click and hold the mouse over the selection until the pointer changes, then drag the selection to the new location in the table and release the mouse button.

Unit D

Word 2000

Formatting a Table

You can improve the appearance of a table by adding borders and shading to rows and columns. Changing the alignment of text in a table can also make your tables more attractive and readable. You can format tables automatically with the Table AutoFormat feature, which provides a variety of preset table formats, or you can use the buttons on the Tables and Borders toolbar to apply a variety of formatting effects to your tables. Table D-1 describes some of the buttons on the Tables and Borders toolbar. Karen uses the Table AutoFormat command to apply borders, shading, and special formatting to the table, then she changes the alignment of text in the table.

Steps

QuickTip

You can also click the Table AutoFormat button on the Tables and Borders toolbar to open the Table AutoFormat dialog box.

1. With the insertion point in the table, click **Table** on the menu bar, then click **Table AutoFormat**

   The Table AutoFormat dialog box opens, as shown in Figure D-9.

2. Scroll the list of formats, then click **Grid 8**

   The Preview box shows a sample table formatted with the Grid 8 format option. You can modify the preset formats to highlight important elements in your tables. By default, Word applies special formatting to heading rows and the first column of a table. To emphasize the meeting times in the agenda, you'll apply special formatting to the last column of the table.

3. Make sure the **Heading rows** and **First column check boxes** are selected under Apply special formats to, then click the **Last column check box** to select it

   In the Preview box, the last column of the sample table now appears in bold. AutoFormat automatically adjusts the width of columns in a table to span the width of the page. To retain the column width you set earlier, you'll turn off the AutoFit feature.

4. Clear the **AutoFit** checkbox, then click **OK**

   The table is formatted with the settings you selected.

Trouble?

Click the More Buttons button on the Formatting toolbar to locate buttons that are not visible on your toolbar.

5. Select the **last column**, click the **Align Right button** on the Formatting toolbar, then deselect the column

   The meeting times are right-aligned. You could also use the alignment buttons on the Tables and Borders toolbar to change the alignment of text in cells. Compare your table to Figure D-10.

6. Type your name at the top of the page, press **[Enter]**, click the **Save button** on the Standard toolbar, then click the **Print button** on the Standard toolbar

7. Click **File** on the menu bar, then click **Close**

TABLE D-1: Buttons on the Tables and Borders toolbar

button	use to	button	use to
Line Style	Determine the line style of borders	**Draw Table**	Draw a table or cells
Line Weight	Determine the thickness of borders	**Eraser**	Erase or remove a border between cells
Border Color	Determine the color of borders	**Merge Cells**	Combine selected cells into a single cell
Outside Borders	Add or remove individual borders	**Split Cells**	Divide a cell into multiple cells
Shading Color	Determine the shade color or pattern of cells	**Insert Table**	Insert new rows, columns, cells, or a new table; determine column width
Align Top Left	Change the alignment of text in a cell	**Distribute Rows Evenly**	Make rows the same height
Change Text Direction	Change the orientation of text	**Distribute Columns Evenly**	Make columns the same width

FIGURE D-9: Table AutoFormat dialog box

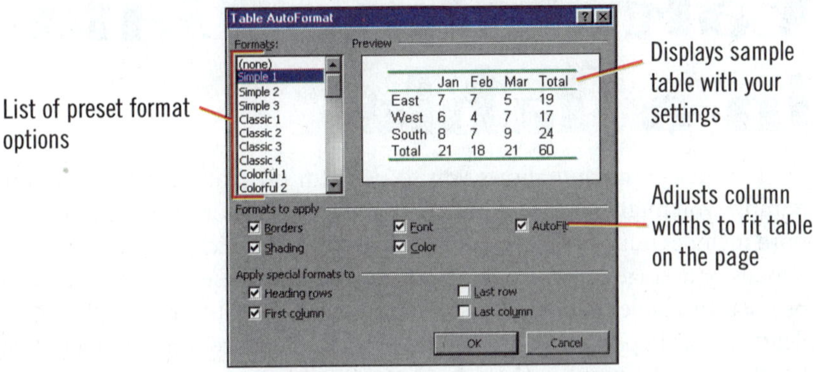

FIGURE D-10: Formatted table

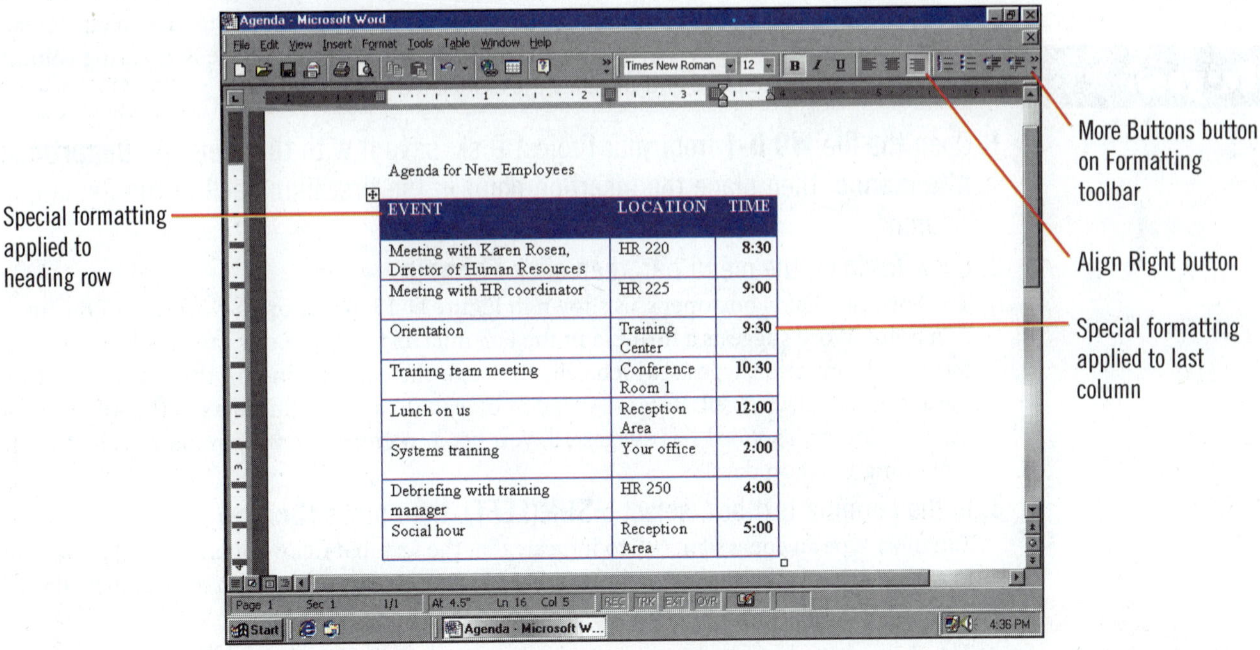

CLUES TO USE

Changing borders and shading in a table

You can add, remove, or alter the borders and shading in a table using the buttons on the Tables and Borders toolbar, shown in Figure D-11, which appears when you click the Tables and Borders button on the Standard toolbar. To change the shading of cells, select the cells you want to format, click the Shading Color list arrow on the Tables and Borders toolbar, then click the shade color and intensity you want to apply to the selected cells. To add or remove borders from a table, select the cells you want to format, then click the Outside Borders list arrow on the Tables and Borders toolbar (or the Formatting toolbar). From the list of border buttons, click the button that corresponds to the border you want to add or remove. For example, if you want to remove borders from around all the cells in your table, you would select the table, click the Outside Borders list arrow, then click the All Borders button. The border buttons are toggle buttons, which means that you can use them to turn borders on and off. When you remove a border from a table, a gridline appears on the screen. The **gridline** is a light gray line that represents the edge of the cell, but does not print.

FIGURE D-11: Tables and Borders toolbar

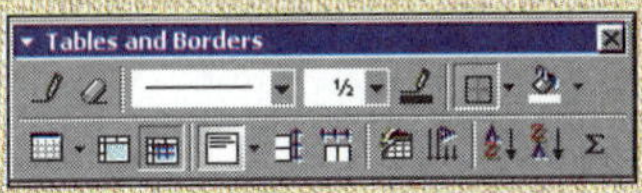

Unit D

Word 2000

Calculating Data in a Table

The Formula command allows you to perform calculations using the numbers in a table. For example, you might want to add the numbers in a row or column to display a total in your table. Word includes built-in formulas that make it easy to quickly perform standard calculations (such as totals or averages). Table D-2 describes several of these formulas. You can also enter your own formulas in a table. To do this, you refer to cells in the table using cell references. A **cell reference** identifies a cell's position in the table. Each cell reference contains a letter (A, B, C....) to identify its column and a number (1, 2, 3....) to identify its row. For example, the cell reference for the first cell in the first row of a table is A1, the second cell in the first row is B1, and so on, as shown in Figure D-12. You can create formulas to multiply, divide, add, and subtract the values of cells. When you change the numbers in a table, you can easily recalculate values associated with those numbers. Karen has created a table for tracking employee attendance that includes columns for the number of vacation days allowed, taken, and remaining. To calculate each employee's remaining vacation days, she enters a formula in each cell of the Remaining column. She then edits data in the table and updates the associated calculation.

Steps

1. Open the file **WD D-1** from your Project Disk, save it with the filename **Department Attendance**, then place the insertion point in the first blank cell in the Remaining column
2. Click **Table** on the menu bar, then click **Formula**
   The Formula dialog box opens, as shown in Figure D-13. Based on the location of the insertion point, Word suggests a formula in the Formula text box—in this case, the built-in SUM formula. Word also suggests which cells to use in the calculation—in this case, the cells to the left of the selected cell. Because you do not want to add the numbers in the Allowed and Taken columns, as Word has suggested, you need to enter a new formula to calculate the remaining vacation days.
3. In the Formula text box, select **=SUM(LEFT)**, then press **[Delete]**
   You must type an equal sign, "=", to indicate that the text that follows it is a formula. You want to enter a formula that subtracts the number of vacation days taken from the number allowed.
4. Type **=D2 – E2**, then click **OK**
   The dialog box closes and 16 appears in the current cell. This is the difference between the value in the fourth column, second row (cell D2) and the fifth column, second row (cell E2).
5. Press **[↓]**, to move the insertion point to **cell F3** (the last cell in the third row), then repeat Steps 2 through 4 using **=D3 – E3** as the formula
   The cells D3 and E3 are the third cells in the fourth and fifth columns. To calculate the other values in the Remaining column, you need to insert a similar formula in each of the empty cells.
6. Press **[↓]**, repeat Steps 2 through 4 using **=D4 – E4** as the formula, then enter the formula for each remaining cell, using **=D5 – E5** and **=D6 – E6** as the formulas
7. Select **7** in cell E6 (the last cell of the fifth column), then type **14**
   If you change a number that is part of a formula, you need to recalculate the formula.
8. Press **[Tab]** to move to the next cell, then press **[F9]**
   Pressing [F9] updates the calculation in the selected cell. "10" now appears in cell E7, as shown in Figure D-14.
9. Deselect the text, then click the **Save button** on the Standard toolbar

QuickTip

Use a plus sign (+) to represent addition; a minus sign (-) for subtraction; an asterisk (*) for multiplication; and a slash (/) for division.

FIGURE D-12: Cell references in a table

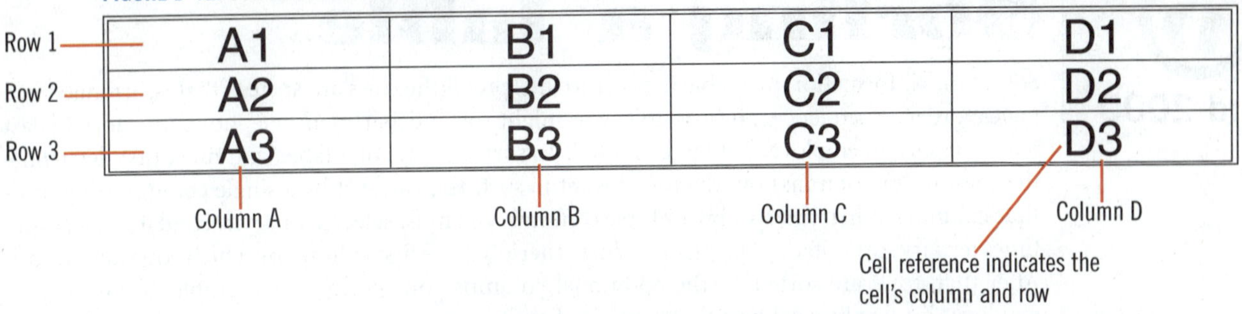

FIGURE D-13: Formula dialog box

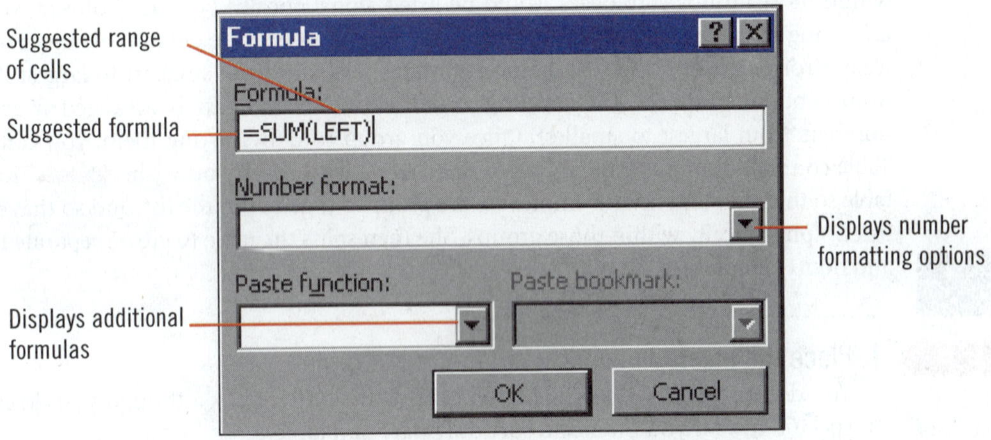

FIGURE D-14: Calculated cells in a table

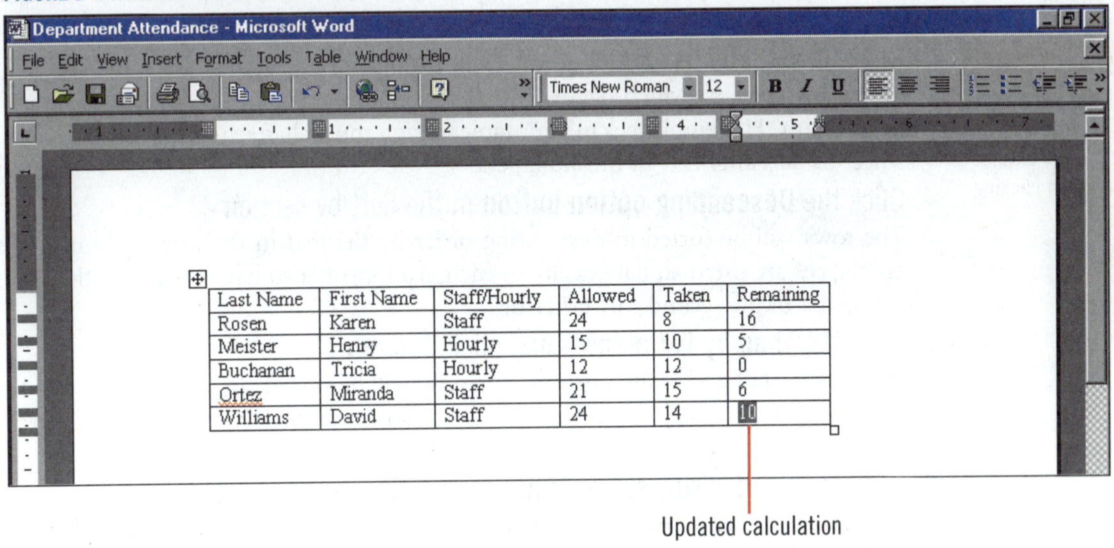

TABLE D-2: Table functions

function	description
Average	Calculates the sum of specified cells, then divides the sum by the number of cells included in the calculation
Count	Displays the number of cells in a specified range of cells
Product	Multiplies the values in specified cells
Sum	Totals the values of cells above or to the left of the current cell

Sorting a Table

Sometimes information in a table is easier to interpret if the rows are **sorted**, that is, arranged in a logical order or sequence. For example, you might sort a department telephone directory by last name, or sort an employee list by date hired. To sort the rows of a table, you must first determine the column (or columns) by which you want to sort. You can sort by a single column or by multiple columns. When you sort by multiple columns, you must select primary, secondary, and sometimes tertiary sort criteria. The primary sort criterion is the first column by which you want to sort. After that, rows are sorted by the additional columns you specify. For example, if you sort an employee list first by a column that contains department names and second by a column that contains employee names, the rows with the same department name would be grouped together, and within those groups employees would be listed alphabetically. For each column, you can sort in ascending or descending order. Sorting in **ascending order** (the default) arranges rows alphabetically (from A to Z) if the sort column contains text, and from smallest to largest if the sort column contains numbers. **Descending order** is the reverse: text is arranged from Z to A and numbers from largest to smallest. Once you group rows by sorting them, you can use the Split Table command on the Table menu to divide a table in two if you wish. Karen sorts the table so that staff and hourly employees are grouped together in the list, and so that employees are listed alphabetically within those groups. She then splits the table to create separate tables for staff and hourly employees.

Steps

QuickTip

You can also click the Sort Ascending or Sort Descending buttons on the Tables and Borders toolbar to sort a table by the selected column.

QuickTip

You can also sort lists and paragraphs by selecting them, clicking Table on the menu bar, and then clicking Sort.

1. Place the insertion point anywhere in the table
   You do not need to select the table to sort the entire table, although you do need to select specific rows if you intend to sort only part of a table.
2. Click **Table** on the menu bar, then click **Sort**
   The Sort dialog box opens, as shown in Figure D-15. In this dialog box, you specify how you want your table sorted. The Sort by drop-down list includes all the columns in the table. You want to sort the table by the information in the Staff/Hourly column, the third column.
3. Click the **Sort by list arrow**, then click **Column 3**
   You want the staff (which begins with "S") employees to appear before the hourly (which begins with "H") employees in your table, so you must change the sort order to descending, since "S" falls after "H" in the alphabet.
4. Click the **Descending option button** in the Sort by section
   The rows will be sorted in descending order by the text in the third column. So that the employees are listed alphabetically in each group, you also have to specify the column and sort order of the second sort criterion.
5. Click the **Then by list arrow**, then click **Column 1**
   Within the Staff and Hourly groups, the rows will be sorted alphabetically by the text in the first column. Your table includes a row of column headings (the first row) that you do not want included in the sort.
6. Click the **Header row option button**, click **OK**, then deselect the table
   The table is sorted based first on the values in the Staff/Hourly column, and then by the values in the Last Name column, as shown in Figure D-16. The first row of the table (containing the column headings) is not included in the sort. Now that the table is sorted, you can split the table into two separate tables.
7. Place the insertion point in the **Tricia Buchanan row**, click **Table** on the menu bar, then click **Split Table**
   The table is divided into two tables separated by a blank line, as shown in Figure D-17.
8. Click the **Save button** on the Standard toolbar

FIGURE D-15: Sort dialog box

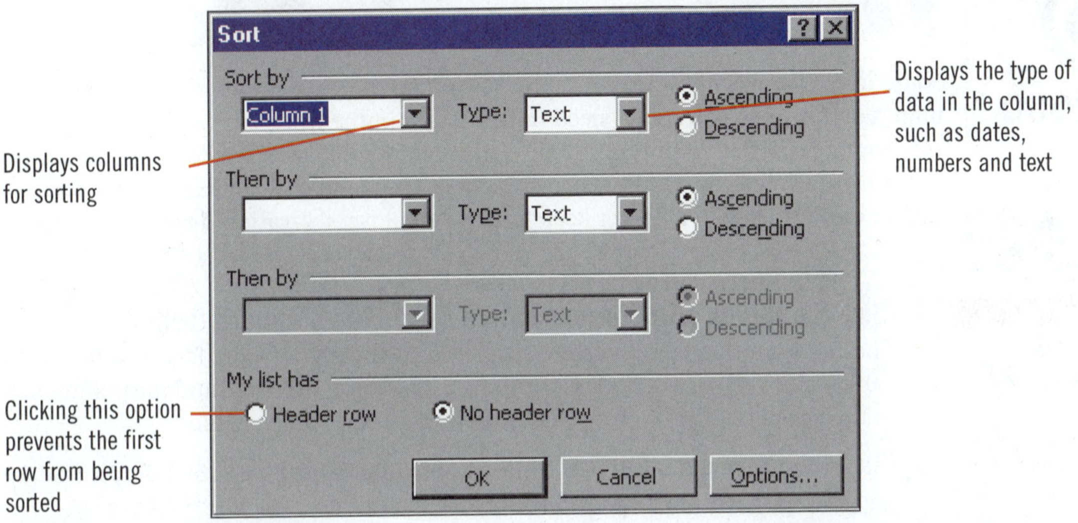

FIGURE D-16: Sorted table

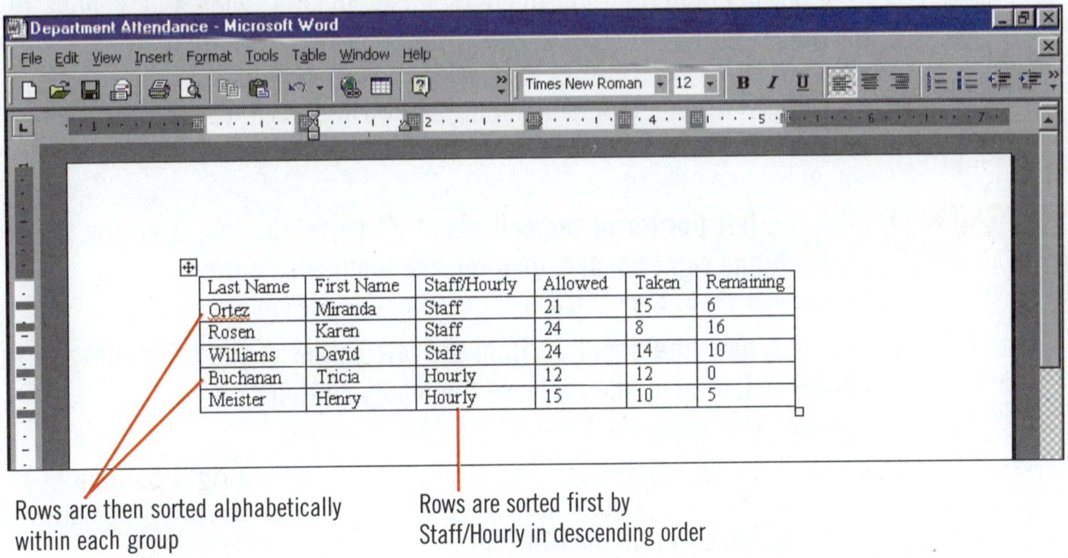

FIGURE D-17: Split table

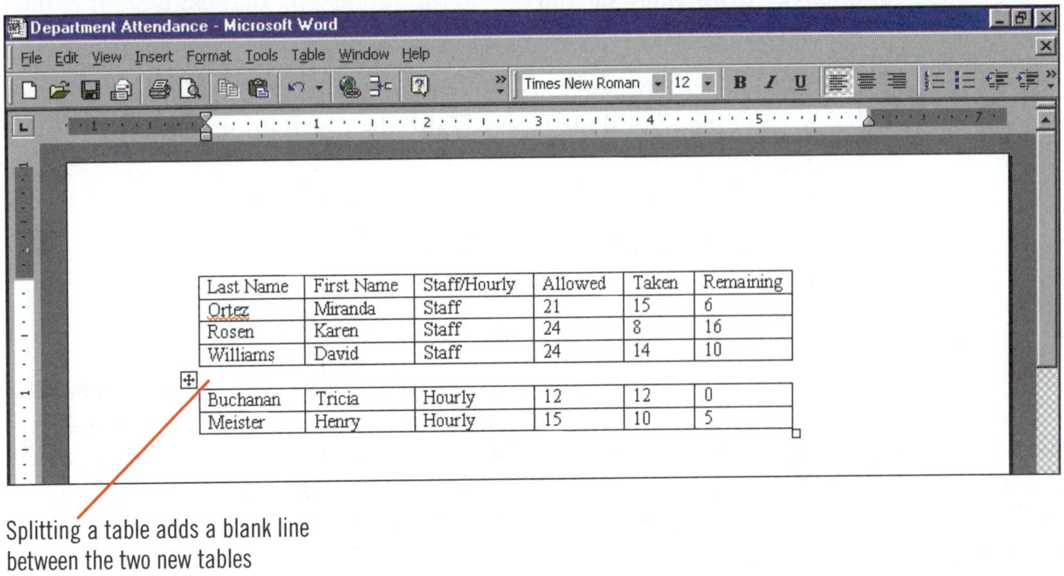

Unit D

Word 2000

Drawing a Table

Sometimes you may not want your table to contain the same number of cells in each row or column. For example, you might need only one cell in the header row or an extra cell in the last column to display an important total. Word's Draw Table feature allows you to customize your tables by drawing cells exactly where you want them. Karen uses the Draw Table feature to create a table to help her keep track of employees' vacation days and personal days.

Steps

QuickTip

If the Office Assistant opens, click Cancel.

Trouble?

Move the Tables and Borders toolbar by clicking its title bar and dragging it if it blocks the area in which you want to work.

QuickTip

If you want to remove a line you drew in a table, click the Eraser button on the Tables and Borders toolbar, then click and drag along the line you want to erase.

1. Click the **Tables and Borders button** on the Standard toolbar
   The Tables and Borders toolbar is displayed, as shown in Figure D-17. Notice that the Draw Table button on the Tables and Borders toolbar is indented and the pointer has changed to the Pencil pointer. You use this pointer to draw a new table.
2. Click the **Down scroll arrow** until you see mostly blank space on your screen
   You'll draw a new table in this blank space in your document.
3. Place the pointer at the **left margin** near the 2" mark on the vertical ruler, click and drag down and to the right to create a cell about 4" wide and 3" high, then release the mouse button
   As you drag, dotted lines that represent the cell border appear. Use the vertical and horizontal rulers as guides for determining the size of the cell. The first cell you draw using the Pencil pointer represents the outside border of the table. Next, you'll create smaller cells within the first cell.
4. Click the **left border** of the cell about ½" below the top, drag the pointer straight across to the **right border**, then release the mouse button
   You created a row. Next you'll create a column in the table.
5. Click the **new line** about 1" from the left border of the table, drag to the **bottom border** of the table, then release the mouse button
   Compare your table with Figure D-19.
6. Keeping the top row intact, draw a line that splits the **right column** in half
   The table now has three columns in the second row. The first row is a single column. Next, you'll add more rows to the table.
7. Draw **four lines** across the **second row** to create five new rows, each about ½" high
8. Click the **Draw Table button** on the Tables and Borders toolbar to deactivate the Pencil pointer
9. Place the insertion point in the first row, type **Allowable Absences**, press **[Tab]** twice, type **Vacation Days**, press **[Tab]**, then type **Personal Days**
   Compare the structure of your table to the table shown in Figure D-20. In the next lesson you will use the Tables and Borders toolbar to modify the structure of the table and to format it.
10. Click the **Save button** on the Standard toolbar

Clues to Use

Rotating text in a table

When a column heading is much wider than the contents of the other cells in the column, you can improve the appearance of the table by displaying the column heading vertically (rather than horizontally) in a cell. To rotate text in a cell, select the text, then click the Change Text Direction button on the Tables and Borders toolbar. Click the button once to rotate the text 90°. Click the button again to change the direction of the vertical text, or to rotate it another 180°. Click the button a third time to return the text to its horizontal position.

FIGURE D-18: Tables and Borders toolbar

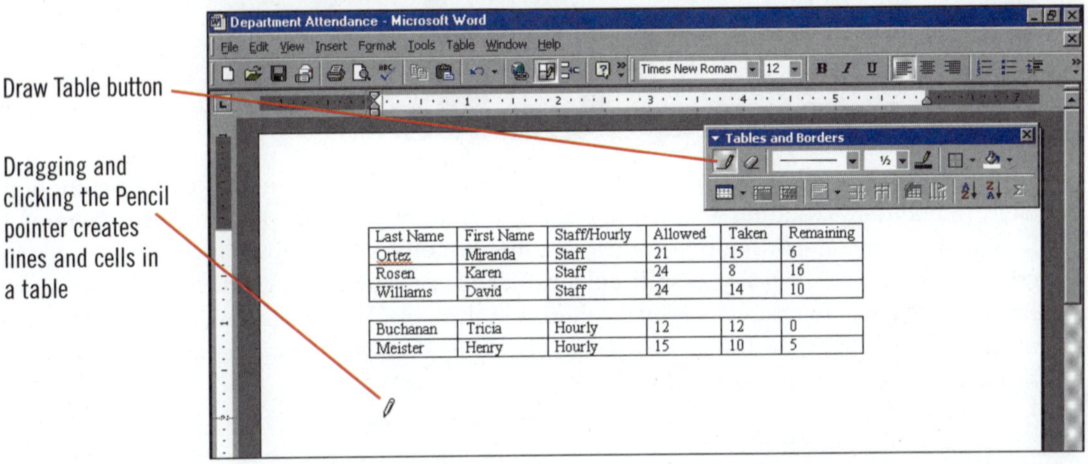

FIGURE D-19: New column

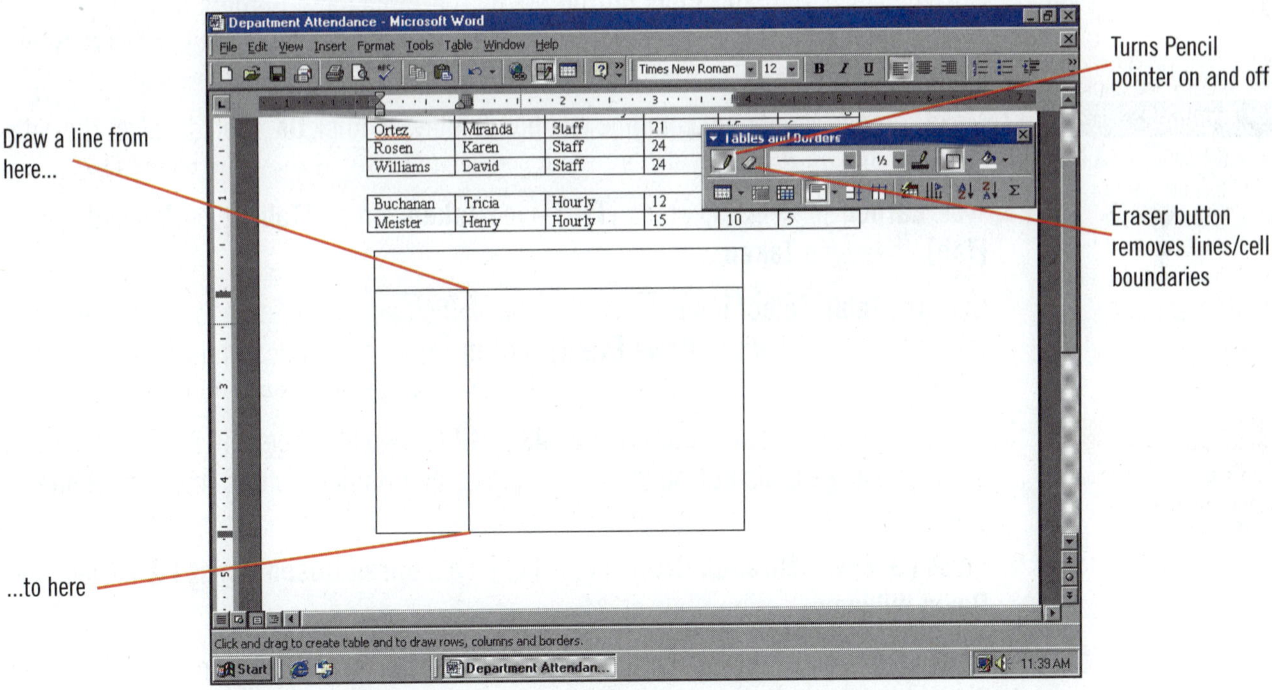

FIGURE D-20: New rows and columns in a table

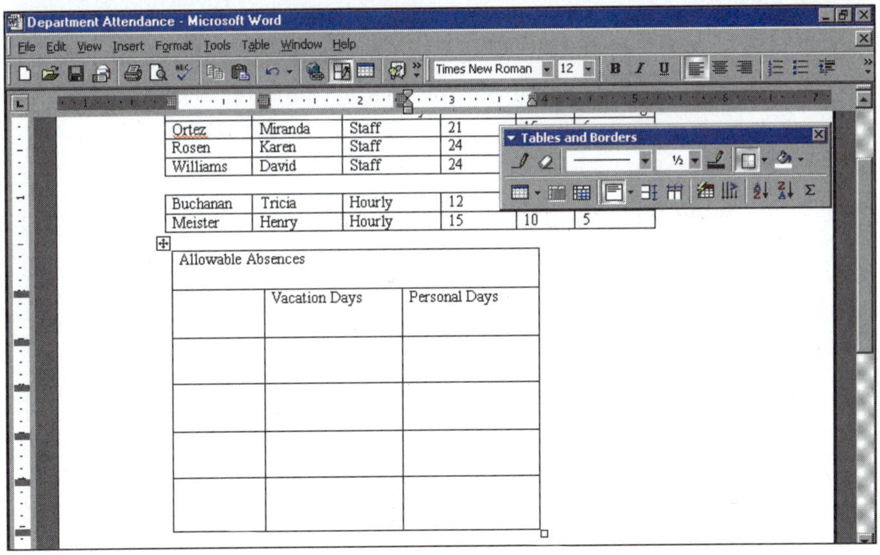

Unit D

Word 2000

Splitting and Merging Cells

You can also use the buttons on the Tables and Borders toolbar to modify the structure of a table. In addition to adding or deleting rows and columns, you can change the structure of a table by merging or splitting cells. When you **merge cells**, you combine two or more cells to create one larger cell. When you **split cells** you divide a single cell to create two or more separate cells. To create additional columns in the table, Karen splits existing cells. She also merges two cells to create a single cell. After completing the structure of her table, she adds text, formats the table, and prints her document.

Steps 1 2 3 4

1. Select the **8 cells** below the headings in the second and third columns (cells B3 to C6), then click the **Split Cells button** on the Tables and Borders toolbar
   The Split Cells dialog box opens, as shown in Figure D-21. You can split selected cells into rows or columns or both. You'll split the two columns into four columns.
2. Make sure the Number of columns text box displays **4,** click **OK**, then deselect the cells
   The columns are evenly divided into four smaller columns, as shown in Figure D-22.
3. Type **Earned** in cell B3, press **[Tab]**, type **Taken**, press **[Tab]**, type **Earned**, press **[Tab]**, then type **Taken**
4. Click the **Table Select icon** at the upper-left corner of the table to select the table, then click the **Distribute Rows Evenly button** on the Tables and Borders toolbar
   The rows are now all the same height. You can merge cells that you want to combine.
5. Deselect the table, select **cells A2** and **A3** (the first two blank cells in the first column), click the **Merge Cells button** on the Tables and Border toolbar, then type **Name**
   The two cells merge to become one cell.
6. Press **[↓]**, type **Miranda Ortez**, press **[↓]**, type **Karen Rosen**, press **[↓]**, then type **David Williams**
7. Select the entire table, click the **Align Top Left list arrow** on the Tables and Borders toolbar, click the **Align Center Left button**, then click in the table
   The text in each cell is left-aligned, but centered vertically.
8. Click the **Table AutoFormat button** on the Tables and Borders toolbar, scroll to the bottom of the Formats list in the Table AutoFormat dialog box, click **Elegant**, then click **OK**
   Compare your table to Figure D-23.
9. Close the Tables and Borders toolbar, type your name at the bottom of the document, click the **Save button** on the Standard toolbar, then click the **Print button** on the Standard toolbar
10. Click **File** on the menu bar, then click **Exit**

Trouble?

If the border between cells B2 and C2 is not aligned with the border between cells C3 and D3, adjust the width of the columns in the second row.

QuickTip

You can also click Table on the menu bar, then click Merge Cells to combine cells, or click Split Cells to divide cells.

FIGURE D-21: Split Cells dialog box

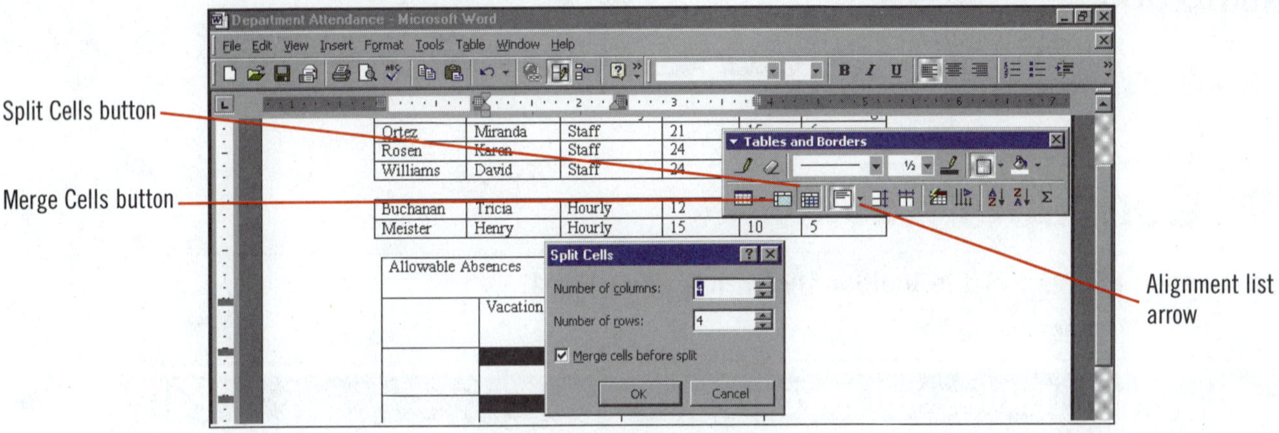

FIGURE D-22: Split cells in a table

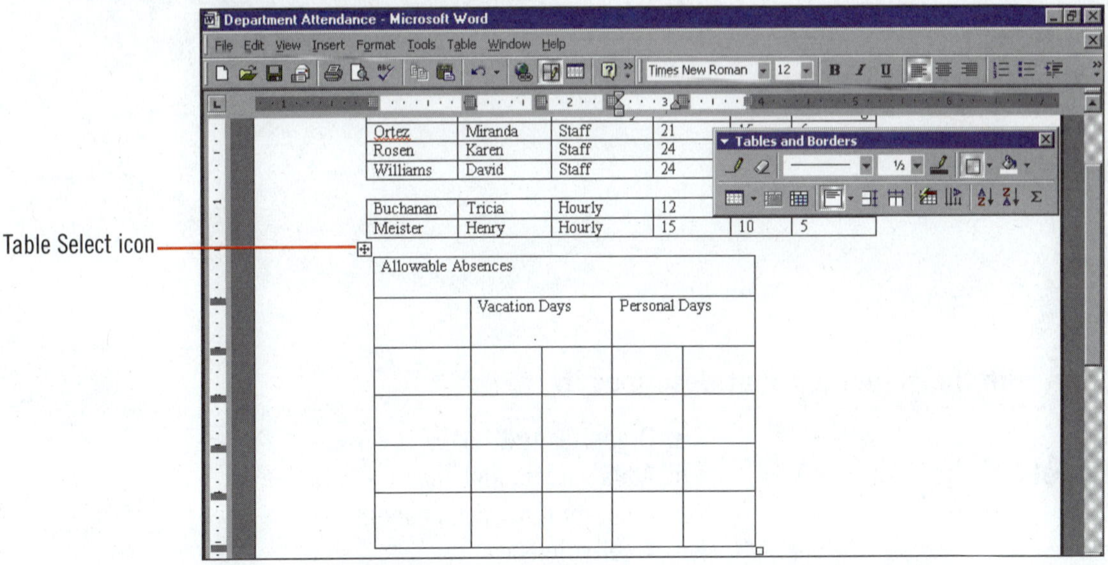

FIGURE D-23: Completed table

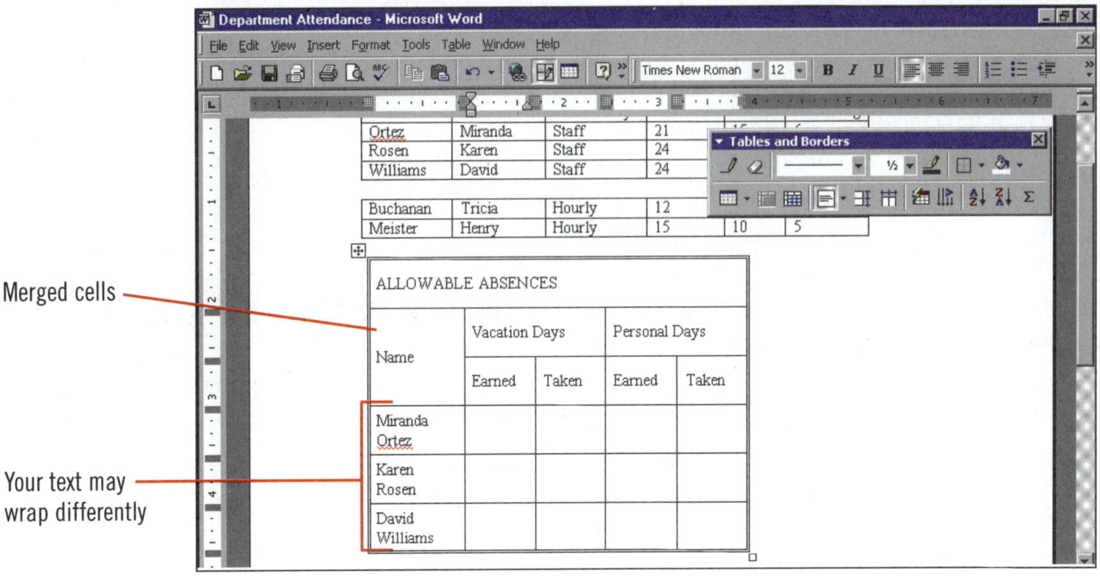

Word 2000 Practice

► Concepts Review

Label each element of the toolbar shown in Figure D-24.

FIGURE D-24

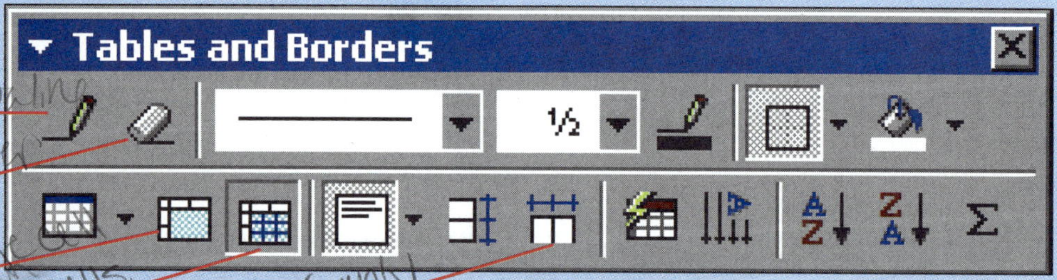

1

2

3

4

5

Match each term with the statement that describes it.

6. Gridline
7. Table AutoFormat
8. B3
9. Cell
10. Descending order
11. Ascending order

a. Organizes text from Z to A
b. Adds borders and shading to tables
c. A non-printing cell boundary
d. A cell reference
e. Organizes text from A to Z
f. The intersection of a row and a column

Select the best answer from the list of choices.

12. Which of the following is NOT a way to create a table in Word?
- **a.** Select tabbed text and click the Insert Table button
- **b.** Click the Insert Table button and drag to select the number of rows and columns you want
- **c.** Click the Tables and Borders button, then drag the Pencil pointer
- **d.** Click Table on the menu bar, then click Table AutoFormat

13. Which statement best describes the commands on the pop-up menu that displays when you right-click a table?
- **a.** The pop-up menu contains only the commands found on the Table menu
- **b.** The pop-up menu contains the commands you are likely to use most often when working in a table
- **c.** The pop-up menu contains Table AutoFormat commands you can use to design a table
- **d.** The pop-up menu contains the command you use to insert calculations in a table

14. **Which statement best describes how to delete only the text inside a row?**
   a. Select the row, then press [Delete]
   b. With the insertion point in the row, click Table on the menu bar, click Delete Cells, then click Delete Entire Row
   c. Select the row, then click the Cut button
   d. Select the row, then press [Shift][Delete]

15. **To break a table into two separate tables, you**
   a. Insert a new row and erase its borders.
   b. Click the Split Cells button.
   c. Click Table on the menu bar, then click Split Table.
   d. Create a new blank table below the table you want to separate, move the text to the new table, then delete the blank rows from the first table.

16. **To add a new blank row to the bottom of a table, you**
   a. Place the insertion point in the last row, click Table on the menu bar, click Insert, then click Rows Above.
   b. Select the last row, click Table on the menu bar, then click Split Cells.
   c. Place the insertion point in the last cell of the last row, then press [Tab].
   d. Place the insertion point in the last row, then press [Shift] [↓].

17. **Which of the following does NOT adjust the width of a column?**
   a. Double-clicking the right border of a column
   b. Clicking the Right Border button
   c. Dragging a column border
   d. Specifying a column width on the Column tab in the Table Properties dialog box

18. **Which of the following is NOT true of the Table AutoFormat command?**
   a. You can apply special formatting to the last column
   b. You can apply special formatting to the last row
   c. You can see an example of the format in the Table AutoFormat dialog box
   d. You can sort by column or row

19. **Which of the following is a valid cell reference for the first cell in the third column?**
   a. C1
   b. A3
   c. 1C
   d. 3A

20. **Which of the following is NOT true about sorting rows in a table?**
   a. The Sort command always sorts all the rows in a table
   b. You can sort a table by more than one column
   c. You can specify not to sort the header row
   d. You can choose the order in which you want rows sorted

Word 2000

Skills Review

1. Create a table.

a. Start Word, type your name at the top of the new document, then press [Enter] twice.
b. Use the Insert Table button to create a table that contains 4 rows and 3 columns.
c. Enter the following text in the table:

N	New	Create a new document
O	Open	Open a document
D	Delete	Clear selected text
S	Save	Save a document

d. Add two new rows to the bottom of the table and enter the following text:

Y	Repeat	Redo the last action
Z	Undo	Undo the last action

e. Save the document as "Quick Table" to your Project Disk.

2. Adjust table rows and columns

a. Adjust the width of the first two columns to fit the text.
b. Drag the right border of the last column to the 2½" inch mark on the horizontal ruler.
c. Select the entire table, and distribute the rows evenly.
d. Center the table on the page, then save your changes to the table.

3. Add and delete rows and columns.

a. Add a new row to the bottom of the table.
b. Type "P," press [Tab], type "Print," press [Tab], then type "Print the current document."
c. Delete the third row of the table.
d. Move the last row so that it becomes the fourth row.
e. Insert a new column between the first and second columns.
f. With the first row selected, insert a new first row at the top of the table.
g. In the first cell of the new row, type "CTRL+," press [Tab], type "Menu," press [Tab], type "Command," press [Tab], then type "To do this."
h. In the new second column, type "File" in the first four cells in the Menu column.
i. Type "Edit" in the remaining cells in the Menu column.
j. Save your changes to the table.

4. Format a table.

a. Display the Tables and Borders toolbar. (*Hint*: Click the Tables and Borders button on the Standard toolbar.)
b. Format the table in the Grid 3 preset format.
c. Change the shade color of the first row to Lavender. (*Hint*: Use the Shading Color list arrow on the Tables and Borders toolbar.)
d. Format the text in the top row in bold.
e. Add inside horizontal borders to the table. (*Hint*: Select the table, click the Outside Borders list arrow, then click the Inside Horizontal Border button.)
f. Center the text in the first 3 columns of the table.
g. Save and print the table, then close the document.

5. Calculate data in a table.

- **a.** Open the file WD D-2 from your Project Disk and save it as "Travel Details."
- **b.** Type your name at the top of the document, then press [Enter] twice.
- **c.** In the second cell in the Expense Total column, enter a formula that calculates the sum of the values of the cells to the left. In the Formula dialog box, click the Number format list arrow, then click 0.00.
- **d.** Repeat Step 5c for the remaining cells in the Expense Total column.
- **e.** Replace the Transportation value in the January column with "122.00".
- **f.** Update the transportation calculation in the Expense Total column.
- **g.** Save your changes.

6. Sort a table.

- **a.** Sort the table in descending order by the values in the Expense Total column.
- **b.** Sort the table alphabetically by the Expenses column, making sure not to include the heading row in the sort.
- **c.** Apply the Classic 2 preset format, then save your changes.

7. Draw a table.

- **a.** Insert several blank lines under the Travel Details table, then use the Pencil pointer to draw a cell 2" high and 3" wide.
- **b.** Draw three lines to create four rows each about ½" high, within the outside border of the new table.
- **c.** Add a vertical line to divide the four rows into two columns.
- **d.** Enter the following text in the table:

Agenda	
8:30	Opening Ceremonies
10:00	
12:00	Group Luncheon

- **e.** Save your changes.

8. Split and merge cells.

- **a.** Split the empty cell in the third row into two columns, then enter the following in the two new cells: Meeting A for Advisors; Meeting B for Committee Members.
- **b.** Merge the cells in the first row.
- **c.** Adjust the width of the first column so that it is about ½" wide.
- **d.** Adjust the width of the second and third columns in the third row so that they are about the same size.
- **e.** Center the text vertically and horizontally within each cell. (*Hint*: Use the Tables and Borders toolbar to align the text.)
- **f.** Change the direction of the times listed in the first column, so that the text is vertically aligned from bottom to top.
- **g.** Format the table using the Colorful 2 preset format, then center the table on the page.
- **h.** Save, print, close the document, and exit Word.

Independent Challenges

1. As the director of marketing for ReadersPlus publishing company, you are responsible for projecting sales for a new book series for beginning readers called "Everyone Reads!" Your manager has asked you to present your sales projections at the upcoming sales meeting. You use Word to prepare a table for your presentation.

To complete this independent challenge:

- **a.** Start Word and create a new document called "Projected Sales" on your Project Disk.
- **b.** At the top of the document, type your name and "Projected Sales" (on separate lines), then center these lines.

c. Create a table with five rows and five columns.
d. Enter the following text:

Everyone Reads!	West	East	Midwest	South
Anthologies Only	5000	7000	5800	7200
Supplements Only	2400	3500	4000	1100
Anthologies with Guides	6800	6700	9400	8200
Complete Package	6500	7500	6300	7700

e. Adjust the width of the first column so that the text in each cell fits on one line.
f. Add a new row to the bottom of the table, then type "Total" in the first cell.
g. Enter a formula in each remaining cell in the last row to calculate the sum of the cells above it.
h. Center the entire table horizontally on the page.
i. Format the table with the Columns 1 preset format.
j. Right-align the numerical values in the table and left-align the first column.
k. Center the column headings, make them bold, and change the shading of the first row to light yellow.
l. Preview, save, print, then close the document.

2. After attending a personal productivity seminar, you decide to become more organized by creating an electronic "To Do" list, a document that you can complete each week. You use Word's Draw Table feature to create the blank "To Do" list.
To complete this independent challenge:

a. Start Word and create a new document called "To Do List" on your Project Disk.
b. At the top of the document, type your name and "To Do List" (on separate lines), then center these lines.
c. Use the Draw Table button to create a table that contains seven rows and one column (about 5" wide and 5" long). Refer to Figure D-25 as a guide to help you complete the remaining steps.
d. Draw a line that divides all but the top row into two columns.
e. Make all the rows the same height.
f. In the top row, type "Things To Do: Week of."
g. Starting with the second row in the first column, type the days of the week, starting with "Monday." In the last row, type "Weekend."
h. Change the direction of the text in the first column so that it is vertically aligned from bottom to top.
i. Make each row 1" high.
j. Adjust the width of the first column to fit the text.
k. Format the table with the Columns 4 preset format.
l. Center the table on the page.
m. Center the text in the first column.
n. Center the text in the top row both vertically and horizontally, then increase the font size to 20 points. Apply bold formatting to all the text in the table.
o. Preview, save, print, then close the document.

FIGURE D-25

3. As a co-chair of the class reunion entertainment committee, you are responsible for keeping track of registration and fees paid for upcoming events. To make it easier to track and update your registration statistics, you create a table showing the distribution of attendees among events, and add formulas to help you calculate registration income.
To complete this independent challenge:

a. Start Word, open the file WD D-3 from your Project Disk, and save it as "Reunion Costs."
b. At the top of the document, insert your name and "Reunion Costs" (on separate lines). Add a blank line underneath, then center these lines.

c. Convert the tabbed text to a table.
d. Add a row to the end of the table, and enter "Variety Show" as the event, with 120 attendees at $7 per person.
e. Calculate the total for each row, using a multiplication formula. (*Hint:* For the first row, type "=B2*C2" in the Formula dialog box.)
f. Sort the table rows so that the events are listed in alphabetical order.
g. Add a new row to the bottom of the table and type "Grand Total" in the first cell in this row.
h. Calculate the total of the values in the Total column.
i. Merge the first three cells in the last row.
j. Format the table with the 3D Effects 1 preset format.
k. Format all the rows to be ½" high, and adjust the width of the last column to fit the text.
l. Left, center-align the text in all the cells vertically, and right-align the text in the columns that contain numbers.
m. Preview, save, print, then close the document.

WEB WORK

4. You are an intern in the Human Resources department at MediaLoft. One of your assignments is to create a memo to all employees that outlines MediaLoft's holidays and events. Rather than type the information, you decide to copy the holidays and events from MediaLoft's intranet site, and then format the table and add more information to it.
To complete this independent challenge:

a. Start Word, click File on the menu bar, click New, then double-click the Elegant Memo template on the Memos tab in the New dialog box.
b. Enter the following in the memo template:
TO: MediaLoft employees
FROM: Your Name
SUBJECT: MediaLoft holidays and events
CC: Karen Rosen
c. Save the document with the filename "MediaLoft Holidays" on your Project Disk.
d. Connect to the Internet, go to the MediaLoft intranet site at http://www.course.com/illustrated/MediaLoft, then click the link for the Human Resources page.
e. Copy the schedule of holidays from the Human Resources page on the intranet site to the body of the memo. Be sure to include the heading "Company Holidays and Events." (Replace the template text in the body of the memo.)
f. Sort the table by type in descending order, and then by date.
g. Split the table to separate holidays and events.
h. Insert a new row at the top of the holidays table and type "MediaLoft Holidays" in the first cell.
i. Insert new row at the top of the event table and type "MediaLoft Events" in the first cell.
j. Copy the second row (column headings) of the holidays table to become the new second row of the events table.
k. Delete the Type column in each table.
l. Add a column to the right end of the events table, type "Location" in the second row, then enter the following in the Location column: "Majestic Towers Hotel," "Civic Center," "Pacific View Park," "Majestic Towers Hotel."
m. Adjust the column widths in each table to fit the text, then merge the cells in the first row of each table.
n. Apply the Classic 2 preset format to each table.
o. Add inside borders to each table.
p. Center the heading for each table, bold the column headings, then center the tables on the page.
q. Preview, save, print, then close the document.

► Visual Workshop

Create the table shown in Figure D-26 and save it as "Activity Prices" on your Project Disk. Be sure to align the text and the table as shown in the figure. (*Hint*: Make each row 1" high and use the List 7 preset format.)

FIGURE D-26

Your Name
Extreme Fitness

Activity	Price	Sales	Total
Aerobic Classes	$15.00	89	$1335.00
Basketball	$7.00	152	$1064.00
Racquetball	$10.00	214	$2140.00
Swimming	$10.00	345	$3450.00
Total for 2000		**800**	**$7989.00**

Word 2000

Unit E

Formatting Pages

Objectives

- MOUS ► Change document margins
- MOUS ► Create headers and footers
- MOUS ► Modify headers and footers
- MOUS ► Insert page numbers
- MOUS ► Insert page breaks
- MOUS ► Create sections
- MOUS ► Create columns
- MOUS ► Balance columns

In addition to formatting text and paragraphs, you can format the pages of your documents. Page formatting includes determining the size and orientation of the paper as well as setting the document margins. In a multiple page document you can also create headers and footers, add page numbers, insert breaks to control the flow of text, and arrange text in columns. Alice Wegman is the marketing manager at MediaLoft. Alice knows that people who belong to book groups tend to buy a lot of books. Alice wants to interest MediaLoft customers in reading and buying more books, so she creates a newsletter promoting book groups that she intends to distribute in MediaLoft stores. She uses Word's page formatting features to make her newsletter attractive and easy to read.

Unit E

Word 2000

Changing Document Margins

In a document, the blank area between the edge of the text and the edge of a page is called the **margin**. When you create a new document, it contains preset default margins. You can adjust a document's margins to change the appearance of the document or to manipulate the amount of text on a page. To adjust margins, you can change the settings on the Margins tab of the Page Setup dialog box, or you can use the rulers. Alice plans for her newsletter to be a four-page document. She has already written and edited the text and completed most of the font formatting. Now she needs to format the pages. She begins by opening the document and changing the default margins.

Steps

QuickTip

If the title flows onto two lines, select Book News, then reduce the font size until Book News fits on one line.

Trouble?

Click the More Buttons button on the Standard toolbar to locate buttons that are not displayed on your toolbar.

QuickTip

To display more than six pages of a document in the Print Preview window, drag the lower-right corner of the Multiple Pages grid to expand the grid.

1. Start **Word**, open the file **WD E-1** from your Project Disk, then save it as **Book News**
   The file opens in Print Layout view, which displays the text as it will appear on a printed page.
2. Click **File** on the menu bar, click **Page Setup**, then click the **Margins tab** if necessary
   The Page Setup dialog box opens, as shown in Figure E-1. You can use this dialog box to set the document margins, to change the paper size and orientation of your document, to change the paper source on your printer, and to set other page layout options. You want to change the size of all four document margins.
3. Click the **Top down arrow** three times until .7" appears, then click the **Bottom down arrow** three times until .7" appears
   Notice that the margins change in the Preview area of the Page Setup dialog box.
4. Click the **Left down arrow** until .7" appears, then click the **Right down arrow** until .7" appears
   On the Margins tab, you can choose to add a **gutter** to your document to allow extra space for a binding at the top or on the left side of a page. You can also create facing pages. **Facing pages** are the left and right pages of a double-sided document, such as a book or a magazine. Documents with facing pages have **mirror margins**—inside and outside margins that are a mirror image of each other—rather than left and right margins. For this brief newsletter, you'll use left and right margin settings.
5. Click **OK**
   All four document margins change to .7".
6. Click the **Print Preview button** on the Standard toolbar, then click the **One Page button** on the Print Preview toolbar if necessary
   The first page appears in Print Preview. Note that you can also change a document's margins in Print Preview (or in Print Layout view) by dragging the edges of the rulers. You want to see the new margin settings applied to the whole document.
7. Click the **Multiple Pages button** on the Print Preview toolbar, select **2x3 Pages** (third box in the bottom row) on the grid that appears, then click
   Six pages of the document display in the Print Preview window.
8. Click , select **1x2 Pages** (second box in the top row), then click
   The first two pages of the document appear side by side in Print Preview, as shown in Figure E-2. You can scroll down to see the other pages of the document.
9. Scroll to see the other pages in the document, click **Close** on the Print Preview toolbar, then click the **Save button** on the Standard toolbar

FIGURE E-1: Margins tab in Page Setup dialog box

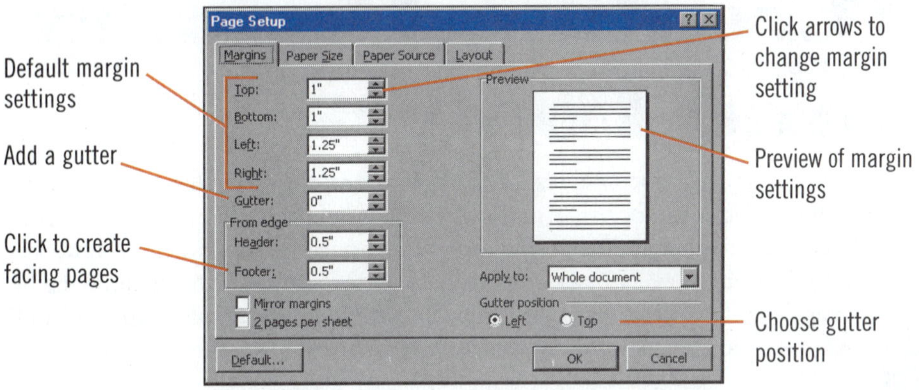

FIGURE E-2: Preview of newsletter

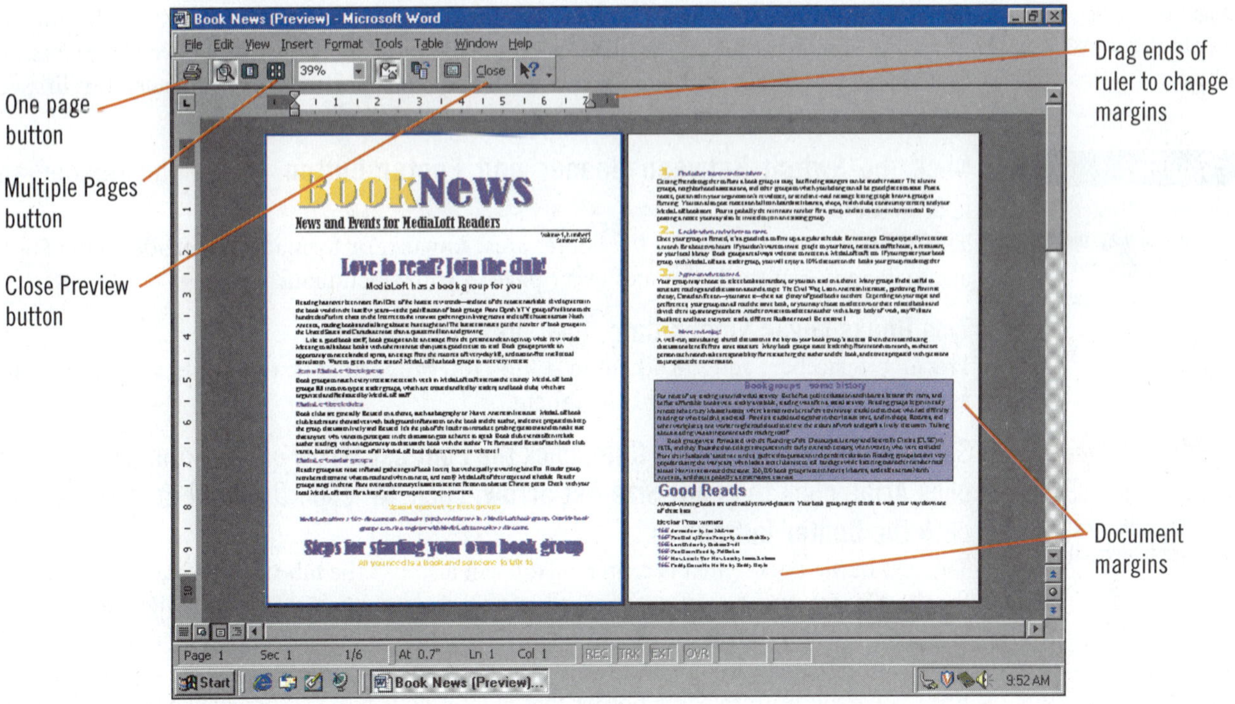

Clues to Use

Changing paper size and orientation

By default, the documents you create in Word use the standard 8 ½ x 11" paper size with a portrait orientation. **Portrait** orientation means that a page is taller than it is wide. Using the Paper Size tab in the Page Setup dialog box shown in Figure E-3, you can change the orientation of a page to **landscape**, so that it is wider than it is tall. On this tab you can also select a different paper size, such as legal or envelope, or you can create a custom paper size. To change the page orientation, click the option button for the orientation that you want, portrait or landscape. To change the paper size, select a predefined paper size or type custom measurements .

FIGURE E-3: Paper Size tab in Page Setup dialog box

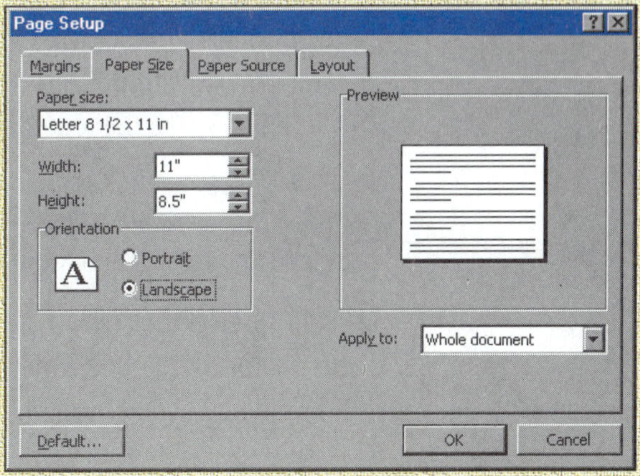

Unit E

Word 2000

Creating Headers and Footers

In multiple page documents, the top or bottom of every page typically contains information, such as a page number, title, author's name, or graphic element, that appears on every page. A **header** is text that appears at the top of every page of a document. A **footer** is text that appears at the bottom of every page. You create headers and footers by opening the headers and footers areas from the View menu and then inserting text or graphics in the header or footer area. Alice adds a footer that includes text and a border to her newsletter.

Steps 1 2 3 4

QuickTip

You cannot edit the body of the document while the Header and Footer areas are open.

Trouble?

If the Header and Footer toolbar is in your way, move it by clicking its title bar and dragging it to a new location.

QuickTip

In a header or footer, click [Tab] once to center-align text and twice to right-align text.

1. Click **View** on the menu bar, then click **Header and Footer**

   The Header area opens and the document text is dimmed, as shown in Figure E-4. The Header and Footer toolbar also opens. The Header and Footer toolbar includes buttons for inserting standard text into headers and footers and for navigating between headers and footers in a document. In a later lesson you'll add a page number to the header, but first you want to create a footer for the newsletter.

2. Click the **Switch Between Header and Footer button** on the Header and Footer toolbar

   The insertion point moves to the Footer area. Any text or formatting you add to the Footer area will appear at the bottom of every page in your document.

3. Type **Books Music Videos Cafe**, then press **[Spacebar]**

   Pressing [Spacebar] adds an accent to "Café". You can format text in headers and footers just as you would format text in the document.

4. Select **Books Music Videos Café**, click the **Font list arrow** on the Formatting toolbar, click **Arial**, click the **Font Size list arrow**, click **14**, click the **Bold button**, then click the **Center button**

   The text in the Footer area is centered. You can also use the tab stops displayed on the ruler for the Header and Footer areas to align text. A center tab stop and a right tab stop for Header and Footer areas are set by default. If you change the margins in a document, you need to adjust the tab stops in the Header and Footer areas to match the new margin settings. Next you want to add a border that will set your footer off from the rest of the text.

5. Click the footer text to deselect it, click **Format** on the menu bar, click **Borders and Shading**, click the **Borders tab** if necessary, click the **Custom box** in the Setting area, make sure the **top line** is selected in the Style list, make sure the color is set to **Automatic**, click the **Width list arrow**, click the **1 ½ pt line**, click the **Top border button** in the Preview area, make sure **Paragraph** is selected in the Apply to list box, compare your dialog box to Figure E-5, then click **OK**

   A thin line spans the top of the footer.

6. Click **Close** on the Header and Footer toolbar, then scroll to the bottom of page 1

   Closing the Header and Footer toolbar closes the Header and Footer areas. The footer you created appears at the bottom of the page, as shown in Figure E-6. The footer text is dimmed.

7. Click the **Print Preview button** on the Standard toolbar, then scroll down to see the footer at the bottom of every page

8. Click **Close** on the Print Preview toolbar, then save your changes

FIGURE E-4: Header area

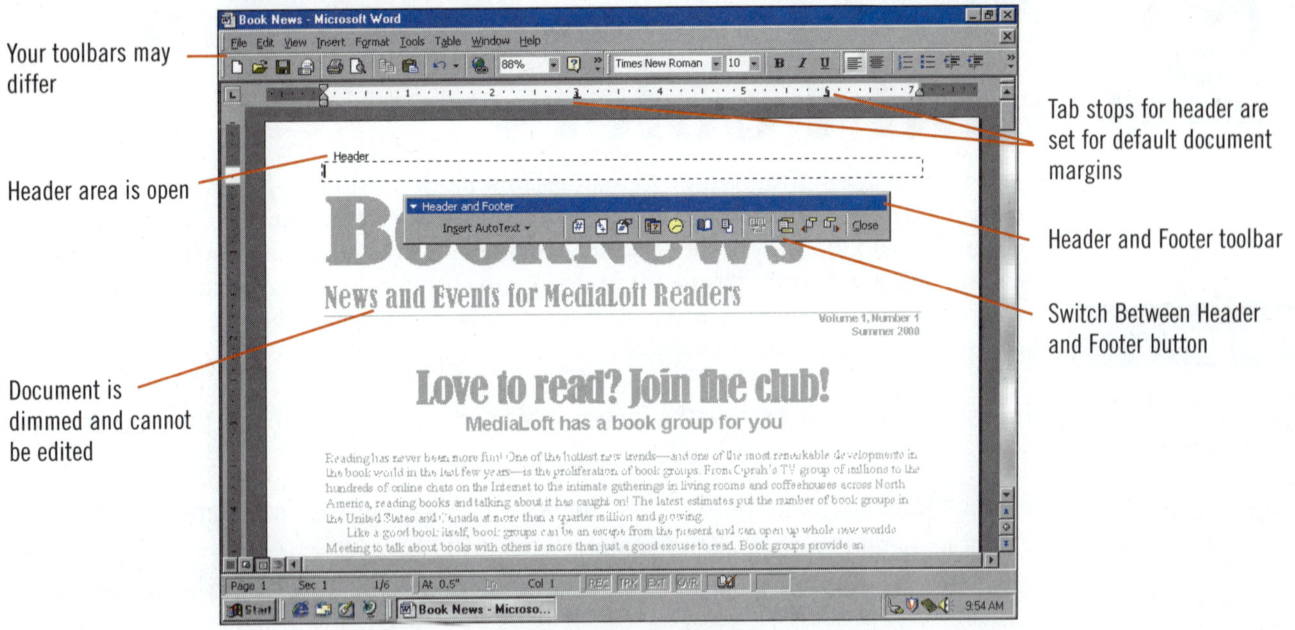

FIGURE E-5: Borders and Shading dialog box

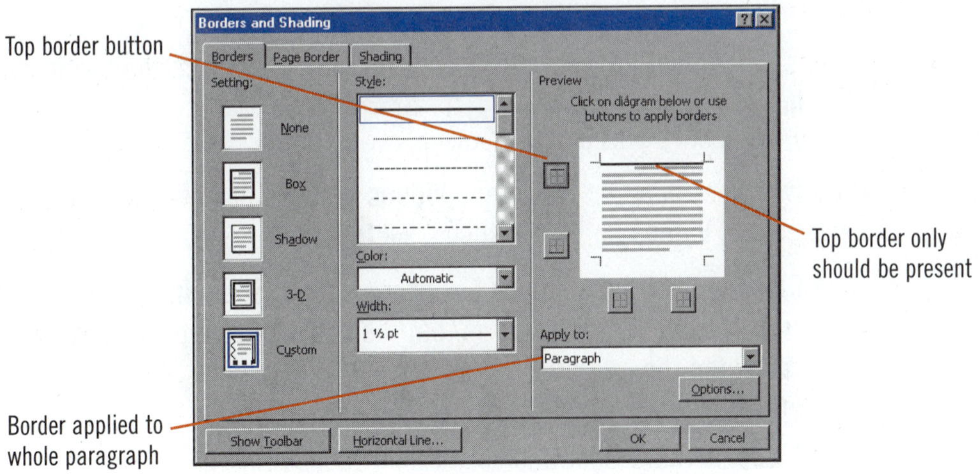

FIGURE E-6: Footer in the document

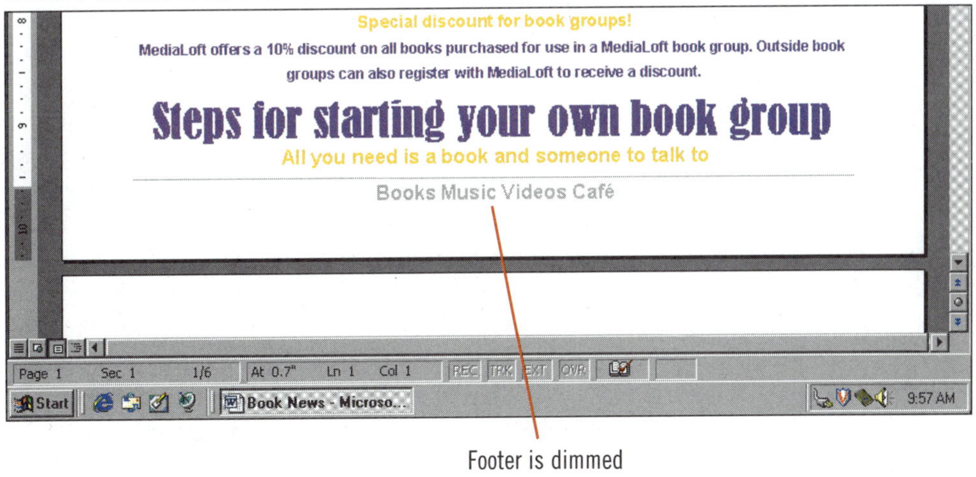

Unit E

Word 2000

Modifying Headers and Footers

If you want to change the text or formatting in a header or footer, you must first open the Header and Footer areas. You can use the Header and Footer command on the View menu to open headers and footers, or, when you are working in Print Layout view, you can double-click the area you want to edit. Alice decides the footer would look better if it included a graphic element between the words. She inserts a small circle symbol between the words in the footer to give the newsletter more style.

Steps

QuickTip

To specify the distance of the header or footer from the edge of the page, change the Header and Footer settings on the Margins tab in the Page Setup dialog box.

1. Position the pointer over the **footer** at the bottom of the first page, then double-click
   The Footer area opens. You can now edit the footer.
2. Place the insertion point between **Books** and **Music** in the Footer area, click **Insert** on the menu bar, then click **Symbol**
   The Symbol dialog box opens, as shown in Figure E-7. In addition to keyboard characters, many fonts include symbols.You can click the Font list arrow in the Symbol dialog box to see the fonts on your computer that include symbols. **Symbols** are special characters, such as bullets, foreign language characters, and simple graphics that you can insert into a document. A trademark symbol ™, a function symbol *f*, and a paragraph mark ¶ are just a few examples of the kinds of symbols you can add.

QuickTip

When you click a symbol, it enlarges so you can see it better.

3. Make sure **Symbol** appears in the Font list box, then click the **circle symbol**, then click **Insert**
   The circle symbol is added to the footer between "Books" and "Music".

QuickTip

Be sure to click two times slowly. Do not double-click.

4. Click two times between **Music** and **Videos** in the footer, click **Insert**, click two times between and **Videos** and **Café**, then click **Insert**
5. Click **Close** in the Symbol dialog box, then use the **[Spacebar]** to add a space before or after each symbol as needed, so that there is a single space between each side of the symbol and the words
   Compare your document with Figure E-8.
6. Click **Close** on the Header and Footer toolbar, scroll to the bottom of the page to see your changes to the footer, then save your changes

CLUES TO USE

Creating headers and footers for specific pages

Sometimes you will not want headers and footers to appear on the first page of a document, for example, a title page. Alternatively, you may want to include different information in the header or footer for the first page. Sometimes you will also want to create different headers and footers for facing pages. For example, if you were formatting the pages of a book, you might want the title of the book to appear at the top of every left (or even-numbered) page, and the title of the current chapter to appear at the top of every right (or odd-numbered) page. You can easily create different odd and even or different first page headers and footers using the Layout tab in the Page Setup dialog box. Click File on the menu bar, click Page Setup, then click the Layout tab. On the Layout tab, select the Different odd and even check box or the Different first page check box (or both), then click OK. When you open headers and footers, you will have different header and footer areas for each option you selected (for example, a First Page header area, an Odd Page header area, and an Even Page header area). You must enter text in each area where you want a header or footer to appear. You can use the Show Previous, Show Next, and Switch Between Header and Footer buttons on the Header and Footer toolbar to navigate between the different header and footer areas in your document.

FIGURE E-7: Symbol dialog box

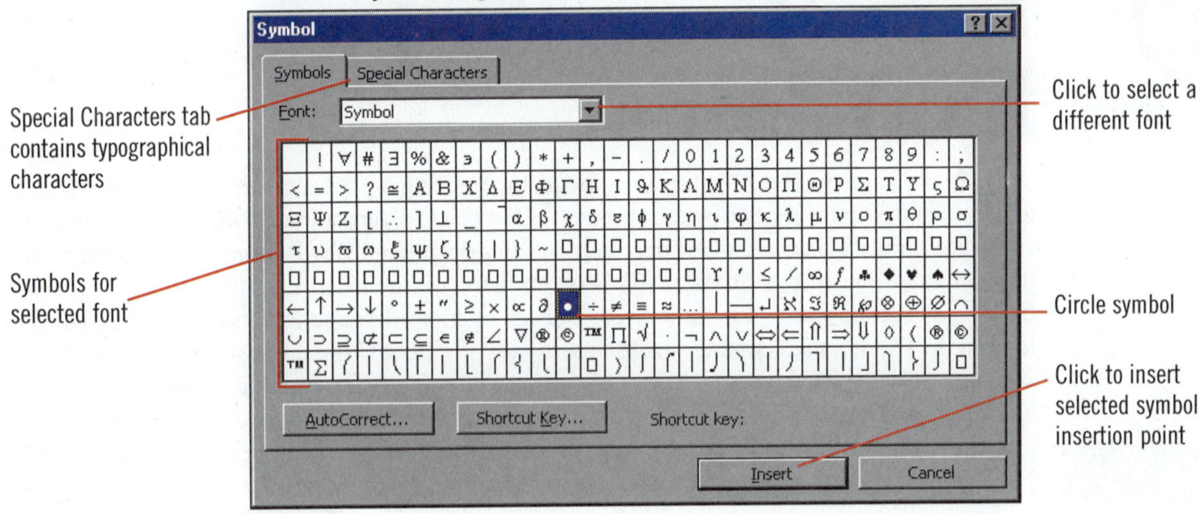

FIGURE E-8: Symbols added to footer

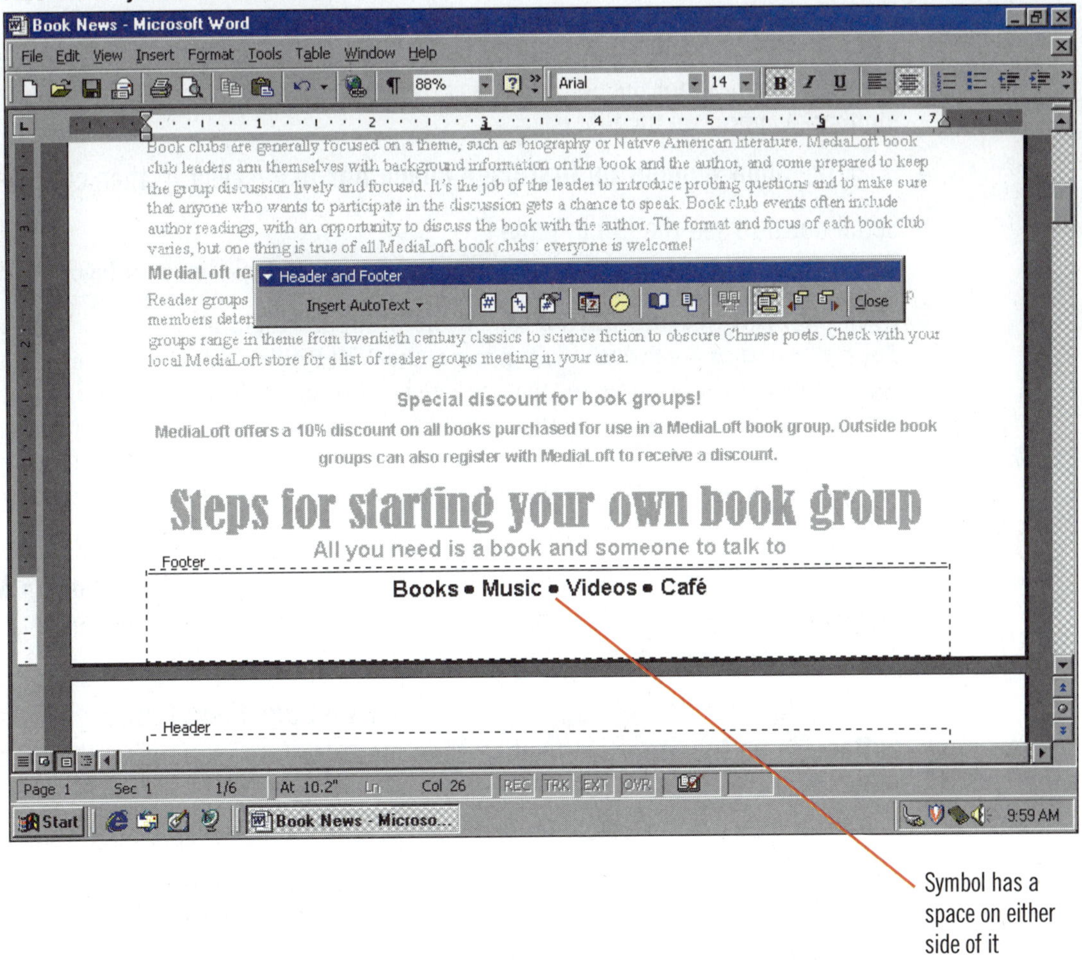

Inserting Page Numbers

You can add page numbers to your documents by inserting a page number field in the header or footer. A **field** is an instruction or code that serves as a placeholder for information that changes, such as a page number. When you insert page numbers in a document, Word automatically numbers each page for you. You can use the Page Numbers command on the Insert menu to add a page number field to a header or footer automatically, or you can open headers and footers and then use the buttons on the Header and Footer toolbar to insert page numbers. Using the Page Numbers command, you can also change the number format of your page numbers (for example, to Roman numerals), and you can start your page numbering with a number other than 1. Alice wants to include a page number at the top of every page of her newsletter except the first page. She uses the Page Numbers command on the Insert menu to add page numbers to her newsletter.

Steps

1. **Press [Ctrl][Home], click Insert on the menu bar, then click Page Numbers**
   The Page Numbers dialog box opens, as shown in Figure E-9. You can use the options in the Page Numbers dialog box to specify the position and the alignment of page numbers in the document. You want to add page numbers to the header.

QuickTip

To change or modify the number format of your page numbers, or to start numbering your document with a number other than 1, click Format in the Page Numbers dialog box, or click the Format Page Number button on the Header and Footer toolbar, then select from the options in the Page Number Format dialog box.

2. **Click the Position list arrow, then click Top of Page (Header)**
   The Preview box shows the page number right-aligned in the upper-right corner of the page. Because the finished newsletter will be folded so that pages 2 and 3 appear next to each other, you want the page numbers to be located on the outside edges of each page in the document.
3. **Click the Alignment list arrow, then click Outside**
   The Preview box shows two pages, each with a page number in the outside corner at the top. Since the masthead for the newsletter is at the top of the first page, you don't want the page number to appear on the first page.
4. **Click the Show number on first page check box to deselect it, then click OK**
5. **Scroll down to see the top of page 2**
   The number "2" appears in the header at the top of page 2, as shown in Figure E-10.
6. **Click the Print Preview button on the Standard toolbar**
   The first two pages of the document appear in the Print Preview window. Notice that there is no page number on the first page and that the footer is also gone. When you deselect the Show number on first page check box in the Page Numbers dialog box, Word creates a different header and footer for the first page. The header and footer on the first page remain blank until you enter text in the First Page header and/or footer areas. You still want the footer to appear on the first page.

QuickTip

To remove page numbers from a document, open headers and footers, then delete the page number field.

7. **Click Close on the Print Preview toolbar, scroll to the bottom of page 2, double-click the footer to open the Footer area, use the selection bar to select Books • Music • Videos • Café, then click the Copy button on the Standard toolbar**
   The footer text is copied to the Clipboard.
8. **Scroll up to the bottom of page 1, click in the First Page Footer area, click the Paste button on the Standard toolbar, then press [Delete] to remove the extra paragraph that was added**
   The text is copied to the footer for the first page. Be sure your footer matches the one shown in Figure E-11.
9. **Click Close on the Header and Footer toolbar, click the Print Preview button, scroll the document to see the page numbers and footers on all pages, close Print Preview, then save your changes**

FIGURE E-9: Page Numbers dialog box

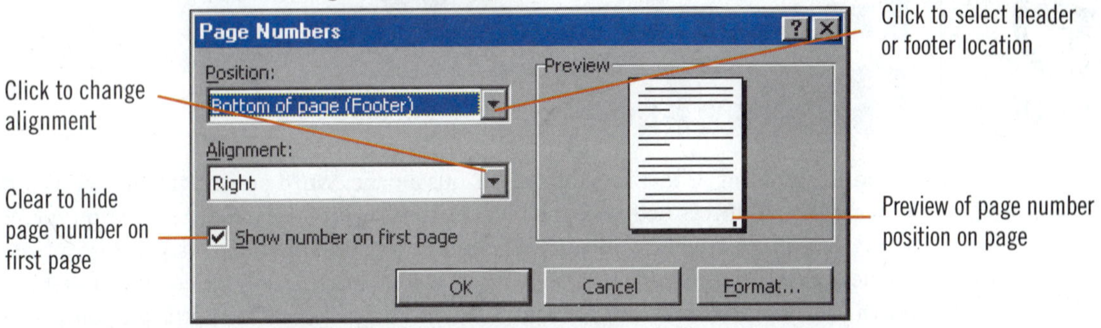

FIGURE E-10: Page number in header

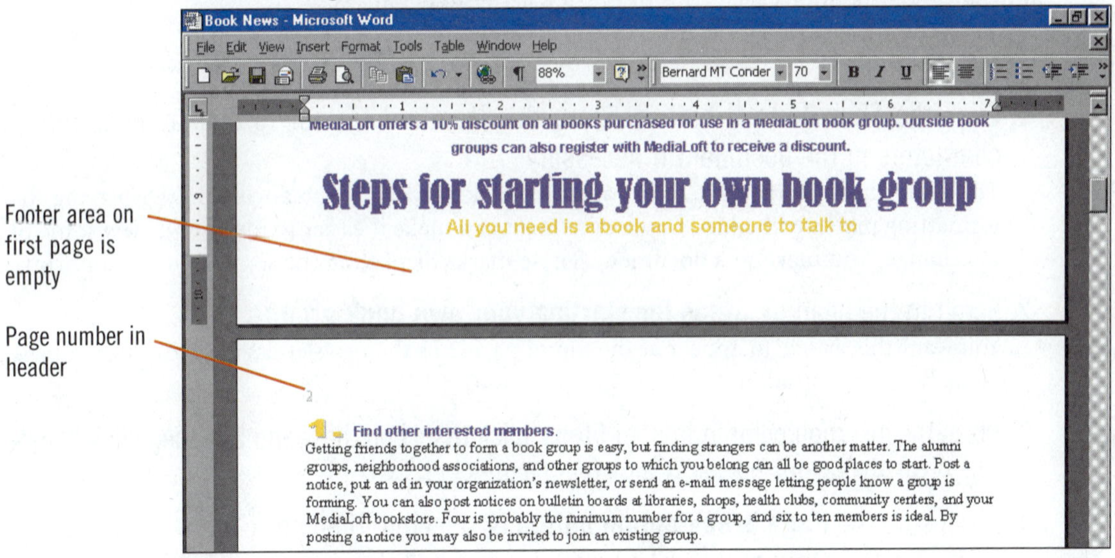

FIGURE E-11: First page footer

CLUES TO USE

Inserting the date and time into a document

You can easily insert the current date and time into your document in a variety of formats using the Date and Time command on the Insert menu. The date and time information is linked to your computer's clock, so the information should always be current. To add the current date or time to a document, click Insert on the menu bar, then click Date and Time. In the Date and Time dialog box, select the date and time format you want to use from the list of available formats. If you want to insert the date and time as a field that will be updated automatically when you open or print a document, select the Update automatically check box. If you want the current date and time to remain in the document as static text, clear the Update automatically check box. Click OK to insert the date and time at the location of the insertion point. You can also use the Insert Date and Insert Time buttons on the Header and Footer toolbar to insert the current date and time into a header or footer.

Unit E

Word 2000

Inserting Page Breaks

When the amount of text in a document fills a page, Word automatically inserts a **page break**, a separator that forces text after the break to appear on the next page. As you type, Word inserts a **soft page break** when you reach the end of a page, which allows you to continue typing on the next page. You can also manually insert a page break, sometimes called a **hard page break**, into a document to force text to begin on a new page. Alice is planning for the finished newsletter to be four pages long. Before arranging the text on the pages, she inserts page breaks at the location she wants each page of the newsletter to begin.

Steps

QuickTip

Page breaks, section breaks, and column breaks are always visible in Normal view.

QuickTip

If the heading flows onto two lines, select the heading, then reduce the font size until the heading fits on one line.

Trouble?

If pressing [Ctrl][Enter] creates more than one hard page break, press [Backspace] to delete the unwanted hard page breaks.

1. Click the **Show/Hide ¶ button** ¶ on the Standard toolbar to display nonprinting characters in the document if necessary
   The nonprinting paragraph, space, and tab marks appear in the document. Displaying the formatting marks embedded in the document can make it easier to insert and view some of the changes you make to a document. These marks display on the screen but do not print.
2. Scroll to the heading **Steps for starting your own book group**
   You want this article to appear at the top of page 2 in the newsletter, so you'll insert a page break before the heading.
3. Place the insertion point in front of **Steps**, click **Insert** on the menu bar, then click **Break**
   The Break dialog box opens, as shown in Figure E-12.
4. Make sure the **Page break option button** is selected, then click **OK**
   Word inserts a hard page break before the heading and moves all the text after the break to the beginning of the next page, as shown in Figure E-13. The page break appears on the screen as a dotted line.
5. Scroll down to the heading **Good Reads**, then place the insertion point in front of **Good**
   You want the "Good Reads" list to start at the top of a new page.
6. Press and hold **[Ctrl]**, then press **[Enter]**
   Pressing [Ctrl][Enter] inserts a hard page break and the "Good Reads" list moves to the next page.
7. Scroll to the end of the "Good Reads" list on page 4, place the insertion point in front of **MediaLoft Headquarters**, then press **[Ctrl][Enter]**
   The text after "MediaLoft Headquarters" is forced onto the next page.
8. View the document in Print Preview, then save your changes

FIGURE E-12: Break dialog box

Inserts a hard page break

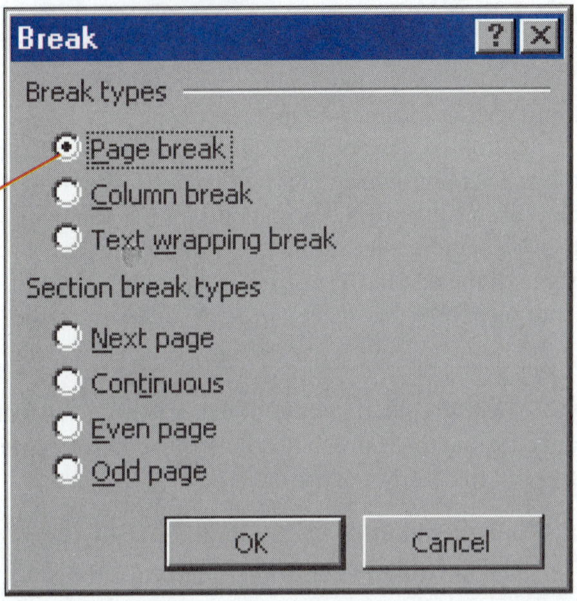

FIGURE E-13: Page break in document

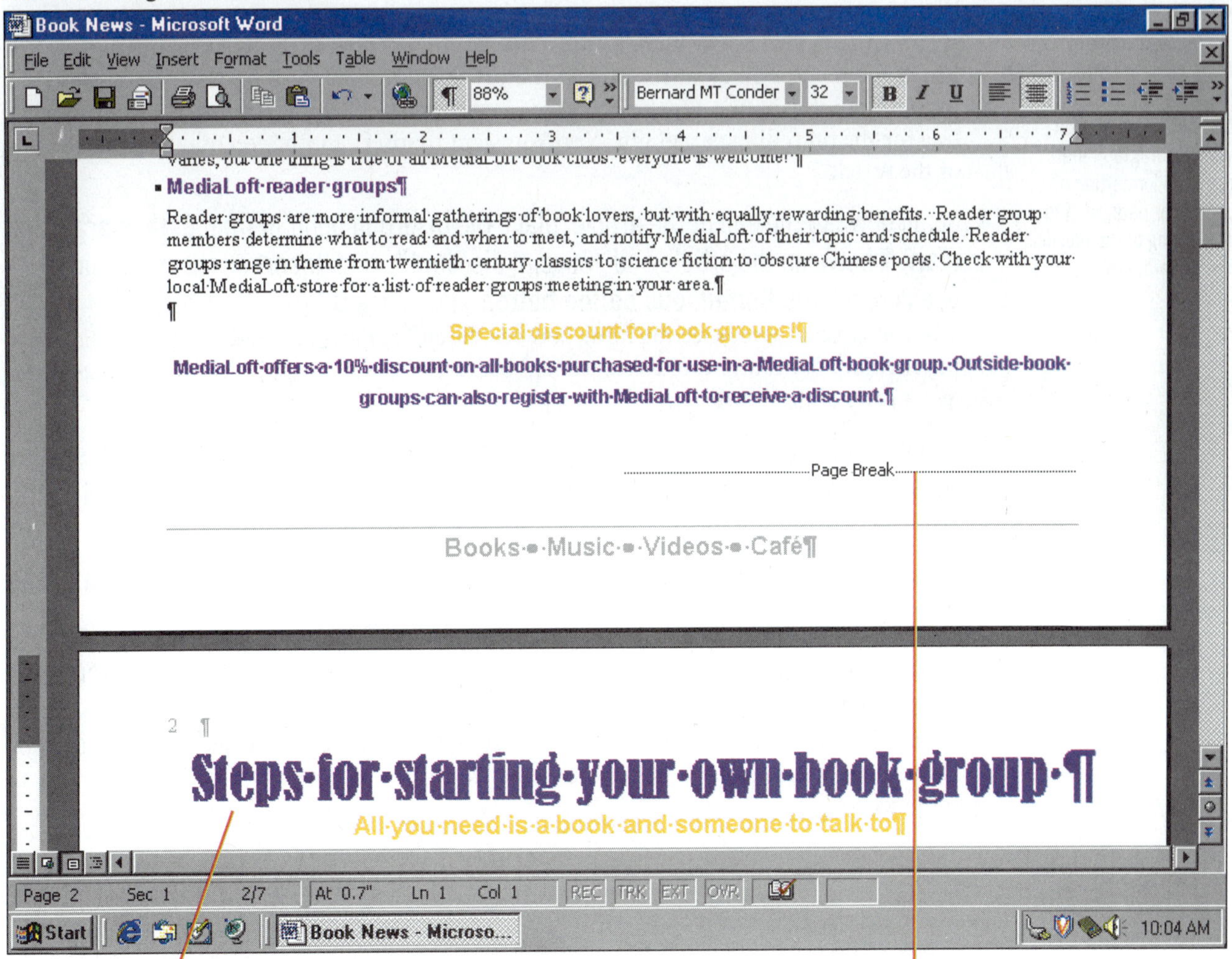

Text after the page break is forced to the top of the next page

Hard page break in document

Unit E

Word 2000

Creating Sections

Each new blank document is one section by default, but you can easily divide a document into more than one section in order to apply different page layout formats to different parts of the document. A **section** is a part of a document that is separated from the rest of the document by **section breaks**. Dividing a document into sections allows you to apply different formats to individual sections of the document. Format options include margins, columns, headers and footers, page size and orientation, page numbering, and other page layout options. Alice wants to format some of the text in the newsletter in columns. She inserts section breaks to divide the document into sections so she can easily apply different formats to different sections.

Steps

Trouble?

Adjust your zoom level as necessary to complete the steps.

Trouble?

If you delete a section break or a paragraph mark by mistake, click the Undo button on the Standard toolbar. Deleting a section break or a paragraph mark changes the formatting of the section or paragraph to the formatting of the previous section or paragraph.

1. Press **[Ctrl][Home]**, click the **Zoom list arrow** on the Standard toolbar, then click **75%**
   You plan to format the "Love to Read" article in two columns, so you'll insert a section break at the top and the bottom of the article.
2. Click in front of **Reading** at the beginning of the first paragraph in the "Love to Read" article, click **Insert** on the menu bar, then click **Break**
   The Break dialog box opens. You can use this dialog box to insert section breaks. You want to insert a continuous section break to begin a new section on the same page, at the location of the insertion point.
3. Click the **Continuous option button**, then click **OK**
   Word inserts a continuous section break (shown as a dotted double line) before "Reading", as shown in Figure E-14. When you insert a section break at the start of a paragraph, Word places the section break at the end of the previous paragraph. A section break stores the formatting information for the preceding section just as a paragraph mark stores formatting for the preceding paragraph. Next you want to insert another section break at the end of the article.
4. Scroll down to the end of the article, place the insertion point in front of the **paragraph mark ¶** between the article and "Special discount", click **Insert** on the menu bar, click **Break**, click the **Continuous option button**, then click **OK**
   Word adds a continuous section break between the end of the article and the "Special discount" information. You continue to create sections because you want to apply different formats to different parts of the newsletter.
5. Scroll to the top of page 2, place the insertion point in front of **Steps**, click **Insert** on the menu bar, click **Break**, click the **Continuous option button**, then click **OK**
   Word adds a continuous section break before the "Steps" article.
6. Scroll to the bottom of the "Steps" article, then insert a **continuous section break** in front of the first paragraph mark under the article
7. Scroll to the "Good Reads" heading at the top of page 3, click in front of **Good**, then insert a **continuous section break**, then save your changes
   Word adds a continuous section break before the "Good Reads" list, as shown in Figure E-15. Notice that the document has six sections. You are ready to apply different formats to some sections.

FIGURE E-14: Section break in document

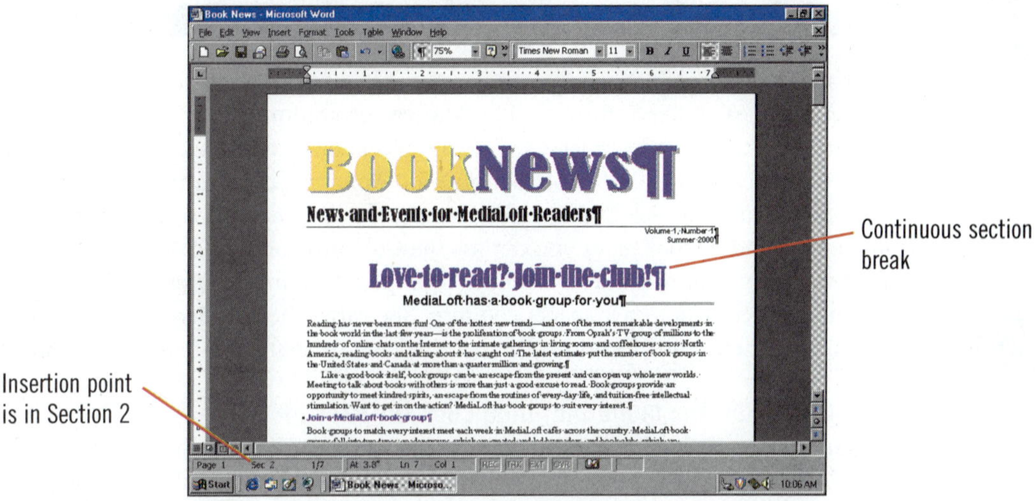

FIGURE E-15: New section break in document

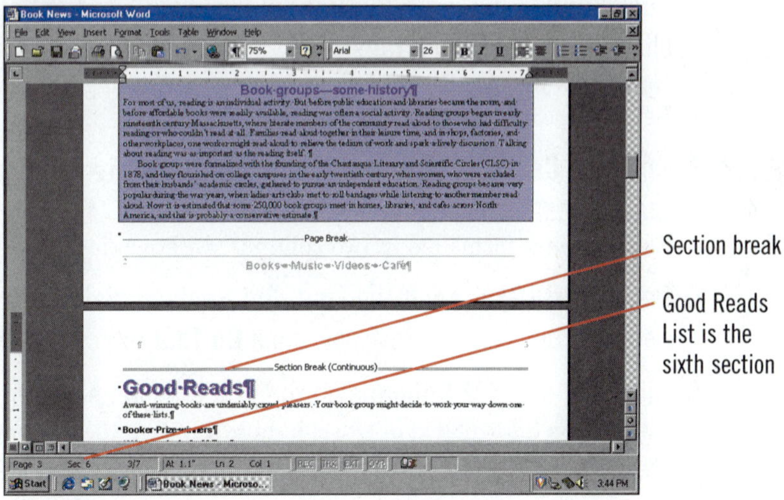

Clues to Use

Aligning text vertically on a page

By default, Word vertically aligns the first paragraph of text on a page with the top margin, but you can change the vertical alignment of text to center it between the top and bottom margins, justify it between the top and bottom margins, or align it with the bottom margin. This is especially useful for pages that are not filled with text, such as the title page of a report. You can change the vertical alignment of all the text in a document, or you can change the vertical alignment of a single section. To change vertical alignment, place the insertion point in the text you want to align, click File on the menu bar, click Page Setup, then click the Layout tab in the Page Setup dialog box, as shown in Figure E-16. Click the Apply to list arrow and select the part of the document whose alignment you want to change. Then click the Vertical alignment list arrow and select the alignment you want: Top, Center, Justified, or Bottom.

FIGURE E-16: Layout tab in Page Setup dialog box

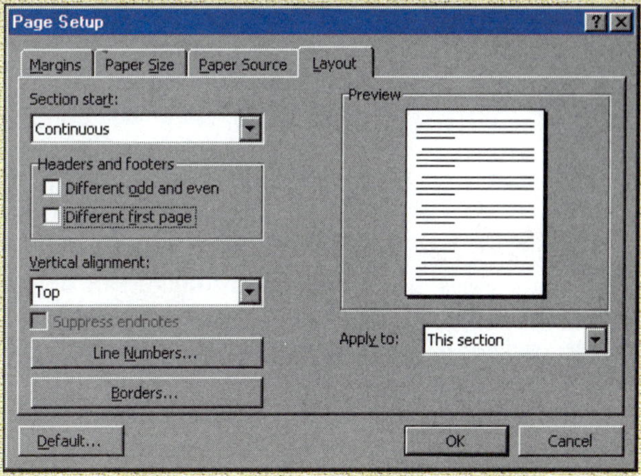

Word 2000

Unit E
Word 2000

Creating Columns

Newspapers and magazines arrange text in columns to make it easier to read and to enable more text to fit on a page. Text that is formatted in **newspaper columns** flows from one column to the next column. In a new Word document, text is arranged in one column that spans the width of the page, but you can create any number of columns. You can apply column formatting to a section, to the whole document, or to selected text. You can create standard size columns using the Columns button on the Standard toolbar, or you can use the Columns command on the Format menu to create columns and to customize the width and appearance of columns. Alice formats several sections in her document in newspaper columns. She varies the number of columns between sections to highlight different articles and make the newsletter interesting to look at and read.

Steps

1. Click **Edit** on the menu bar, then click **Go To**
   The Find and Replace dialog box opens. You can use the Go To command to navigate quickly to a page, section, or other element in a document. Table E-1 describes some ways to navigate quickly through longer documents.
2. Click **Section** in the Go to what list box, type **2** in the Enter section number text box, click **Go To**, then click **Close**
   Notice that the insertion point moved to the beginning of Section 2 (the "Love to Read" article), as indicated on the status bar.
3. Click the **Columns button** on the Standard toolbar, select **2 Columns** in the grid that appears, then click
   The section is formatted in two columns, as shown in Figure E-17.
4. Press **[Ctrl][G]** to open the Find and Replace dialog box, select **2** and type **4** in the Enter section number text box, click **Go To**, then click **Close**
5. Click , select **2 Columns** on the grid that appears, then click
   The section is formatted in two columns. You want the heading and subheading for the article to span the width of the page, so you'll change the headings to be one column.
6. Select **Steps for starting your own book group** and **All you need is a book and someone to talk to** including the paragraph marks, click , select **1 Column** in the grid that appears, click, then deselect the text
   A new section break appears after the heading, as shown in Figure E-18. Section breaks are automatically inserted wherever you apply page layout options that affect only part of a document. Next you'll format the text in Section 7.
7. Press **[Ctrl][G]**, select **4** and type **7** in the Enter section number text box, click **Go To**, click **Close**, click , select **4 Columns** in the grid that appears, then click
   The text in the section is formatted in four columns. However, the page would look better if the columns were wider, with less white space between them and divided by lines.
8. With the insertion point in Section 7, click **Format** on the menu bar, then click **Columns**
   The Columns dialog box opens, as shown in Figure E-19. You can use the Columns dialog box to change the number of columns, adjust the width and spacing of columns, create columns of unequal width, and add lines between columns.
9. Click the **Equal column width check box** to select it, click the **Spacing down arrow** twice until .3 appears, click the **Line between check box** to select it, click **OK**, then save your changes
   Now the columns are wider with lines between them. All the text now fits on four pages.

QuickTip

You can also create columns by clicking Format on the menu bar, clicking Columns, and then selecting the number of columns in the Columns dialog box.

QuickTip

You can also change column width by dragging the column markers on the horizontal ruler.

FIGURE E-17: Section formatted in two columns

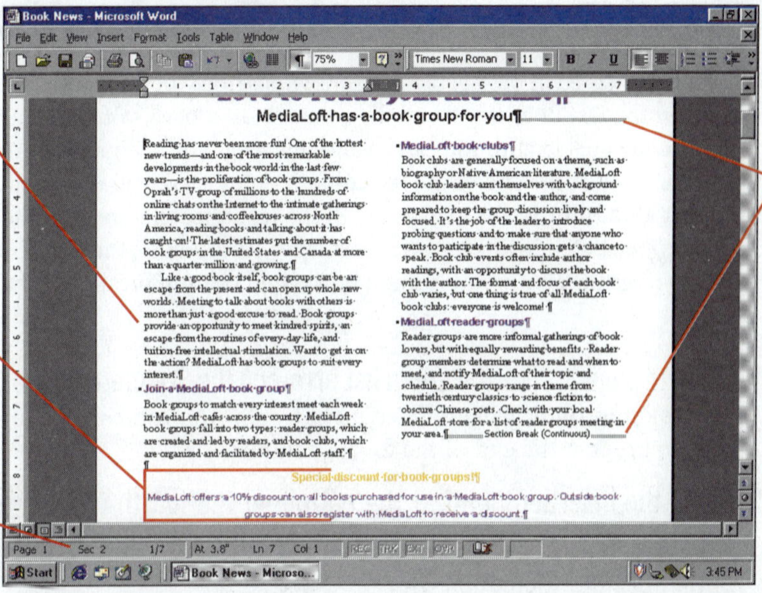

FIGURE E-18: New section break

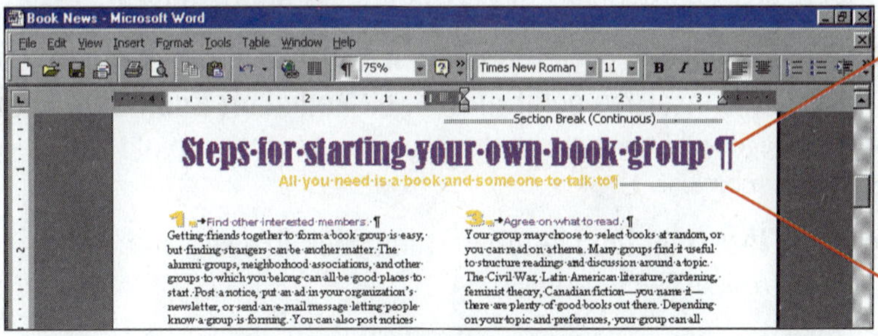

FIGURE E-19: Columns dialog box

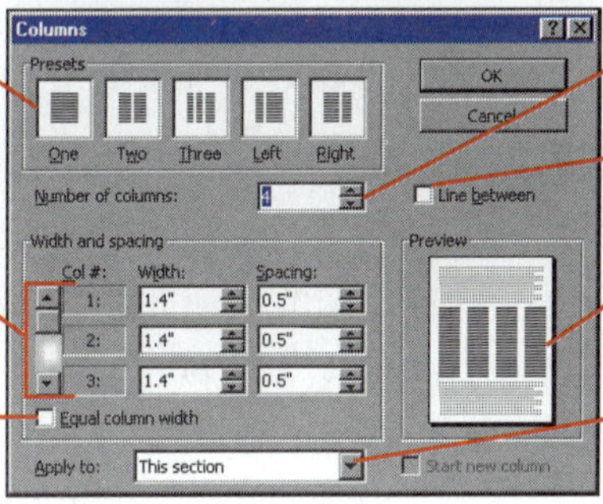

TABLE E-1: Ways to navigate a document

navigation method	description
Go To command	Use the Go To command on the Edit menu to go to a specific item in a document, such as a page, section, line, footnote, bookmark, table, or heading
Browse by object	Click the Select Browse Object button on the vertical scroll bar to open a menu of objects by which you can browse through a document, including pages, sections, tables, graphics, and fields; click the item you want to browse by, then click the Previous Page or Next Page buttons on the scroll bar to continue browsing
Document map	Click the Document Map button on the Standard toolbar to display a list of the headings in a document in the Document Map pane; click a heading in the Document Map to jump to the corresponding heading in the document
Hyperlinks	Click a text or image hyperlink to jump to the file, Web page, or location in the same document to which the hyperlink is connected

Unit E

Word 2000

Balancing Columns

Text that is formatted in newspaper columns wraps from the bottom of one column to the top of the next. When the text does not fill all the columns on a page, you may end up with a page that has columns of unequal length. You can balance the length of unequal columns by inserting a continuous section break at the end of the last column. Another way to control the flow of text in columns is to insert a **column break**, which forces the text after the break to move to the top of the next column. Before finishing her newsletter, Alice adjusts the text flow in the columns on pages 3 and 4 by inserting continuous section breaks and column breaks to balance the columns.

Steps

1. Scroll to page 3, click the **Zoom list arrow** on the Standard toolbar, then click **Whole Page**
   The columns on page 3 are unequal in length. You can balance the columns by inserting a section break at the end of the fourth column.
2. Place the insertion point at the bottom of the fourth column (click at the end of the last line of text), click **Insert** on the menu bar, click **Break**, click the **Continuous** option button, then click **OK**
   The columns on page 3 automatically adjust to become roughly the same length, and the page break moves to below the columns, as shown in Figure E-20.
3. Scroll to page 4, click the **Zoom list arrow** on the Standard toolbar, click **50%**, then place the insertion point in front of **MediaLoft Book Club Events**
   The page will look better if this text appears at the top of the next column, so you'll insert a column break.
4. Click **Insert** on the menu bar, then click **Break**
   The Break dialog box opens.
5. Click the **Column break option button**, then click **OK**
   The text moves to the top of the second column and a column break appears at the bottom of the first column, as shown in Figure E-21. You have finished formatting the newsletter. Before printing, you'll view it in Print Preview.
6. Click the **Print Preview button** on the Standard toolbar
   Pages 3 and 4 display in Print Preview.
7. Scroll up to view pages 1 and 2, click **Close** on the Print Preview toolbar, press **[Ctrl][End]** to move the insertion point to the end of the document, press **[Enter]** twice, then type your name
8. Save your changes, print the document, close the document, then exit Word

Trouble?

Be sure to place the insertion point before the page break. Adjust your zoom level as necessary to complete the steps.

QuickTip

When a page has a column break, inserting a continuous section break will not balance the columns on that page.

Clues to Use

Adding hyphenation

Another way to control text flow in a document is to use hyphenation. **Hyphens** are short dashes used to break words that appear at the end of a line. Hyphenating text eliminates the gaps that often appear in justified paragraphs and reduces ragged right edges in unjustified text. You can insert hyphens manually or you can use the hyphenation feature to hyphenate a document quickly and automatically. To hyphenate a document automatically, click Tools on the menu bar, point to Language, then click Hyphenation. In the Hyphenation dialog box, select the Automatically hyphenate document check box, then set a value in the Hyphenation zone. This zone is the distance between the margin and the end of the last word in a line. The narrower the hyphenation zone, the greater the number of hyphenated words. Click OK to turn on automatic hyphenation.

FIGURE E-20: Balanced columns

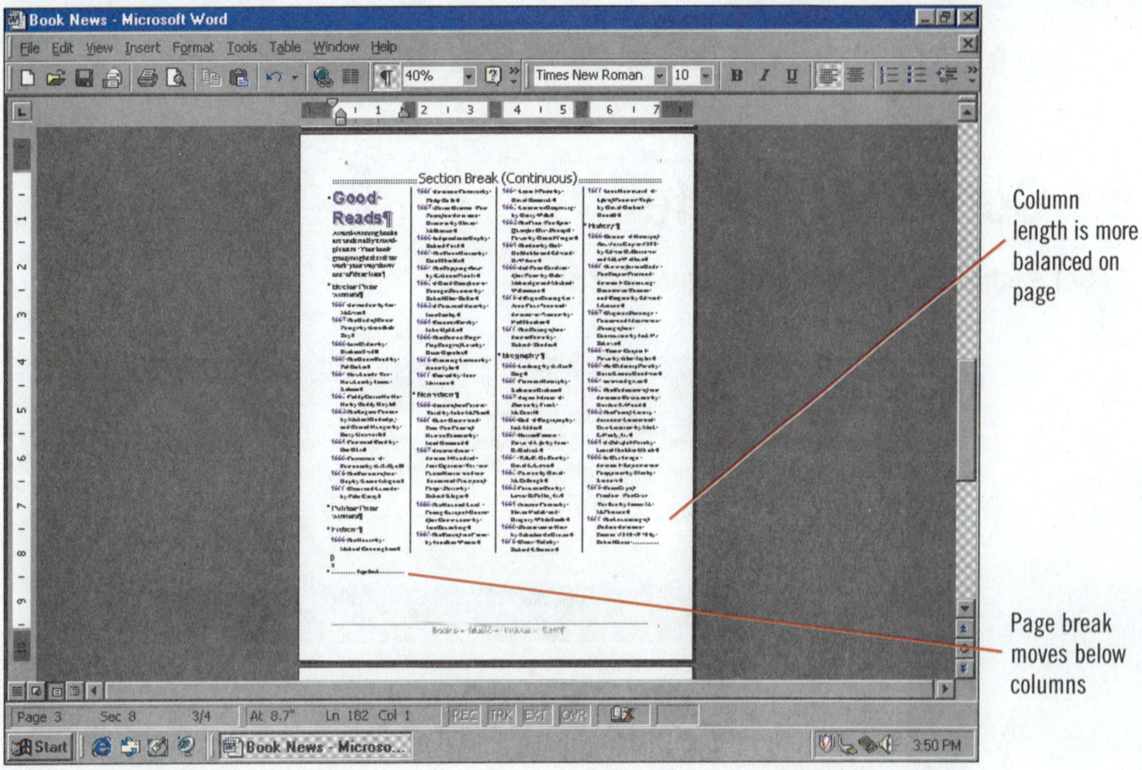

FIGURE E-21: Column break

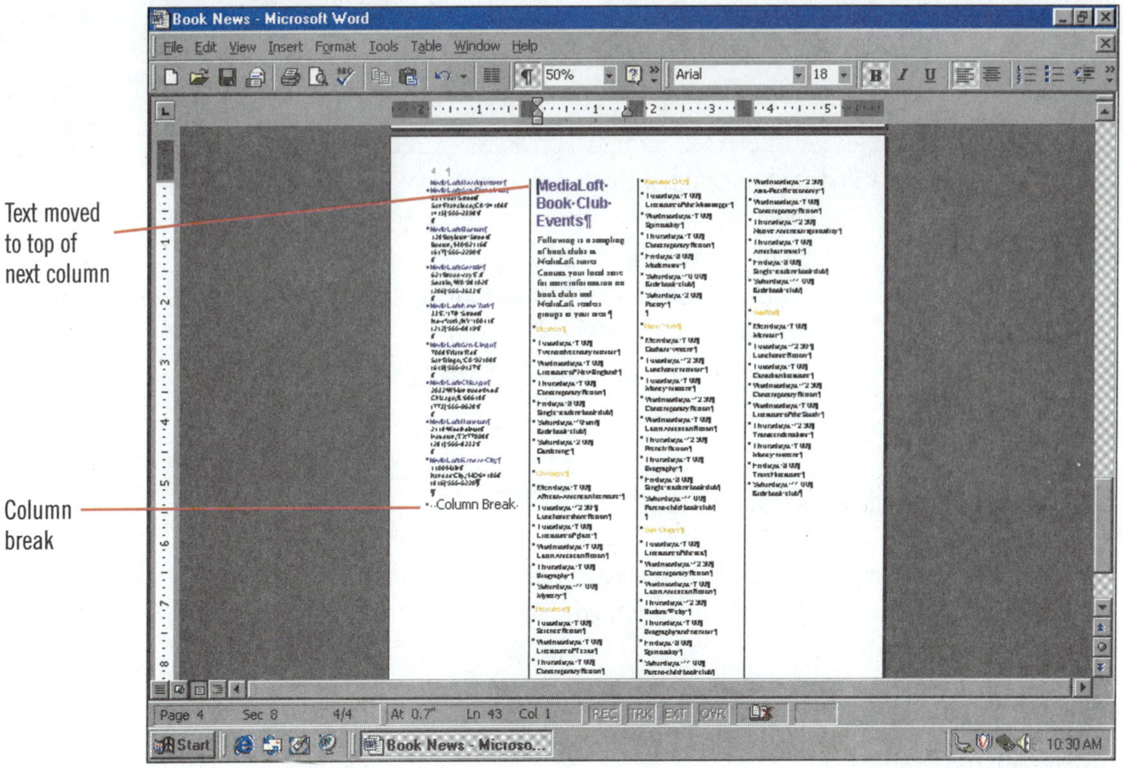

Practice

► Concepts Review

Label each element shown in Figure E-22.

FIGURE E-22

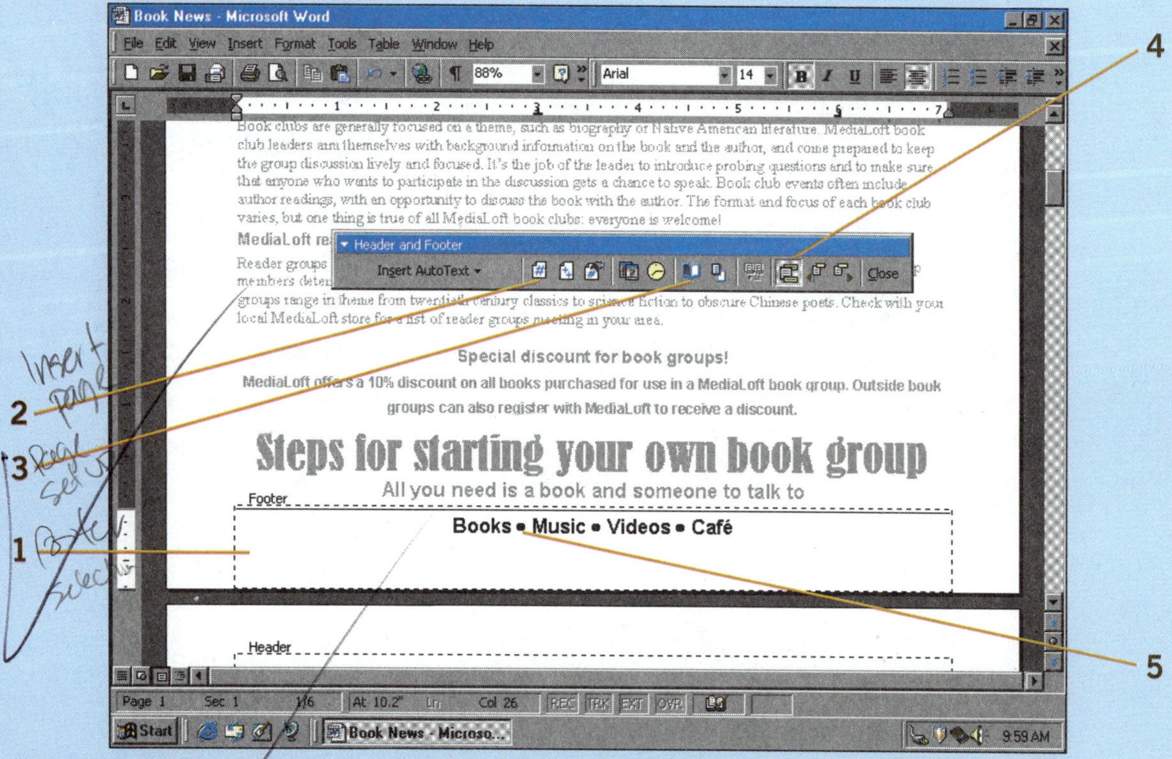

Match each term with the statement that describes it.

6. **Footer**
7. **Header**
8. **Portrait orientation**
9. **Section**
10. **Margin**
11. **Landscape orientation**

a. Text that appears at the top of every page in a document
b. The white space between the edge of the text and the edge of the page
c. A page that is wider than it is tall
d. A part of a document that can be formatted differently (such as in columns) from the rest of the document
e. Text that appears at the bottom of every page in a document
f. A page that is taller than it is wide

Select the best answer from the list of choices.

12. Which of the following options is not available in the Page Setup dialog box?

a. Adjust the margins for the top, bottom, left, and right edges of a document
b. Adjust the tab settings for a header and footer
c. Add a gutter
d. Select the page orientation

13. When you decrease the size of all margins in a document
- **a.** You increase the amount of text that will fit on the page.
- **b.** You decrease the amount of text that will fit on the page.
- **c.** The amount of text that will fit on the page does not change.
- **d.** You change the orientation of the paper.

14. Which of the following is not true about headers and footers?
- **a.** Clicking View and then clicking Header and Footer displays the Header and Footer toolbar
- **b.** You can insert fields in a header or footer
- **c.** You can create a different header or footer for the first page
- **d.** You can edit document text while you are working in headers and footers

15. The easiest way to balance column length on a page is to
- **a.** Change the number of columns on the page.
- **b.** Insert column breaks.
- **c.** Adjust the spacing between columns.
- **d.** Insert a continuous section break at the end of the page.

16. Pressing [Ctrl][Enter] inserts a
- **a.** Soft page break.
- **b.** Hard page break.
- **c.** Continuous section break.
- **d.** Column break.

17. To open headers and footers you
- **a.** Click the Switch Between Header and Footer button on the Header and Footer toolbar.
- **b.** Double-click one of the headers or footers.
- **c.** Click the Show Previous button on the Header and Footer toolbar.
- **d.** Click the Show Next button on the Header and Footer toolbar.

18. A document with mirror margins always has
- **a.** An even number of pages.
- **b.** Right and left margins.
- **c.** Outside and inside margins.
- **d.** A gutter.

19. Which of the following is not a way to insert page numbers in a header or footer?
- **a.** Click the Numbering button on the Formatting toolbar
- **b.** Click the Insert Page Number button on the Header and Footer toolbar
- **c.** Click Page X of Y on the Insert AutoText menu
- **d.** Click Insert on the menu bar, then click Page Numbers

20. To create a document that is 8½ inches high and 11 inches wide
- **a.** Select landscape orientation on the Paper Size tab in the Page Setup dialog box.
- **b.** Adjust the document margins on the Margins tab in the Page Setup dialog box.
- **c.** Change the vertical alignment on the Layout tab in the Page Setup dialog box.
- **d.** Change the width and height settings on the Paper Size tab in the Page Setup dialog box.

Skills Review

1. Change document margins.

a. Start Word and open the document WD E-2 from your Project Disk. Save the document as “Mountain Travel”.

b. Change the document margins to the following settings:

Top	1.3"
Bottom	1.3"
Left	1"
Right	1"

c. View all four pages of the document in Print Preview, then return to Print Layout view.

2. Create headers and footers.

a. Open headers and footers.

b. On the horizontal ruler, drag the right tab stop to align with the right margin at the 6½" mark. Drag the center tab stop to the 3 ¼" mark.

c. In the header, type “Mountain Travel Executive Summary”, click before the text, then press [Tab].

d. Format the header text in 11 point Arial, then bold the text.

e. Add a 1 pt. black border under the header text, making sure to apply the border to the paragraph.

f. Switch to the footer, then adjust the tab stops in the footer to correspond with the new margins you created in Step 1.

g. Press [Tab] twice, then insert today's date using the Date and Time command on the Insert menu. Select any date format you like, and deselect the Update automatically check box in the Date and Time dialog box if necessary.

h. Close headers and footers, then view the document in Print Preview.

3. Modify headers and footers.

a. Double-click the header to open the Header area.

b. Click between “Travel” and “Executive” in the header, then use the Symbol command on the Insert menu to open the Symbol dialog box.

c. Click the Font list arrow and select the Almanac MT font.

d. In the second row, click the Sun symbol (12th from the left), then click Insert. (*Hint*: If the Almanac MT font is not installed on your computer, insert a symbol of your choice.)

e. Close the Symbol dialog box. Add a space before and after the symbol as needed.

f. Select the symbol in the header and change the font size to 36.

4. Insert page numbers.

a. Switch to the Footer area.

b. Click the Format Page Number button on the Headers and Footers toolbar, change the number format to lower-case Roman numerals, then click OK.

c. Click the Insert Page Number button on the Header and Footer toolbar.

d. Close headers and footers.

e. View the page numbers in Print Preview.

5. Insert page breaks.

a. Use the Go To command to navigate to the top of page 3.

b. Scroll up, then insert a page break before the heading “Communications”.

6. Create sections.

a. Use the Go To command to navigate to the top of page 1.

b. On the first page, insert a next page section break before “Finance”.

c. Click inside the first section, then change the vertical alignment of the first section to center. (*Hint*: Use the Layout tab in the Page Setup dialog box.)

7. **Create columns.**
   a. Click in Section 2.
   b. Using the Columns button, format Section 2 in two columns.
   c. Using the Columns command, change the spacing between the columns to .4". Make sure the new columns are of equal width.
   d. Add a line between the columns.
   e. View all five pages of the document in Print Preview.

8. **Balance columns.**
   a. Hyphenate the document using the automatic hyphenation feature. (*Hint*: Click Tools on the menu bar, point to Language, then click Hyphenation.)
   b. On page 3, insert a continuous section break before the page break to balance the columns.
   c. Balance the columns on page 5.
   d. Type your name at the bottom of the title page before the section break, then preview the document. Make any necessary adjustments so that the text flows smoothly between columns and from page to page.
   e. Save your changes, print the document, then close it and exit Word.

Independent Challenges

1. You are a member of the board of directors of the North Country Community Association, a local organization devoted to helping children in your community. One of the organization's most successful programs is the North Country Project, a mentoring program that matches individual children with an adult who spends time each week with the child in school. You have agreed to take responsibility for a print publicity campaign to recruit new volunteers. You begin by drafting text for a brochure that describes the program and encourages adults to participate. When printed, this brochure will be folded in thirds.

To complete this independent challenge:

a. Start Word, open the document WD E-3 on your Project Disk and save it as "North Country".
b. View each page of the document in Print Preview to get a feel for its contents.
c. Change the page orientation of the document to landscape, then change the zoom level to Whole Page.
d. Change all the document margins to .5".
e. Format the entire document in three columns of equal width, with .4" between columns.
f. Insert a column break before the "Q" for the first question "What is the North Country Project?"; then insert another column break before the "Q" for the question "What does a volunteer do with a child at school?"
g. Insert a next page section break before the heading "The North Country Community Association".
h. At the bottom of the third column on the first page, before the section break, type "To learn more, call 555-7635." Change the font size of the new text to 28, center it, then bold the text. Format the new text in one column.
i. On the second page, add your name to the last sentence in the first column as the person to contact, then insert a column break at the bottom of the column.
j. Insert another column break in the second column, which is empty.
k. In the third column, type "The North Country Project", press [Enter], then type "One-to-One In-School Mentoring Program". This column will become the front cover of your brochure when it is printed and folded.
l. Now that the layout of the brochure is complete, use fonts, font colors, symbols, and paragraph formatting to improve the appearance of your brochure. Be sure to format the third column on the second page so that it is an eye-catching cover for the brochure.
m. Preview, save, print, then close the document.

2. You are writing a book on the arts that will be published by a small book publisher. Each chapter in your book provides an introduction to one of the arts and introduces a few prominent artists in the field. Your publisher requires that you submit your manuscript as camera-ready copy—in other words, the book's pages need to be formatted as the printed book will look. The publisher has provided a set of page layout guidelines that you must follow to format the pages of your manuscript.

To complete this independent challenge:

- **a.** Start Word, open the file WD E-4 on your Project Disk, and save it as "Chapter 2".
- **b.** Change the font of the entire document to 11-point Bookman Old Style. If this font is not installed on your computer, choose a different serif font.
- **c.** Change the alignment of all the text in the document to justify it, then turn on automatic hyphenation. (*Hint*: To justify the text, use the Select All command, then the Justify button on the Formatting toolbar.)
- **d.** Change the font size of the chapter heading to 16 points, then bold the heading.
- **e.** Go to the top of the document, then press [Enter] ten times.
- **f.** Change the paper size to 5½" wide and 8" tall.
- **g.** Change the top and bottom margins to be .9" each, and the right and left margins to be .5". Create mirror margins and add a .4" gutter on the left to allow room for the book's binding.
- **h.** Use the Layout tab in the Page Setup dialog box to create different headers and footers for odd and even pages.
- **i.** Open the header and footer areas. In the Odd Page Header area, type "Chapter 2", insert a decorative symbol of your choice, then type "A Brief History of Architecture".
- **j.** Right-align the text in the odd page header, change the font to Bookman Old Style, and italicize the text.
- **k.** Switch to the even page header, then type the title of the book, "An Introduction to the Arts" in the Even Page Header area.
- **l.** Insert the same decorative symbol after the title in the even page header, then type your name.
- **m.** Left-align the title in the even page header, change the font to Bookman Old Style and italicize the text.
- **n.** Insert page numbers that are centered in the footer. Change the font of the page numbers to Bookman Old Style. Be sure to insert a page number in both the odd and even page footers.
- **o.** Format the page numbers so that the first page of Chapter 2 begins on page 15. (*Hint*: Use the Format Page Number button on the Header and Footer toolbar.)
- **p.** Preview, save, print, then close the document.

3. You are the office manager at Swift Forestry, a Vermont firm that specializes in forest management consulting services for people who own forested land. You are trying to expand your business to attract clients from neighboring states and provinces, so you create a flyer advertising Swift Forestry that you intend to circulate in New York, New Hampshire, and Quebec. Your flyer includes a map so that potential clients can find your offices.

To complete this independent challenge:

- **a.** Start Word, open the file WD E-5 on your Project Disk, then save it as "Swift Forestry".
- **b.** Use the Zoom list arrow on the Standard toolbar to switch to Two Pages view.
- **c.** Insert a next page section break after the contact information, then change the page orientation of the second page to landscape.
- **d.** Change the left and right margins on the first page to 1". Change the top and bottom margins on the second page to be .7".
- **e.** On the first page, format the list above the address in two columns. Change the zoom level if necessary to better see your work.
- **f.** Insert a symbol in front of each item in the list to create a bullet. Browse the symbols that are available on your computer and choose a symbol that is appropriate to the content of the flyer. (*Hint*: Use a hanging indent as needed to be sure a second line of a bulleted item is aligned under the first line of that item.)

g. Add a footer to the document that includes your name aligned on the left and "Printed on recycled paper" aligned on the right. Insert the symbol for recycling or a symbol of your choice in front of the text. Adjust the tab stops so the text is properly aligned on the right.
h. Use different fonts, font colors, symbols, borders, and shading to improve the appearance and appeal of the first page of the flyer.
i. Preview, save, print, then close the document.

4. You work in the human resources department at MediaLoft. Your supervisor has asked you to create a handout for MediaLoft employees that explains the benefits of investing in a 401(k) plan. The information you need to include in the handout is posted on MediaLoft's intranet site. An intranet is a group of connected networks owned by a company or organization that is used for internal purposes. Intranets use Internet software to handle the data communications, such as e-mail and Web pages, within an organization. These pages often provide company-wide information. As with all intranets, the MediaLoft intranet limits access to MediaLoft employees.

To complete this independent challenge:

a. Start Word.
b. Connect to the Internet and use your browser to go to the MediaLoft intranet site at http://www.course.com/illustrated/MediaLoft. Click the link for the Human Resources page, then click the link for Frequently Asked Questions.
c. Select all the text on the Frequently Asked Questions page and copy it to the Clipboard. Switch to Word and paste the text from the Clipboard into a new blank document. Disconnect from the Internet when you have copied the information to Word.
d. Save the document with the filename "401K" to your Project Disk.
e. Make all four document margins 1", change the alignment of the text in the document from left-aligned to justified, then turn on automatic hyphenation.
f. Create mirror margins, then create different headers/footers for odd- and even-numbered pages.
g. Insert a page number at the outside margin and the date at the inside margin of the header. (*Hint*: The outside margin is on the left on an even-numbered page and on the right on an odd-numbered page.)
h. Use the AutoText menu on the Header and Footer toolbar to insert the filename in the even page footer, then add your name to the odd page footer. Center the text in the footers.
i. Format the entire document in two columns of equal width, with .3" of space between the two columns.
j. Select the heading "401(k) Plans", change the font size to 36, center the text, and format the heading in one column. (*Hint*: When changing the number of columns, use the selection bar to select text.)
k. Select the heading "Frequently Asked Questions" and the paragraph under it, and format the selected text in one column.
l. Insert a next page section break before the headings "401(k) Advantages" and "What is a mutual fund?"
m. Click in front of "What is a mutual fund?", type "More Questions", then press [Enter].
n. Center the headings "401(k) Advantages" and "More Questions", change their font size to 26, and format them in one column.
o. Study the layout and text flow of each page of the document. Use page breaks, column breaks, section breaks, and other page formatting options to improve the appearance of your document.
p. Use the Go To command to go to the top of the document, then browse the document by section. (*Hint*: Click the Select Browse Object button on the vertical scroll bar, click Browse by Section, then click the Next Section arrows below the Select Browse Object button to browse the document.)
q. Save your changes, then print and close the document.

▶ Visual Workshop

Open the file WD E-6 on your Project Disk and save it as "Miller Street". Format the file as shown in Figure E-23. (*Hint:* Set the right and left margins to 6".) Add your name to the bottom of the list of artists, save the file, then print a copy.

FIGURE E-23

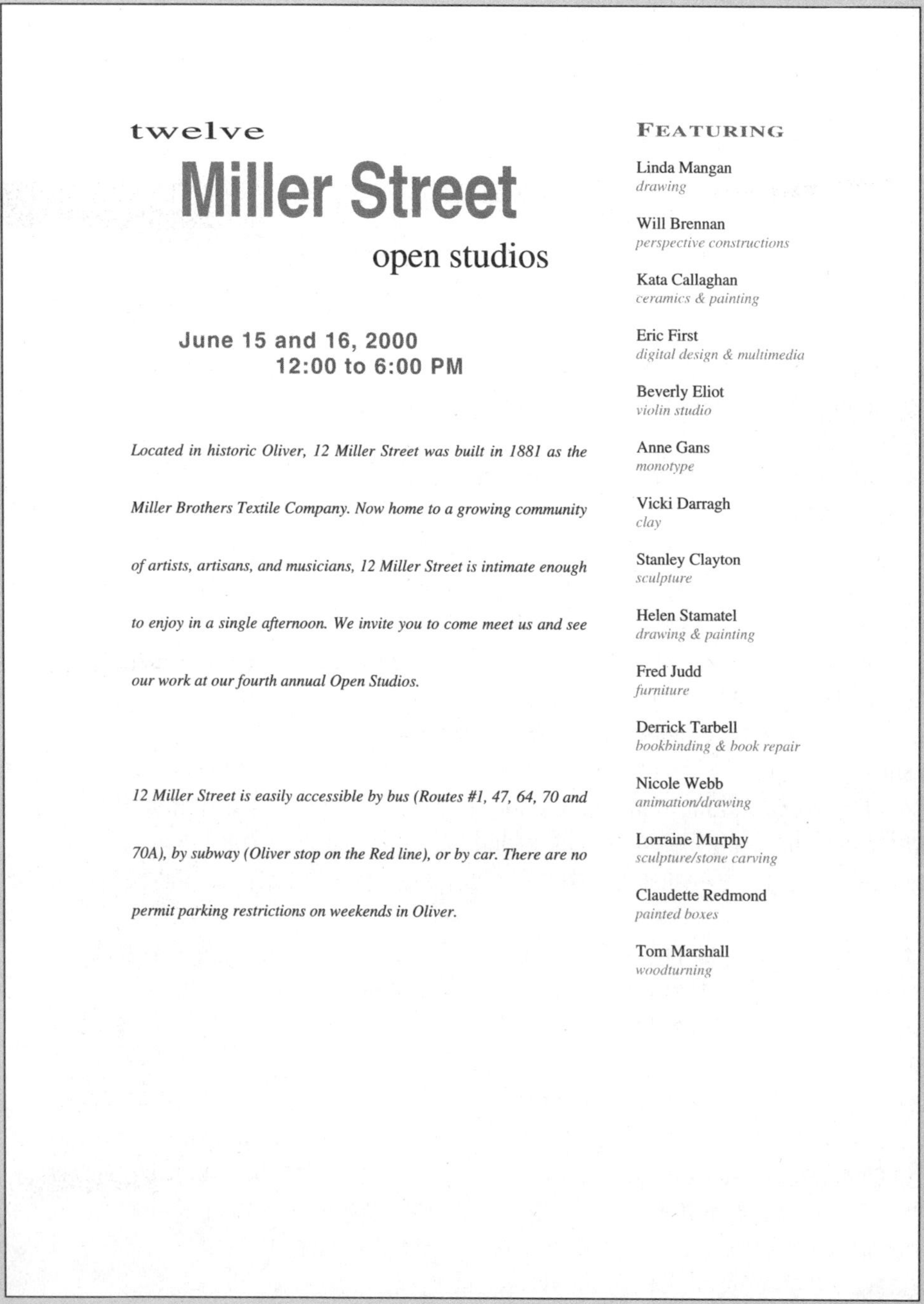

twelve

Miller Street

open studios

June 15 and 16, 2000
12:00 to 6:00 PM

Located in historic Oliver, 12 Miller Street was built in 1881 as the Miller Brothers Textile Company. Now home to a growing community of artists, artisans, and musicians, 12 Miller Street is intimate enough to enjoy in a single afternoon. We invite you to come meet us and see our work at our fourth annual Open Studios.

12 Miller Street is easily accessible by bus (Routes #1, 47, 64, 70 and 70A), by subway (Oliver stop on the Red line), or by car. There are no permit parking restrictions on weekends in Oliver.

FEATURING

Linda Mangan
drawing

Will Brennan
perspective constructions

Kata Callaghan
ceramics & painting

Eric First
digital design & multimedia

Beverly Eliot
violin studio

Anne Gans
monotype

Vicki Darragh
clay

Stanley Clayton
sculpture

Helen Stamatel
drawing & painting

Fred Judd
furniture

Derrick Tarbell
bookbinding & book repair

Nicole Webb
animation/drawing

Lorraine Murphy
sculpture/stone carving

Claudette Redmond
painted boxes

Tom Marshall
woodturning

Word 2000

Unit F

Adding

Graphics

Objectives

- MOUS ► Insert clip art graphics
- ► Wrap text around graphics
- ► Move and resize graphics
- MOUS ► Insert pictures from files
- MOUS ► Draw AutoShapes
- MOUS ► Insert text boxes
- MOUS ► Draw lines
- MOUS ► Create WordArt
- MOUS ► Use Click and Type

By adding graphics to a document you can create dramatic effects. Graphics can illustrate a point, break up the monotony of large blocks of text, and make your documents visually interesting. Word provides many built-in graphic images, called clip art, that you can add to your documents. You can also insert graphics that are created in other programs. You can also use the drawing feature in Word to create your own graphics. The marketing department at MediaLoft sponsors a variety of in-store events to encourage customers to visit MediaLoft and browse. Alice Wegman needs to create several flyers to advertise upcoming events at the San Francisco store. She uses clip art and Word's drawing features to make her flyers colorful and appealing.

Unit F
Word 2000

Inserting Clip Art

Adding clip art to your documents is a fun way to illustrate your ideas and create documents that have a powerful effect. **Clip art** is a collection of graphic images that you can insert in documents. Clip art files are stored in the Microsoft ClipGallery, which is a library of pictures, recorded sounds, and motion clips that comes with Word and is shared by all Office applications. Clip art images in the ClipGallery are organized in categories. You can browse the ClipGallery by category to find a clip art image (or "clip") that meets your needs, or you can perform a search to locate all the clips that match a keyword or topic. If you are connected to the Internet, you can also download clip art from Clips Online, a Microsoft Web site for ClipGallery users, into your ClipGallery. Alice has begun working on a flyer advertising readings for children at MediaLoft. To give the flyer some personality, she illustrates it with clip art.

Steps

QuickTip

To return personalized toolbars and menus to the default settings, click Tools on the menu bar, click Customize, click Reset my usage data on the Options tab, click Yes, then click Close.

Trouble?

If the categories do not display on your Picture tab, click the All Categories button on the ClipGallery toolbar.

QuickTip

You can also drag a clip from the ClipGallery into a document to insert it.

1. Start **Word**, open the file **WD F-1** from your Project Disk, then save it as **Readings Flyer**
   The document opens in Print Layout view.
2. Scroll down, then click in front of **Wednesday**
   You want to insert a clip art image near Wednesday.
3. Click **Insert** on the menu bar, point to **Picture**, then click **Clip Art**
   The ClipGallery opens, which displays the pictures, sounds, and motion clips that are available with Word. You can also click the Insert Clip Art button on the Drawing toolbar to open the ClipGallery.
4. Click the **Pictures tab** if necessary
   The clip art pictures are organized in categories. Word includes many default categories, but you can add your own categories to the ClipGallery as well. You can scroll to see all the categories in your ClipGallery.
5. Click the **Cartoons** category
   The clips in the Cartoons category appear on the Pictures tab, as shown in Figure F-1.
6. Click the **owl clip** in the top row
   A menu with four buttons appears when you select a clip art image. You can use this menu to insert the selected clip, preview it, add it to another category, or search for similar clips.
7. Click the **Insert Clip button**
   The clip is inserted in the document at the location of the insertion point. The ClipGallery remains open, which is useful if you want to insert more than one clip art image into a document. Some of the clips in your ClipGallery may be stored on your Office 2000 CD. When you click the Insert Clip button, if a message appears saying the file is stored on a disc, insert your Office 2000 CD, then click Retry.
8. Click the **Close button** on the ClipGallery title bar
   The owl image appears in the document at the location of the insertion point, as shown in Figure F-2. Notice that the image is larger than you want it to be and that it displaced the text when it was inserted. When you insert an image, it is part of the line of text in which it was inserted (an **inline** graphic). To allow graphics to be placed near text without being part of a line of text, you must apply text wrapping to the graphic. You will learn how to wrap text around graphic objects in the next lesson.
9. Click the **Save button** on the Standard toolbar

FIGURE F-1: Cartoons clips in Microsoft ClipGallery

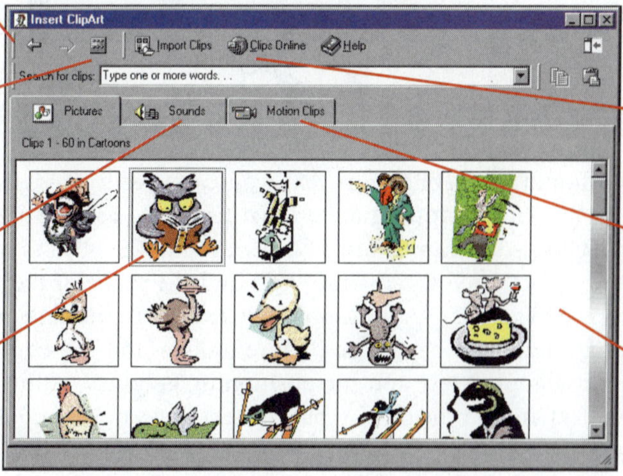

FIGURE F-2: Clip art image in the document

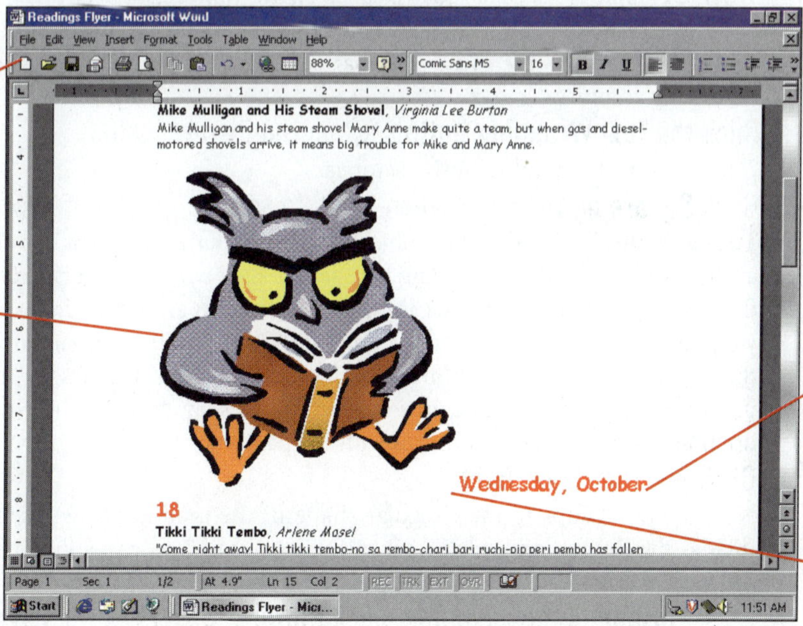

CLUES TO USE

Downloading clips from the Microsoft ClipGallery Live Web site

For an even broader range of clips to illustrate your documents, you can download images from the ClipGallery Live Web site. To get clips from the Microsoft ClipGallery Live Web site, click the Clips Online button on the ClipGallery toolbar, then click OK. This launches your browser and connects you to the site. Once you have read and accepted the License Agreement, which specifies how you are permitted to use clips from the site, the ClipGallery Live window opens. You can view the clips by type (clip art, photos, sounds, and motions), search by keyword, or browse the clips by category. Figure F-3 shows clips found using the keyword "Australia."

FIGURE F-3: Microsoft ClipGallery Live Web site

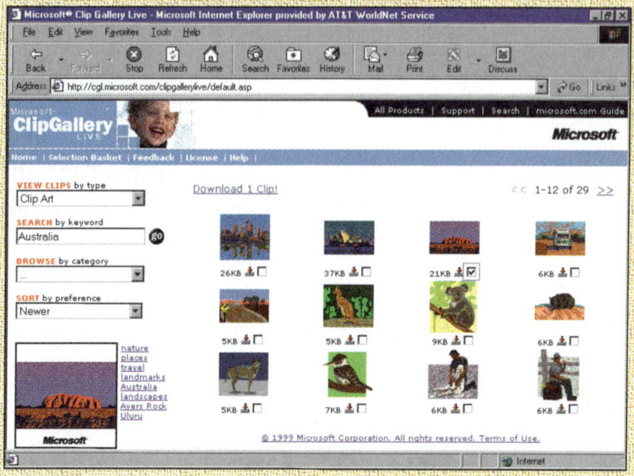

Unit F

Word 2000

Wrapping Text Around Graphics

When positioning a graphic near text, you can specify how you would like the text to wrap around the graphic. **Wrapping** means that text flows around a graphic object rather than over it. You can choose to wrap text in a square around the object's frame, wrap it above and below the graphic object, or you can wrap it around the shape of the graphic itself. When you apply text wrapping to an inline graphic object, it becomes a **floating** graphic. You can move a floating graphic anywhere on a page. The Picture toolbar and the Format Picture dialog box contain options for wrapping text and for positioning graphics within text. Alice wraps the document text around the owl so that the text flows more smoothly on the page.

Steps

Trouble?

If your Picture toolbar does not open, click View on the menu bar, point to Toolbars, then click Picture. If necessary, move the toolbar by dragging its title bar to a new location.

QuickTip

The anchor symbol appears when nonprinting characters are displayed.

1. Click the **Show/Hide ¶ button** on the Standard toolbar to display nonprinting characters if necessary, then click the **owl graphic** to select it
   When a graphic is selected, squares called **sizing handles** appear on all four sides and corners of the object. Before you wrap text around an inline graphic, its sizing handles are black. When you select a graphic, the Picture toolbar also opens. The Picture toolbar includes buttons for modifying graphics.
2. Click the **Text Wrapping button** on the Picture toolbar
   A menu of text wrapping options appears.
3. Click **Square** on the menu, then scroll to see the graphic if necessary
   The text wraps to the sides of the object frame so that the graphic is set off in the text as a square, as shown in Figure F-4. The sizing handles are now white, which indicates that the graphic is a floating object. Usually the first thing you should do after inserting a graphic is to apply text wrapping to it so that it becomes a floating graphic. Notice that an anchor symbol appears in the upper-right corner of the graphic object, next to the "Wednesday" paragraph. The anchor indicates the graphic is anchored to the "Wednesday" paragraph. When a graphic object is **anchored** to a paragraph, it moves with the paragraph if the paragraph moves.
4. Click , then click **Tight**
   Now the text wraps to the irregular shape of the graphic image itself. However, the image divides the lines of text, making it difficult to read. You can adjust text wrapping so that it only wraps to one side of an image.
5. Click **Format** on the menu bar, click **Picture,** then click the **Layout tab**
   The Layout tab in the Format Picture dialog box includes several Wrapping style options as well as options for aligning graphic images horizontally between the margins. You want to use the more advanced options.
6. Click **Advanced**, then click the **Text Wrapping tab**
   The Text Wrapping tab in the Advanced Layout dialog box, shown in Figure F-5, includes options for changing the wrapping style, determining which sides of the object to wrap text around, and changing the spacing between the edge of the image and the edge of the text. You want to wrap the text around the right side of the image only.
7. Click the **Right only option button** in the Wrap text area, click the **Right up arrow** in the Distance from text area once so that **.2"** displays, click **OK**, then click **OK**
   The text wraps around the right side of the image only, as shown in Figure F-6. The text, which originally fit on one page, now flows to page 2 because the graphic was added.
8. Deselect the graphic, click , then save your changes

FIGURE F-4: Text wrapped in a square around image

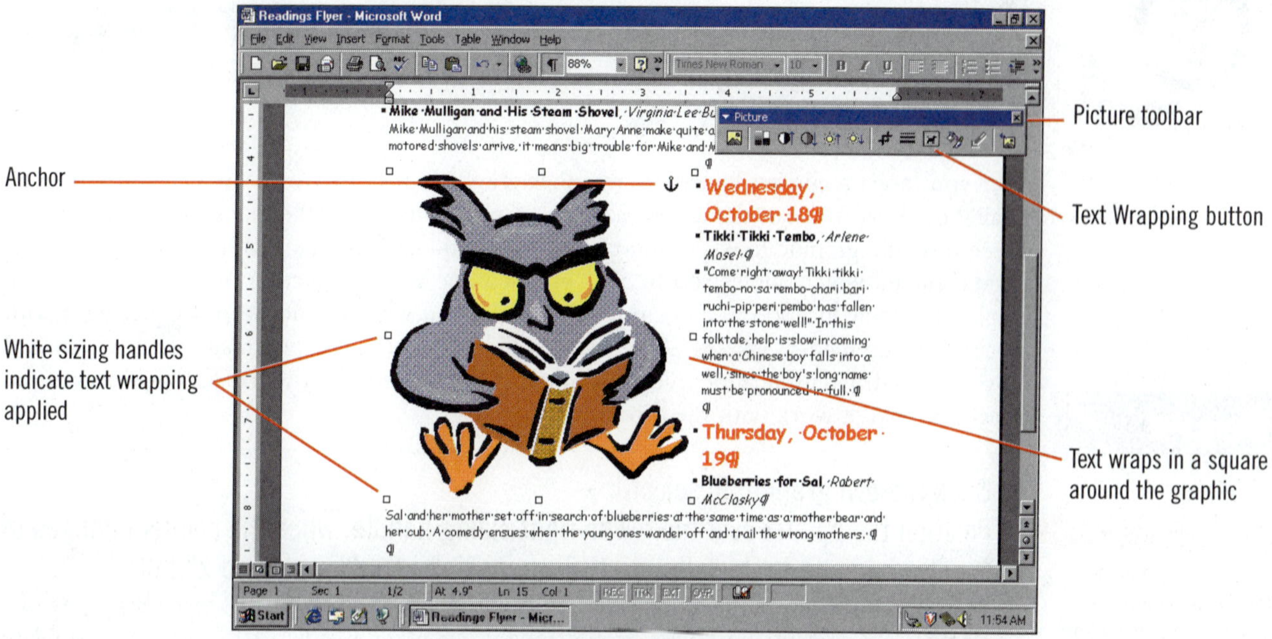

FIGURE F-5: Text Wrapping tab in Advanced Layout dialog box

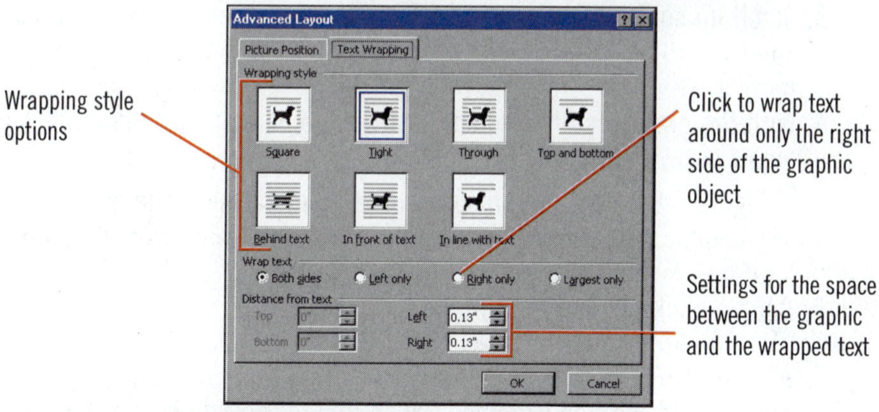

FIGURE F-6: Text wrapped tightly to the right of the image

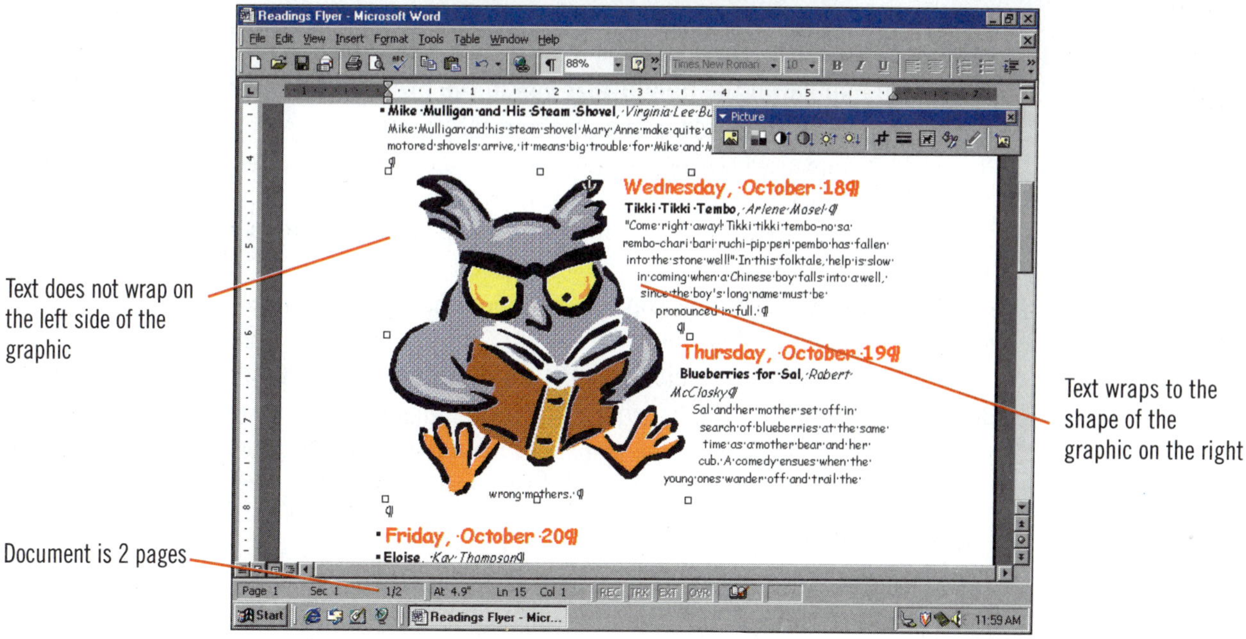

Unit F
Word 2000

Moving and Resizing Graphics

After you insert a clip art image or any other graphic object in Word, you can resize it to be smaller or larger. You can change the size of a graphic object using the mouse, which allows you to see how the graphic looks as you change it, or you can use the Picture command on the Format menu, which allows you to alter precisely the size of a picture. You can also move a graphic to a new location in a document by dragging it with the mouse, or by placing it with precise measurements. Alice reduces the size of the clip art image she inserted and moves it to a different location in the document. She then adjusts the size and position of the image to make it work with the flow of text.

Steps 1 2 3 4

1. Click the **owl graphic** to select it
2. Position the pointer over the **lower-right sizing handle**, when the pointer changes to ↘, drag up and to the left until the graphic is about **2"** wide and **2"** tall
   The size of the image is reduced, as shown in Figure F-7. Dragging a corner sizing handle changes the size of the object proportionally; in other words, its height and width are reduced or enlarged by the same percentage. Next you want to move the graphic up the page.
3. Scroll up so that "Monday" and the graphic appear in the document window
   You want to move the graphic to the left of the text "Monday". You can drag a graphic to move it.
4. With the graphic still selected, position the pointer over the graphic, when the pointer changes to ✥, drag the graphic up so its top aligns with the top of **Monday** as shown in Figure F-8, release the mouse button, then deselect the graphic
   The graphic is now located to the left of "Monday". You decide the graphic would look better if it were slightly larger.
5. Double click the **owl graphic**
   The Format Picture dialog box opens. You can double-click any graphic object to open the Format Picture dialog box, where you can choose from a variety of options for sizing, positioning, coloring, and wrapping text around the object.
6. Click the **Size tab**
   The Size tab allows you to enter precise measurements for a graphic. You can also enter a percentage by which you want to reduce or enlarge the graphic proportionally.
7. Select the number in the **Height text box** in the Size and rotate area, type **2.75**, then click in the **Width text box** in the Size and rotate area
   The width automatically changes to 2.64" when you click the Width text box. When the Lock aspect ratio check box is selected, you only need to enter a height or a width. Word automatically calculates the other measurement to keep the resized graphic proportional to the original.
8. Click **OK**
   The graphic is enlarged. Now you can reposition the graphic to make it work with the flow of text and make your flyer more eye-catching.
9. Drag the graphic to the left so that the right edge of the graphic frame aligns at about the **2"** mark on the horizontal ruler, then deselect the graphic
   Notice that you can position the graphic in the margin now that text wrapping is applied. Compare your flyer with Figure F-9 and make any necessary adjustments.
10. Save your changes

QuickTip

Dragging a side, top, or bottom sizing handle changes only the height or width of the graphic so that the object's proportions change.

QuickTip

You can also click Format on the menu bar, then click Picture to open the Format Picture dialog box.

FIGURE F-7: Resized graphic

FIGURE F-8: Owl graphic being dragged to new location

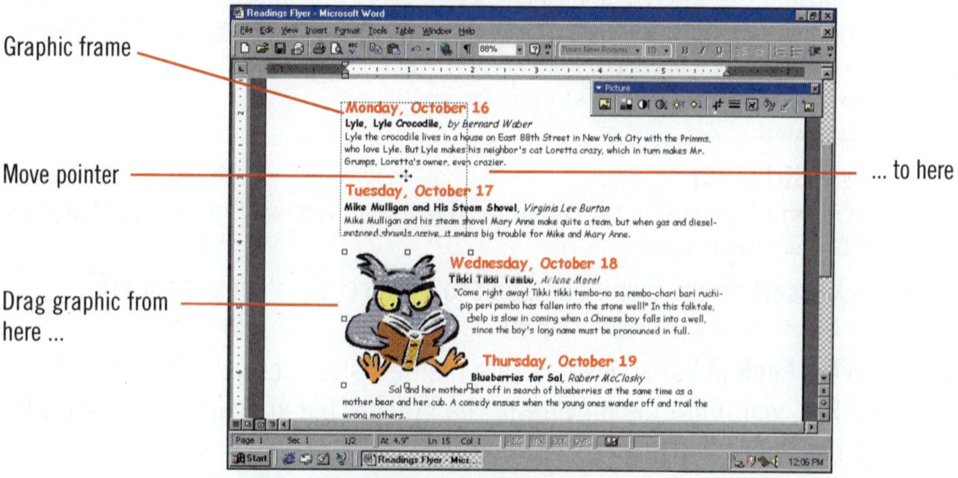

FIGURE F-9: Resized graphic moved

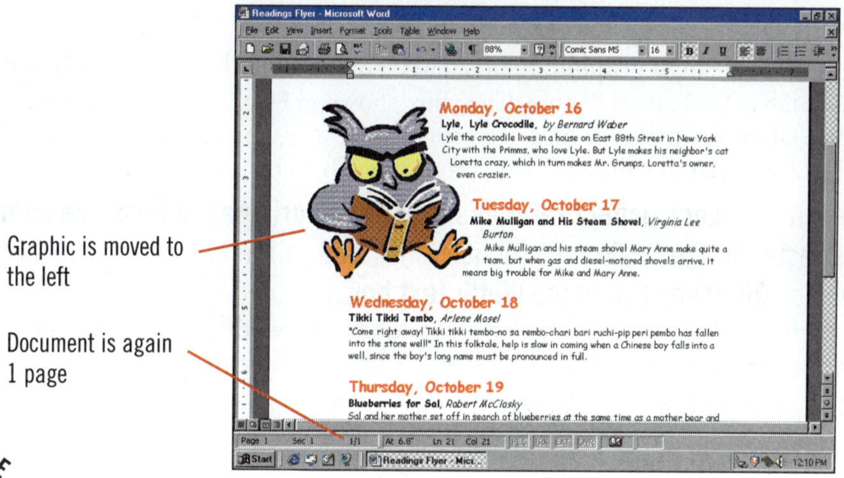

CLUES TO USE

Moving inline and floating graphics

When working with graphics it is important to understand that usually you will need to change an inline graphic to a floating graphic to be able to move it where you want in a document. When you insert a graphic in a document, it is automatically inserted as an inline graphic, which makes it part of the document's text. Inline graphics have black sizing handles and can only be moved to another location in the text – you can't move an inline graphic to a blank area of a page. Floating graphics, on the other hand, have white sizing handles and can be moved anywhere on a page, independent of a document's text. To change an inline graphic to a floating graphic, you must apply a text wrapping style to the graphic, *even if there is no text on the page.* To change an inline graphic to a floating graphic, use the Text Wrapping button on the Picture toolbar or double-click the graphic, click the Layout tab in the Format Picture dialog box, select a text wrapping style other than "In line with text", then click OK.

Unit F
Word 2000

Inserting Pictures from Files

In addition to the clip art graphics that come with Word, you can insert graphics that were scanned or created in other graphics programs into your documents. Most graphics created in other programs have a bitmapped format. **Bitmapped graphics** are composed of many small dots, called **pixels**, that contain information about color and intensity. Some of the more common file extensions for bitmapped graphics are .gif, .tif, .jpg, and .bmp, but there are many others as well. You can insert graphics created in other graphics programs into your documents using the Picture, From File command on the Insert menu. Alice wants to add the MediaLoft logo to the flyer. The logo graphic was created in another graphics program, so Alice needs to insert the graphic file into the document.

Steps

1. Press **[Ctrl][End]**
   The insertion point is at the end of the document. You want to add the MediaLoft logo near the contact information.
2. Click **Insert** on the menu bar, point to **Picture**, then click **From File**
   The Insert Picture dialog box opens.
3. Use the **Look in list arrow** to locate the files stored on your Project Disk, click the file **WD F-2**, wait until the preview of the graphic file appears in the Insert Picture dialog box, then click **Insert**
   The logo graphic is inserted at the location of the insertion point. Since the logo is too big to fit on page 1, it is now on page 2. You want to reduce the size of the logo so that it will fit at the bottom of page 1.
4. Double click the **logo graphic**, then click the **Size tab** in the Format Picture dialog box
   The Size tab in the Format Picture dialog box, shown in Figure F-10, opens. You already used the Size tab to enter precise measurements to size a graphic. Now you will use it to scale graphics. You want to reduce the logo proportionally to be 20% of its current size.
5. Make sure the **Lock aspect ratio** and **Relative to original picture size check boxes** are selected in the Scale area, double-click **100** in the Height text box in the Scale area, type **20**, then click in the **Width text box**
   Because the Lock aspect ratio check box is selected, the width automatically changes to 20% when you click the Width text box. You also want to wrap the text around the graphic.
6. Click the **Layout tab**, click **Tight** in the Wrapping style area, click **OK**, then scroll down to locate the logo graphic in the document
   The logo is much smaller, but still on page 2. You'll need to drag the logo to position it to the right of the text at the bottom of page 1.
7. Select the **logo graphic** if necessary, then drag it up to the bottom of page 1 so that its right edge is even with the right margin, as shown in Figure F-11
   The text wraps to the left of the logo and the flyer is once again just one page.
8. Replace the name **Alice Wegman** with your name, then click the **Print Preview button** on the Standard toolbar
   Compare your flyer with Figure F-12.
9. Close Print Preview, save your changes, click the **Print button** on the Standard toolbar, then close the file
   A copy of the flyer prints.

FIGURE F-10: Size tab in Format Picture dialog box

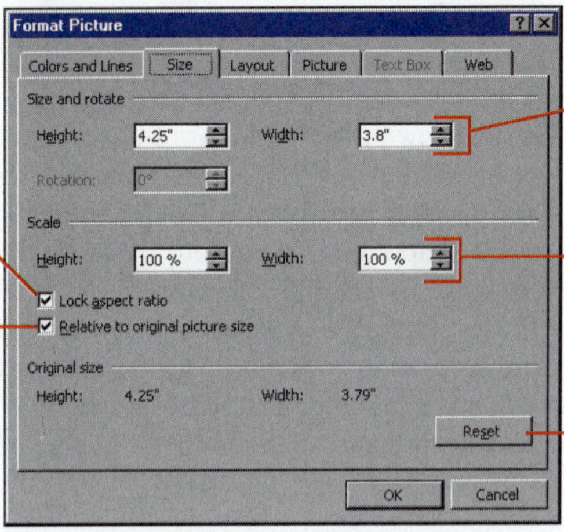

FIGURE F-11: Logo graphic being dragged to a new location

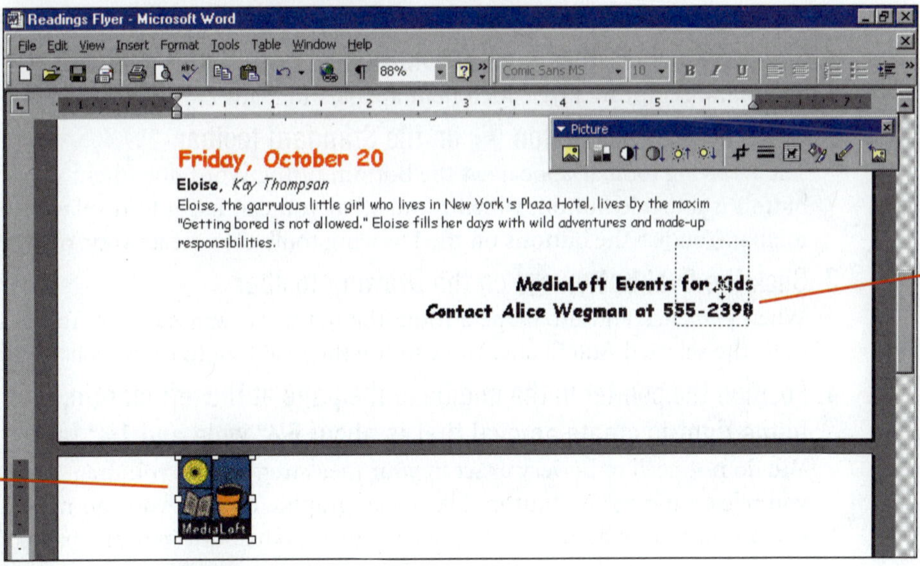

FIGURE F-12: Completed Readings flyer

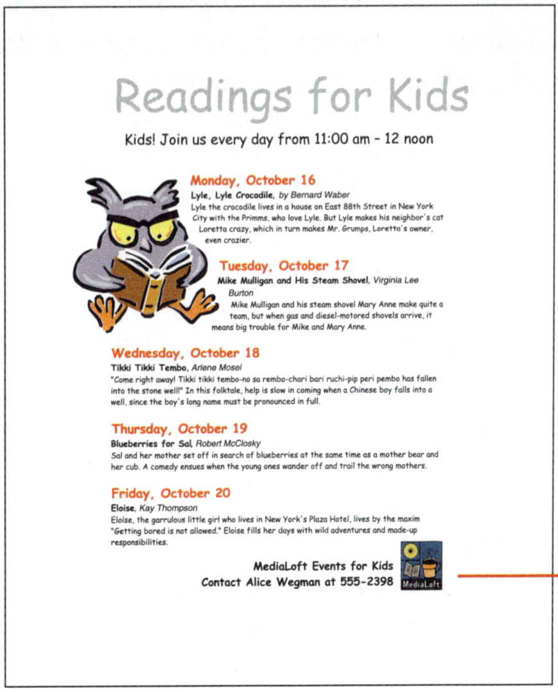

Unit F

Word 2000

Drawing AutoShapes

You are not limited to clip art and graphics created in other programs to illustrate your documents. You can also create your own graphics in Word using the drawing tools on the Drawing toolbar. The Drawing toolbar includes tools for drawing lines and shapes, as well as tools for applying color, shadows, and fills to the images you create. Using the AutoShapes button on the Drawing toolbar, you can create simple shapes quickly without having to draw them from scratch. **AutoShapes** include squares, triangles, ovals, block arrows, lightening bolts, stars, banners, and other fun designs. Once you insert a shape, you can resize it, rotate it, color it, or combine it with other shapes to create more complex graphics. The marketing department has invited the author of a new book about paper sculpture for kids to demonstrate several projects at MediaLoft. Alice uses AutoShapes to make the flyer she creates for the event colorful and eye-catching.

Steps 1 2 3 4

1. Click the **New Blank Document button** on the Standard toolbar, save the new document as **Sculpture Flyer** to your Project Disk, click the **Zoom list arrow** on the Standard toolbar, then click **Whole Page**
   The blank Sculpture Flyer document appears in Print Layout view.
2. Click the **Drawing button** on the Standard toolbar
   The Drawing toolbar appears at the bottom of the Word document window. The Drawing button is a toggle button, which means that you can use it to display or hide the Drawing toolbar. You use the buttons on the Drawing toolbar to create your own graphic images.
3. Click the **Oval button** on the Drawing toolbar
   When you click an AutoShape button, the pointer changes to +. You drag this pointer to draw the selected AutoShape. You can use the oval tool to draw ovals and circles.
4. Position the pointer in the middle of the page at the left margin, then drag down and to the right to create an oval that is about **6½" wide** and **1¾" tall**
   You do not need to be very exact in your measurements as you drag. An oval appears when you release the mouse button. Like other graphic objects, you can move, resize, and wrap text around AutoShapes. You'll move the oval to the bottom of the page.
5. Position the pointer over the **oval shape**, then when the pointer changes to ✥, drag the oval down so that its bottom edge is about **1"** from the bottom edge of the page
6. Click **AutoShapes** on the Drawing toolbar, point to **Stars and Banners**, then click the **Explosion 2 button** on the menu that appears
   The AutoShapes menu contains the categories of lines and shapes that you can easily draw. You can point to each item on the menu to view the different AutoShapes that come with Word.
7. Click about **¼"** in from the upper-left corner of the page, then drag to create a shape that is about **4"** wide and **4"** high
   Compare your shapes with Figure F-13. You can move or resize your shapes if necessary so that your flyer resembles the figure. Next you want to add color to your shapes.
8. With the star shape selected, click the **Fill Color list arrow** on the Drawing toolbar, click **Red** (1st box, 3rd row), click the **Line Color list arrow**, click the **Yellow box** (3rd box, 4th row), click the **Line Style button**, then click the **4½ pt solid line**
   The star shape is filled with red and outlined with a 4½ point yellow line.
9. Click the **oval shape**, click , click **Violet** (7th box, 3rd row), click , click , then click the **4½ pt solid line**, compare your flyer with Figure F-14 and make adjustments as needed, and save your changes

Trouble?

Click the More Buttons button on the Standard or Formatting toolbar to locate buttons that are not displayed on your toolbar.

QuickTip

Pressing [Shift] while you drag with the Oval tool creates a circle.

QuickTip

To check or change the exact size of a shape you draw, double-click the shape, then check the measurements on the Size tab in the Format AutoShape dialog box.

QuickTip

When you select a new color, the active color changes.

FIGURE F-13: AutoShapes in document

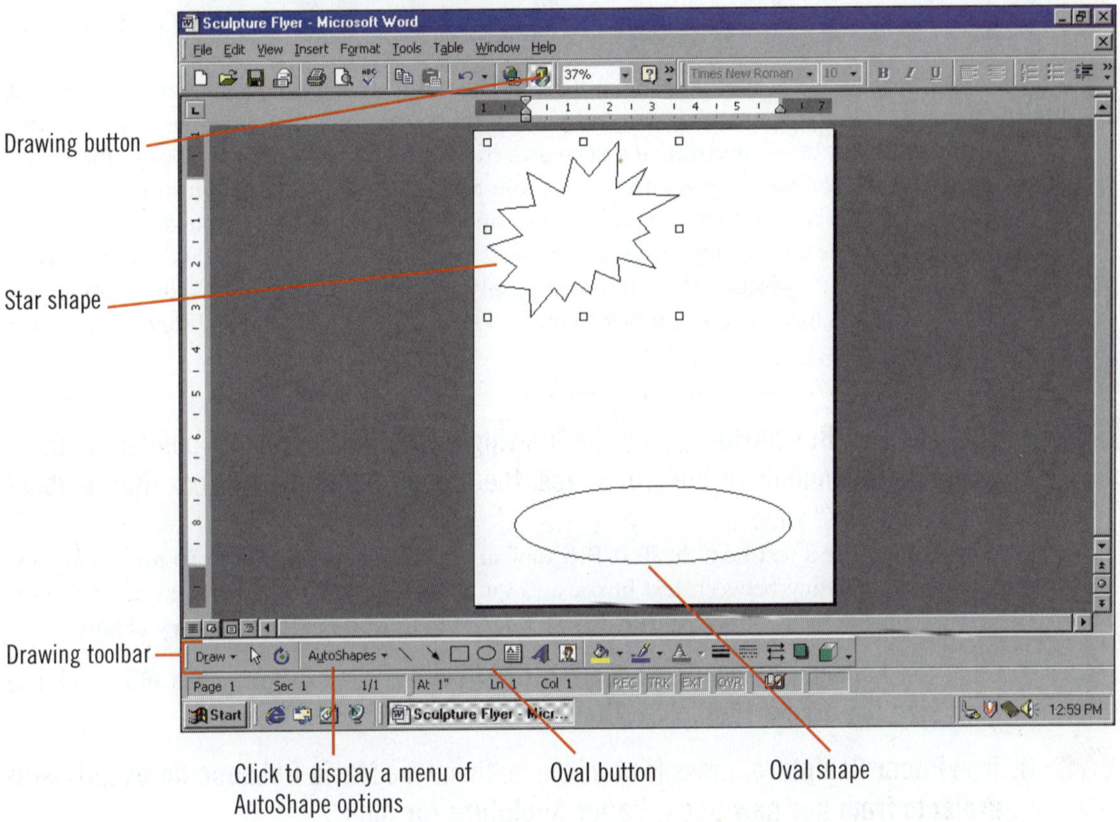

FIGURE F-14: Colors applied to AutoShapes

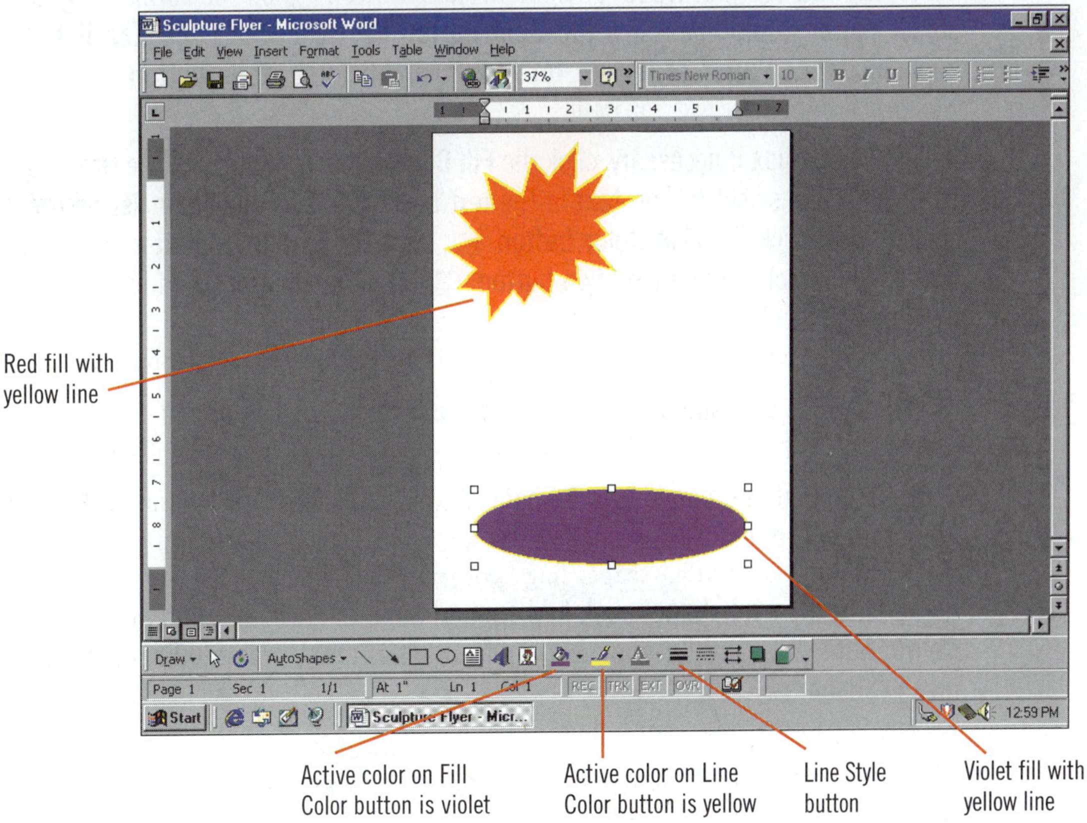

Unit F
Word 2000

Inserting Text Boxes

When you want to add text to your documents as a graphic image, you can create a text box. A **text box** is a container into which you can place text and graphics. For example, if you wanted to create a **pull quote** — decorative text in an article that you set off by wrapping the article text around it — you would place the pull quote text in a text box. You can draw a text box around existing text or graphics, or you can draw an empty text box and add text or graphics to it. Like other graphic objects, text boxes can be resized, moved, and enhanced using the tools on the Drawing toolbar. Alice draws an empty text box and adds information about the event to it. She then formats the text box to make it stand out. Finally, she adds text boxes to the oval and star shapes.

Steps 1 2 3 4

Trouble?

If your Text Box toolbar does not appear, click View on the menu bar, point to Toolbars, then click Text Box.

1. Click the **Text Box button** on the Drawing toolbar, place the + pointer about ½" below the left-middle of the star shape, then drag to create a text box that is about **3" high and 5½" wide**
   When you create a text box, the Text Box toolbar appears. It contains buttons for linking text boxes, for navigating between text boxes, and for changing the direction of text in a text box. Before typing in the text box, you'll change the font and font size of the text you will type.
2. Click the **Font list arrow** on the Formatting toolbar, click **Comic Sans MS**, click the **Font Size list arrow**, then click **26**

QuickTip

To change the margins in a text box, double-click the patterned frame of the text box, click the Text Box tab in the Format Text Box dialog box, then change the margin settings.

3. Type **Paper Sculpture**, press **[Enter]** twice, then type **Maria DeLeone helps kids with projects from her new book, Paper Sculpture for Kids**
   If the text does not all fit in the text box, drag a corner of the text box to enlarge it. You can format text in a text box just as you would format text elsewhere in a document.
4. Select the text you just typed, click the **Center button** on the Formatting toolbar, select **Paper Sculpture**, click the **Bold button**, click the **Font Size list arrow**, click **36**, select **Paper Sculpture for Kids**, then click the **Italic button**
   Next you'll format the text box itself
5. Select the **text box** if necessary, click the **Fill Color list arrow** on the Drawing toolbar, click **Blue**, select **all the text** in the text box, click the **Font Color list arrow**, click **Yellow**, click the **Line Color button**, click the **Line Style button**, click the **6 pt solid line**, click the **Dash Style button**, click **Square Dot** (third line down), then deselect the text box
   Compare your text box with Figure F-15. You can also enter text in AutoShapes.

QuickTip

You can also create an empty text box by clicking the Text Box button, and then clicking once in the document window.

6. Right-click the **star shape**, then click **Add Text** on the pop-up menu
   The shape changes to a text box. You can add text or graphics inside the shape.
7. Change the font and font size to **24 point Comic Sans MS**, type **MediaLoft Events for Kids!**, select the text, click , click , click , then deselect the graphic
   If the text does not fit in the shape, drag a corner of the shape to enlarge it.
8. Right-click the **oval shape**, click **Add Text**, change the font and font size to **26 point Comic Sans MS**, type **October 21st, 1:00**, press **[Enter]**, type **MediaLoft Café**, then press **[Spacebar]**
   Pressing [Spacebar] adds the accent to "Café".
9. Select the text in the oval shape, click , click , click , deselect the shape, then save your changes
   Compare your flyer with Figure F-16.

FIGURE F-15: Formatted text box

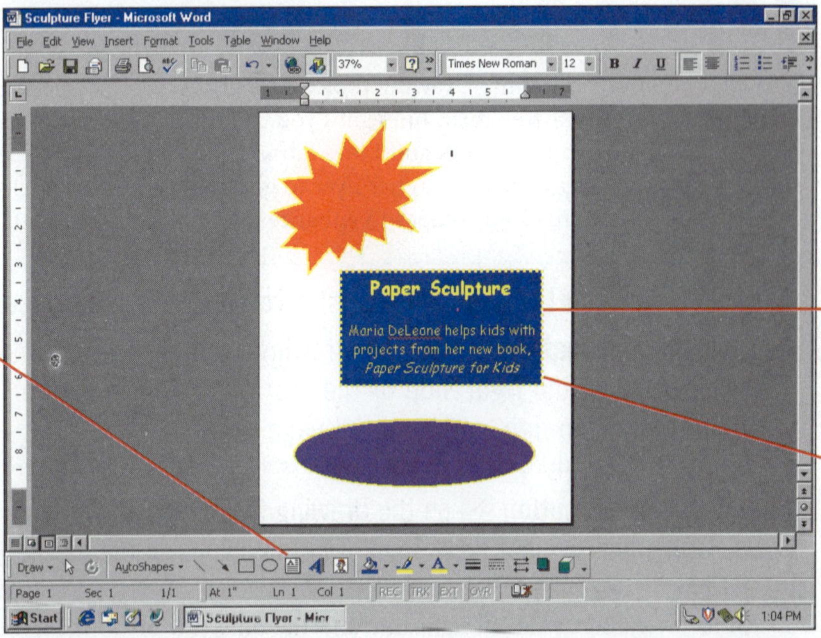

Text Box button

Text box is blue with yellow text

Line around text box is yellow square dots

FIGURE F-16: Text in AutoShapes

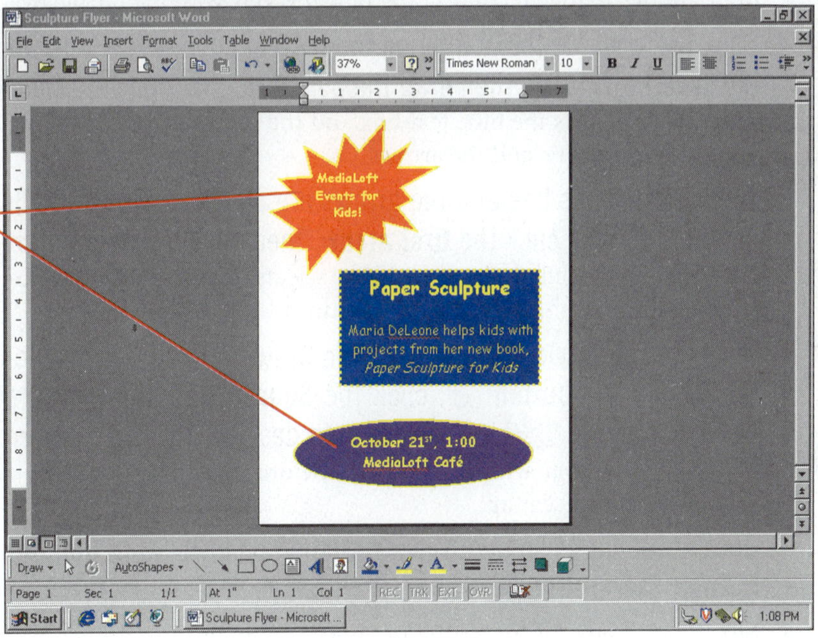

Text is added to AutoShapes

CLUES TO USE

Creating callouts

When you want to draw a reader's attention to a specific item in a document, you can create a callout to that item. A **callout** is a graphic object that contains text and a line that points to the item you want to call attention to. To create a callout, click AutoShapes on the Drawing toolbar, point to Callouts, then click a callout style on the menu. Position the pointer in the location you want to call out in the document, then drag the pointer to the location where you want the callout text to appear. After you release the mouse button, type the callout text in the text box, then deselect the callout shape. You can format a callout using the tools on the Drawing toolbar. To resize a callout, select it, then drag its sizing handles. To reposition the callout text, select the callout text box, then drag it to a new location. To change the location the callout points to, select the callout line, then drag a yellow sizing handle to a new location.

Unit F

Word 2000

Drawing Lines

Lines that you draw using the Drawing toolbar are also graphic objects. You can draw straight lines, arrows, curved, or free-form lines, and you can format lines using any of the tools on the Drawing toolbar or on the Colors and Lines tab in the Format AutoShape dialog box. Alice adds several decorative lines to her flyer to give it a stylish look. Before finishing her flyer, she also adds several small star shapes to enhance the finished document.

Steps

1. Click **[Ctrl][Home]**, click the **Zoom list arrow** on the Standard toolbar, then click **50%**
2. Click the **Line button** on the Drawing toolbar, position the + pointer at the inside point on the right side of the star as shown in Figure F-17, then drag the pointer to the top right corner of the page
   A straight line in the default format appears. Next you'll draw an arrow.
3. Click the **Arrow button** on the Drawing toolbar, position the + pointer at the right end of the line you just drew, then drag the pointer to the top-middle edge of the blue text box
   An arrow connects the straight line and the blue text box. When you draw an arrow, the arrowhead appears at the end of the line when you release the mouse button. Next, you'll draw another arrow to connect the blue text box with the purple oval.
4. Click, position the pointer on the bottom edge of the **blue text box** about ½" from the lower-left corner, then drag the pointer to the top-middle edge of the **purple oval**
   An arrow connects the blue text box and the purple oval. Next you'll change the line style and color of the line and the arrows.
5. Scroll so that the line and the arrows are all visible, click the **line** to select it, press and hold **[Shift]**, click the **first arrow**, then click the **second arrow**
   Pressing [Shift] while you select objects selects several objects at once. Now you can format all three lines with the same format settings.
6. Click the **Line Style button** on the Drawing toolbar, click the **6 pt solid line**, click the **Dash Style button**, click the **Square Dot** (third dash style), click the **Line Color list arrow**, click **Red**, then deselect the line and arrows
   Compare your flyer with Figure F-18. Before finishing your flyer, you'll add a few more AutoShapes to spice it up.
7. Click **AutoShapes** on the Drawing toolbar, point to **Stars and Banners**, then click the **5-Point Star button**
8. Position the pointer under the red star shape, drag to draw a 5-point star shape that is about 1/2" high and 1/2" wide, click the **Fill Color list arrow** on the Drawing toolbar, then click the **Yellow box**
   A yellow star shape appears under the red star shape.
9. Repeat step 8 to draw 6 more 5-point stars in other white areas of the flyer, right-click one of the stars, click **Add Text**, type your initials, then enlarge the star if necessary to fit your initials
   Your initials will identify the flyer as yours when you print it.
10. Preview your flyer in Print Preview, compare it to Figure F-19, save your changes, print a copy of the flyer, then close the file

QuickTip

To resize a line, drag a sizing handle. To move a line, place the pointer over the line, when the pointer changes to , drag the line to a new location.

QuickTip

Double-click the Line or Arrow buttons to draw more than one line or arrow. When you are finished, click the button again to return to the I-beam pointer.

QuickTip

You can also format lines using the Colors and Lines tab in the Format AutoShape dialog box. Double-click a line to open the Format AutoShape dialog box.

QuickTip

You can also use the Copy and Paste commands to create a copy of the graphic and then drag the copy to a new location.

FIGURE F-17: Line drawn in flyer

FIGURE F-19: Completed Sculpture flyer

FIGURE F-18: Formatted line and arrows

CLUES TO USE

Drawing curved, freeform, and scribble lines

In addition to the straight lines and arrows that you can draw using the Line and Arrow buttons, you can also use the AutoShapes menu to draw curved, freeform, and scribble lines in your documents. Click AutoShapes on the Drawing toolbar, point to Lines, then click the Curve, Freeform, or Scribble buttons. Lines and shapes drawn using the Curve and Freeform Line tools are connected by nodes. Click the location where you want the line to begin, move the mouse pointer to draw a curved or freeform line, click to create a node, move the mouse again to create another line, and so on. When you are finished drawing the line or shape, double-click to turn off the line tool. The Scribble tool works more like a pencil on paper: to draw a line, press the mouse button, and then move the mouse pointer to draw as you would draw with a pencil. When you have finished drawing, click to turn off the Scribble tool and deselect the graphic.

Unit F

Word 2000

Creating WordArt

WordArt is another powerful graphics tool that you can use to give your documents visual flair and impact. **WordArt** is a graphic object that contains specially formatted text. Text in WordArt objects is formatted in unique shapes, orientations, and patterns that you can easily modify and customize. You create WordArt using the WordArt button on the Drawing toolbar. Alice needs to create a third flyer to advertise weekly musical performances in the MediaLoft Café. She creates a WordArt object to headline the flyer and to draw the attention of readers.

Steps

1. Click the **New Blank Document button** on the Standard toolbar, save the new document as **Music Flyer** to your Project Disk, click the **Zoom list arrow** on the Standard toolbar, then click **Page Width**
   You'll insert the WordArt object at the top of the page.
2. Click the **Insert WordArt button** on the Drawing toolbar
   The WordArt Gallery dialog box opens, as shown in Figure F-20. The WordArt Gallery displays the various styles you can choose for your WordArt text.
3. Click the second style in the third row from the top, then click **OK**
   The Edit WordArt Text dialog box opens. In this dialog box you type the text you want to format as WordArt. If desired, you can also change the font and font size of the WordArt text.
4. Type **Music at MediaLoft**, then click **OK**
   The WordArt object appears in the document with the settings you choose and the WordArt toolbar appears. The WordArt toolbar contains buttons for creating and modifying WordArt objects. It opens whenever a WordArt object is selected. You want to enlarge the WordArt object so that it spans the width of the page.
5. Position the pointer over the lower-right corner sizing handle until the pointer changes to ↘, press **[Ctrl]**, then drag down and to the right so that the object is about **2"** tall and **5½"** wide
   Pressing [Ctrl] while you drag to resize an object keeps the object's center fixed in place. As you drag to resize an object, it can be difficult to gauge the size of the object using the rulers. If you want to check or change the exact size of the WordArt graphic, you can select it, click the Format WordArt button on the WordArt toolbar, and then click the Size tab in the Format WordArt dialog box. The exact height and width of the selected object appear in the Size and rotate area on the Size tab. Next you'll move the WordArt object to the top of the page.
6. Position the pointer over the WordArt text, and when the pointer changes to ✥, drag the object so that its top is about **.8"** from the top of the page and it is centered
   Use the rulers to help you place the object. The upper-middle sizing handle should be centered on the page and just above the top margin. Compare your document with Figure F-21 and make any necessary adjustments. Once you create, size, and position your WordArt object, it's simple to change its style, shape, color, and other formatting options to achieve the look you want.
7. Click the **WordArt Same Letter Heights button** on the WordArt toolbar
   The upper- and lower-case letters change to become the same height.
8. Click the **WordArt Gallery button** on the WordArt toolbar, click the second style in the fourth row from the top, then click **OK**
   The WordArt changes to a new style.
9. Click the **WordArt Shape button** on the WordArt toolbar, then click the **Double Wave 1 button** on the menu that appears
   The shape of the WordArt text changes. Compare your document with Figure F-22. You might want to experiment with several different WordArt shapes before saving the document.
10. Deselect the WordArt, then save your changes

QuickTip

To change the color of WordArt text, click the Format WordArt button on the WordArt toolbar. In the Format WordArt dialog box, select from the options on the Colors and Lines tab.

FIGURE F-20: WordArt Gallery dialog box

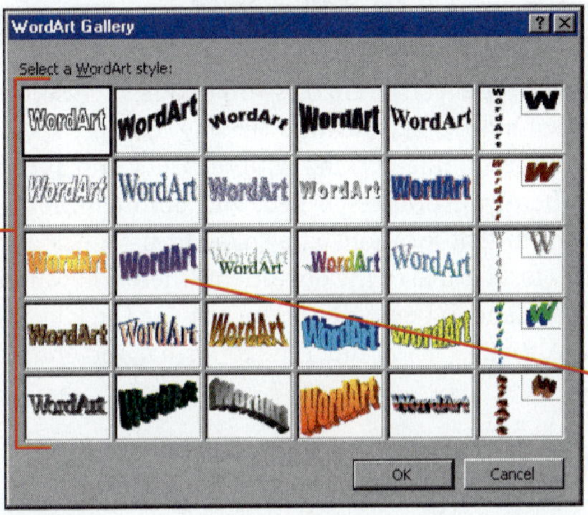

FIGURE F-21: WordArt in document

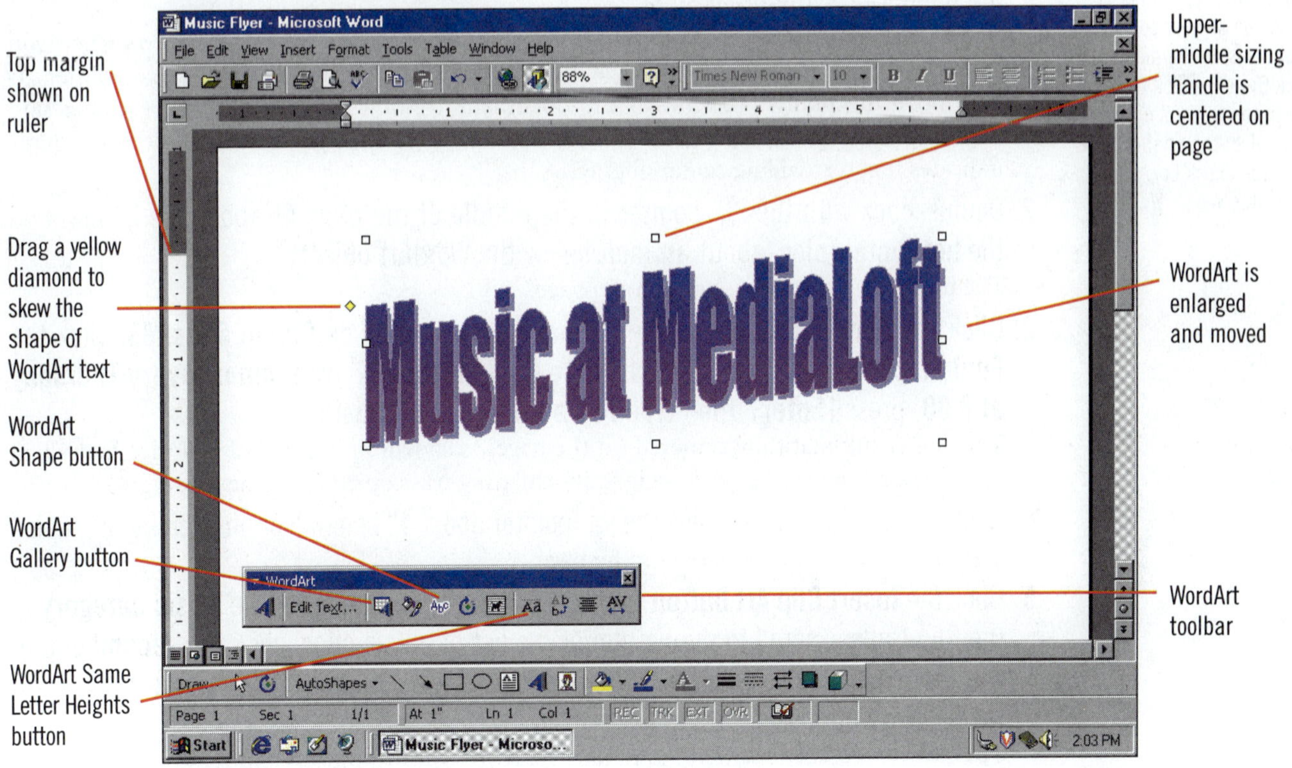

FIGURE F-22: Modified WordArt

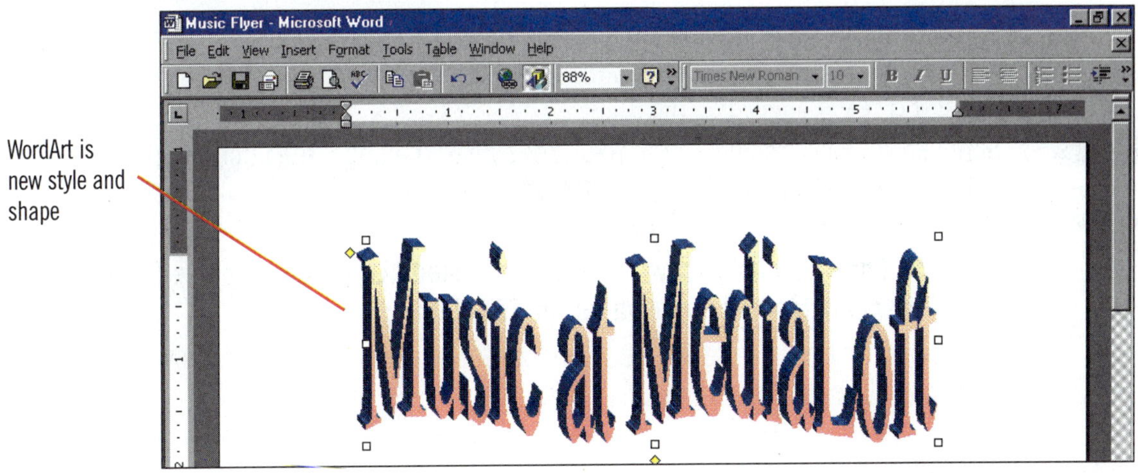

Word 2000

Unit F

Word 2000

Using Click and Type

Word's **Click and Type** feature enables you to quickly insert text, graphics, tables, and other items in a blank area of a document without having to apply special formatting, such as alignment or indents, to the item. Double-clicking with the Click and Type pointer places the insertion point in the location where you double-clicked, and automatically applies the formatting necessary to position an item in that location. The shape of the Click and Type pointer indicates the format settings in effect for the area of the document where you want to insert an item. Table F-4 describes the different Click and Type pointers. You can use Click and Type in Print Layout or Web Layout view. Alice uses Click and Type to format and enter text and clip art in her flyer.

Steps

Trouble?

If Click and Type is not turned on on your computer, click Tools on the menu bar, click Options, click the Edit tab in the Options dialog box, select the Enable click and type check box, then click OK.

1. Click a blank area under the WordArt in the middle of the document, then slowly move the pointer over the blank area

   Notice that the I-beam pointer changed to one of the Click and Type pointers when you clicked. Clicking once in a blank area of the screen enables the Click and Type pointer. As you move the pointer around in the document window, the pointer shape changes to indicate how text will be formatted in that area of the document. For example, the shape indicates that text will be center-aligned.

2. Double-click with the pointer in the middle of the page at about the 3" mark on the horizontal ruler (about an inch below the WordArt object)

   The insertion point is centered on the page.

3. Click the **Font list arrow** on the Formatting toolbar, click **Comic Sans MS**, click the **Font Size list arrow**, click **24**, click the **Bold button**, type **Join us every Thursday at 8:00**, press **[Enter]**, then type **For an evening of music**

   The text is automatically centered on the page, as shown in Figure F-23. Notice that when you pressed [Enter], the center-aligned formatting was copied to the next paragraph.

4. Scroll down, then double-click the pointer about **1"** below "For an evening of music"

   The insertion point is centered on the page.

5. Click the **Insert Clip Art button** on the Drawing toolbar, click the **Music category** in the Clip Gallery, scroll to the bottom of the list of music clips, click the **second clip in the last row** (a gold and black graphic showing a guitar and a keyboard), click the **Insert Clip button**, then close the ClipGallery

   The clip art graphic is centered on the page. If you click to the left and right of the graphic, you'll notice the Click and Type pointer change to or to indicate formatting for wrapping text around a graphic.

6. Scroll down, double-click the pointer about **1"** below the graphic, type **MediaLoft Cafe**, then press **[Spacebar]** to add the accent to Café

   The text is center-aligned on the page.

Trouble?

If you double-click outside the margin, the Page Setup dialog box may open. If so, click Cancel, move the pointer until the appears, then double-click again.

7. Scroll down, move the pointer to the right side of the page, then double-click the pointer about **1"** below "MediaLoft Café"

   The insertion point is aligned with the right margin.

8. Click the **Font Size list arrow**, click **18**, type **MediaLoft Events,** press **[Enter]**, then type **For schedules call [your name] at 555-2398.**

9. Preview your flyer in Print Preview, compare it with Figure F-24, save your changes, print a copy of the flyer, then close the file

FIGURE F-23: Center-aligned text

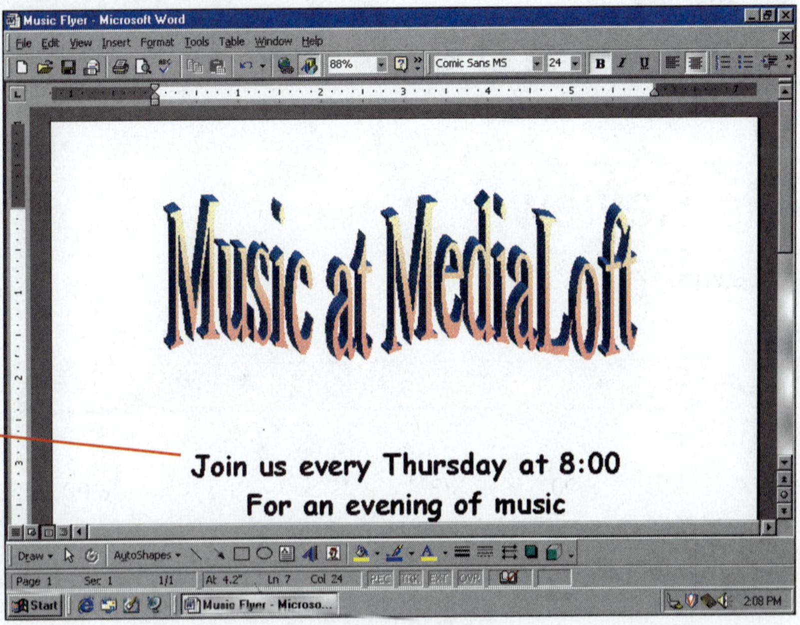

FIGURE F-24: Completed Music flyer

TABLE F-4: Click and Type pointers

pointer shape	use to apply
	A center-aligned tab stop; text that you type is centered on the page
	A right-aligned tab stop; text that you type is right-aligned on the page
	A left-aligned tab stop; text that you type is left-aligned on the page
	A left indent
	Left text wrapping
	Right text wrapping

Practice

Concepts Review

Label each button shown in Figure F-25.

FIGURE F-25

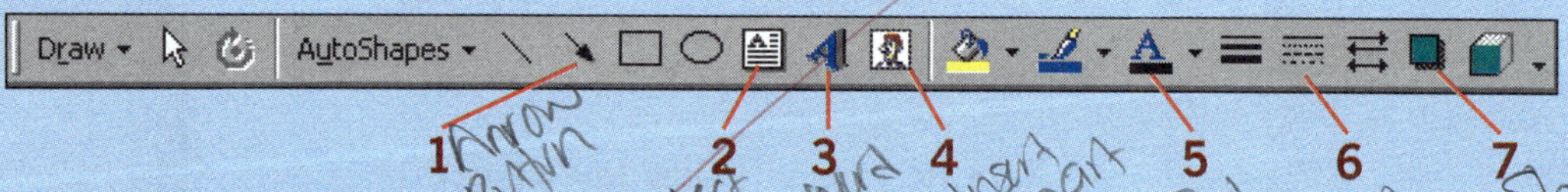

Match each term with the statement that describes it.

8. **Sizing handles**
9. **Clip art**
10. **Bitmapped graphics**
11. **AutoShapes**
12. **Text box**
13. **WordArt**

a. Graphics composed of specially formatted text
b. Graphics you can draw and format using the Drawing toolbar
c. Squares that indicate an object is selected
d. Graphics created in other programs and composed of pixels
e. A collection of graphic image files
f. Container into which you can place text and graphics

Select the best answer from the list of choices.

14. To insert an AutoShape, you click

a. Insert on the menu bar, then click AutoShape.
b. AutoShapes on the Drawing toolbar.
c. Format on the menu bar, then click AutoShape.
d. Draw on the Drawing toolbar.

15. To create a graphic that contains text, you can

a. Create a WordArt object.
b. Create a text box.
c. Right-click an AutoShape, then click Add Text.
d. All of the above.

Skills Review

1. Insert clip art graphics

a. Start Word, open the file WD F-3 from your Project Disk, then save it as "Edifice Inc".
b. Click Insert on the menu bar, point to Picture, then click Clip Art.
c. In the Buildings category, click the Leaning Tower of Pisa clip in the first row of clips, then click the Insert Clip button.
d. Click the Leaning Tower of Pisa clip again, click the Find similar clips button, then click Artistic Style.
e. Scroll down, select the clip showing the man climbing the ladder, click the Insert Clip button, then close the ClipGallery. (*Hint*: Choose another appropriate clip if this clip is not available.)

2. Wrap text around graphics

a. Click the Zoom list arrow, then click 50%.
b. Select the leaning tower graphic and click the Text Wrapping button on the Picture toolbar.
c. Apply tight text wrapping to the graphic.
d. Select the ladder graphic and apply square text wrapping to it.

3. Move and resize graphics

a. Resize the leaning tower clip art graphic proportionally so it is about 1½" wide. (*Hint*: Change the zoom level if necessary to better see the graphic.)
b. Resize the ladder clip art graphic proportionally so it is about 1½" wide.
c. Move the ladder clip art graphic to the left of the heading "Safety". Adjust the position of the graphic so that the top of the graphic is aligned with the top of the "Safety" heading, the left side of the graphic is even with the left margin, and the text for the Safety section wraps smoothly around the graphic.
d. Move the leaning tower clip art graphic to the left of the heading "Sound Construction" on the second page. (*Hint*: You can use cut and paste to move graphics from one page to another page.)
e. Adjust the position of the graphic so that the top of the graphic is aligned with the top of the "Sound Construction" heading, the left side of the graphic is even with the left margin, and the text for the Sound Construction section wraps smoothly around the graphic.

4. Insert pictures from files

a. On the first page, place the insertion point in front of "Edifice", click Insert on the menu bar, point to Picture, click From File, then insert the graphic file WD F-4 from your Project Disk.
b. Resize the column graphic so it is about 1½" wide, then wrap the text in a square around it, adjusting the size and position of the graphic if necessary so the text wraps smoothly around it.

5. Draw AutoShapes

a. Display the Drawing toolbar if necessary, click AutoShapes, point to Block Arrows, then click the Up Arrow shape.
b. On the right side of the "Balancing the Books" section, draw an arrow that is about 2¼" tall and 1¾" wide.
c. Adjust the position of the arrow so that the right side of the graphic object is aligned with the right margin, and the top of the arrow is aligned with the top of the "Balancing" heading, then wrap the text tightly around the arrow shape.
d. Fill the arrow with Pale Blue fill, and apply Shadow Style 16. (*Hint*: Click the Shadow button on the Drawing toolbar. Position the pointer over a menu option to see a ScreenTip with its name.)
e. Adjust the position of the arrow so that the text wraps smoothly around it and the shadow does not fall off the page.
f. Scroll to the second page, click AutoShapes, point to Basic Shapes, then click the Sun shape.
g. On the right side of the "Environment First" section, draw a sun shape that is about 2" wide and 2" tall. Align the right edge of the sun shape with the right margin.
h. Wrap the text tightly around the sun shape so that the text only wraps to the left of the shape.
i. Fill the sun shape with Light Yellow.

6. Insert text boxes

a. Scroll to the bottom of the document, draw a text box that is about 3½" wide and 1¼" tall, and center it on the page about 1" below the last line of text.
b. Inside the text box, type "Edifice Inc", press [Enter], type "100 Massachusetts Avenue", press [Enter], then type "Cambridge, MA 02139".
c. Select the text, center it, and change the font size to 20.
d. Fill the text box with Light Yellow and change the line around it to 2¼ points.
e. Scroll to the first page, right click the arrow shape, click Add Text, type "Revenues are up 15%.", center the text, then change the font to 11 point Arial.

7. Draw lines

a. Scroll to the top of the document, then draw a straight line that is 6" long above the heading "Edifice Inc".
b. Adjust the position of the line so that it is about ½" above the heading "Edifice Inc," and centered on the page.
c. With the line selected, click the Arrow Style button, then click the Arrow 7 style.
d. Change the line style to a 3 pt solid line, then change the line color to Indigo.

8. **Create WordArt**
   a. Select and cut the heading "The Cutting Edge", then click the Insert WordArt button on the Drawing toolbar.
   b. Select the fourth WordArt style in the fourth row from the top, click OK, press [Ctrl][V] to paste the heading "The Cutting Edge" in the Edit WordArt Text dialog box, then click OK.
   c. Resize the WordArt to be about 5" wide and 1½" tall, wrap text around the top and bottom of the WordArt object, then move it above the double-arrow line, centered on the page.
   d. Click the WordArt Shape button on the WordArt toolbar and select a different shape for the WordArt.
9. **Use Click and Type**
   a. Press [Ctrl][End], click once, position the right-align Click and Type pointer about 1" below the text box, double-click, then type your name.
   b. Save the document, view it in Print Preview, make adjustments as needed, print a copy, then close the document.

Independent Challenges

1. As marketing assistant for the Boston Tourism Authority, it's your job to create publications that promote Boston for tourists. You have written the text for a flyer, and now you want to add graphics to spice it up.

To complete this independent challenge:

a. Start Word, open the file WD F-5 from your Project Disk and save it as "Boston".
b. Insert a WordArt graphic with the text "Boston" as a heading for the flyer.
c. Resize the WordArt to be about 6" long and 2" high, center it at the top of the page, and wrap text using the top and bottom wrapping style. Experiment with WordArt styles and shapes to achieve the look you want.
d. In the middle of the page, draw a text box that is about 2" wide and 2.5" high. Apply square text wrapping to the text box. Position the text box so it is centered between the columns on the page.
e. In the text box, type "Make Boston your next vacation destination!" in 11-point Arial bold, then center the text.
f. Click in front of "Make" in the text box, press [Enter], place the insertion point in the blank paragraph above "Make", then insert a relevant clip art graphic at the location of the insertion point. (*Hint*: In the ClipGallery, look in the Buildings category, or type "city" in the Search for text box, then press [Enter]. Square-shaped clips will look best.)
g. Leave the graphic as an inline graphic. Reduce or enlarge the size of the graphic if necessary so that the text and the graphic both fit in the text box.
h. Add your name to the last sentence, save the document, print the document, then close it.

2. You have just started your own software consulting business. Your first project is to create a letterhead for your business.

To complete this independent challenge:

a. Start Word, create a new blank document, then save it as "Letterhead" to your Project Disk.
b. Switch to Print Layout view if necessary. Change the left document margin to 2" and the top and bottom margins to .5".
c. Open the ClipGallery and select a clip to use as your company logo. Insert the clip, resize it to be 1" wide, and set the text wrapping to tight. Move the clip to the upper-left corner of the page.
d. Zoom to view the whole page, then draw a straight vertical line from the top margin to the bottom margin of the page. (*Hint:* Hold the [Shift] key to draw a straight line.) Set the text wrapping to tight for the line, then move it so it is about 1¾" from the left edge of the page.
e. Zoom to view the page width, then draw a text box that is about 1" wide and 2" long.
f. Change the font and font size to 8-point Arial, type your name in the text box, press [Enter], type "Software Consulting", press [Enter], then type your address and telephone number. Select the text in the text box and right-align it using the Align Right button.

g. Set the text wrapping for the text box to tight, resize the text box so that all the text fits, then move the text box under the clip art on the left side of the line. Try to align the right edge of the text with the right edge of the clip art graphic. With the text box selected, click the Line Color list arrow, then click No Line.
h. Preview, save, print, then close the document.

3. You are a graphic designer. An electric company, Daly Electric, has hired you to design a business card for their company. You create three different designs for the business card to show your client.

To complete this independent challenge:

a. Start Word, create a new blank document, then save it as "Business Cards" to your Project Disk.
b. In the Page Setup dialog box, change the paper size of the document to 3.5" x 2", then change the margins to .25". Switch to Print Layout view and change the zoom level to whole page.
c. Create three business cards with different designs. Each card will be a different page in the document. Press [Ctrl][Enter] to insert hard page breaks to create three pages.
d. Each card should include the name of the company, Daly Electric, the company's address and phone number, and the name of an employee. You can use your name and address for the sample cards. Position the text on the business cards using text boxes and Click and Type.
e. On the first card, create a design using AutoShapes and lines.
f. On the second card, include a WordArt graphic. Change the font size of the WordArt so it fits on the business card.
g. On the third card, insert a clip art graphic. Remember to wrap text around any graphic that you insert.
h. Use the fonts, colors, lines, and other tools on the Drawing toolbar to enhance your three business card designs.
i. Save the document, print the document, then close it.

WEB WORK

4. You are a designer in the marketing department at the MediaLoft Chicago store. Your boss has asked you to design a bookmark that will be distributed to MediaLoft customers when they buy books. The bookmark should include an eye-catching graphic, the store's address, its hours of business, and the MediaLoft logo.

To complete this independent challenge:

a. Start Word, create a new blank document, then save it as "Bookmark" to your Project Disk.
b. In the Page Setup dialog box, change the paper size of the document to 2.5" x 7", then change the margins to .25". Switch to Print Layout view and change the zoom level to whole page.
c. Connect to the Internet and use your browser to go to the MediaLoft intranet site at http://www.course.com/illustrated/MediaLoft. Click the About MediaLoft link, then click the link for MediaLoft Chicago. Write down the store address, phone number, and store hours posted on the intranet site.
d. Insert a clip art graphic with a book theme. Use one of the clips in the ClipGallery or download a clip from the Microsoft ClipGallery Live Web site.
e. Apply text wrapping to the clip to make it a floating graphic, then move it to the bottom of the page.
f. Insert the WD F-2 file, the MediaLoft logo, from your Project Disk. Set the text wrapping to square, reduce the size of the logo to about ½", then move it to the upper-left corner of the page.
g. Using Click and Type, type "MediaLoft Chicago" to the right of the logo, then type the store hours, address, and phone number so that they are centered in the bookmark. Apply font formatting to improve the appearance of the text.
h. Use AutoShapes, lines, and color to enhance your bookmark.
i. Disconnect from the Internet, type your name in the bookmark, save your changes, and then print and close the document.

► Visual Workshop

Create the flyer shown in Figure F-26 and save it as "Movies Flyer" to your Project Disk. Type your name on the flyer before printing it.

FIGURE F-26

Word 2000

Unit G

Creating a Web Page

Objectives

- Plan a Web publication
- MOUS Create a Web page
- MOUS Apply themes
- Add graphics to a Web page
- MOUS Save a document as a Web page
- MOUS Insert hyperlinks
- Edit hyperlinks
- MOUS Preview a Web page

By creating Web pages in Word, you can create online documents that others can read over the Internet or an intranet. In this unit you'll learn how to create a new Web page, apply themes and formatting to Web pages, and work with graphics on a Web page. You'll also learn how to convert an existing print document to a Web page, create and edit hyperlinks, and preview a Web page in a browser.

One of MediaLoft's marketing goals is to increase its presence as a retailer of CDs and other music-related products. With this in mind, Alice Wegman is creating a Web site for MediaLoft employees to keep them updated on the marketing department's efforts, as well as trends in the retail music industry. The Web site will be posted on the MediaLoft intranet site and updated as necessary.

Unit G

Word 2000

Planning a Web Publication

A **Web page** is a document that is stored on the World Wide Web or an intranet, and viewed on a computer using a Web browser. You can create a Web page from scratch in Word, or you can convert an existing document to a Web page. Web pages often contain highlighted text or graphics called **hyperlinks** that open other Web pages when you click them. A group of associated Web pages that are linked together with hyperlinks is called a **Web site** or **Web publication**. The first page of a Web site that opens when you view the site in a browser is called the **home page**. The home page often serves as a table of contents for the Web site. Before you create a Web site, it is important to plan its content and organization. Alice's music Web site will include a home page that contains hyperlinks to the other Web pages in the Web site. Before creating the Web pages for the newsletter, Alice plans their content and organization and the tasks involved in creating them.

Details

Determine the purpose of the Web site

You can use a Web site to communicate information, collect information, or make a transaction. Alice's Web site will communicate MediaLoft's marketing program for music products to MediaLoft employees.

Sketch each Web page

Identify the information you want to include in your Web site and then sketch each page, including the links between pages. Alice identifies the documents she wants to include on the intranet site and then sketches the layout of each Web page. Her sketch is shown in Figure G-1.

Create each Web page

Create a new document and enter the Web page text, or convert an existing document to a Web page. Word includes a Web Page Wizard and templates for creating many standard types of Web pages. Alice will use a blank Web page template to create her Web site's home page, Music Notes. She will also convert an existing document to a Web page and add it to the Web site.

Format each Web page

Word includes visual themes that you can apply to any Web page. You can also create your own design for Web pages using backgrounds, lines, graphics, bullets, and other Word formatting features. Alice will select a theme and apply it to each page in her Web site to give it a cohesive look.

Save each Web page document

Web pages are saved in HTML (Hypertext Markup Language) format so that they can be viewed on the Web. Alice will use standard Word formatting features to design the layout of her Web pages before saving them in HTML format.

Format hyperlinks

Use hyperlinks to connect the pages of your Web site to each other. You can also create hyperlinks to sound and video clips, to other files on your computer, or to other Web pages. Alice will add hyperlinks linking the home page to a Web page that she creates from an existing Word document, to a Web page on the Internet, and to the MediaLoft intranet site.

View Web pages using a browser

Confirm that your Web pages are readable and correctly formatted and check that the links between Web pages work by viewing your Web site in your Web browser. Alice will use Web Page Preview to check each of her Web pages and test the links between pages.

FIGURE G-1: Alice's Web page sketch

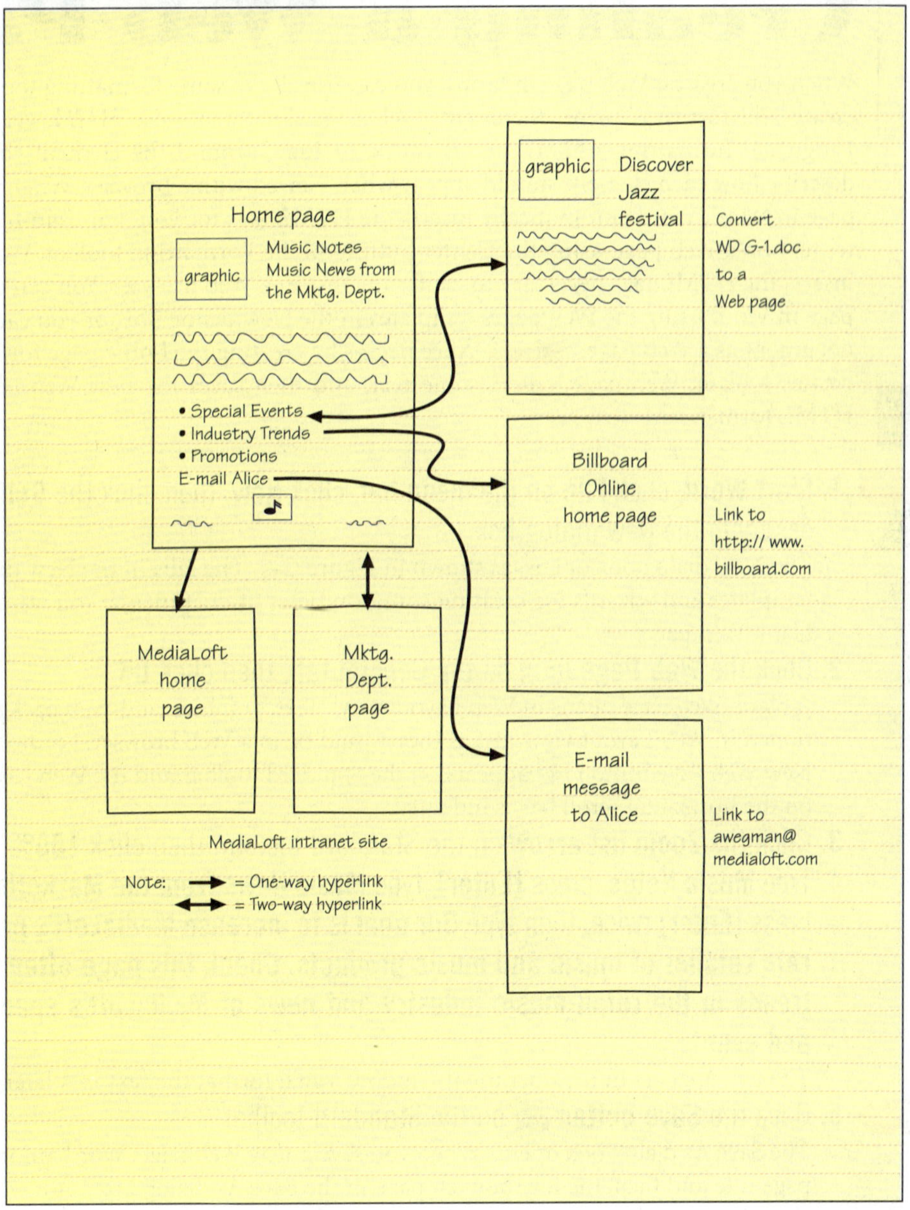

CLUES TO USE

Understanding the vocabulary of Web pages

When creating and working with Web pages, it is important to understand the following terms:

- **Home page:** the first Web page of a Web site to open when you view the site in a browser
- **Hyperlink:** highlighted text or graphic on a Web page that opens another Web page when you click it
- **Hypertext Markup Language** (HTML): the programming language used to create Web pages
- **Internet:** a communications system that connects computers and computer networks around the world
- **Intranet:** a network that connects computers in a local area and is used for internal purposes only
- **Web browser:** a software program used to access and display Web pages
- **Web page:** a document that is stored on the Web or an intranet and viewed on a computer using a Web browser
- **Web site** (or Web publication): a group of associated Web pages that are linked to each other by hyperlinks
- **World Wide Web** (the Web): a subset of the Internet that contains Web pages

Unit G

Word 2000

Creating a Web Page

When you create a Web page in Word, you can use all the same formatting tools that you use to create and format a print document. Web page documents use **HTML** (Hypertext Markup Language) formatting. HTML places codes, or **tags**, around the elements of a Web page to describe how each element should appear when viewed with a browser. When you create a Web page in Word, Word automatically inserts the HTML tags for you. For example, when you center text on a Web page using the Center button on the Formatting toolbar, Word automatically inserts the HTML tags necessary to center the text in a Web browser. You can create a new Web page in Word using the Web pages templates in the New dialog box, or you can save an existing document as a Web page. Alice begins by creating the home page for her Web site. She creates a blank Web page, enters some text, and then saves the new Web page document in HTML format.

Steps

QuickTip

To return personalized toolbars and menus to the default settings, click Tools on the menu bar, click Customize, click Reset my usage data on the Options tab, click Yes, then click Close.

1. Start **Word**, click **File** on the menu bar, click **New**, then click the **General tab** if necessary in the New dialog box
   The New dialog box opens, as shown in Figure G-2. The tabs in the New dialog box include templates and wizards for creating common types of documents. You want to create a new, blank Web page.
2. Click the **Web Page icon** on the General tab, then click **OK**
   A blank Web page opens in Web Layout view. Text, graphics, and Web backgrounds are positioned in Web Layout view just as they would be in a Web browser. For now, notice that the New Web Page button appears on the Standard toolbar and the Web Layout View button on the horizontal scroll bar is indented.
3. Click the **Zoom list arrow** on the Standard toolbar, then click **100%** if necessary
4. Type **Music Notes**, press **[Enter]**, type **Music News from the Marketing Department**, press **[Enter]** twice, then type **Our goal is to increase MediaLoft's profile as a first-rate retailer of music and music products. Check this page often for updates on trends in the retail music industry and news of MediaLoft's special promotions and events.**
   The text appears in the document window. You'll format the text in a later lesson.

QuickTip

The page title displays in the browser title bar when the Web page is published to the Web, so it is important that the page title of a Web page is descriptive of its contents.

5. Click the **Save button** on the Standard toolbar
   The Save As dialog box opens. When you save a new Web page, Word automatically enters a page title and filename for the Web page in the Save As dialog box. You want to change the page title to indicate that it is the home page for the Music Notes Web site.
6. Click **Change Title**
   The Set Page Title dialog box opens.
7. Click after Music Notes in the Page title text box, press **[Spacebar]**, type **Home Page**, then click **OK**
   The Page title changes to "Music Notes Home Page". Notice that the Save as type list box displays "Web Page" as the file type. Web pages are automatically saved in the file format—HTML—suitable for publishing a document on the Web or an intranet. You want to save the Web page with the filename "Music Notes Home" to your Project Disk.
8. Click after Music Notes in the File name text box, press **[Spacebar]**, type **Home**, then use the **Save in list arrow** to display the drive or folder that contains your Project Disk
   Compare your Save As dialog box with Figure G-3.
9. Click **Save**
   The Web Page document is saved to your Project Disk.

FIGURE G-2: General tab in New dialog box

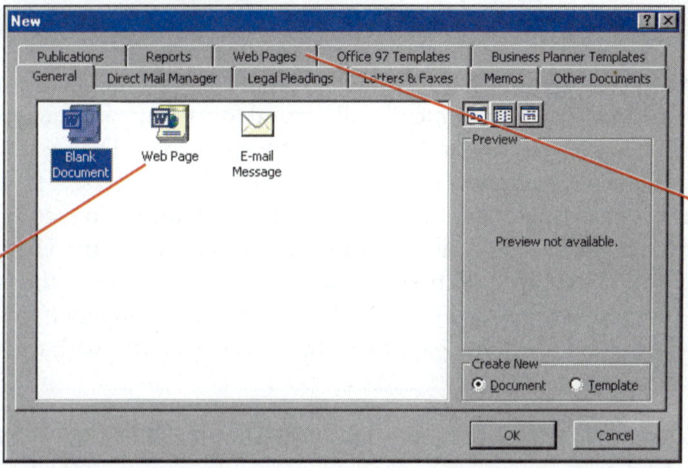

FIGURE G-3: Save As dialog box

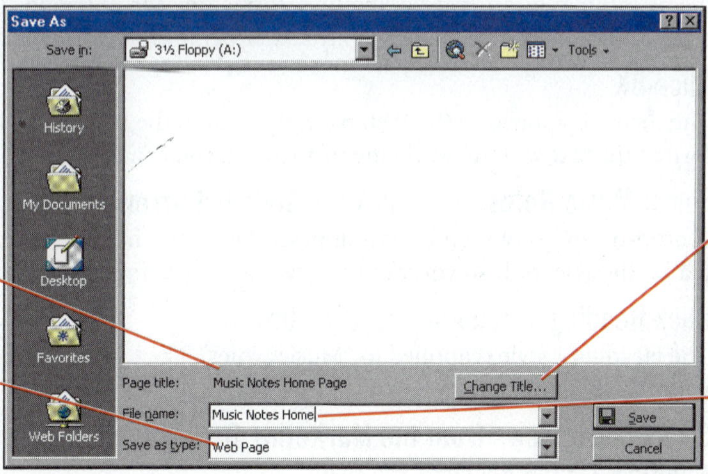

CLUES TO USE

Using the Web Page Wizard

You can also use the Web Page Wizard to create Web pages based on Word's Web page templates. To start the Web Page Wizard, click File on the menu bar, click New, click the Web Pages tab in the New dialog box, then double-click the Web Page Wizard icon. The wizard opens. Click Next, enter a title and location for your Web site in the first of 5 wizard dialog boxes, then click Next. In the second dialog box, shown in Figure G-4, you can choose to include or not include frames on your Web pages. **Frames** contain hyperlinks and other navigation elements that help users to navigate a group of associated Web pages. Some browsers do not support frames, so if you are creating a Web site that will have a large audience, you may want to create pages without frames. Continue working through the Web Page Wizard to add pages to the Web site, organize the pages in the Web site, and apply a visual theme to the Web site. When you are satisfied with your selections, click Finish. The first Web page appears in the Word document window. You can customize the Web pages using Word's formatting features.

FIGURE G-4: Web Page Wizard dialog box

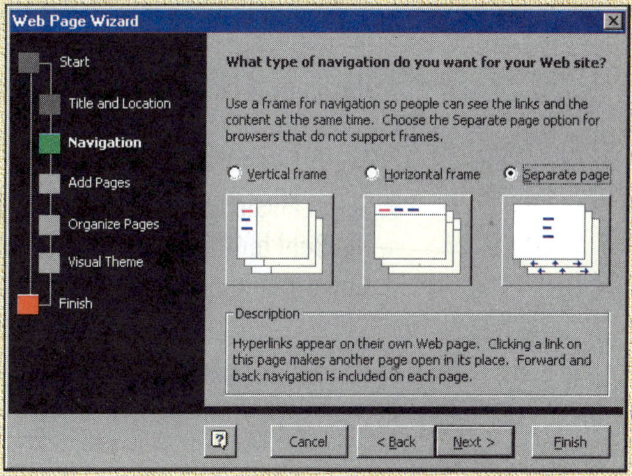

Unit G

Word 2000

Applying Themes

To give to your Web site a unified look, you can apply a theme to your Web pages. A **theme** is a predefined set of design elements, colors, and fonts that you can apply to Web pages and e-mail messages to give your documents a common visual look. Themes include designs for Web backgrounds, bullets, and lines, and styles for text and hyperlinks. A **style** is a predefined set of font settings, font attributes, font colors, and paragraph formatting settings that you can apply to text to format it quickly and easily. You can apply a theme using the Theme command on the Format menu. You can apply styles to text using the Style list arrow on the Formatting toolbar. Alice chooses a theme for the Music Notes Web site and applies it to the home page. She also formats the text on the home page using the styles that come with the theme.

Steps

1. Click **Format** on the menu bar, click **Theme**, then click **Artsy** in the Choose a Theme list box
   A sample of the Artsy theme appears in the Theme dialog box, as shown in Figure G-5. The theme includes a textured background, formatting for lines and bullets, and text formatting styles for headings, bulleted lists, body text, hyperlinks, and other text elements of a Web page.
2. Click **OK**
   The theme is applied to the Web page. By default, the Normal style is applied to the text. To format the text with other theme formatting, you can apply styles to the text.
3. Select **Music Notes**, then click the **Style list arrow** on the Formatting toolbar
   A drop-down list of theme styles appears. Each style name on the drop-down list is formatted in the style itself so you can preview the style before applying it.
4. Click **Heading 1**, then deselect the text
   The Heading 1 style is applied to "Music Notes". The text is now formatted in 24-point Arial with a gold font color.
5. Select **Music News from the Marketing Department**, click the **Style list arrow**, click **Heading 3**, then deselect the text
   The text is formatted in purple 14-point Arial.
6. Click at the end of the last paragraph, press **[Enter]** twice, type **Special Events**, press **[Enter]**, type **Industry Trends**, press **[Enter]**, type **Promotions**, press **[Enter]** twice, select the three new lines of text, click the **Bullets button** on the Formatting toolbar, then deselect the text
   The paragraphs are formatted as a bulleted list using the theme's special bullets. You also want to add a horizontal line to the Web page.
7. Press **[Ctrl][End]**, click the **Tables and Borders button** on the Standard toolbar, click the **Outside Border list arrow** on the Tables and Borders toolbar, click the **Horizontal Line button**, then close the Tables and Borders toolbar
   A horizontal line formatted in the theme design is added to the Web page. Once you have applied styles to text, you can customize the formatting to suit your purposes.
8. Select **Music Notes**, click the **Font Size list arrow** on the Formatting toolbar, click **36**, click the **Bold button** , click the **Italic button** , select **Music News from the Marketing Department**, click the **Font Size list arrow**, click **18**, click , then deselect the text
   Compare your Web page with Figure G-6.
9. Save your changes to the Web page
   A folder called Music Notes Home_files is automatically created on your Project Disk when you save the formatting changes you applied to the Web page in this lesson. The folder contains all the files—such as the theme, bullets, and styles—used in the Web page.

Trouble?

Some themes may be stored on your Office 2000 CD. When you click a theme, if a message appears saying you need to install the theme, insert your Office 2000 CD, then click Install.

Trouble?

Click the More Buttons button on the Formatting toolbar to locate buttons that are not visible on your toolbar.

QuickTip

Double-click a line object to open the Format Horizontal Line dialog box, which you can use to change the size or alignment of a horizontal line.

FIGURE G-5: Artsy theme in Theme dialog box

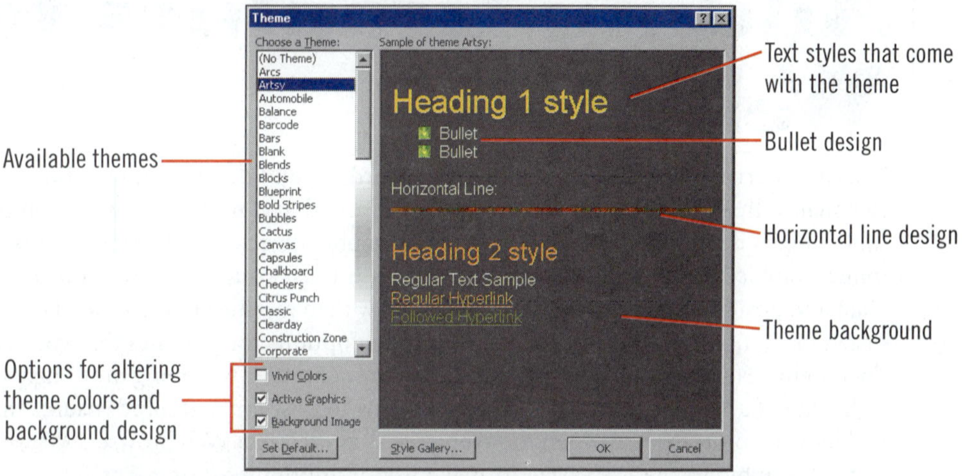

FIGURE G-6: Theme and styles applied to Web page

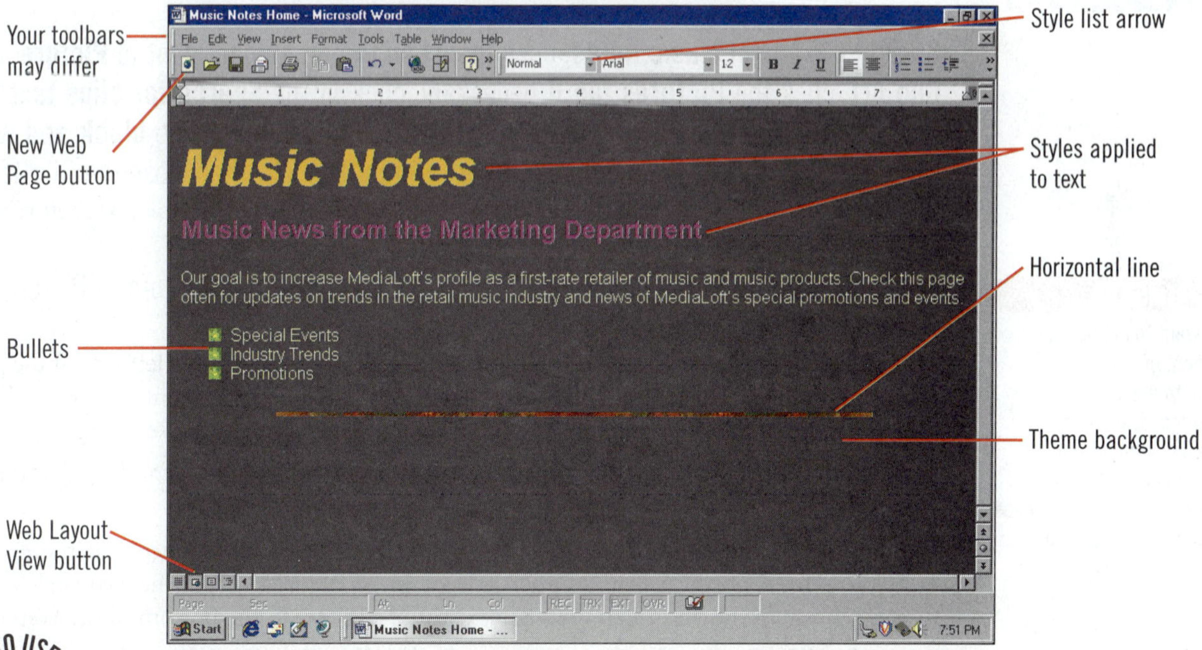

Clues to Use

Adding backgrounds to Web pages

Backgrounds sit behind the text and graphics on a Web page to give your Web pages a colorful and interesting look. Word's themes include background designs, but you can also design your own backgrounds for Web pages. To add or change the background of a Web page, click Format on the menu bar, then point to Background. A color palette appears. If you want to use a solid color for a background, select a color from the palette or click More Colors to create a custom color. For more background design options, click Fill Effects on the color palette. The Fill Effects dialog box opens. The tabs in the Fill Effects dialog box allow you to choose between gradients, textures, or patterns as a background, or to select a picture file to use as a background for your Web page. Click the tab with the type of background you want, then select from the options for styles and colors on that tab. The Texture tab is shown in Figure G-7.

FIGURE G-7: Texture tab in Fill Effects dialog box

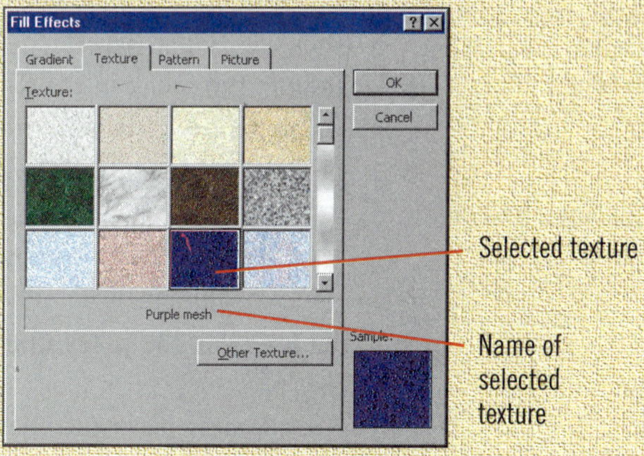

Unit G

Word 2000

Adding Graphics to a Web Page

You can insert clip art, bitmapped graphics, WordArt, and drawing objects into your Web pages to enhance their appearance. You can also add sound and motion clips to Web pages to create multi-media documents. When you insert a graphic object on a Web page, it is inserted as an inline graphic. To make it a floating graphic you must wrap text around it. Floating graphics align and position differently in Web Layout view than in other Word views. This is because Web browsers do not support all the same formatting options for graphics that you can use in print documents. For example, floating graphics with square text wrapping only align with the left or right side of a Web page. Using Web Layout view to position a graphic ensures that the graphic will look as you want it to when the Web page is viewed in a Web browser. Alice adds a clip art graphic to the Web page to make it look more interesting. For fun, she also inserts a sound clip so that people can listen to music as they read the Music Notes Web site.

Steps

1. Click at the end of **Music Notes**, click **Insert** on the menu bar, point to **Picture**, click **Clip Art**, click the **Pictures tab** if necessary, click in the **Search for clips text box**, type **CD**, press **[Enter]**, scroll down the list of CD clips, select the **black and white CD image** in the third row, click the **Insert clip button**, then close the ClipGallery
   The CD graphic is inserted to the right of "Music Notes", in line with the text. Before moving the graphic, you'll change it to a floating graphic.
2. Select the **CD graphic**, double-click it, click the **Layout tab** in the Format Picture dialog box, click the **Square** wrapping style, then click **OK**
   The graphic becomes a floating graphic and automatically moves to the left side of the page. Floating graphics are right- or left-aligned on Web pages. If you want to center-align a graphic, you use an inline graphic. Next you'll resize the graphic to make it larger.
3. Position the pointer over the **lower-right sizing handle**, then drag the sizing handle so that the graphic is about **2¼"** wide
   You can use the horizontal ruler to help you resize the graphic. Notice that the graphic jumps to a fixed position in the upper-left corner of the Web page when you release the mouse button, as shown in Figure G-8. Next you'll add text to the bottom of the Web page.
4. Press **[Ctrl][End]**, click the **Style list arrow**, click **Heading 4**, click the **Bold button** on the Formatting toolbar, then click the **Center button**
5. Type **June is Jazz Month! Double-click the music icon to hear some cool jazz...**, then press **[Enter]**
   The text is formatted in the Heading 4 style, bolded, and centered on the page. You'll insert a sound clip of some jazz music at the location of the insertion point.
6. Click, click **Insert** on the menu bar, point to **Picture**, click **Clip Art**, click the **Sounds tab**, click in the **Search for clips text box**, type **jazz**, then press **[Enter]**
   The jazz music clips appear on the Sounds tab.
7. Scroll down, click the **jazzy** clip in the last row, click, then close the ClipGallery
   The jazzy clip is inserted below the line of text, as shown in Figure G-9. The clip remains centered because it is an inline graphic. To play a sound clip, you can double-click its icon. You must have a sound system and speakers installed on your computer to be able to play a sound file.
8. Double-click the **jazzy clip icon**, listen to the music, then save your changes to the Web page
   As the music plays, the jazzy clip icon changes to show the progress of the music clip, as shown in Figure G-10.

QuickTip

If you want to change the alignment of the floating graphic to make it right-aligned, you can double-click the graphic to open the Format Picture dialog box, and then change the horizontal alignment setting on the Layout tab.

QuickTip

If you want to position text or a floating graphic precisely on a Web page, you can create a table and insert the text and graphics in table cells.

QuickTip

If you are unable to insert or play a sound clip, read the remaining step to understand how a sound clip is played, then save your changes.

FIGURE G-8: Clip art graphic in Web page

FIGURE G-9: Jazz clip in Web page

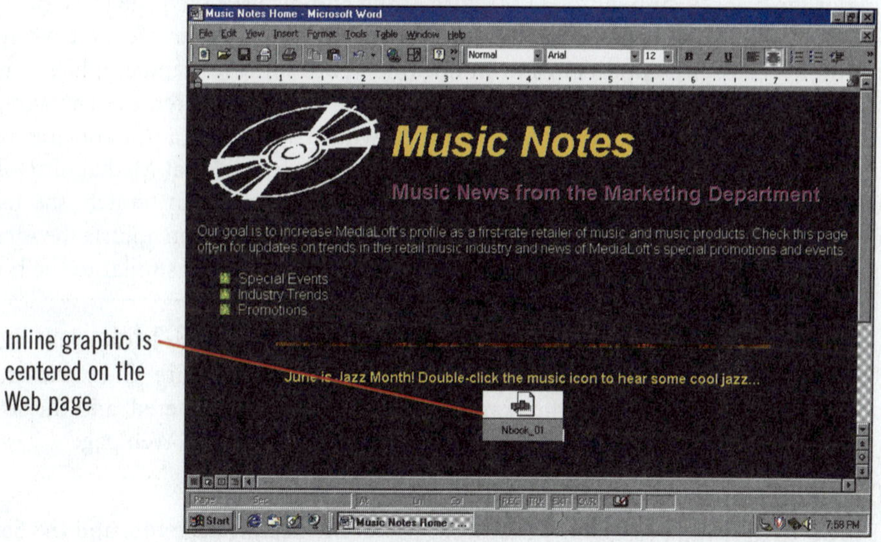

FIGURE G-10: Jazz clip playing

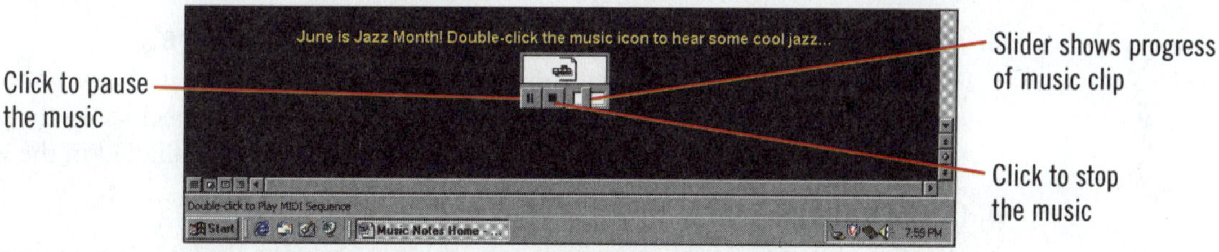

Word 2000

CLUES TO USE

Copying and moving Web pages

When you save a document as a Web page in HTML format, each graphic in the document is automatically converted to a GIF, JPEG, or PNG format file and placed in a supporting folder that contains all the files used in the Web page. This folder is created automatically when you create a new Web page or save a print document as a Web page. It contains the files for the graphics, backgrounds, bullets, horizontal lines, and other elements used on a Web page. The supporting folder is saved in the same location as the HTML document, and it has the same name as the HTML document file plus the suffix "files". For example, the supporting folder that was automatically created when you saved the Music Notes Home HTML file on your Project Disk is called the Music Notes Home_files folder, and it too is located on your Project Disk. When you copy or move a Web page to a new location on your computer, you must be careful to copy all the files associated with that Web page—in other words, you must copy the supporting folder in addition to the HTML document file. If you change file locations, you might need to update the links to those graphics as well. If a browser cannot locate the graphic image files associated with a Web page, the browser will display a placeholder instead of a graphic. If you see a placeholder when you open a Web page you copied or moved, you'll know you need to go back and copy or move the supporting files associated with that Web page too, or you may need to update the graphic links.

Unit G

Word 2000

Saving a Document as a Web Page

As you learned in the preceding lessons, you can create a Web page by opening a new blank Web page, adding content, and then saving the Web page. You can also convert an existing Word document to a Web page by opening it and saving it as a Web page. When you save an existing print document as a Web page, Word saves the document as an HTML file and creates a supporting folder that contains all the files associated with the Web page. Word converts the content and formatting of the print document to HTML formatting and displays the page in Web Layout view. Web Layout view shows the document as it will look in a Web browser. Most formatting appears in a browser exactly as it appears in a print document, but some text and graphics may look different when you view them on a Web page. For example, columns are removed and graphics with certain kinds of text wrapping will change position when you convert a print document to a Web page. Alice wants to add a Web page about a jazz festival that MediaLoft is sponsoring to her Music Notes Web site. Rather than create the Web page from scratch, she uses a press release she wrote about the festival and saves it as a Web page. She then adjusts the formatting of the new Web page and applies the Artsy theme so that the page looks similar to the home page.

Steps 1 2 3 4

1. **Click File on the menu bar, click Open, then open the file WD G-1 from your Project Disk**
   The document opens in Print Layout view as shown in Figure G-11. Notice that the document is two pages long, the graphic on the first page is centered, and the second page is formatted in two columns. You'll save the print document as a Web page.

2. **Click File on the menu bar, then click Save as Web Page**
   The Save As dialog box opens. "Discover Jazz" is the default page title and the Save as type list box displays "Web Page", indicating that the file will be saved in HTML format. You'll rename the file to match the page title.

3. **Type Discover Jazz in the File name text box, then click Save**
   A dialog box informing you that some of the formatting features in the print document will not display in a Web browser opens as shown in Figure G-12. Specifically, the graphic with text wrapped around it in the press release will be left- or right-aligned in the Web page.

4. **Click Continue**
   Word saves a copy of the document as a Web page to your Project Disk, and the document appears in Web Layout view. Notice that the graphic is now left-aligned on the Web page. If you scroll down the page, you'll also notice that there are no margins on the Web page, the document is one long page, and the text is formatted in a single column.

5. **Click Format on the menu bar, click Theme, click Artsy in the Choose a Theme list box, then click OK**
   The Artsy theme is applied to the document. If you scroll down the page, you'll notice that text that was formerly black in the print document is now white on the Web page.

6. **Scroll to the top of the page, select the graphic, then drag it to the upper-left corner of the Web page**
   The graphic jumps into place in the upper-left corner when you release the mouse button.

7. **Click the Show/Hide ¶ button on the Standard toolbar, click in front of the first paragraph mark ¶ under festival, press [Delete] seven times, then click ¶**
   Compare your Web page with Figure G-13.

8. **Save your changes to the Web page, then close the file**
   The Music Notes Home file appears in the document window.

FIGURE G-11: Discover Jazz print document in Print Layout view

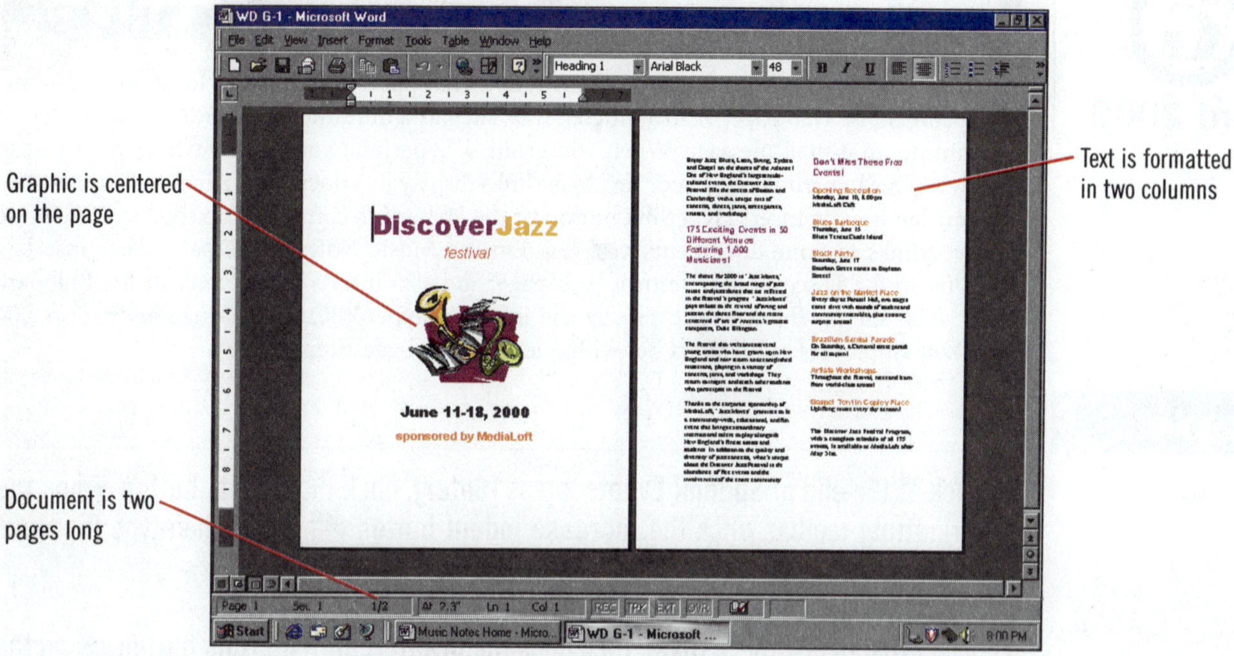

FIGURE G-12: Microsoft Word dialog box

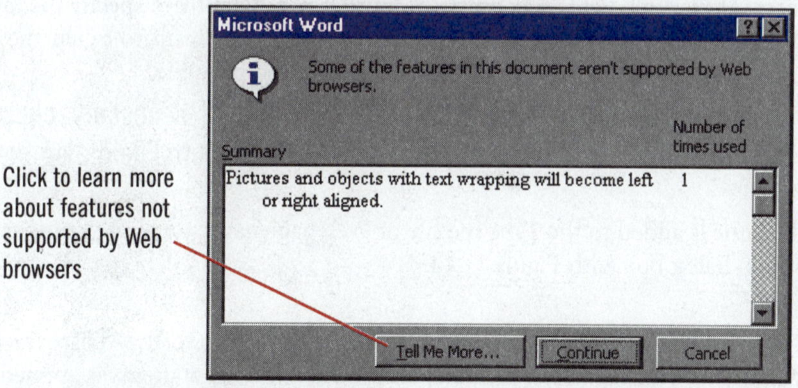

FIGURE G-13: Formatted Web page

Unit G

Word 2000

Inserting Hyperlinks

Hyperlinks can link or "jump" to a document, to a Web page, to a different location in the current document or Web page, or to a different file, such as a multimedia file. You can also create a hyperlink to an e-mail message. When you create a hyperlink, you specify where you want to jump when the hyperlink is clicked. Text hyperlinks display in a document as colored, underlined text. You can use the Insert Hyperlink button or the Hyperlink command on the Insert menu to add hyperlinks to your documents. On the Music Notes home page, Alice inserts a hyperlink to the Discover Jazz festival Web page. She also inserts a hyperlink to the Billboard Online Web site on the Internet. Finally she inserts a hyperlink to her e-mail address so that MediaLoft employees can contact her with questions or suggestions.

Steps

1. Click at the end of **Special Events**, press **[Enter]**, click the **Bullets button** on the Formatting toolbar, click the **Increase indent button** twice, then type **Discover Jazz festival**

   You will create a hyperlink using this text.

2. Select **Discover Jazz festival**, then click the **Create/Edit Hyperlink button** on the Standard toolbar

   The Insert Hyperlink dialog box opens. You use this dialog box to specify the location of the file, the Web address, or the e-mail address you want to jump to when the hyperlink is clicked. You'll add a hyperlink to the Discover Jazz Web page file.

3. Click **Existing File or Web Page** in the Link to area if necessary, click **File** in the Browse for area, select the **Discover Jazz** file in the Link to File dialog box, then click **OK**

   The filename is added to the Type the file or Web page name text box. Compare your Insert Hyperlink dialog box with Figure G-14.

4. Click **OK**

   Word automatically applies orange, underlined formatting to the "Discover Jazz festival" hyperlink. This is the text style for a hyperlink when the Artsy theme is applied. Next, you'll add another hyperlink to a Web page on the Internet.

5. Click at the end of **Industry Trends**, press **[Enter]**, click , click twice, type **Billboard charts of top hits**, select the text, then click

   The Insert Hyperlink dialog box opens.

6. Type **http://www.billboard.com/charts** in the Type the file or Web page name text box

   Compare your Insert Hyperlink dialog box with Figure G-15. You just entered the Web address, or **URL** (Uniform Resource Locator), for the Web page containing the Billboard charts of top music hits.

7. Click **OK**

   The new hyperlink appears on the Web page. Next, you'll create a hyperlink to an e-mail address.

8. Click under **Promotions**, press **[Enter]**, type **Contact Alice Wegman, Marketing Manager**, press **[Enter]**, select **Alice Wegman**, then click

   The Insert Hyperlink dialog box opens.

9. Click **E-mail Address** in the Link to area, type **awegman@medialoft.com** in the E-mail address text box, then click **OK**

   "Alice Wegman" is formatted as a hyperlink, as shown in Figure G-16. You'll test your hyperlinks in a later lesson.

10. Save your changes to the Web page

QuickTip

You can create a hyperlink to a graphic by selecting the graphic, then clicking the Create/Edit Hyperlink button.

QuickTip

If you don't know the URL of a Web page, you can click Browse in the Insert Hyperlink dialog box to open your browser and search the Web for the page you want.

FIGURE G-14: Insert Hyperlink dialog box with hyperlink to file

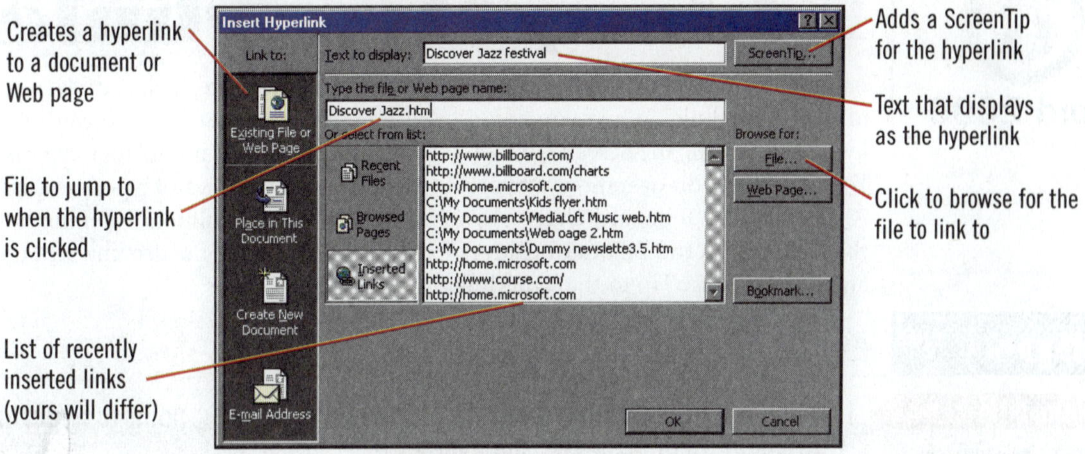

FIGURE G-15: Insert Hyperlink dialog box with hyperlink to Web address

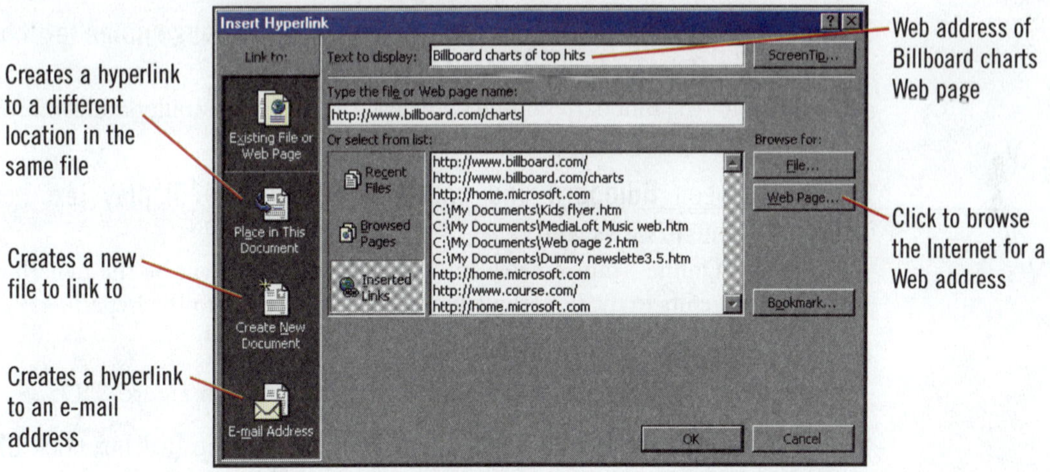

FIGURE G-16: Hyperlinks in Web page

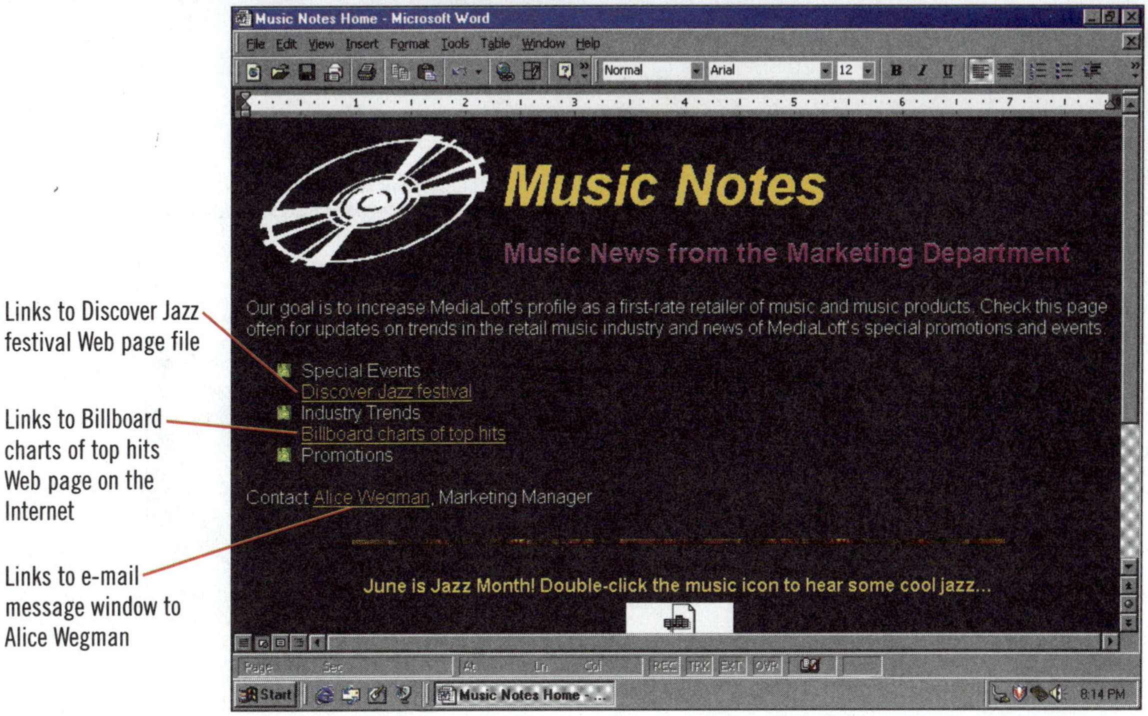

Unit G

Word 2000

Editing Hyperlinks

As the information on your Web page changes, you'll need to change, update, and remove some of your hyperlinks. When you edit a hyperlink, you can change the hyperlink destination, the hyperlink text, or the ScreenTip that displays when a reader points to a hyperlink in a browser. You can easily edit or remove a hyperlink in Word using the Edit Hyperlink command. Alice edits the "Billboard charts" hyperlink to link to the Billboard Online home page, rather than directly to the Billboard charts of top hits Web page. She also changes the hyperlink text and adds a ScreenTip to the hyperlink.

Steps

QuickTip

To remove a hyperlink, right-click it, point to Hyperlink on the pop-up menu, then click Remove Hyperlink.

1. Right-click the **Billboard charts of top hits hyperlink**, point to **Hyperlink** on the pop-up menu, then click **Edit Hyperlink**

   The Edit Hyperlink dialog box opens. You'll change the destination of the hyperlink by changing the Web address to which it jumps.

2. Click at the end of the URL in the Type the file or Web page name text box, then press **[Backspace]** seven times to delete "/charts"

   The URL for the Billboard Online home page is http://www.billboard.com. You also want to change the text that displays the hyperlink.

3. Click between **Billboard** and **charts** in the Text to display text box, then type **Online—music news and**

   "Billboard Online—music news and charts of top hits" will be the hyperlink text. Before saving your edits to the hyperlink, you'll add a ScreenTip to the hyperlink.

4. Click **ScreenTip**

   The Set Hyperlink ScreenTip dialog box opens as shown in Figure G-17.

5. Type **Billboard charts and news online** in the ScreenTip text box click **OK**, click **OK** in the Edit Hyperlink dialog box, then save your changes to the Web page

   The revised hyperlink text appears in the Web page as shown in Figure G-18. The ScreenTip for the hyperlink will appear when the Web page is viewed in a browser, but it does not appear in Word. You'll preview the Web page in your browser in the next lesson.

CLUES TO USE

Sending a Word document via e-mail

Another way to share information with others via the Internet or a local network is to e-mail a copy of a Word document directly from Word. To e-mail a document, open the document, then click the E-mail button on the Standard toolbar. An e-mail header opens at the top of the document window, as shown in Figure G-19. Type the e-mail addresses of the recipients in the To and Cc boxes, separated by semi-colons, or click the icons next to the To and Cc boxes to open and use your address book. When you are ready to send the file, click the Send a Copy button on the e-mail header toolbar. Word e-mails a copy of the file to the recipients using your default e-mail program.

FIGURE G-19: Document with e-mail header

FIGURE G-17: Set Hyperlink ScreenTip dialog box

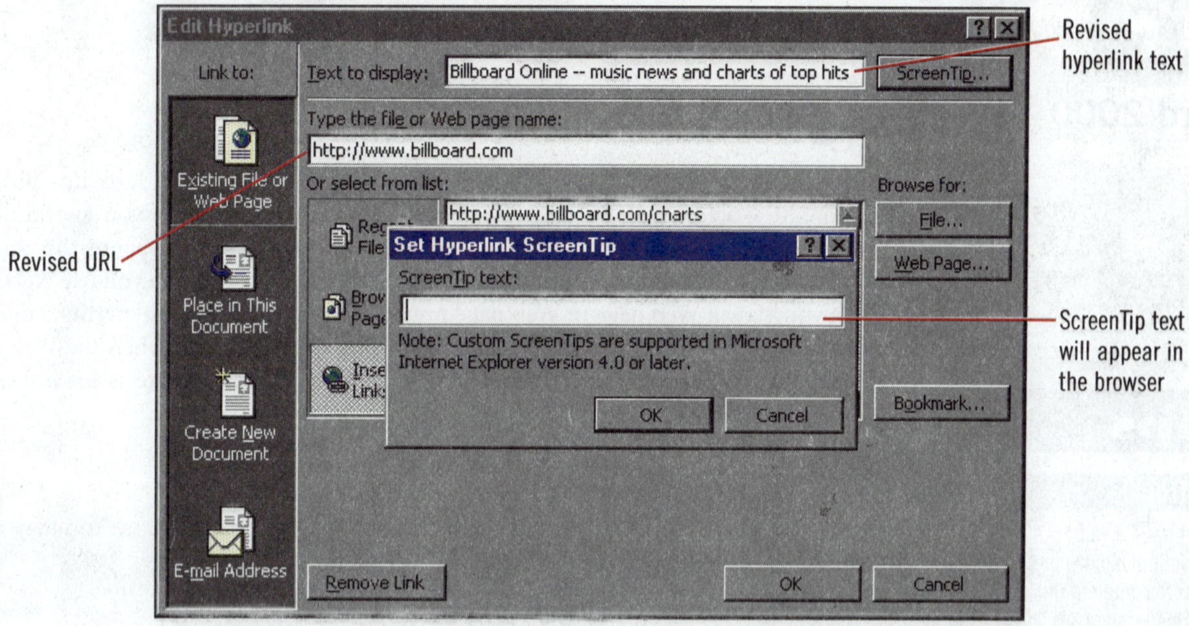

FIGURE G-18: Edited hyperlink in Web page

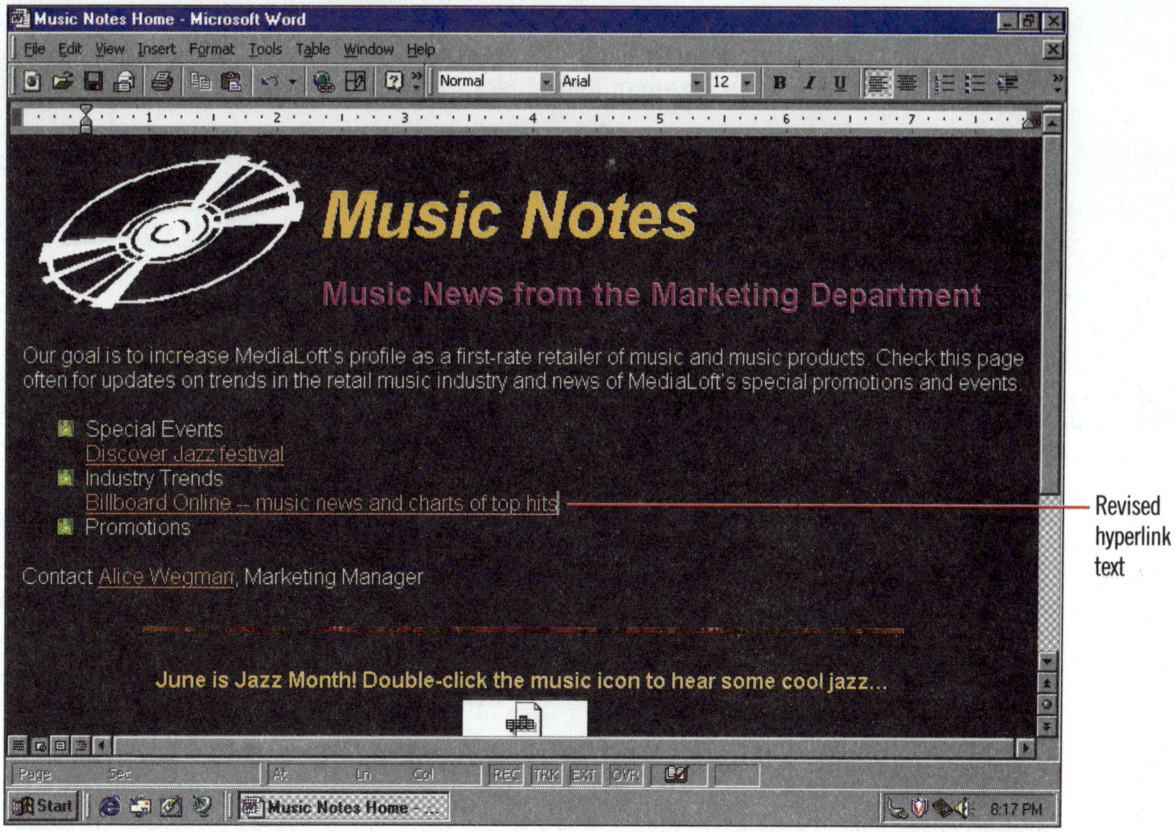

Word 2000

Previewing a Web Page

Word's Web page preview feature allows you to see how your document will look in a browser so that you can edit it before publishing it to the Web or an intranet. When you view a document in Web page preview, Word makes a copy of the document and then opens the copy in your browser. If your browser is not open already, it opens automatically when you use Web page preview. When you view a Web page in Web page preview, you can test your hyperlinks to see if they work correctly. You can also view the HTML tags for your Web pages when the Web page is open in the browser. Alice previews her Web site in her browser, tests the links, and views the HTML source code for the Web pages.

Steps

Trouble?

You must have a Web browser installed on your computer to complete this lesson. This lesson uses the Internet Explorer 5 browser. If you are using a different Web browser, your screens may not match the figures in this lesson and some features used in the lesson may not be available.

1. **Click File on the menu bar, then click Web Page Preview**
   The default browser opens and displays the Web page in the browser window. You may need to maximize your browser window.
2. **Click the Discover Jazz festival hyperlink**
   The Discover Jazz page opens in the browser window, as shown in Figure G-20. You can scroll down the Web page to check its formatting before returning to the Music Notes home page. The browser toolbar contains buttons for navigating between Web pages.
3. **Click the Back button on the browser toolbar**
   The Music Notes home page displays in the browser window. Notice that the color of the Discover Jazz festival hyperlink has changed to olive green. The olive green color is the style for a hyperlink that has been followed when a Web page is formatted using the Artsy theme.
4. **Point to the Billboard Online hyperlink**
   The ScreenTip you created for the hyperlink appears when you point to the hyperlink. If you are able to connect to the Internet, you can click the Billboard Online hyperlink to test it. The Billboard Online home page will open in your browser window. When you have finished viewing the Billboard Web site, you can click the Back button on the browser toolbar to return to the Music Notes home page. Next you'll test the e-mail hyperlink.
5. **Click the Alice Wegman hyperlink**
   A new mail message to Alice Wegman opens, as shown in Figure G-21. You could type a message in the message area and click the Send button to send the message to Alice. However, you'll close the message and continue exploring your Web site in the browser.
6. **Click the Close button on the message title bar, click View on the menu bar, then click Source**
   The HTML code for the Web page appears in the Music Notes Home Notepad window, as shown in Figure G-22. If you are familiar with HTML code, you can edit your Web page by changing the HTML tags in this window. Otherwise you can edit your Web pages using Word.
7. **Close the Music Notes Home Notepad window, then click the Edit button on the browser toolbar**
   The Music Notes Web page appears in the Word document window.
8. **Scroll to the bottom of the page, click under the jazzy music clip, double-click with the Click and Type pointer, then type your name**
9. **Save your changes to the Web page, print it, close the file, exit Word, then close your browser**
   You have finished your work on the Web page. Later, Alice will add a hyperlink to the marketing department Web page and the MediaLoft home page before sending her Web pages to the MediaLoft network administrator to post on the MediaLoft intranet site.

Trouble?

If the Edit button is not available in your browser, click the Word program button on the taskbar, then edit the document in Word.

FIGURE G-20: Discover Jazz festival Web page in the browser window

FIGURE G-21: E-mail message to Alice Wegman

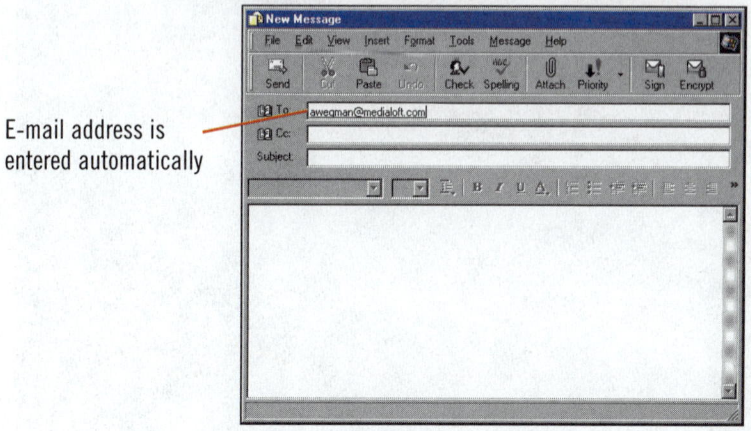

FIGURE G-22: HTML source code for Web page

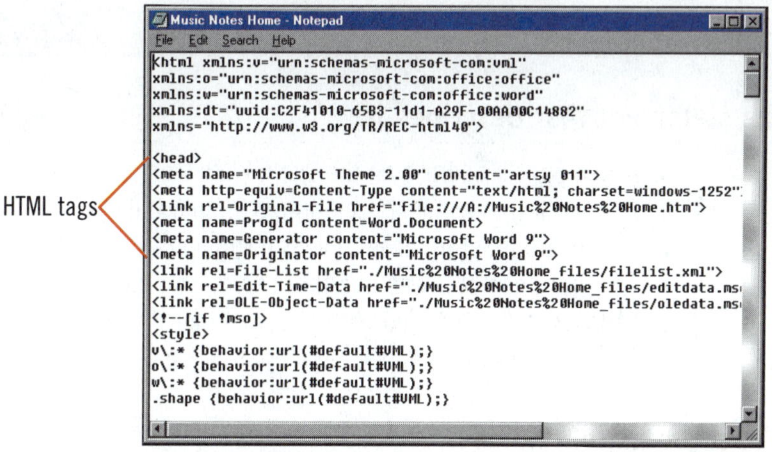

CLUES TO USE

Publishing a Web document to an intranet or the Web

To make your Web pages available on an intranet or over the Web, you need to publish (or post a copy) your Web site to a Web server. In order to post your Web site to an intranet, you must transfer the HTML files and support files to the intranet server on your local network. If you want to publish your Web site on the Internet, you can transfer the files to your Internet Service Provider (ISP), to be posted on your ISP's Web server. Check with your network administrator or your ISP for information on how to transfer your Web pages and the supporting files to the correct server.

Practice

► Concepts Review

Label each element shown in Figure G-23.

FIGURE G-23

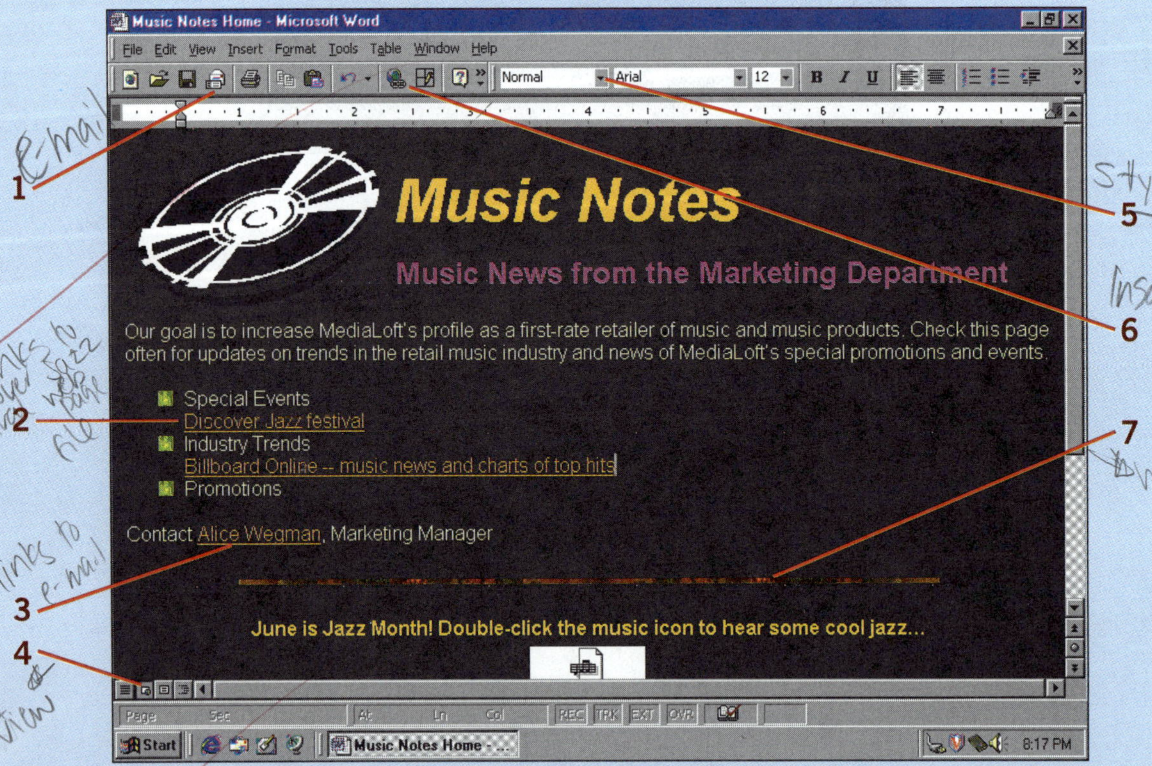

Match each term with the statement that describes it.

8. **Internet**
9. **Intranet**
10. **Hyperlink**
11. **Browser**
12. **URL**
13. **Home page**

a. A Web page's address on the World Wide Web
b. A network that connects computers around the world
c. A software program used to view documents saved in HTML format
d. The first page of a Web site that serves as a table of contents
e. Text or graphic that you click to open other files or Web pages
f. A network that connects computers in a local area

Select the best answer from the list of choices.

14. Hyperlinks can be used to open

a. Web pages.
b. E-mail messages.
c. Files.
d. All of the above.

15. You can position graphics on your Web pages using

a. Web Layout view.
b. Print Layout view.
c. A Web browser.
d. Web Page Preview.

16. **To insert a horizontal line on a Web page**
    a. Click the Line button on the Drawing toolbar.
    b. Click the Horizontal Line button on the Tables and Borders toolbar.
    c. Click the Line Style button on the Drawing toolbar.
    d. Click Format on the menu bar, then click Theme.
17. **To center a graphic on a Web page**
    a. Select the graphic, apply inline text wrapping, then click the Center button.
    b. Select the graphic, apply square text wrapping, then drag it to the center of the page.
    c. Select the graphic, apply square text wrapping, then click the Center button.
    d. Select the graphic, click Format on the menu bar, then click Center.
18. **When you save a print document as a Web page, which of the following is NOT true**
    a. Word creates a folder in the same location as the Web page document.
    b. Word applies HTML tags to the document.
    c. Your browser opens.
    d. The Web page has a filename and a page title.
19. **Web themes include designs for**
    a. Bullets, horizontal lines, graphics, and headings.
    b. Backgrounds, tables, hyperlinks, and bullets.
    c. Bullets, hyperlinks, headings, and frames.
    d. Backgrounds, bullets, horizontal lines, and hyperlinks.
20. **You can convert a print document to an HTML document in Word by**
    a. Clicking File on the menu bar, then clicking Web Page Preview.
    b. Clicking the Web Layout View button.
    c. Creating a hyperlink to the file.
    d. Clicking File on the menu bar, then clicking Save as Web Page.

Skills Review

1. **Create a Web page**
   a. Start Word and create a new blank Web page.
   b. Type "Southeast Computer Solutions", press [Enter], type "Software training for business and home users", then press [Enter] twice.
   c. Save the new document to your Project Disk as a Web page with the page title "Southeast Home Page" and the filename "Southeast Computer Solutions".
2. **Apply themes**
   a. Apply the Straight Edge theme to the Web page.
   b. Select "Southeast Computer Solutions" and apply the Heading 1 style.
   c. Select "Software training …." and apply the Heading 3 style.
   d. Click below the "Software training …" subhead, type "Register now for Office 2000 courses:", then press [Enter].
   e. Type the following list, pressing [Enter] after each program name: Word, Excel, Access, PowerPoint, Internet Explorer, Publisher, FrontPage, PhotoDraw. Press [Enter] twice after "PhotoDraw".
   f. Select the list of programs and apply bullets to it.
   g. Use the Horizontal Line button on the Tables and Borders toolbar to insert a horizontal line under the bulleted list, then close the Tables and Borders toolbar.
   h. Click Format on the menu bar, point to Background, then click Fill Effects.
   i. On the Texture tab in the Fill Effects dialog box, select the Stationery texture (4th texture in top row), then click OK.

3. Add graphics to a Web page

a. Press [Ctrl][Home], click Insert on the menu bar, point to Picture, then click Clip Art.
b. Click the Office category on the Pictures tab, then insert the green and beige computer image in the top row (last clip in the top row).
c. Close the ClipGallery.
d. Drag the lower-right sizing handle to resize the graphic to be about 3" wide.
e. Double-click the graphic.
f. On the Layout tab in the Format Picture dialog box, set the text wrapping to square and set the horizontal alignment to right.

4. Save a document as a Web page

a. Open the file WD G-2 from your Project Disk and scroll the document to get a feel for its content and formatting.
b. Use the Save as Web page command to save the file as a Web page. Change the title of the page and the filename to "Southeast Fall Schedule", then click OK.
c. Read the message about the formatting changes that will occur, then click Continue.
d. Apply the Straight Edge theme to the Web page.
e. Change the background to the Stationery texture.
f. Drag the lower-right sizing handle of the graphic to resize it to be about 1" wide. Double-click the graphic, then apply the In line with text wrapping style to it.
g. Click between the graphic and "Southeast", then press [Enter].
h. Apply the Heading 1 style to "Southeast Computer Solutions".
i. Center the graphic and the heading, then insert a horizontal line under the heading.
j. Select all the text below "All courses begin September 8", including the text in the tables, then change the font size to 12.
k. Bold the name of each software program.

5. Insert hyperlinks

a. Click the Southeast Computer Solutions file button on the taskbar.
b. Click under the horizontal line, type "Fall schedule", press [Enter], type "Office 2000 Certification", press [Enter], then type "Register by e-mail".
c. Select "Fall Schedule", then click the Insert Hyperlink button.
d. Create a hyperlink to the Southeast Fall Schedule file on your Project Disk. (*Hint*: Click File in the Browse for area.)
e. Select "Office 2000 certification", then create a hyperlink to the URL "www.microsoft.com".
f. Select "Register", then create a hyperlink to the e-mail address "register@southeast.com". Type "Register" in the Subject text box.
g. Click the Southeast Fall Schedule file button on the taskbar, press [Ctrl][End], press [Enter], then type "Southeast Computer Solutions Home".
h. Select the text, then create a hyperlink to the Southeast Computer Solutions file on your Project Disk. (*Hint*: Click the Existing File or Web Page icon in the Insert Hyperlink dialog box, then click File.)
i. Save your changes to the file, then close it.

6. Edit hyperlinks

a. Right-click the Register hyperlink, point to Hyperlink, then click Edit Hyperlink.
b. Change the Text to display from "register" to your name.
c. Click ScreenTip, then type "Send a message to Southeast Computer Solutions".
d. Change the e-mail address to your e-mail address. If you don't have an e-mail address, type "[your name]@southeast.com". Click OK to close the Edit Hyperlink dialog box.
e. Click in front of your name in the Web page, then type "Contact". Click after your name, then type "to register".
f. Save your changes to the Web page.

7. Preview a Web page

a. Click Web Page Preview on the File menu, then maximize your browser window if necessary.
b. Click the Fall Schedule hyperlink.
c. Scroll down the Southeast Fall Schedule page, then click the Southeast Computer Solutions Home hyperlink.
d. If you can connect to the Internet, click the Office 2000 certification hyperlink to test it. Use the Back button on your browser to return to the Southeast Home Page.
e. Click the e-mail hyperlink with your name. If you have an e-mail address, and if you can connect to the Internet to send an e-mail message, type a brief message to yourself, then send the message. Otherwise, close the mail message window.
f. Click View on the menu bar, click Source, look at the HTML tags for the Web page, then close the Notepad window.
g. Close the browser window to return to Word.
h. Print a copy of the Southeast Computer Solutions file, then close the file.

Independent Challenges

1. You work at Seneca Waters, a wetlands preserve and wildlife refuge that is open to the public. Your local chamber of commerce is creating a Web site that will include links to Web pages about attractions for tourists in your area. You create a Web page that briefly describes Seneca Waters for inclusion on the Web site.

To complete this independent challenge:

a. Start Word and create a new, blank Web page. Save your Web page with the title and filename "Seneca Waters" to your Project Disk.
b. Apply the Sumi Painting theme to the Web page.
c. Type "Seneca Waters", press [Enter], type "Wetlands Preserve and Wildlife Refuge", then press [Enter]. Apply the Heading 1 and Heading 2 styles to the heading and subheading, then center the headings.
d. Insert a horizontal line below the headings.
e. Below the line, insert a table with 2 columns and 1 row. (*Hint*: Use the Insert Table button.) Select the table, then center it on the page using the Center button. (*Hint*: To select the table, click the Table Select icon at the upper-left corner of the table, or use the Select Table command on the Table menu.)
f. In the right cell, type "Seneca Waters provides habitat—food, water, cover, and space—for millions of birds and other plants and animals. Visit Seneca waters to see:", then press [Enter].
g. Type the following list, pressing [Enter] after each item: Migratory birds, Endangered species, Native plants and animals, Beautiful wetlands. Format the list with bullets.
h. Click in the left cell, then open the ClipGallery. From the Nature category, insert the clip of the water bird in the first row, then close the ClipGallery.
i. Resize the clip to make it about 1" wide and 1" high, then use the Center button to center the clip in the cell.
j. Drag the border between the cells to the left about an inch. Select the table, click the Horizontal Line list arrow on the Tables and Borders toolbar, then click the No Border button.
k. Below the table, type "Open to the public from sunrise to sunset", apply the Heading 3 style, then center the text.
l. Save your changes to the Web page, preview it in your browser, close the browser, type your name in the bottom-left corner of the Web page, then print a copy of the Web page.
m. If you have the ability to send e-mail, use the E-mail button to send a copy of the Web page to your instructor or to someone else, then close the file.

2. You are the owner of a small bistro called Chez Andre, which specializes in French food with a Cuban twist. You have many loyal customers who call you regularly to inquire about the day's prix fixe dinner special. To make it easier for your customers, you decide to create a small Web site where you can post the prix fixe dinner menu each day.

To complete this independent challenge:

a. Start Word, click file on the menu bar, then click New. On the Web Pages tab in the New dialog box, double-click the Web Page Wizard.
b. Click Next, then type "Chez Andre" for the Web site title. Make sure the Web site location is a folder named "Chez Andre" on your Project Disk, then click Next. (*Hint*: If your Project Disk is in drive A, the Web site location should be A:\Chez Andre\.)
c. Click the Separate page option button, then click Next.
d. In the list of current pages in the Web site, click each listed page, then click Remove Page.
e. Click Add Template Page. In the Web Page Templates dialog box, click Left-aligned Column, then click OK.
f. Click Add Existing File, add the file WD G-3 from your Project Disk, then click Next.
g. Click the Left-aligned Column page in the list of Web pages, then click Rename. Rename the page "Chez Andre".
h. Rename the WD G-3 page "Today's Menu". Click Next.
i. Add the Citrus Punch visual theme to your Web site. (*Hint*: Click Browse Themes.) When you have added the theme, click Next, then click Finish.
j. It may take a few minutes for the Wizard to create the Web site. After the Wizard creates the Web pages, click the Chez Andre hyperlink on the home page.
k. Click the Edit button on the Internet Explorer browser toolbar. In Word, select the main heading placeholder and type "Ooo La La!". Change the font to Lucida Calligraphy, change the font size to 36, and italicize the text. (*Hint*: Select a different font if Lucida Calligraphy is not available.)
l. Select the first section heading and type "Chez Andre". Apply the Heading 1 style to the text and change the font color to black.
m. Select the paragraph under the section heading and type "A Modern French Bistro with a Cuban Twist". Format the text in the Heading 3 style.
n. Select the next paragraph and type "Serving dinner nightly and brunch every Sunday." Press [Enter], then type "Featuring bistro fare, prix fixe dinner specials, and late night Cuban bar food." Format the two sentences with bullets.
o. Under the bulleted list, type, "Eliot Street, Marcellus, New York", press [Enter], then type "Reservations: 315-555-7539".
p. Delete the remaining placeholder text, replace the caption placeholder with your name, then save your changes.
q. Click the Today's Menu hyperlink, then click the Edit button on the browser toolbar.
r. Format all the text except the hyperlink text in the Heading 4 style, change the font to Lucida Calligraphy, then center the text. Change the font size of "Today's Menu" to 36, then add a horizontal line under "Today's Menu".
s. Save your changes to the Web page, then close it.
t. Click the Refresh button on the browser toolbar. Test the other links, then close the browser windows.
u. In Word, print a copy of all the Web pages associated with the Chez Andre Web site, then close all the Web site files.

3. You work for the city of Amherst and have been assigned the task of creating a Web site for the city. You have already sketched your plan for the Web site and drafted the text for the home page and one of the other Web pages on the site. Now you need to format your home page and begin creating the other pages for the Web site.

To complete this independent challenge:

a. Start Word and open the file WD G-4 from your Project Disk. This file will be the Amherst home page. Save the file as a Web page with the page title and filename "Amherst home page" to your Project Disk.
b. Choose a theme for your Web site and apply it to the Amherst home page. Format the page using text styles, horizontal lines, and bullets. Add a clip art graphic to the Web page. If necessary, you can edit the text on the page or move it around to suit your design. When you have finished formatting the page, save your changes.
c. Open the file WD G-5 from your Project Disk. This file will be linked to the Amherst home page. Save the file as a Web page with the page title and filename "Amherst movies" to your Project Disk.

d. Apply the same theme to the Amherst movies Web page, and format it using text styles, horizontal lines, and bullets. Add a clip art graphic to the Web page. If necessary, edit the text on the page or move it around to suit your design.

e. At the bottom of the Web page, type "Amherst home", then use this text to create a hyperlink to the Amherst home page. When you have finished formatting the page, save your changes to the file.

f. Switch to the Amherst home page, scroll to the bottom of the page, then use the text "a weekend at the movies" to create a hyperlink to the Amherst movies Web page.

g. Save your changes to the home page, then preview it in your browser. Test the hyperlinks on both pages, then close the browser window. If necessary, adjust the formatting of your Web pages in Word.

h. Type your name at the bottom of each Web page, save your changes, print a copy of each page, then close the files.

WEB WORK

4. MediaLoft would like to begin selling books and CDs over the Internet. Your boss at MediaLoft has asked you to research the Web sites of other bookstores that sell products online and to draft a plan for a MediaLoft Web site. To create your plan, you'll investigate the Web sites of other bookstores, note the features of each, sketch a plan for a MediaLoft Web site, and then create a Web page that describes the positive and negative features of each Web site you visited and includes a hyperlink to each site. You can use your browser to search for online bookstores or use links from the Research Center on the MediaLoft intranet site. When you have finished your report, you'll e-mail this document to your boss.

To complete this independent challenge:

a. Connect to the Internet, then use your browser to search for online bookstores. You can also go to the MediaLoft intranet site at http://www.course.com/illustrated/MediaLoft, click the Research Center link, then click the Competition: Other Bookstores link to find a list of hyperlinks to online bookstores.

b. Investigate the Web sites of at least 3 different companies. Note the positive and negative features of each site: Is the home page well-organized? Is the layout and design of the site effective? Is it easy to navigate the site? Do the hyperlinks make sense? Is it easy to get information on products and to order a product online? What features make the site interesting and fun? Support your responses with examples from each Web site.

c. Disconnect from the Internet, then sketch a plan for a MediaLoft Web site using the guidelines for planning a Web site presented in this unit. Include a home page for your site and hyperlinks to several other Web pages. Include details about the content of each Web page on the site and describe how these Web pages should be developed. Also include plans for an e-mail hyperlink on your Web site.

d. Start Word and create a new blank Web page. Save the Web page with the page title and filename "Proposal for MediaLoft Web site" to your Project Disk.

e. Type the heading "What MediaLoft can learn from its competition", then type subheadings for each company whose Web site you intend to describe (use at least three). Under each subheading, describe the positive and negative features of each Web site you visited.

f. For each Web site you describe, insert a hyperlink to its home page.

g. If you have an e-mail address, insert a hyperlink to your e-mail address on the Web page.

h. Apply a theme to your Web page, then format it using styles, horizontal lines, bullets, and clip art. Make your Web page attractive and easy to read.

i. Type your name at the bottom of the Web page, save your changes, preview the Web page in your browser, then return to Word and print a copy of the Web page.

j. If you have the ability to send e-mail, use the E-mail button to send a copy of your Web page to your instructor or to someone else, then close the file.

Visual Workshop

Create the Web pages shown in Figure G-24 using the files WD G-6 and WD G-7 from your Project Disk. Save the WD G-6 file with the page title and filename "Pacific Spring Flower Show". Save the WD G-7 file with the page title "Pacific Spring Flower Show Directions" and the filename "Directions". Format the Web pages using the Artsy theme, and create hyperlinks between the Web pages as shown in Figure G-24. Add your name to the Web pages before printing them.

FIGURE G-24

Word 2000

Unit H

Merging Word Documents

Objectives

- Understand mail merge
- MOUS Create a main document
- MOUS Create a data source
- Enter and edit records
- Insert merge fields
- MOUS Perform a mail merge
- MOUS Create labels
- MOUS Sort records

A mail merge combines a standard document, such as a form letter, with customized information, such as a recipient's name and address, to create a set of customized documents. Mail merge is widely used by companies who need to send similar documents to many individuals at once. The recipient's name and other personal information are often added to a standard document to create a more personal impression. The Word Mail Merge Helper guides you step by step through the mail merge process. The marketing department recently surveyed MediaLoft customers. Alice Wegman wants to write to the customers who provided especially helpful feedback. She uses the Mail Merge Helper to create a form letter, enter the customers' names and addresses, perform the mail merge, and generate a mailing label for each envelope.

Unit H

Word 2000

Understanding Mail Merge

When you perform a mail merge, you merge a document that contains standard text with a document that contains unique data for individual people or items. Combining the two documents in a mail merge results in many customized versions of the standard document, each unique to an individual or item. Figure H-1 shows an overview of a mail merge. You can easily create form letters, mailing labels, envelopes, and other types of documents using Word's mail merge feature. Alice plans to produce her thank you letters using mail merge. Before beginning, she reviews the steps for merging documents using the Mail Merge Helper.

Details

Create the main document

The **main document** is the file that includes the text that will appear in every merge document. Text that appears in every version of a merge document is called **boilerplate text**. Later in the mail merge process, you will also insert merge fields into the main document to indicate where the custom information goes.

Create the data source

The **data source** is the file that contains the information, or data, that varies in each merged document. A data source is comprised of data fields and records. A **field** is a category of information—such as first name, last name, address, city, state, or zip code—that every merged document will contain. A **record** is a complete set of information for one individual or one item, such as one person's first name, last name, address, city, state, and zip code. Data source files are actually simple Word tables. Each column in the table represents one data field, such as a first name or zip code. The **header row** of the table contains the names of the data fields, called the **field names**, and each subsequent row in the table is a record. Each record row contains the complete set of data for one individual or one item.

Determine the fields to include in the data source

When you create a data source, you must decide what fields to include. It's important to think of and include all the fields you may need to use before you begin to enter data. For example, some addresses may include a department name or require a second line for an address, while other addresses may be very short. You can always leave a field blank if you don't need it, so it is better to use more fields rather than less fields in your data source. Each record must have the same number of data fields.

Enter the records in the data source

Once you have set up your data source and selected the fields to include, the next step is to enter the information for the records. When you perform a merge, each record is merged with the boilerplate text to create a unique document.

Insert merge fields in the main document

Merge fields are placeholders that indicate where in the main document the data from each record should be placed when the main document and the data source are merged. You must insert merge fields into the main document before performing the merge.

Perform the merge

When the main document and the data source are set up, merging the two documents is as simple as clicking a button. You can choose to merge to a new file, which will contain all the individual versions of the merged document, or to merge directly to a printer, fax, or e-mail.

FIGURE H-1: Mail Merge process

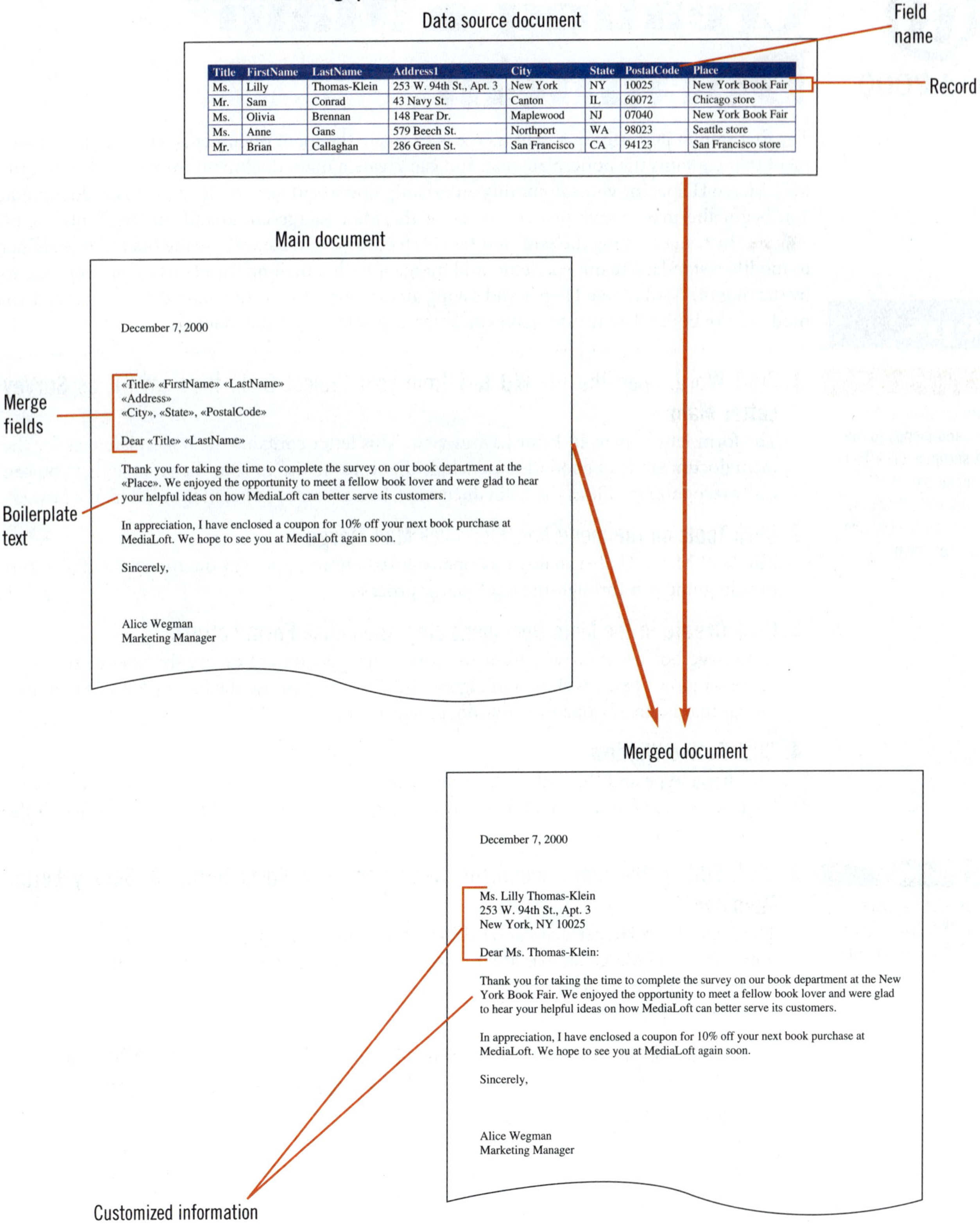

Title	FirstName	LastName	Address1	City	State	PostalCode	Place
Ms.	Lilly	Thomas-Klein	253 W. 94th St., Apt. 3	New York	NY	10025	New York Book Fair
Mr.	Sam	Conrad	43 Navy St.	Canton	IL	60072	Chicago store
Ms.	Olivia	Brennan	148 Pear Dr.	Maplewood	NJ	07040	New York Book Fair
Ms.	Anne	Gans	579 Beech St.	Northport	WA	98023	Seattle store
Mr.	Brian	Callaghan	286 Green St.	San Francisco	CA	94123	San Francisco store

Unit H

Word 2000

Creating a Main Document

The first step in performing a mail merge is to create the main document—the standard document that contains the boilerplate text. You can create a main document from scratch using the Mail Merge Helper, or you can modify an existing document and use it as the main document. You begin the mail merge process by using the Mail Merge command on the Tools menu. Instead of typing the same letter to each customer, Alice will use the Mail Merge Helper to modify a standard thank you letter and merge it with a mailing list of customers. She begins by starting the Mail Merge Helper and saving an existing letter as the main document. She then modifies the boilerplate text to make the letter appropriate for the mailing.

Steps 1 2 3 4

QuickTip

To return personalized toolbars and menus to the default settings, click Tools on the menu bar, click Customize, click Reset my usage data on the Options tab, click Yes, then click Close.

1. Start **Word**, open the file **WD H-1** from your Project Disk, then save it as **Survey Letter Main**

   The form letter opens in Print Layout view. This letter contains the boilerplate text for the main document. It's a good idea to include the word "main" in your filename so that you can easily recognize the file as the main document. You are ready to begin the mail merge process.

2. Click **Tools** on the menu bar, then click **Mail Merge**

   The Mail Merge Helper dialog box opens. Instructions appear at the top of the dialog box to help guide you through the mail merge process.

3. Click **Create** in the Main Document area, then click **Form Letters**

   A message box asking if you want to create a new document or use the document in the active window opens, as shown in Figure H-2. You want to use the Survey Letter Main document that is already open in your document window.

4. Click **Active Window**

   The merge type and the path of the main document appear in the Mail Merge Helper dialog box, as shown in Figure H-3. Before moving on to create the data source, you'll edit the main document letter.

Trouble?

This book assumes your Project Disk is located in drive A. The location of your Project Disk may differ.

5. Click **Edit** in the main document area, then click **Form letter: A:\Survey Letter Main.doc**

   The Mail Merge Helper dialog box closes so that you can make changes to the main document. The Mail Merge toolbar also opens. The Mail Merge toolbar appears in the document window of the main document when you are setting up a mail merge. You'll insert today's date at the top of the letter.

6. Click **Insert** on the menu bar, click **Date and Time**, click the **third date format** in the list of available formats, make sure the **Update automatically check box** is cleared, click **OK**, then press **[Enter]** five times

   Today's date appears at the top of the letter. Clearing the Update Automatically check box ensures that the date is inserted in the document as a static date. In other words, the date will not be updated each time you save or print the document.

7. Scroll down, select **Alice Wegman** in the closing, type your name, then click the **Save button** on the Standard toolbar

   The edited main document appears as shown in Figure H-4. Once you have edited the main document, you are ready to resume the mail merge process. You'll create a data source for the mail merge in the next lesson.

FIGURE H-2: Mail merge message box regarding the main document

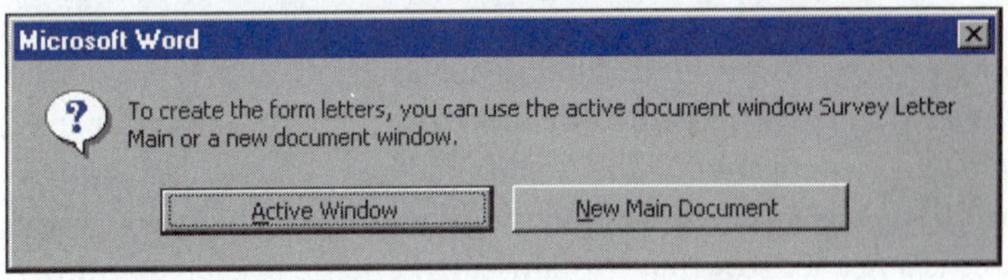

FIGURE H-3: Mail Merge Helper dialog box

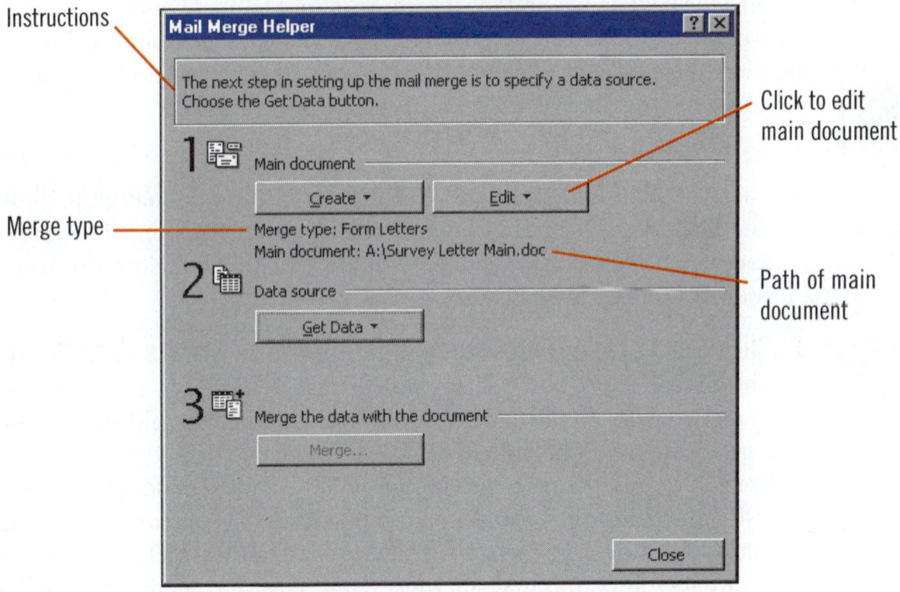

FIGURE H-4: Main document with Mail Merge toolbar

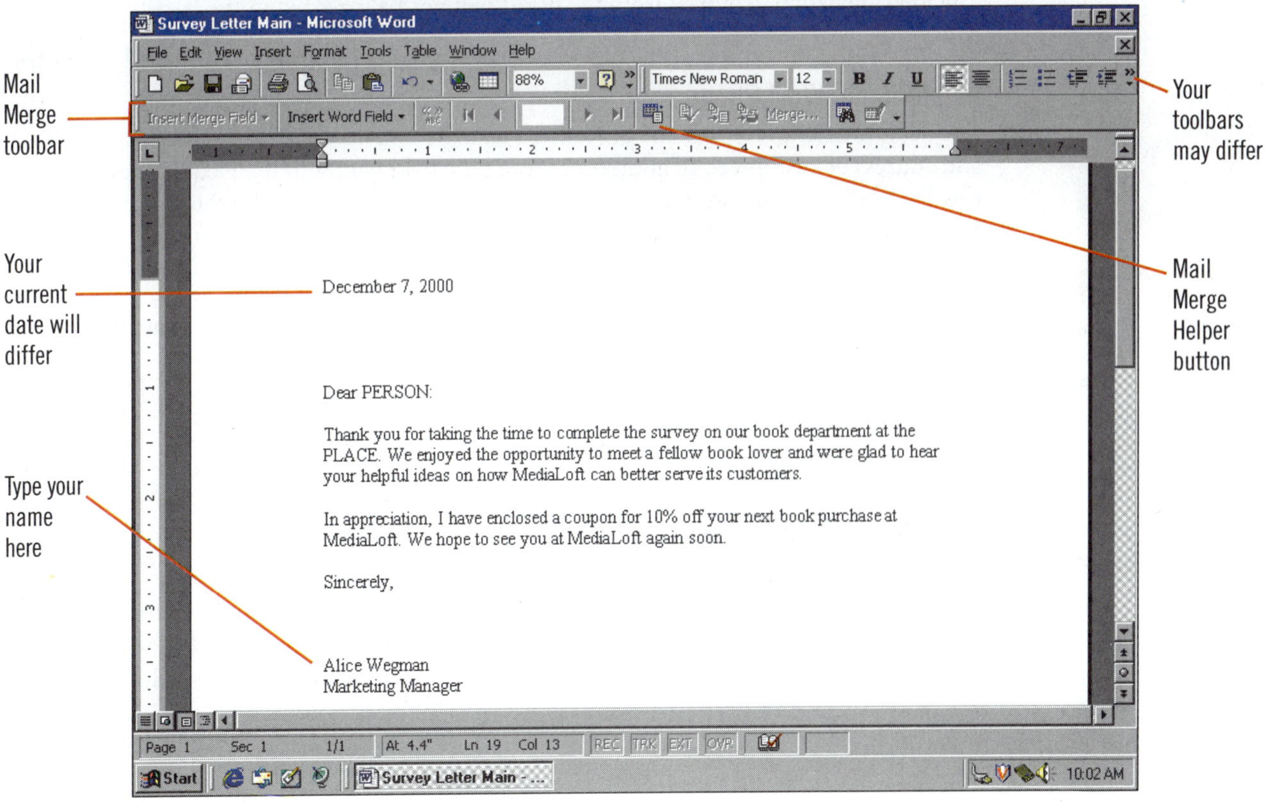

Word 2000

Unit H

Word 2000

Creating a Data Source

Once you have specified a main document, you are ready to create a data source. The **data source document** contains the information that will differ in each version of the merged document. The data source document is actually a table that contains the fields to be used in a mail merge and the records for each individual document you want to create. The first row of the table is a header row that contains a field name in each column. A **field** is a specific item of data, such as a first name or a zip code. The remaining rows of the table contain the records for the mail merge. A **record** is the specific data for an individual or item. When setting up a mail merge, you can create a new data source or you can specify an existing data source that already contains the field names and the records you want to use in your mail merge. Alice creates a new data source for her mail merge. She includes fields for each customer's name, address, and place the customer filled out the survey. She begins by specifying the fields the data source will contain. Later she will enter the records.

Steps

1. Click the **Mail Merge Helper button** on the Mail Merge toolbar
   The Mail Merge Helper dialog box opens with instructions for specifying the data source. Since a data source can be used with more than one main document, you want to design your data source to be flexible.

2. Click **Get Data** in Data Source area, then click **Create Data Source**
   The Create Data Source dialog box opens, as shown in Figure H-5. The Field names in header row list box includes a list of commonly used field names. You can use each field name as is, or you can add or remove a field name from the list. The more field names you use in a record, the more flexibility you have. For example, having the title, first name, and last name fields gives you the option of addressing someone informally by using their first name, or formally by using their title and last name. You'll use some of the field names for your data source, but first you must remove the field names you don't want to use.

   QuickTip
   If you remove a field name by mistake, immediately click Add Field Name to restore it.

3. Click **JobTitle** in the Field names in header row list box, then click **Remove Field Name**
   The JobTitle field is removed from the list. It will not be included in the data source.

4. Repeat Step 3 to remove the following field names: **Company**, **Address2**, **Country**, **HomePhone**, **WorkPhone**
   The fields are removed from the header row list. The remaining fields are for the title, name, and address of customers. In addition to using the field names in the Field names in header row list box, you can add your own field names to create new fields. You want to add one field to your data source for the location the customer filled out the survey.

5. Type **Place** in the Field name text box, then click **Add Field Name**
   "Place" is added to the header row list. After adding all the fields you want to include in your data source, you are ready to save the data source file.

   QuickTip
   Field names must start with a letter, contain no spaces, and be unique within the same data source document. They can be up to 40 characters long.

6. Click **OK**
   The Save As dialog box opens. It's a good idea to include the word "Data" in your filename so that you can easily recognize the file as the data source file.

7. Type **Survey Data**, make sure the Save in list box displays the location of your Project Disk, then click **Save**
   When you click Save, a message box reminding you that the data source contains no records opens, as shown in Figure H-6. In this message box, you can choose to edit the data source or edit the main document. You'll add records to the data source in the next lesson.

FIGURE H-5: Create Data Source dialog box

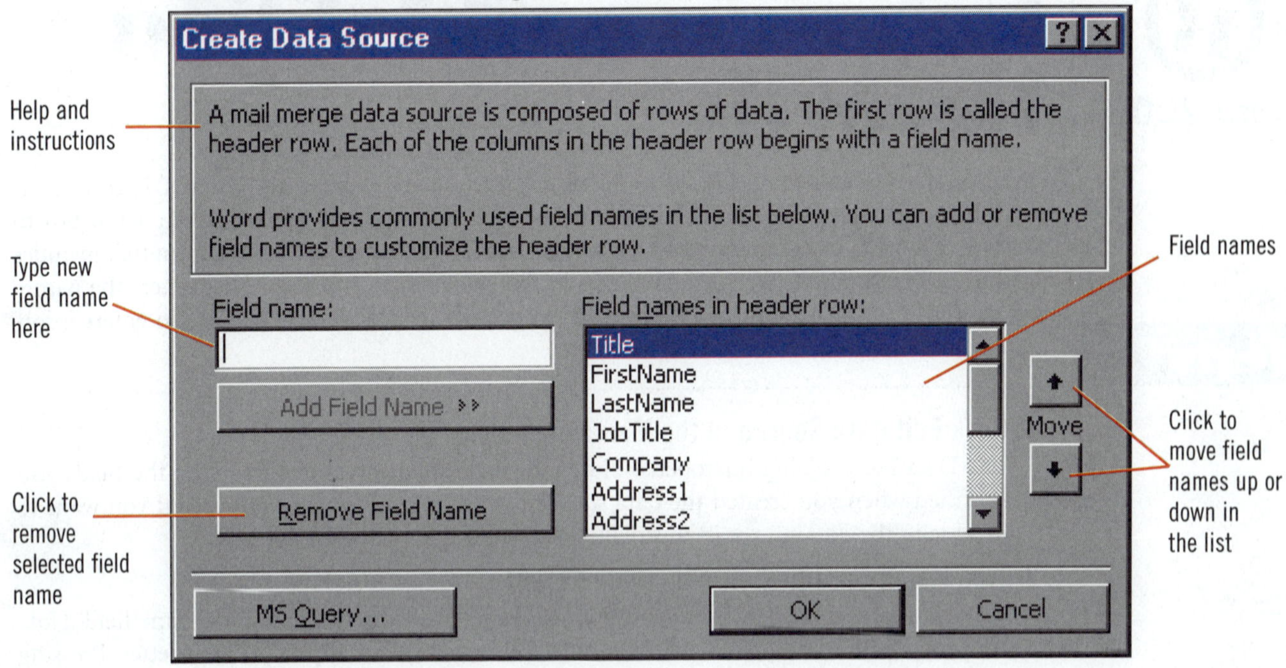

FIGURE H-6: Mail merge message box regarding the data source

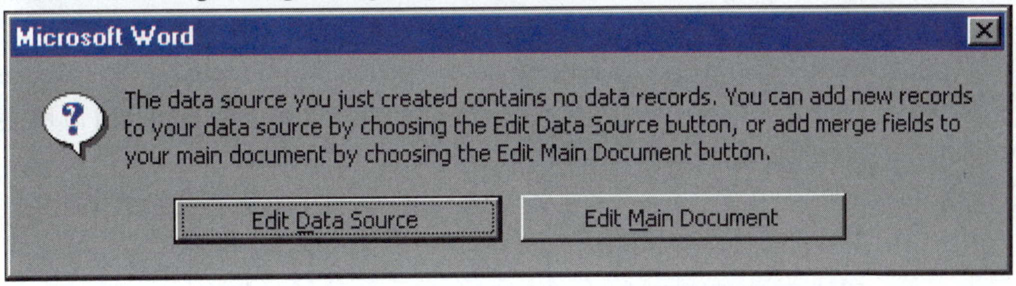

CLUES TO USE

Changing the order of field names

The order of field names in the data source does not matter, but it is convenient to arrange the field names in a logical order to make it easier to enter records in a data source document. To change the order of field names, select the field name that you want to move in the Field names in header row list box, then click the Up or Down arrows to reposition the field name where you want it in the list.

Unit H

Word 2000

Entering and Editing Records

Once you have created the fields for your data source, you are ready to add records. Records contain the information related to each individual or each item. You use the Data Form dialog box to add or edit records in a data source quickly. The Data Form dialog box shows a form that includes text boxes corresponding to the field names in the data source. Alice enters the names and addresses of the customers who provided especially helpful feedback. She also enters information about where they completed the survey.

Steps

1. Click **Edit Data Source** in the Mail merge message box
   The Data Form dialog box opens. The fields included in the dialog box are the fields you specified when you created the data source document.. You enter each record you want to include in the data source in this dialog box.
2. Type **Ms.** in the Title field, then press **[Tab]**
   "Ms." appears in the Title field and the insertion point moves to the FirstName field. Note that you must add a period after the title if you want it to appear in your letter. Pressing [Tab] moves the insertion point to the next field.
3. Type **Lilly**, press **[Tab]**, type **Thomas**, press **[Tab]**, type **253 W. 94th St., Apt. 3**, press **[Tab]**, type **New York**, press **[Tab]**, type **NY**, press **[Tab]**, type **10025**, press **[Tab]**, then type **New York Book Fair**
   Compare your Data Form dialog box with the one shown in Figure H-7.
4. Click **OK**
   Clicking OK closes the Data Form dialog box. You can add additional records to a data source at any time.
5. Click the **Edit Data Source button** on the Mail Merge toolbar
   The Data Form dialog box opens showing the first record added. You'll add four new records.
6. Click **Add New**, then enter the following 4 records, pressing **[Tab]** to move from field to field and pressing **Add New** at the end of each record:

Title	FirstName	LastName	Address1	City	State	PostalCode	Place
Mr.	Sam	Conrad	43 Navy St.	Canton	IL	60072	Chicago store
Ms.	Olivia	Brennan	148 Pear Dr.	Maplewood	NJ	07040	New York Book Fair
Ms.	Anne	Gans	579 Beech St.	Northport	WA	98023	Seattle store
Mr.	Brian	Callaghan	286 Green St.	San Francisco	CA	94123	San Francisco store

   Next, you need to review and save the changes to the data source document.
7. Click **View Source**
   The Survey Data document showing the data records in table format appears in the document, as shown in Figure H-8. The Database toolbar also appears in the document window. Each field name in the header row of the table corresponds to a field in the Data Form dialog box. You can add or change records using this view, or you can click the Data Form button on the Database toolbar to open the Data Form dialog box. Table H-1 describes some of the buttons on the Database toolbar. You notice a mistake in the first record.
8. In the first record, click after **Thomas**, then type **-Klein**
   The data in the LastName field for the first record changes to "Thomas-Klein".
9. Save your changes to the Survey Data file, then close it

QuickTip

You can enter as many characters as you need to in the text boxes in the Data Form dialog box.

Trouble?

If you clicked Add New after adding the last record, click Delete to delete the empty record.

QuickTip

If you need your name on the printed solutions, change "Brian Callaghan" to your name.

FIGURE H-7: Data Form dialog box

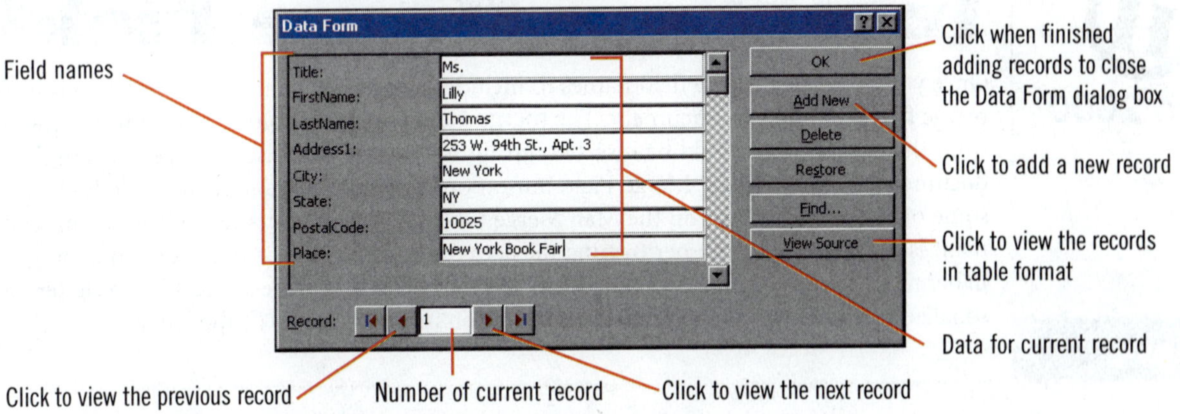

FIGURE H-8: Data records in table format

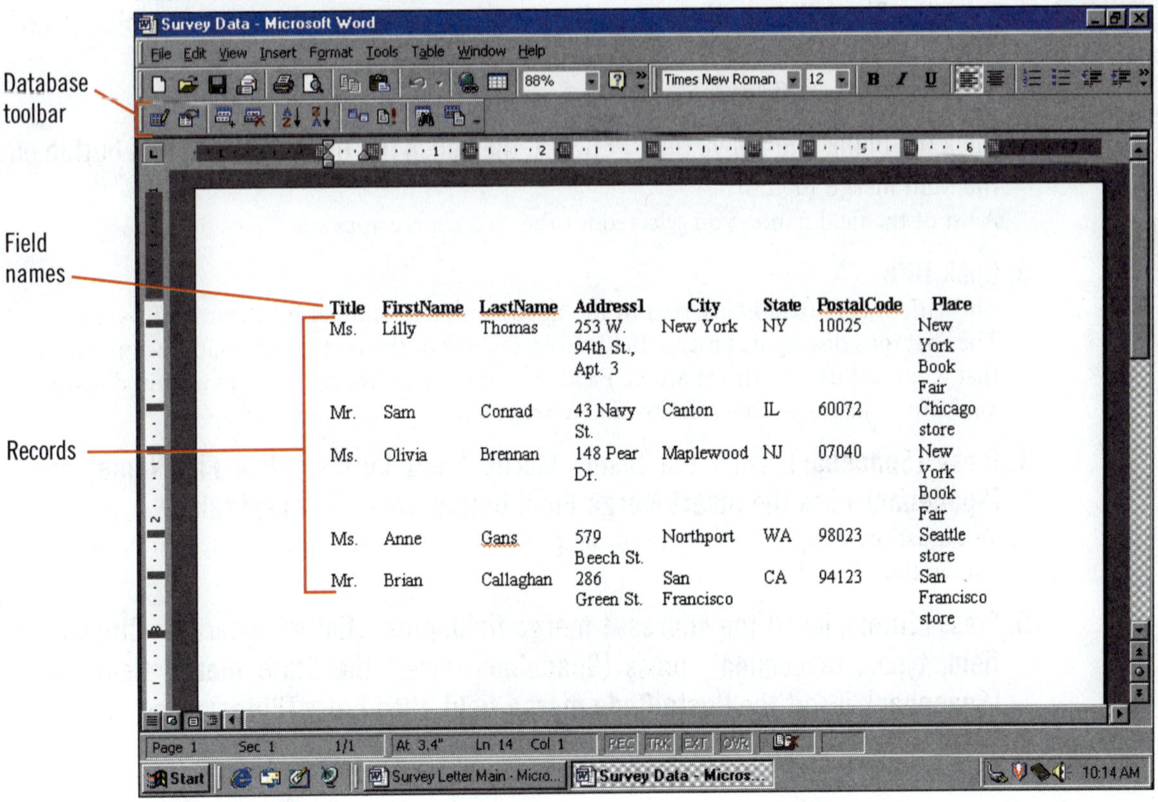

TABLE H-1: Database toolbar buttons

button	name	use to
	Data Form	Open the Data Form dialog box to enter a new record or edit an existing record in the data source
	Manage Fields	Open the Manage Fields dialog box to add, remove, or rename fields in the data source
	Add New Record	Add a new record to the data source table
	Delete Record	Delete a record from the data source table
	Sort Ascending	Sort the records in the data source in ascending order
	Sort Descending	Sort the records in the data source in descending order
	Find Record	Search for a record in the data source
	Mail Merge Main Document	Switch to the main document

Unit H

Word 2000

Inserting Merge Fields

Once you have selected the field names to include in your data source, the next step is to insert merge fields in the main document. The **merge fields** are placeholders that indicate where data from the data source should be inserted during the merge. You insert merge fields in the main document using the Insert Merge Field button on the Mail Merge toolbar. Table H-2 describes some of the other buttons on the Mail Merge toolbar. Inserting merge fields in the main document is the last step before performing the actual merge. Alice inserts the merge fields in her main document. She uses the merge fields to create the inside address for the letters, a personalized salutation, and customized information inside the body of the letter.

Steps

Trouble?

Click the More Buttons button to locate buttons that are not visible on your toolbars.

1. Click the **Show/Hide button** ¶ on the Standard toolbar to display nonprinting characters if necessary
   You'll insert merge fields for the inside address above the salutation in the letter.
2. Click the blank line above Dear PERSON, then click the **Insert Merge Field button** on the Mail Merge toolbar
   A list of the field names you selected for the data source appears.
3. Click **Title**
   The Title merge field is inserted in the document, surrounded by chevrons (<< and >>). The chevrons distinguish merge fields from the rest of the text in the main document. Note that you must use the Insert Merge Field button to insert merge fields in a main document. You cannot just type chevrons around a field name.
4. Press **[Spacebar]**, click the **Insert Merge Field button**, click **FirstName**, press **[Spacebar]**, click the **Insert Merge Field button**, then click **LastName**
   You must press [Spacebar] between merge fields if you want a space to appear between the data in the merged documents.
5. Press **[Enter]**, insert the **Address1 merge field**, press **[Enter]**, insert the **City merge field**, type **,** (a comma), press **[Spacebar]**, insert the **State merge field**, press **[Spacebar]**, insert the **PostalCode merge field**, then press **[Enter]** twice
   Be careful to insert proper punctuation, spacing, and blank paragraphs when you insert merge fields.
6. Double-click **PERSON** in the salutation, insert the **Title merge field**, press **[Spacebar]**, then insert the **LastName merge field**
   The Title merge field replaces the selected text. It can sometimes be useful to add placeholder text when you create a main document to later help you position the merge fields.
7. Select **PLACE** in the first sentence, insert the **Place merge field**, then click ¶
   Compare your document to that shown in Figure H-9 and make any necessary adjustments.
8. Save your changes to the main document

FIGURE H-9: Main document with merge fields

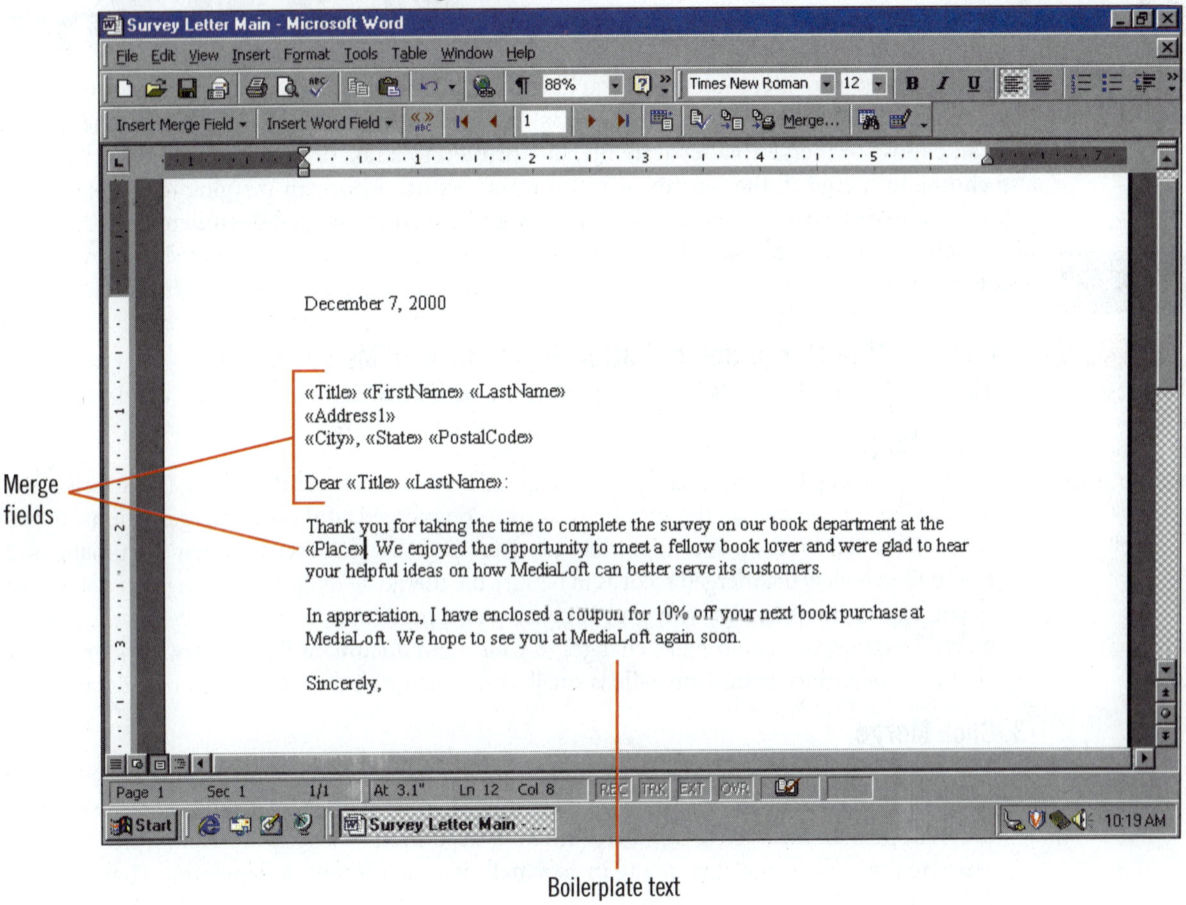

TABLE H-2: Mail Merge toolbar buttons

button	name	use to
	**View Merged Data**	Switch between viewing the main document with merge fields and with merged data
	**First Record**	Go to the first record in a merged document
	**Previous Record**	Go to the previous record in a merged document
1	**Go to Record**	Go to a specific record in a merged document
	**Next Record**	Go to the next record in a merged document
	**Last Record**	Go to the last record in a merged document
	**Mail Merge Helper**	Open the Mail Merge Helper dialog box
	**Check for Errors**	Check for errors in merged documents
	**Merge to New Document**	Merge to a new document and display the merged documents on-screen
	**Merge to Printer**	Print merged documents without reviewing them
Merge...	**Start Mail Merge**	Open the Merge dialog box
	**Find Record**	Search for a record in the merged documents
	**Edit Data Source**	Edit the data source document

Unit H

Word 2000

Performing a Mail Merge

Once your data source is complete and you have inserted merge fields in the main document, performing the actual mail merge is as simple as clicking a button. When you perform the merge, you can choose to merge to a separate file, to a printer, to a fax, or to e-mail addresses. You can also choose to merge all the records or just certain records. Although merging to a separate file requires more disk space, it allows you to review and edit your merged documents before printing or sending them. Alice merges the letter to a separate file so that she can view the results of the mail merge and make any necessary adjustments before printing the letters.

Steps 1 2 3 4

QuickTip

To merge to a file quickly, click the Merge to New Document button on the Mail Merge toolbar. To merge to a printer quickly, click the Merge to Printer button.

1. Click the **Mail Merge Helper button** on the Mail Merge toolbar

   The Mail Merge Helper dialog box opens showing instructions for merging the documents.

2. Click **Merge**

   The Merge dialog box opens as shown in Figure H-10. You can use this dialog box to select the destination for the merge, the specific records to be merged, and other merge options. If you have a large data source, you might identify a few records to merge to a new document. You would then review the merged records to be sure the merge fields appear in the main document as you expect them to and with proper spacing and punctuation. After reviewing the sample merged records, you could make changes to your main document if necessary before merging all the records. Since your source file is small, you'll merge all the records to a new document.

3. Click **Merge**

   The main document and the data source are merged to a new document called Form Letters1, as shown in Figure H-11. The document contains five letters, each addressed to a different person. Each letter in the document is separated by a section break, which you can see when you view the document in Normal view or display non-printing characters in Print Layout view.

QuickTip

If you notice an error in an individual's merge fields, you should make the change in the data source, save the change, and then perform the merge again. This way the next time you use that data source file, the information will be up-to-date.

4. Scroll down and read each letter

   The letters each include the custom information you entered in the data source. If you wanted to, you could edit an individual letter in the merged document file to customize it further. Note that any changes you make to the customized data in the merged document file are not made to the data source file.

5. Click **File** on the menu bar, then click **Save**

   The Save As dialog box opens. If you have a very large data source you may decide not to save the merged file since merged files can take up quite a bit of disk space. Once the main document file and the data source file are created it is simple to merge the files any time you need the merged document. Since your merged file is small, you'll save it with a new filename before printing it.

6. Type **Survey Letter Merged**, make sure the location of your Project Disk is displayed in the Save in list box, then click **Save**

   The document containing the merged letters is saved with the filename "Survey Letter Merged". You can now print the letters.

7. Click **File** on the menu bar, click **Print**, click the **Current Page option button** in the Print range area in the Print dialog box, then click **OK**

   The first of five letters prints.

8. Close all open Word files, saving changes when prompted

FIGURE H-10: Merge dialog box

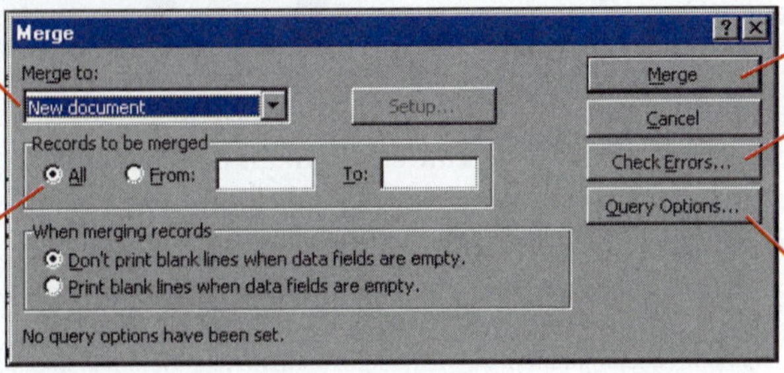

FIGURE H-11: Merged documents

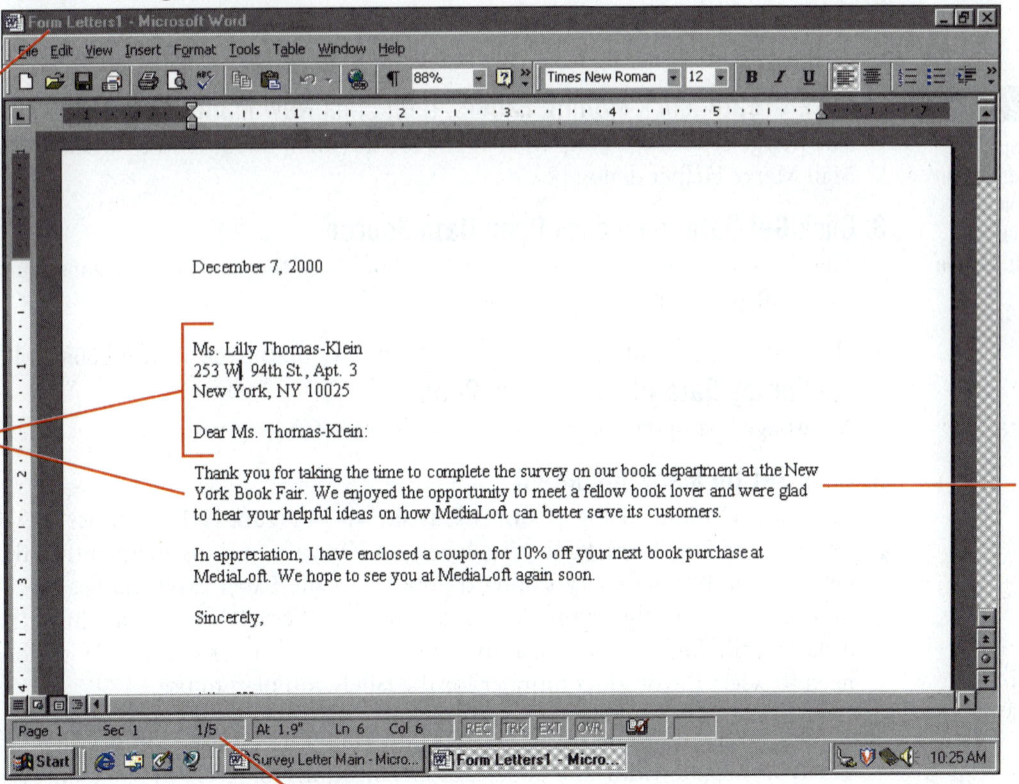

CLUES TO USE

Previewing merged documents

It's a good idea to preview a merge document before performing the merge to make sure that the printed documents will appear as you want them to. To preview a merged document, click in the main document, then click the View Merged Data button on the Mail Merge toolbar. The data from the first record in the data source appears in place of the merge fields in the main document window, and it appears just as it will in the printed document. Check the document to make sure that the merge fields, punctuation, and spacing all appear in the preview as you want them to appear in the final merge. To view the data from other records, you can click the arrow buttons , , , on the Mail Merge toolbar, or type a record number in the Go to Record box 1 on the Mail Merge toolbar. To make adjustments to the main document, click the View Merged Data button again to view the merge fields in the main document, make the necessary adjustments, then save the main document. The View Merged Data button is a toggle button. You can use it to switch between viewing the merge fields and previewing the merged data.

Unit H

Word 2000

Creating Labels

You can also use a data source to create labels or print envelopes for a mailing. To create labels or print envelopes, you must create a new main document, attach the existing data source, select the format for your labels or envelopes, and then merge the files. Word includes many standard formats for labels, envelopes, post cards, nametags, disk labels, and other types of label documents that you can create using a mail merge. Alice wants to create labels to mail the merged letters. She creates a new main document for the labels and attaches the data source.

Steps 1 2 3 4

1. Click the **New Blank Document button** on the Standard toolbar, click **Tools** on the menu bar, then click **Mail Merge**

   The Mail Merge Helper dialog box opens. You'll create a new main document for the mailing labels.

2. Click **Create**, click **Mailing Labels**, then click **New Main Document**

   The merge type and a temporary name for the main document, Document4, appear in the Mail Merge Helper dialog box.

   Trouble?
   The number following the filename "Document" will differ depending on the number of files you have opened during this session of Word.

3. Click **Get Data**, then click **Open Data Source**

   The Open Data Source dialog box opens. You'll use the Survey Data data source document you created earlier.

4. Make sure the location of your Project Disk is displayed in the Look in list box, click the **Survey Data** file, then click **Open**

   A message box opens, prompting you to finish setting up your main document.

5. Click **Set Up Main Document**

   The Label Options dialog box opens, as shown in Figure H-12. You use this dialog box to select a standard format for your labels and specify options for printing the labels. The default brand name Avery standard appears in the Label products list box. The Product number box lists the many standard types of Avery labels for mailings, name badges, diskettes, file folders, post cards, business cards, and other types of label documents. You need to select the product number for the labels you plan to use.

6. Scroll down the Product number list box, then click **5161 – Address**

   The type, height, width, and paper size specifications for Avery 5161 – Address labels appear in the Label information area of the dialog box.

7. Click **OK**

   The Create Labels dialog box opens. In this dialog box, you insert the merge fields for the labels.

8. Click **Insert Merge Field** in the Create Labels dialog box, click **Title**, press **[Spacebar]**, then enter the remaining merge fields, spacing, and punctuation as shown in Figure H-13

   Be careful to enter the punctuation and spacing accurately so that your labels are punctuated properly when you perform the merge.

9. Click **OK**

   The Mail Merge Helper dialog box displays the filename and location of the data source and the merge options in effect.

10. Click **Close**

    The label main document with the merge fields inserted appears in the document window. You'll sort the records to be merged and perform the merge in the next lesson.

FIGURE H-12: Label Options dialog box

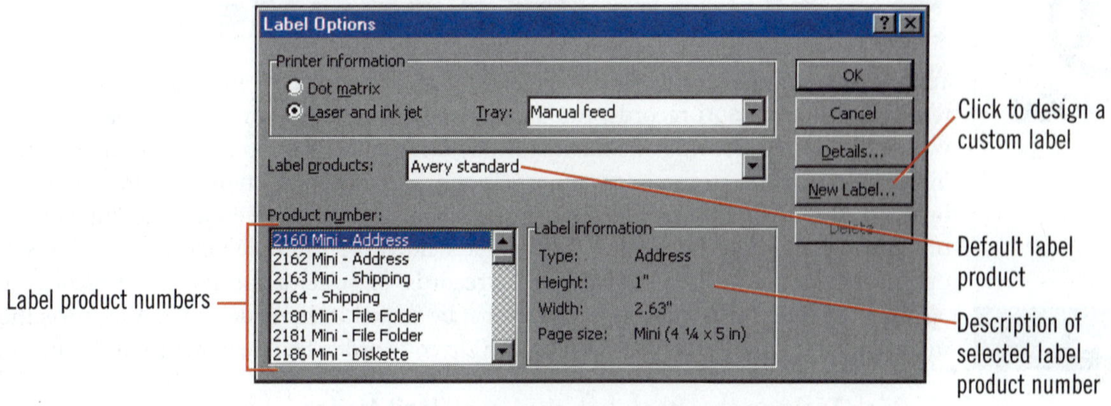

FIGURE H-13: Create Labels dialog box

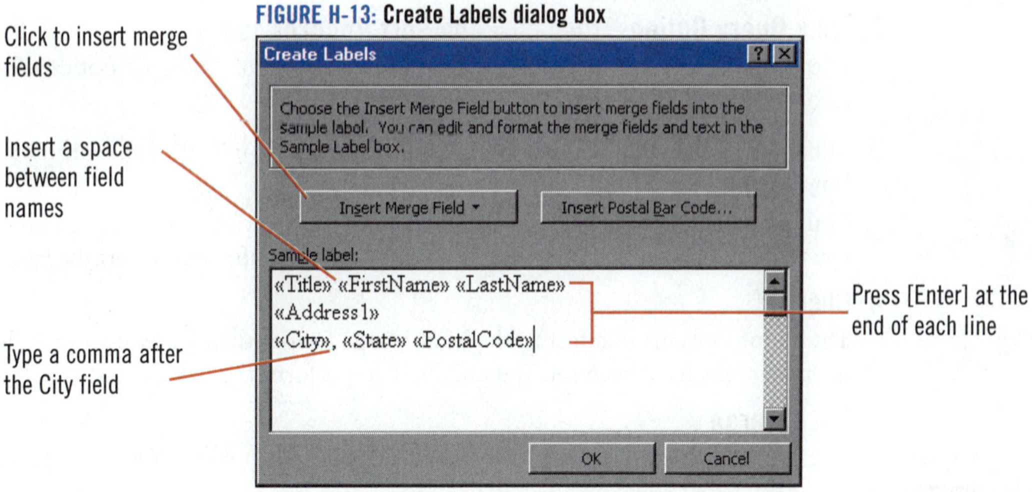

CLUES TO USE

Printing envelopes and labels

You don't need to perform a mail merge to print envelopes and labels in Word. You can easily format and print individual envelopes and labels using the Envelopes and Labels command on the Tools menu. The Envelopes and Labels dialog box includes an Envelopes tab and a Labels tab. On the Envelopes tab, shown in Figure H-14, type the recipient's address in the Delivery address box and the return address in the Return address box. Before printing the envelope, click Options to open the Envelope Options dialog box, where you can select an envelope size, format the font and position of the text on the envelope, and set the printing options. Click OK to close the dialog box. When you are ready to print the envelope, insert an envelope in your printer as shown in the Feed area on the Envelopes tab, then click Print. You can also print an individual label. On the Labels tab in the Envelopes and Labels dialog box, type the address for the label in the Address box, click Options to select the label product number in the Label Options dialog box, click OK, then click Print.

FIGURE H-14: Envelopes tab in Envelopes and Labels dialog box

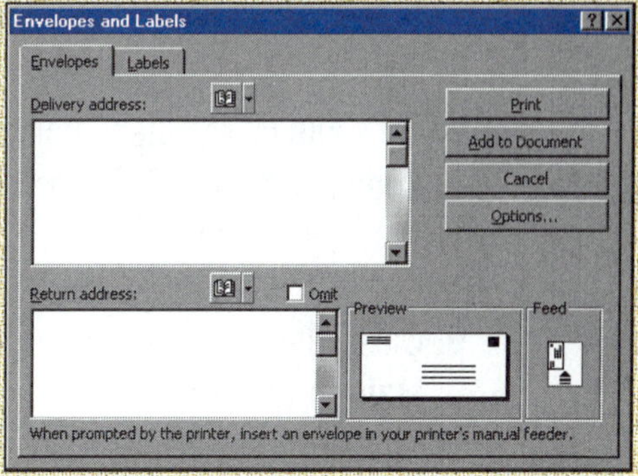

Unit H

Word 2000

Sorting Records

You can determine the order in which Word merges the records in a data source by sorting the records. When you **sort** records, you arrange them in a logical order or sequence. For example, you might sort the records of a mailing list by last name or by zip code. You can sort the records in a data source by setting a query option. In the query option, you indicate the criteria (or fields) by which you want to sort, and then choose to sort the records in either ascending or descending order. You can sort a data source by a single field or by multiple fields. When you set a query option, you can also apply a **filter** to the records, or select a specific set of records to merge. All bulk mailings at MediaLoft must be sorted in zip code order. Alice sorts the records in the data source so that the labels merge in zip code order. She then merges and prints the labels.

Steps

1. Click **Tools** on the menu bar, then click **Mail Merge**

   The Mail Merge Helper dialog box opens. You'll sort the records before performing the merge.

2. Click **Query Options,** then click the **Sort Records tab**

   The Sort Records tab in the Query Options dialog box contains options for sorting the records in a data source.

3. Click the **Sort by list arrow**, scroll down the list of field names, then click **PostalCode**

   Compare your Sort Records tab with Figure H-15. You can sort by more than one criteria if you want. Since you are using a small data source, it is sufficient to sort the labels by zip code.

4. Click **OK**

   The list of Options in effect in the Mail Merge Helper dialog box now includes a note that query options have been set. You are ready to perform the merge.

5. Click **Merge**

   The Merge dialog box opens with the default options in effect. You'll merge all the records.

6. Click **Merge**

   The records are merged to a new document in zip code order as shown in Figure H-16. The temporary name of the new document is Labels2. The labels are arranged in the document in a Word table. You may or may not be able to see the table borders depending on your table settings. Now that the labels are in a new Word document, you can format them as you wish.

7. Click **Edit** on the menu bar, click **Select All**, click the **Font Size list arrow** on the Formatting toolbar, click **14**, click the **Bold button** B, then deselect the labels

   The labels are formatted in 14-point bold text. To make formatting changes that affect only the fields in a document, apply the formatting changes to the merge fields in the main document. Before applying formatting, select the merge field by clicking and dragging over the chevrons and field name. Do not make formatting changes to the data source document because those changes will be lost when the merge is performed. You can now save the labels.

8. Click **File** on the menu bar, click **Save**, save the file with the filename **Survey Labels Zip Code Merge** to your Project Disk, then click the **Print button** on the Standard toolbar

   The labels print. If you want to print the labels on label paper, you should use Avery 6151–Address label paper.

9. Close the file, save the label main document file with the filename **Survey Labels Main** to your Project Disk, close the file, then exit Word

   The sort options you specified for the data source are saved along with the main document file. When you open the data source file, the records will be sorted in zip code order.

QuickTip

If you want to see the borders around the labels, click Table on the menu bar, then click Show Gridlines.

FIGURE H-15: Sort Records tab in Query Options dialog box

Sort in ascending order by postal code

FIGURE H-16: Merged labels in zip code order

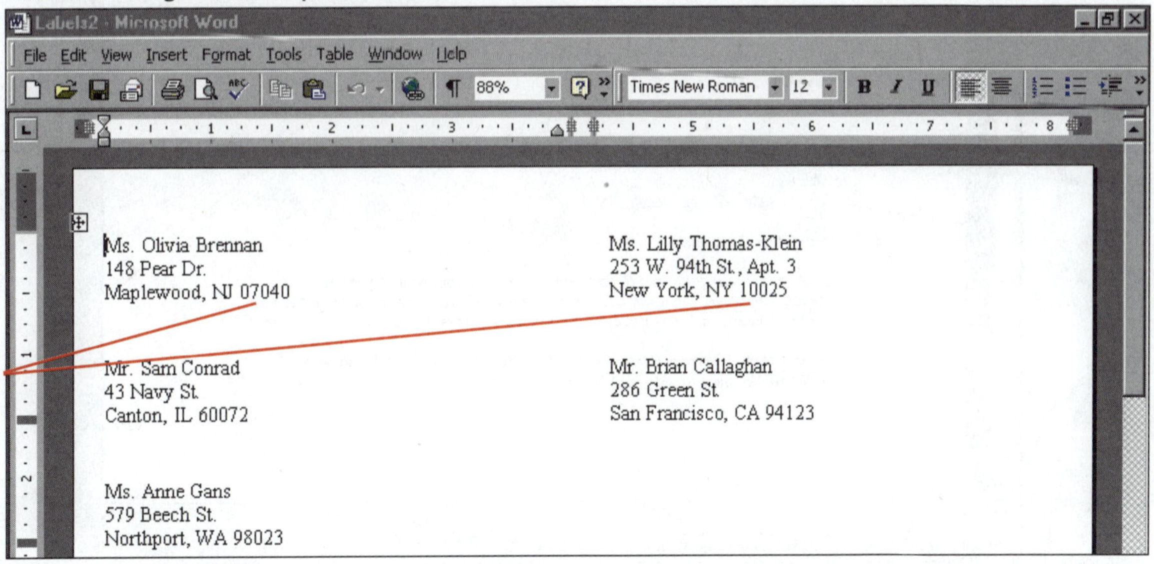

Labels are organized by zip code

Word 2000

CLUES TO USE

Filtering the records to be merged

Sometimes you do not want to send a document to all the individuals in a data source. For example, you might want to send a letter to only those customers who live in California. Using the Filter Records tab in the Query Options dialog box shown in Figure H-17, you can apply a **filter** to the records so that only the records that meet the criteria you specify merge. To filter records, click the Field list arrow on the Filter Records tab, select a data field, click the Comparison list arrow, then select a comparison phrase. A comparison phrase indicates how a field should be evaluated in relation to the criteria you enter in the Compare to text box. For example, to filter for the records of people living in California, you would select the field name "State" in the Field list box, select the phrase "Equal to" in the Comparison list box, then type "CA" (the abbreviation for California) in the Compare to text box. You can specify up to six filter criteria on the Filter Records tab. When you finish setting filter criteria, click OK.

FIGURE H-17: Filter Records tab in Query Options dialog box

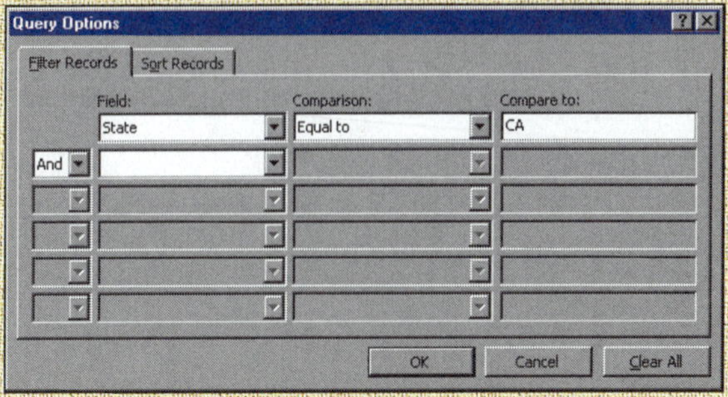

Word 2000

Practice

► Concepts Review

Label each element shown in the main document window in Figure H-18.

FIGURE H-18

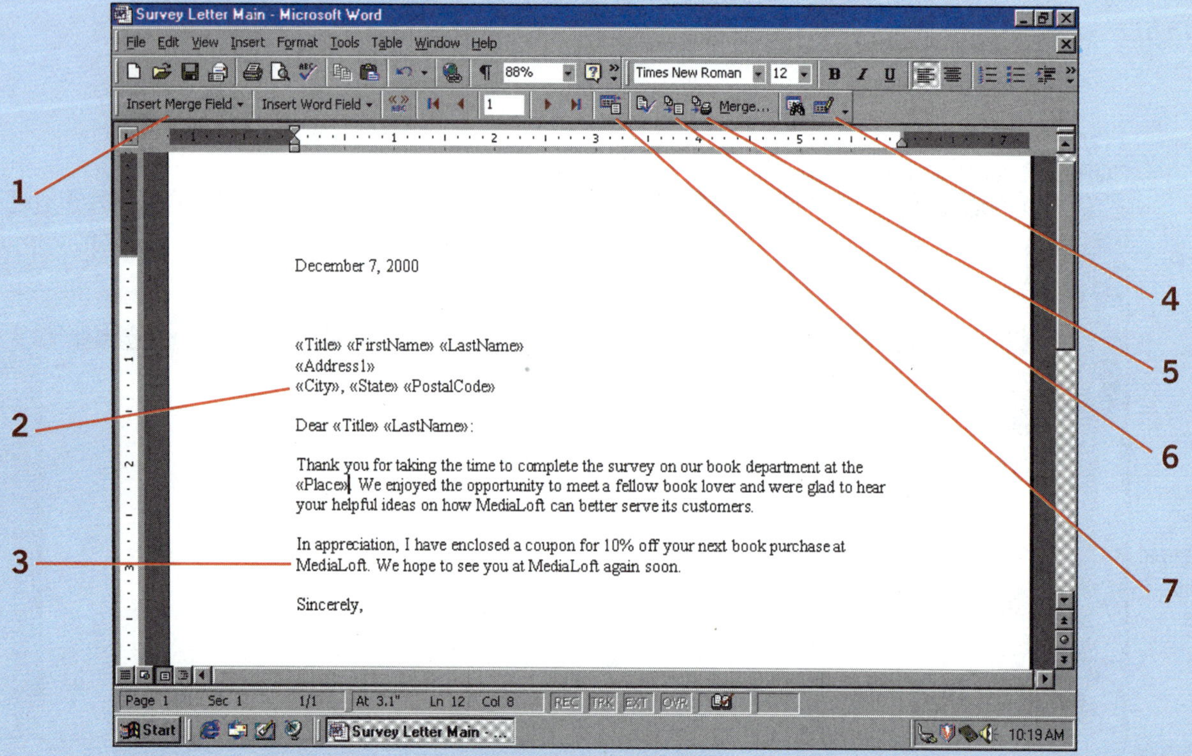

Match each term with the statement that describes it.

8. Data source	**a.** The entire collection of data related to an item or individual
9. Record	**b.** A file that contains the customized information that differs in each merged document
10. Merge field	**c.** A category of information in a data source
11. Main document	**d.** The text that is the same for each version of a merged document
12. Boilerplate text	**e.** Criteria used to select a group of records to be merged
13. Filter	**f.** A command used to show the data source in table format
14. View Source	**g.** A file that contains the standard text for all versions of the merged document
15. Field	**h.** The placeholder inserted into a main document to show where the customized data should be merged

Select the best answer from the list of choices.

16. Which statement best describes a benefit of showing records in table format?
- **a.** You can add merge fields to the main document.
- **b.** You can view one data record at a time.
- **c.** You can edit the merged document.
- **d.** You can add or delete records from the data source.

17. Which of the following tasks cannot be accomplished using the Query Options dialog box?
- **a.** Sort records by fields in ascending or descending order.
- **b.** Save query specifications for future merge operations.
- **c.** Select fields to be included in the merge operation.
- **d.** Select records to be included in the merge operation.

18. To set up a mail merge, you must first
- **a.** Insert merge fields in a document.
- **b.** Click Tools on the menu bar, then click Mail Merge.
- **c.** Click View on the menu bar, point to Toolbars, then click Mail Merge.
- **d.** Click Tools on the menu bar, then click Merge Documents.

19. To place merge fields in a document
- **a.** Insert chevron symbols around the field names in the main document.
- **b.** Click the Insert Merge Field button on the Mail Merge toolbar.
- **c.** Click the New Merge Field button on the Mail Merge toolbar.
- **d.** Click the Manage Fields button on the Database toolbar.

20. The header row of a data source contains
- **a.** Records.
- **b.** Boilerplate text.
- **c.** Field names.
- **d.** Filters.

Skills Review

1. Create a main document
- **a.** Start Word, open the file WD H-2 from your Project Disk, then save it as "Ideas Main".
- **b.** Open the Mail Merge Helper dialog box by clicking Tools on the menu bar, then clicking Mail Merge.
- **c.** Click Create, then create a form letter main document using the Ideas Main document in the active window.
- **d.** Click Edit, then type your name in the From line of the memo. Click the Subject placeholder, then type "NEWSLETTER IDEAS".
- **e.** Save your changes to the main document.

2. Create a data source

a. Click the Mail Merge Helper button on the Mail Merge toolbar.
b. Create a new data source by clicking Get Data, then clicking Create Data Source.
c. In the Field names in header row list box, remove all the field names except FirstName, LastName, and JobTitle.
d. Add a field called "MailStation" using the Add Field Name button, then click OK.
e. Name the data source file "Ideas Data" and save it to your Project Disk.

3. Enter and edit records in a data source

a. Click Edit Data Source to add records to the data source document.
b. Enter the following records, clicking [Enter] or [Tab] to move from field to field, and clicking Add New between records:

FirstName	LastName	JobTitle	MailStation
James	Quirk	Marketing Manager	34
Elizabeth	Martinez	Customer Service Manager	18
Scott	Silver	Vice President of Sales	4
Peter	Hendry	Charter Sales Liaison	45
Miranda	Ortez	Vice President of Marketing	35
Monica	Sims	Director of Advertising	20
Lorraine	Crow	Director of Development	32
Isaac	Parsons	Human Resources Manager	22

c. Click OK after entering the last record.
d. Click the Edit Data Source button on the Mail Merge toolbar, then click View Source.
e. Compare the data source table to the table in Step b, save your changes to the data source file, then close it.

4. Insert merge fields

a. Display the non-printing characters in the main document, then click after the tab character that follows To:.
b. Click the Insert Merge Field button on the Mail Merge toolbar, then click FirstName.
c. Press [Spacebar], then insert the LastName merge field.
d. Type (a comma), press [Spacebar], then insert the JobTitle merge field.
e. Click after the tab character that follows MAILSTATION:, then insert the MailStation merge field.
f. Save your changes to the main document.

5. Perform a mail merge

a. Click the Merge to New Document button on the Mail Merge toolbar.
b. Scroll through the merged memos to check for errors.
c. Save the merged document with the filename "Ideas Merge" to your Project Disk.
d. Print one page of the document, then close the Ideas Merge document and the Ideas Main document, saving any changes.

6. Create labels

a. Open a new blank document.
b. Click Tools on the menu bar, then click Mail Merge.
c. Click Create, click Mailing Labels, then click New Main Document.
d. Click Get Data, click Open Data Source, select the Ideas Data file on your Project Disk, then click Open.
e. Click Set Up Main Document.

f. Click 5161–Address in the Product number list box in the Label Options dialog box, then click OK.
g. In the Create Labels dialog box, click Insert Merge Field, then click FirstName.
h. Press [Spacebar], then insert the LastName merge field.
i. Press [Enter], then insert the JobTitle merge field.
j. Press [Enter], type "Mail station", press [Spacebar], then insert the MailStation merge field.
k. Click OK, then click Close in the Mail Merge Helper dialog box.
l. Save the labels main document as "Ideas Labels Main" to your Project Disk.

7. Sort records

a. Click the Mail Merge Helper button on the Mail Merge toolbar.
b. Click Query Options, then click the Sort Records tab.
c. Click the Sort by list arrow, click LastName, then click OK.
d. Click Merge in the Mail Merge Helper dialog box.
e. In the Merge dialog box, make sure New Document is selected, then click Merge.
f. Select all the labels, then change the font size to 14.
g. Change the name in the first label to your name, then save the merged labels with the filename "Ideas Labels Merge" to your Project Disk.
h. Print the labels
i. Close all open files, saving changes when prompted.

Independent Challenges

1. You are a marketing assistant at Nomad, Ltd., a small adventure travel company. Rather than respond individually to every request for information that you get from customers, you keep a running mailing list of the customers who call or write for information, and then every few weeks you set aside time to answer all the requests at once. When you send information to customers, you send a standard form letter about upcoming Nomad adventure tours along with a copy of Nomad's newsletter. You merge this standard letter with the mailing list you created so that the letter has a personal touch.

To complete this independent challenge:

a. Start Word, open the file WD H-3 from your Project Disk, type your name in the closing, then save the file as "Nomad Main" to your Project Disk.
b. Open the file WD H-4 from your Project Disk, save it as "Nomad Data" to your Project Disk, then close the file.
c. Open the Mail Merge Helper, then create a form letter main document using the active window.
d. Use the Nomad Data file from your Project Disk as the data source.
e. Insert merge fields in the main document. Replace the words in all caps in the letter with merge fields with the same name. Be sure to use proper spacing and punctuation between the merge fields.
f. Open the Mail Merge Helper, then sort the records to be merged in zip code order.
g. Merge the form letter and data source to a new document.
h. Scroll through each letter in the merge document and make any necessary adjustments.
i. Save the merge file with the filename "Nomad Merge" to your Project Disk.
j. Print one letter from the merge file, then close the file.
k. Open the Mail Merge Helper, then create a new mailing label document.
l. Use the Nomad Data file from your Project Disk as the data source, then set up the main document.
m. Use Avery 5161 – Address labels, then insert the merge fields in the sample label using correct spacing and punctuation.
n. Sort the records to be merged in zip code order, then merge the label main document and the data source to a new document.
o. Scroll down the label merge document and make any necessary adjustments. Add your name and mailing information to the label merge document as the last label.

p. Save the label merge document with the filename "Nomad Label Merge" to your Project Disk, print the document, then close it.
q. Save the label main document with the filename "Nomad Label Main" to your Project Disk, then close it.
r. Close the Nomad Main letter, saving any changes.

2. You are a writer and you have just finished writing the last chapter of a novel called *Blizzard.* You must send off a disk containing the manuscript to your publisher right away. You have written a quick cover letter to accompany your manuscript. Now you'll use Word to create a label for the disk. You'll also address an envelope to mail the cover letter and disk. You must be able to print envelopes on your printer to complete the second part of this independent challenge.

To complete this independent challenge:

a. Start Word, click Tools on the menu bar, then click Envelopes and Labels.
b. On the Labels tab, click Options, then select the Avery 5096 – Diskette label in the Label Options dialog box.
c. In the Printer area, select the appropriate option for your printer in the Tray list box (Manual feed or the appropriate printer tray), then click OK.
d. In the Address box, type your name, press [Enter], type "Final chapter of Blizzard", press [Enter], type "Copyright [your name]", press [Enter], then type today's date.
e. In the Print area, select the Single label option button.
f. Insert label paper in the appropriate tray in your printer or in your printer's manual feeder, then click Print. You can also print a label on plain paper.
g. Click Tools on the menu bar, then click Envelopes and Labels.
h. On the Envelopes tab, type the following in the Delivery address box: Helff Publishers, Inc. 475 E. 23rd St., Suite 19, New York, NY 10027 Attn: Helen Grimes, Editorial Department
i. Type your name and address in the Return address box, then click Options.
j. On the Envelope Options tab, make sure the Envelope size is set to Size 10, then change the font of the delivery address and return address to Times New Roman. (*Hint*: Click Font in both places on the Envelope Options tab.)
k. Click the Printing Options tab, select the appropriate option for your printer in the Feed from list box (Manual feed or the appropriate printer tray), then click OK.
l. If you are able to print envelopes on your printer, insert an envelope in the appropriate tray for your printer as shown in the Feed area on the Envelopes tab, then click Print. (*Note:* If you are asked if you want to save the return address as the default address, click No.)

3. As the circulation manager at Finance News, Inc., you are responsible for distributing your company's newsletters and bulletins to subscribers. As a result of a new tax law in Massachusetts, your company has just published a special bulletin reporting on financial news of interest to your Massachusetts subscribers. You need to create mailing labels to send the bulletin to all your subscribers with Massachusetts addresses.

To complete this independent challenge:

a. Start Word, open the file WD H-5 from your Project Disk, then save it with the filename "Subscriber Data". This file will be the data source for your merge.
b. Open the Mail Merge Helper and create a new mailing label main document. Use the Subscriber Data file as the data source.
c. Set up the main label document using Avery 5161 – Address labels.
d. Insert the merge fields in the label document using proper spacing and punctuation.
e. Set query options for the merge so that only records with Massachusetts (or "MA") in the state field are merged. On the Filter Records tab, select State as the field, select Equal to as the Comparison, then type "MA" in the Compare to text box.
f. Merge the label document and the filtered data source to a new document.
g. Add your name as a label to the label merge document, save it with the filename "Subscriber Labels MA Merge" to your Project Disk, print the labels, then close the file.

h. Save the main document with the filename "Subscriber Labels Main" to your Project Disk, then close the file.
i. Close the data source file.

4. You are an assistant in the marketing department at the MediaLoft San Diego store. One of your responsibilities is to write press releases for upcoming in-store events. To complete this task more efficiently, you decide to use mail merge to create your press releases. You'll create a main document that contains the boilerplate text for the press releases and then merge it with a data source that includes the information on each upcoming event. The event information you need for next month's events is posted on the MediaLoft intranet site. You'll print the information from the intranet site and then enter it in your data source.

To complete this independent challenge:

a. Connect to the Internet and use your browser to go to the MediaLoft intranet site at http://www.course.com/illustrated/MediaLoft. Click the About link, click the MediaLoft San Diego link, then click the In-store Events link.
b. Print a copy of the In-store Events page, then disconnect from the Internet. You'll use the information on this page to create a data source for the press release mail merge.
c. Start Word and open the file WD H-6 from your Project Disk. Save the file as "Press Release Main".
d. Click the Show/Hide button to display non-printing characters. Click the blank line under "Contact", type your name, click the blank line under your name, then type "619-555-9137".
e. Select "DATE", then insert today's date using the Insert Date and Time command. Select the Update Automatically check box so that the date is updated each time the merge is performed.
f. Select "HEADLINE", type "In-store Events at MediaLoft", then center the headline text.
g. Select "BODY", then type "On DATE, MediaLoft San Diego will host a MediaLoft EVENT TYPE at TIME in the MediaLoft Café. The EVENT TYPE will feature DESCRIPTION. The event is free and open to the public. For more information call 555-9137."
h. Save your changes to the main document.
i. Open the Mail Merge Helper, click Create, click Form Letters, then click Active Window.
j. Click Get Data, click Create Data Source, then remove all the field names in the Field names in header row list box.
k. Add the following field names: Date, Time, EventType, and Description.
l. Save the data source with the filename "Press Release Data" to your Project Disk.
m. Referring to the table you printed from the MediaLoft intranet site, enter the eight records in the data source. Enter the first and second records as follows:

Date	Time	EventType	Description
November 5	7:00 p.m.	Author's Talk	John West reading from his new novel Filling Time
November 8	7:00 p.m.	Fiction Discussion Group	discussion of Jane Hampton's The Ides of March

(*Note:* In the Date field you must include the month. In the Description field you must be careful to enter the data so that it will complete the sentence "The event features…".)

n. When you have entered all eight records in the data source, save your changes to the data source file.
o. In the main document file, replace the placeholder text you typed with the merge fields of the same names, then save your changes.
p. Use the View Merged Data button to preview the merge document and check the press releases for correct usage, spacing, and punctuation. Make any necessary adjustments to the main document and the data source document, then save your changes.
q. Merge all the records to a new file, then save the merged file with the filename "Press Release Merge" to your Project Disk.
r. Read through the merged press releases and make any necessary adjustments. (*Hint*: Italicize the titles of books.)
s. Print the first two pages of the merge file, then close all files, saving changes when prompted.

► Visual Workshop

Using the Mail Merge Helper, create the nametags shown in Figure H-19. Name the main document "Nametags Main", name the data source document "Nametags Data", name the merged nametags document "Nametags Merge", and save all the files to your Project Disk. Add a record to the data source that includes your name. Print the nametags after performing the merge. (*Hint:* Create a mailing label main document. In the Label Options dialog box, select the 5095 – Name Badge product number. In the main document, increase the font size of the label text to 18 points, center the text, and boldface the field names for the name.)

FIGURE H-19

Louis Benoit
Director of Marketing
Computer Solutions, Inc.

Meredith Campbell
Vice President of Sales
VirtualWorld, Inc.

Gabriel Lee
Creative Director
Cyber Games Enterprises

Hannah Wadlington
President
Online Marketing, Inc.

Word 2000 MOUS Certification Objectives

Below is a list of the Microsoft Office User Specialist program objectives for Core Word 2000 skills showing where each MOUS objective is covered in the Lessons and Practice. This table lists the Core MOUS certification skills covered in the units in this book (Units A-H). For more information on which Illustrated titles meet MOUS certification, please see the inside cover of this book.

MOUS Standardized Coding Number	Activity	Lesson page where skill is covered	Location in lesson where skill is covered	Practice
W2000.1	**Working with text**			
W2000.1.1	Use the Undo, Redo, and Repeat command	WORD B-6	Clues to Use	Skills Review
W2000.1.2	Apply font formats (Bold, Italic and Underline)	WORD C-4	Steps 2–8	Skills Review, Independent Challenges 1–4
W2000.1.3	Use the SPELLING feature	WORD B-14	Steps 3–7	Skills Review, Independent Challenges 1, 2, 4
W2000.1.4	Use the THESAURUS feature	WORD B-15	Clues to Use	Skills Review, Independent Challenge 2
W2000.1.5	Use the GRAMMAR feature	WORD B-14	Steps 3–7	Skills Review, Independent Challenges 1, 2, 4
W2000.1.6	Insert page breaks	WORD E-10	Steps 1–8	Skills Review, Independent Challenges 1, 4
W2000.1.7	Highlight text in document	WORD C-4	Clues to Use	Independent Challenge 2
W2000.1.8	Insert and move text	WORD B-10	Steps 1–9	Skills Review, Independent Challenges 1–4
W2000.1.9	Cut, Copy, Paste, and Paste Special using the Office Clipboard	WORD B-8 WORD B-10 WORD B-12	Details Steps 1–6 Steps 1–6	Skills Review, Independent Challenges 1–4
W2000.1.10	Copy formats using the Format Painter	WORD C-6	Clues to Use	Skills Review
W2000.1.11	Select and change font and font size	WORD C-2	Steps 3–8	Skills Review, Independent Challenges 1–4, Visual Workshop
W2000.1.12	Find and replace text	WORD B-18	Steps 1–6	Skills Review, Independent Challenges 1, 4
W2000.1.13	Apply character effects (superscript, subscript, strikethrough, small caps and outline)	WORD C-4	Steps 4–8	Skills Review, Independent Challenges 1, 4
W2000.1.14	Insert date and time	WORD E-9	Clues to Use	Skills Review, Independent Challenge 4
W2000.1.15	Insert symbols	WORD E-6	Steps 2–5	Skills Review, Independent Challenges 1, 2, 3
W2000.1.16	Create and apply frequently used text with AutoCorrect	WORD B-16	Steps 1–5	Skills Review, Independent Challenge 3

MOUS Standardized Coding Number	Activity	Lesson page where skill is covered	Location in lesson where skill is covered	Practice
W2000.2	**Working with paragraphs**			
W2000.2.1	Align text in paragraphs (Center, Left, Right and Justified)	WORD C-6	Steps 1–4	Skills Review, Independent Challenges 1–4, Visual Workshop
W2000.2.2	Add bullets and numbering	WORD C-16	Steps 1–7	Skills Review, Independent Challenges 1, 2, Visual Workshop
W2000.2.3	Set character, line, and paragraph spacing options	WORD C-4 WORD C-10 WORD C-12	QuickTip Steps 1–5 Steps 1–7	Skills Review, Independent Challenges 3, 4, Visual Workshop
W2000.2.4	Apply borders and shading to paragraphs	WORD C-18	Steps 1–7, Clues to Use	Skills Review, Independent Challenges 2, 3, 4, Visual Workshop
W2000.2.5	Use indentation options (Left, Right, First Line and Hanging Indent)	WORD C-8	Steps 1–6, Clues to Use	Skills Review, Independent Challenges 1, 2, 3
W2000.2.6	Use TABS command (Center, Decimal, Left and Right)	WORD C-14	Steps 1–7	Skills Review, Independent Challenges 2, 3
W2000.2.7	Create an outline style numbered list	WORD C-17	Clues to Use	
W2000.2.8	Set tabs with leaders	WORD C-14	Steps 3–7	Skills Review
W2000.3	**Working with documents**			
W2000.3.1	Print a document	WORD A-12	Steps 5–6	Skills Review, Independent Challenges 1–4, Visual Workshop
W2000.3.2	Use print preview	WORD A-12	Steps 1–4	Skills Review, Independent Challenges 1–4
W2000.3.3	Use Web Page Preview	WORD G-16	Steps 1–7	Skills Review, Independent Challenges 1–4, Visual Workshop
W2000.3.4	Navigate through a document	WORD E-15	Table E-3	Skills Review, Independent Challenges 1–4, Visual Workshop
W2000.3.5	Insert page numbers	WORD E-8	Steps 1–6	Skills Review, Independent Challenges 2, 4
W2000.3.6	Set page orientation	WORD E-3	Clues to Use	Independent Challenges 1, 3
W2000.3.7	Set margins	WORD E-2	Steps 2–9	Skills Review, Independent Challenges 1–4, Visual Workshop
W2000.3.8	Use GoTo to locate specific elements in a document	WORD E-14	Steps 1–7	Skills Review, Independent Challenges 2, 4
W2000.3.9	Create and modify page numbers	WORD E-8	Quick Tip Step 2, Step 7	Skills Review, Independent Challenge 2
W2000.3.10	Create and modify headers and footers	WORD E-4 WORD E-6	Steps 1–9 Steps 1–6 Clues to Use	Skills Review, Independent Challenges 2, 4
W2000.3.11	Align text vertically	WORD E-12	Clues to Use	Skills Review, Independent Challenge 4

MOUS Standardized Coding Number	Activity	Lesson page where skill is covered	Location in lesson where skill is covered	Practice
W2000.3.12	Create and use newspaper columns	WORD E-14	Steps 1–8	Skills Review, Independent Challenges 1, 3, 4, Visual Workshop
W2000.3.13	Revise column structure	WORD E-14 WORD E-16	Steps 3–9 Steps 1–6	Skills Review, Independent Challenges 1, 3, 4, Visual Workshop
W2000.3.14	Prepare and print envelopes and labels	WORD H-15	Clues to Use	Independent Challenge 2
W2000.3.15	Apply styles	WORD G-6	Steps 3–8	Skills Review, Independent Challenges 1–4, Visual Workshop
W2000.3.16	Create sections with formatting that differs from other sections	WORD E-12	Steps 1–7	Skills Review, Independent Challenges 1, 3, 4, Visual Workshop
W2000.3.17	Use click & type	WORD F-18 WORD F-19	Steps 1–8 Table F-1	Skills Review, Independent Challenges 3, 4, Visual Workshop
W2000.4	**Managing files**			
W2000.4.1	Use save	WORD A-10	Steps 1–4	Skills Review, Independent Challenges 1–4, Visual Workshop
W2000.4.2	Locate and open an existing document	WORD B-4	Steps 2–5	Skills Review, Independent Challenges 1, 2
W2000.4.3	Use Save As (different name, location or format)	WORD B-4	Steps 6–7	Skills Review, Independent Challenges 1, 2
W2000.4.4	Create a folder	WORD B-4	QuickTip	
W2000.4.5	Create a new document using a Wizard	WORD B-3	Clues to Use	Independent Challenge 4
W2000.4.6	Save as Web Page	WORD G-4 WORD G-10	Steps 5–9 Steps 1–4	Skills Review, Independent Challenges 1–4, Visual Workshop
W2000.4.7	Use templates to create a new document	WORD B-3	Clues to Use	Visual Workshop
W2000.4.8	Create Hyperlinks	WORD G-12 WORD G-14	Steps 2–9 Steps 1–5	Skills Review, Independent Challenges 2, 3, 4 Visual Workshop
W2000.4.9	Use the Office Assistant	WORD A-14	Steps 1–8	Skills Review, Independent Challenges 1, 3
W2000.4.10	Send a Word document via e-mail	WORD G-15	Clues to Use	Skills Review, Independent Challenges 1, 4
W2000.5	**Using tables**			
W2000.5.1	Create and format tables	WORD D-2	Steps 4–10	Skills Review, Independent Challenges 1, 2, 3, Visual Workshop
W2000.5.2	Add borders and shading to tables	WORD D-8	Steps 1–5, Clues to Use	Skills Review, Independent Challenges 1–4, Visual Workshop
W2000.5.3	Revise tables (insert & delete rows and columns, change cell formats)	WORD D-6	Steps 1–5	Skills Review, Independent Challenges 1–4

MOUS Standardized Coding Number	Activity	Lesson page where skill is covered	Location in lesson where skill is covered	Practice
W2000.5.4	Modify table structure height and width)	WORD D-4	Steps 1–4	Skills Review, Visual Workshop
W2000.5.5	Rotate text in a table	WORD D-14	Clues to Use	Skills Review, Independent Challenge 2
W2000.6	Working with pictures and charts			
W2000.6.1	Use the drawing toolbar	WORD F-10 (AutoShapes)	Steps 2–9	Skills Review, Independent Challenges 1,4, Visual Workshop
		WORD F-12 WORD F-13 (Text Boxes)	Steps 1–9 Clues to Use	Skills Review, Independent Challenges 1–4, Visual Workshop
		WORD F-14 (Lines)	Steps 2–9 Clues to Use	Skills Review, Independent Challenges 2,3,4, Visual Workshop
		WORD F-16 (WordArt)	Steps 2–9 QuickTip	Skills Review, Independent Challenge 3, Visual Workshop
W2000.6.2	Insert graphics into a document (WordArt, Clip Art, Images)	WORD F-2 (Clip Art)	Steps 1–7 Clues to Use	Skills Review, Independent Challenges 1–4 Visual Workshop
		WORD F-8 (Images)	Steps 2–8	Skills Review, Independent Challenge 4
		WORD F-16 (WordArt)	Steps 1–9	Skills Review, Independent Challenges 1, 3, Visual Workshop

Project Files List

To complete many of the lessons and practice exercises in this book, students need to use a Project File that is supplied by Course Technology and stored on a Project Disk. Below is a list of the files that are supplied, and the unit or practice exercise to which the files correspond. For information on how to obtain Project Files, please see the inside cover of this book. The following list only includes Project Files that are supplied; it does not include the files students create from scratch or the files students create by revising the supplied files.

Unit	File supplied on Project Disk	Location file is used in unit
Word Unit A	No files supplied	
Word Unit B	WD B-1.doc	Lessons
	WD B-2.doc	Skills Review
	WD B-3.doc	Independent Challenge 1
	WD B-4.doc	Independent Challenge 2
Word Unit C	WD C-1.doc	Lessons
	WD C-2.doc	Skills Review
	WD C-3.doc	Independent Challenge 1
	WD C-4.doc	Independent Challenge 2
Word Unit D	WD D-1.doc	Lessons
	WD D-2.doc	Skills Review
	WD D-3.doc	Independent Challenge 3
Word Unit E	WD E-1.doc	Lessons
	WD E-2.doc	Skills Review
	WD E-3.doc	Independent Challenge 1
	WD E-4.doc	Independent Challenge 2
	WD E-5.doc	Independent Challenge 3
	WD E-6.doc	Visual Workshop
Word Unit F	WD F-1.doc	Lessons
	WD F-2.jpg	Lessons, Independent Challenge 4
	WD F-3.doc	Skills Review
	WD F-4.bmp	
	WD F-5.doc	Independent Challenge 1

Unit	File supplied on Project Disk	Location file is used in unit
Word Unit G	WD G-1.doc	Lessons
	WD G-2.doc	Skills Review
	WD G-3.doc	Independent Challenge 2
	WD G-4.doc WD G-5.doc	Independent Challenge 3
	WD G-6.doc WD G-7.doc	Visual Workshop
Word Unit H	WD H-1.doc	Lessons
	WD H-2.doc	Skills Review
	WD H-3.doc WD H-4.doc	Independent Challenge 1
	WD H-5.doc	Independent Challenge 3
	WD H-6.doc	Independent Challenge 4

Word 2000

Glossary

Alignment The horizontal position of text relative to page margins or tab stops; for example, left, center, or right.

Anchor Formatting feature that attaches a graphic object to a paragraph so that the graphic object moves with the paragraph if the paragraph moves.

Application See *Program.*

Ascending order The sequence in which items are sorted from smallest to largest, or from A to Z.

AutoCorrect A feature that automatically corrects misspelled words and grammatical errors as you type. Word provides many entries for common mistakes, but you can also add your own.

AutoFit A table formatting feature that automatically adjusts the width of a table to fit to the document margins.

AutoRecover A feature that automatically saves document changes in a temporary file at specified intervals, so that you can recover some of your changes if power to your computer is interrupted.

AutoShape A drawing object, such as a circle, rectangle, triangle, or callout that is created using the Drawing toolbar.

Bitmap A file format for graphics that is composed of pixels.

Boilerplate text Text that appears in every version of a merge document.

Bold Formatting in which text appears thicker and darker.

Border A vertical or horizontal line that you can add to the top, bottom or sides of paragraphs; also the line that divides cells in a table. You can format borders with different line styles and colors.

Bullet A small graphic symbol, usually a round or square dot, often used to identify items in a list.

Callout A graphic object that calls attention to something in a document; contains text and a line that points to the item to which you want to call attention.

Cell The intersection of a row and a column in a table.

Cell reference An address or name that identifies a cell's position in a table; it consists of a letter that identifies the cell's column and a number that identifies its row; for example, cell B3.

Center A form of paragraph alignment in which the lines of text are centered between the left and right margins.

Character spacing A form of character formatting that allows you to expand or condense the amount of space between characters, adjust the width (or scale) of characters, raise or lower characters, and adjust kerning.

Click To press and release a mouse button in one motion.

Click and Type A feature that allows you to quickly insert text, graphics, tables, and other items in a blank area of a document without having to apply formatting such as alignment and indents.

Clip art A collection of pictures, sound clips, and motion clips that you can insert into a document.

Clipboard A temporary storage area for cut or copied items that are available for pasting. See *Office Clipboard.*

Clipboard toolbar A toolbar that shows the contents of the Office Clipboard; contains buttons for copying and pasting items to and from the Office Clipboard.

Column A vertical arrangement of cells in a table.

Column break A break inserted manually to force text to move to the top of the next column.

Copy A command that copies a selected part of a document and places it on the Clipboard.

Cut A command that removes a selected part of a document and places it on the Clipboard.

Data source In a mail merge, the document that contains the variable information to be merged with the boilerplate text of the main document.

Default The original setting, such as page margins or tab spacing, set by the program.

Delete To remove selected text or a graphic from a document.

Descending order The sequence in which rows are sorted from Z to A or from largest to smallest.

Dialog box A window that opens when more information is needed to carry out a command.

Document window The rectangular area of the Word program window where you view and work on a document.

Drag To hold down the mouse button while moving the mouse.

Edit To add, delete, or change text and graphics.

Facing pages The left and right pages in a two-page spread of a double-sided document, such as a book or a magazine.

Field An instruction or code inserted into a document that serves as a placeholder for information that changes, such as a date or a page number.

Field name In a mail merge, the names of the data fields in the header row of a data source.

File An electronic collection of information that has a unique name, distinguishing it from other files. In Word, all documents are stored as files.

Filename The name assigned to a file; the name you assign to a document when you save it to a disk.

Filter To isolate a set of records that meet certain criteria; used to select a specific set of records to merge.

Floating graphic A graphic object that has text wrapping applied to it and can be placed anywhere on a page.

Folders Subdivisions of a disk that work like a filing system to help you organize files.

Font The typeface or design of a set of characters (letters, numerals, symbols, and punctuation marks).

Font effects Enhanced formatting you can apply to text, such as bold, italics, shadows, or all caps.

Font size The size of text, measured in points (pts). The larger the number of points, the bigger the font size.

Footer Text that appears at the bottom of each page in a document.

Format The appearance of a document, including color, font, attributes, borders, and shading.

Format Painter A feature used to copy the formatting applied to one set of text to another.

Formatting toolbar A toolbar that contains buttons for the most frequently used formatting commands.

Formula A set of instructions used to perform numeric calculations (adding, multiplying, averaging, etc.).

Frame A bordered area on a Web page that contains hyperlinks and other navigation elements to help users navigate a Web site.

Global replace Replacing all occurrences of specific text in a document without having to review and change each occurrence individually.

Graphics A picture, chart, or drawing in a document.

Gutter Extra margin space left for a binding at the top or on the left side of a page.

Hanging indent A paragraph format in which the first line of a paragraph starts farther to the left than the subsequent lines.

Hard page break A page break inserted manually to force text to begin on a new page.

Header Text that appears at the top of each page in a document.

Header row In a mail merge, the first row of the data source table that contains the names of data fields.

Home page The first page that a visitor to a Web site usually sees. The home page usually links to other pages in the Web site, and other pages link back to the home page.

Horizontal ruler A graphical bar across the top of the document window that you can use to place and align text.

Hyperlink Text or an object in a document that, when clicked, opens another site or Web page.

Hypertext Markup Language (HTML) The language used to describe the content and format of Web pages.

Hyphens Short dashes used to break words that appear at the end of a line.

Indent The distance between the beginning or end of a line of text and the page margins. A paragraph can have left, right, first-line, and hanging indents.

Indent markers Movable buttons on the horizontal ruler that determine the indent settings for the selected paragraph.

Inline graphic A graphic object that is part of a line of text; the default setting for a graphic before text wrapping is applied.

Insertion point A blinking vertical line in the document window that indicates where text will appear when you type.

Internet A communications system that connects computers and computer networks located around the world using telephone lines, cables, satellites, and other telecommunications media.

Intranet A computer network that connects computers in a local area only, such as computers in a company's office.

Italics Formatting in which the text appears slanted.

Justify A form of paragraph alignment in which both the left and right edges of a paragraph are flush with the margins.

Kerning A form of character formatting that allows you to adjust the space between standard combinations of characters, such as "W" followed by "a".

Keyboard shortcut A combination of keys or function keys you can press to perform an operation in Word. Using keyboard shortcuts is often faster than using the menus and commands.

Landscape orientation Horizontal page orientation; a page that is wider than it is tall.

Left-align A form of paragraph alignment in which the left edge of a paragraph is even, usually flush with the left margin.

Line spacing The amount of space between lines of text, measured in lines or points.

Lowercase The small letters of a character set (a, b, c, d...).

Mail merge A feature that combines a main document, such as a form letter, with a data source, such as recipients' names and addresses, to create a set of customized documents.

Main document In a mail merge, the document that contains the merge fields and the boilerplate text.

Margin The empty space between the edge of the text, or the printed area, and the edge of the page. A document's margins are visible in Print Preview or Print Layout view.

Menu bar A bar beneath the title bar that contains menus that list the program's commands.

Merge Combining two or more cells in a table to form a single cell.

Merge field In mail merge, a placeholder that indicates where in the main document the data from each record should be placed when the main document and the data source are merged.

Mirror margins Inside and outside margins that mirror each other in a document with facing pages.

More Buttons button The button you click to display toolbar buttons that are not currently visible.

Newspaper columns Columns of text in which text flows from the bottom of one column to the top of the next column.

Non-printing characters Marks displayed on the screen to indicate characters that do not print, such as tab characters or paragraph marks. You can control the display of non-printing characters with the Show/Hide ¶ button on the Standard toolbar.

Normal view The document view in which you do not see the edges of the page; useful for most editing and formatting tasks.

Office Assistant An animated character that appears to offer tips, answer questions, and provide access to the program's Help system.

Office Clipboard A temporary storage area shared by all Office programs that can be used to cut, copy and paste multiple items within and between Office programs. The Office Clipboard can hold up to 12 items collected from any Office program. See also *Clipboard toolbar.*

Open The operation of retrieving and displaying a document in the document window.

Overtype mode A feature that lets you replace, or overwrite, existing text as you type.

Page break A separator that forces all text after the break to appear on the next page of a document.

Paragraph spacing The amount of space between paragraphs, measured in points.

Paste A command that inserts cut or copied items into a document from the Clipboard.

Pixels Small dots that comprise a bitmapped graphic image and contain information about color and intensity.

Point The unit of measurement for fonts and space between paragraphs and text characters. There are 72 points per inch.

Portrait orientation Vertical page orientation that is taller than it is wide.

Print Layout view A view that mimics the look of a printed page; especially useful for viewing margins, alignment, and text flow.

Print Preview A command you can use to display the document as it will look when printed.

Program Task-oriented software (such as Excel or Word) that enables you to perform a certain type of task such as data calculation or word processing.

Pull quote Decorative text in a document that is set off by wrapping document text around it.

Record In a mail merge, a complete set of data for one individual or one item, such as one person's first name, last name, address, city, state, and zip code.

Redo A command that repeats a reversed edit or formatting change; only reversed changes can be repeated with the Redo command.

Replace The command you use to locate and change a specific occurrence of text. Also, refers to the operation of selecting and typing over existing text to replace it.

Reset usage data An option that allows personalized toolbars and menus to be returned to their default settings.

Right-align A form of paragraph alignment in which only the right edge of a paragraph is even, usually flush with the right margin.

Row A horizontal arrangement of cells in a table.

Sans serif font A font whose characters do not include serifs, the small strokes at the ends of the characters. Arial is a sans serif font.

Save The command used to permanently store your document and any changes you make to a file on a disk. See also *Filename.*

ScreenTip A pop-up label that appears when you point to a button. It provides descriptive information about the button.

Scroll To move within a window to display parts of a document that are not currently visible.

Scroll bars Bars at the right and bottom edges of the document window used to view different parts of a document not currently visible in the document window.

Scroll box The movable box in the scroll bars that you drag to move around in a document.

Search To use the Find command to locate specific text in a document.

Section A part of a document that is separated from the rest of the document by section breaks.

Section break A separator that divides a document into sections that can be formatted differently from other sections.

Select To highlight text with the mouse. Most formatting and editing commands in Word require that you select the text that you want to format or edit.

Selection bar An unmarked column at the left edge of a document window that can be used to select text. In a table, each cell, row, and column also has its own selection bar.

Serif font A font that has small strokes (called serifs) at the ends of the characters. Times New Roman and Palatino are serif fonts.

Shading A background color or pattern you can apply to text, tables, or graphics.

Sizing handle Squares that appear on the corners and sides of a selected object and are used to resize an object.

Soft page break An automatic page break that Word inserts at the bottom of a page.

Sort An operation that arranges rows in a table (or paragraphs of text) in a sequence, such as chronological, alphabetical, or numerical order.

Sort criterion The detail of a table or list by which rows or paragraphs are sorted, for example, last name.

Split cells A command used to divide a cell in a table into two or more cells.

Standard toolbar The toolbar containing buttons that perform some of the most frequently used commands.

Status bar A bar at the bottom of the Word window that indicates the current page number and section number, the total number of pages in the document, and the vertical position (in inches) of the insertion point.

Style A predefined set of character and paragraph formatting settings that you can apply to text to format it quickly and easily.

Superscript Formatting in which the text is raised above and is several points smaller than adjacent text. Copyright and trademark symbols, as well as certain notations in equations, are often superscripted.

Symbols Special characters such as bullets and foreign language characters that you can insert into a document.

Tab A key you press to position text so that it is located at a specific horizontal position in a document.

Tab leaders A solid or dotted line that appears in front of tabbed text.

Tab stop A measured position used for placing and aligning text horizontally at a specific location in a document. Word has five kinds of tab stops, left-aligned (the default), centered, right-aligned, decimal, and bar.

Table A grid of rows and columns divided by borders; commonly used to display text, numbers, or other items for quick reference and analysis.

Table AutoFormat A feature that includes preset formats that can be applied to format a table with shading, fonts, and borders.

Tags HTML codes that describe how each element on a Web page should appear when viewed with a browser.

Template A formatted document that contains placeholder text you can replace with your own text. Word includes templates for creating memos, letters, faxes, and other kinds of commonly used documents.

Text box A graphic object that is a container for text and graphics.

Text wrapping Formatting that forces text to flow around a graphic object rather than over it and changes an inline graphic to a floating object.

Theme A predefined set of Web backgrounds, bullets, horizontal lines, colors, and styles that you can apply to Web pages and e-mail messages to give documents a common visual look.

Title bar The bar at the top of a window that displays the program name and the filename of the current document.

Tone The feeling of a document, affected by its content and visual appearance.

Toolbar A bar that contains buttons that give you quick access to the most frequently used commands. Word includes many different toolbars related to specific tasks. For example, the Tables and Borders toolbar contains buttons that are useful when you create tables.

Undo A command that reverses previous edits or formatting changes you made to a document; you can undo up to 100 previous actions.

Uppercase The capital letters of a character set (A, B, C, D…).

Vertical alignment The placement of text on a page or in a cell in relation to the top, bottom, or center of the page or cell.

Vertical ruler A graphical bar at the left edge of the document window in Print Layout view.

View A format for displaying a document in the document window that offers features useful for working on different types of documents. Word includes four views: Normal, Outline, Print Layout, and Web Layout.

View buttons Buttons on the horizontal scroll bar that allow you to switch between views.

Web browser A software program used to access and display Web pages.

Web page A document that is stored on the World Wide Web or an intranet and viewed on a computer using a Web browser.

Web site A group of associated Web pages that are linked together with hyperlinks.

Wizard An interactive set of dialog boxes that guides you through the process of creating a document; it asks you questions about document preferences and creates the document according to your specifications.

Word processing program A software application used to create documents efficiently.

WordArt A graphic object that contains text formatted in unique shapes, special colors, and patterns.

Wordwrap A feature that automatically moves the insertion point to the next line of a paragraph as you type.

World Wide Web (Web or WWW) A part of the Internet containing Web pages that are linked together.

Index

Index

Index

Index